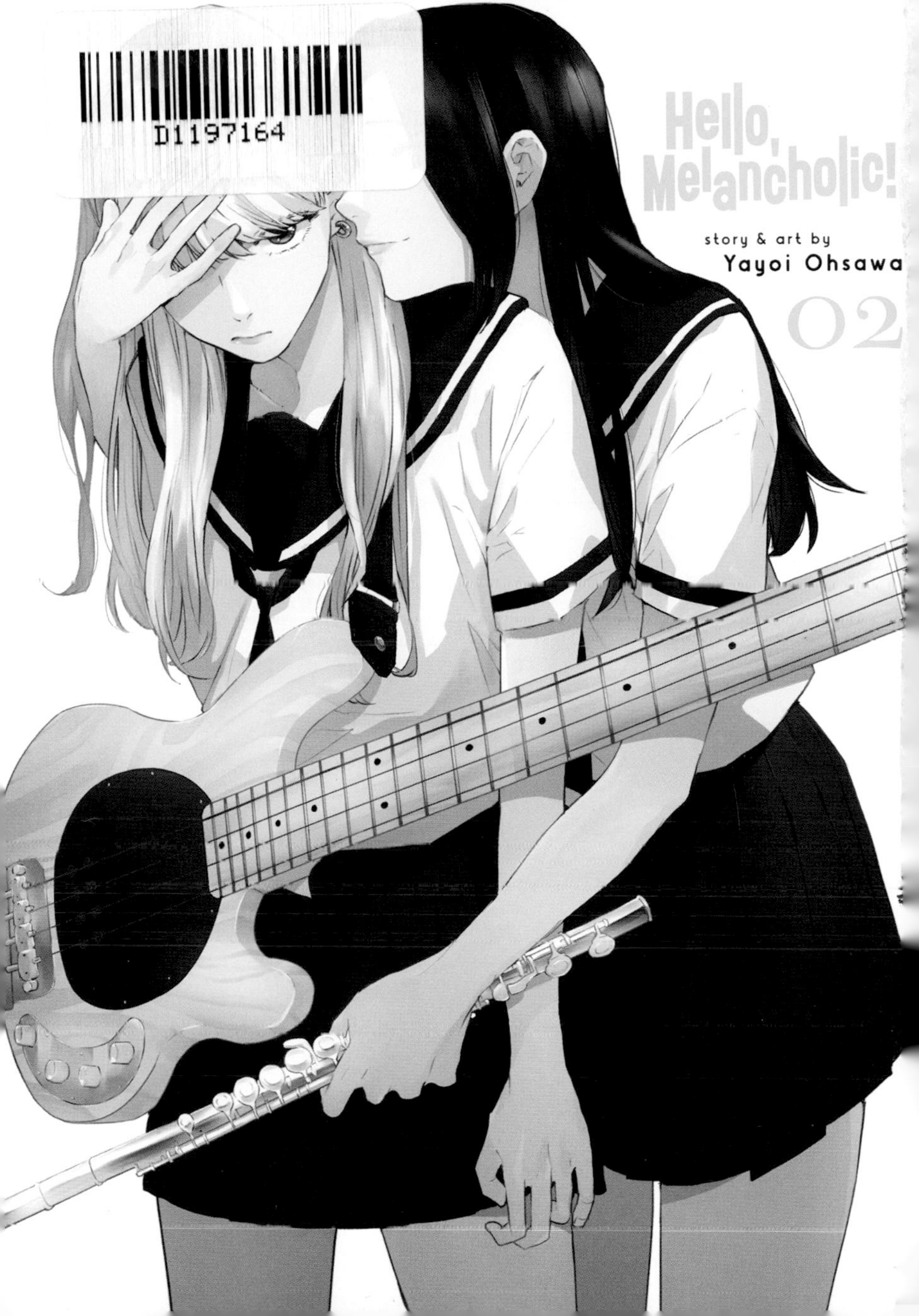
Hello, Melancholic!
story & art by
Yayoi Ohsawa
02

Hello, Melancholic!

story & art by
Yayoi Ohsawa

CONTENTS

SEVEN SEAS ENTERTAINMENT PRESENTS

Hello, Melancholic!

story and art by **YAYOI OHSAWA**   **VOLUME 2**

TRANSLATION
Margaret Ngo

ADAPTATION
Marykate Jasper

LETTERING
Mo Harrison

COVER DESIGN
H. Qi

PROOFREADER
Leighanna DeRouen

COPY EDITOR
B. Lillian Martin

SENIOR EDITOR
Jenn Grunigen

PRODUCTION DESIGNER
Christina McKenzie

PRODUCTION MANAGER
Lissa Pattillo

PREPRESS TECHNICIAN
Melanie Ujimori

PRINT MANAGER
Rhiannon Rasmussen-Silverstein

EDITOR-IN-CHIEF
Julie Davis

ASSOCIATE PUBLISHER
Adam Arnold

PUBLISHER
Jason DeAngelis

HELLO, MELANCHOLIC! Vol. 2
© 2020 Yayoi Ohsawa. All rights reserved.
First published in Japan in 2020 by Ichijinsha Inc., Tokyo.
Publication rights for this English edition arranged through Kodansha Ltd., Tokyo.

Seven Seas press and purchase enquiries can be sent to Marketing Manager Lianne Sentar at press@gomanga.com. Information regarding the distribution and purchase of digital editions is available from Digital Manager CK Russell at digital@gomanga.com.

Seven Seas and the Seven Seas logo are trademarks of Seven Seas Entertainment. All rights reserved.

ISBN: 978-1-63858-340-0
Printed in Canada
First Printing: July 2022
10 9 8 7 6 5 4 3 2 1

READING DIRECTIONS

This book reads from *right to left*, Japanese style. If this is your first time reading manga, you start reading from the top right panel on each page and take it from there. If you get lost, just follow the numbered diagram here. It may seem backwards at first, but you'll get the hang of it! Have fun!!

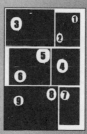

track5

Kiss Me

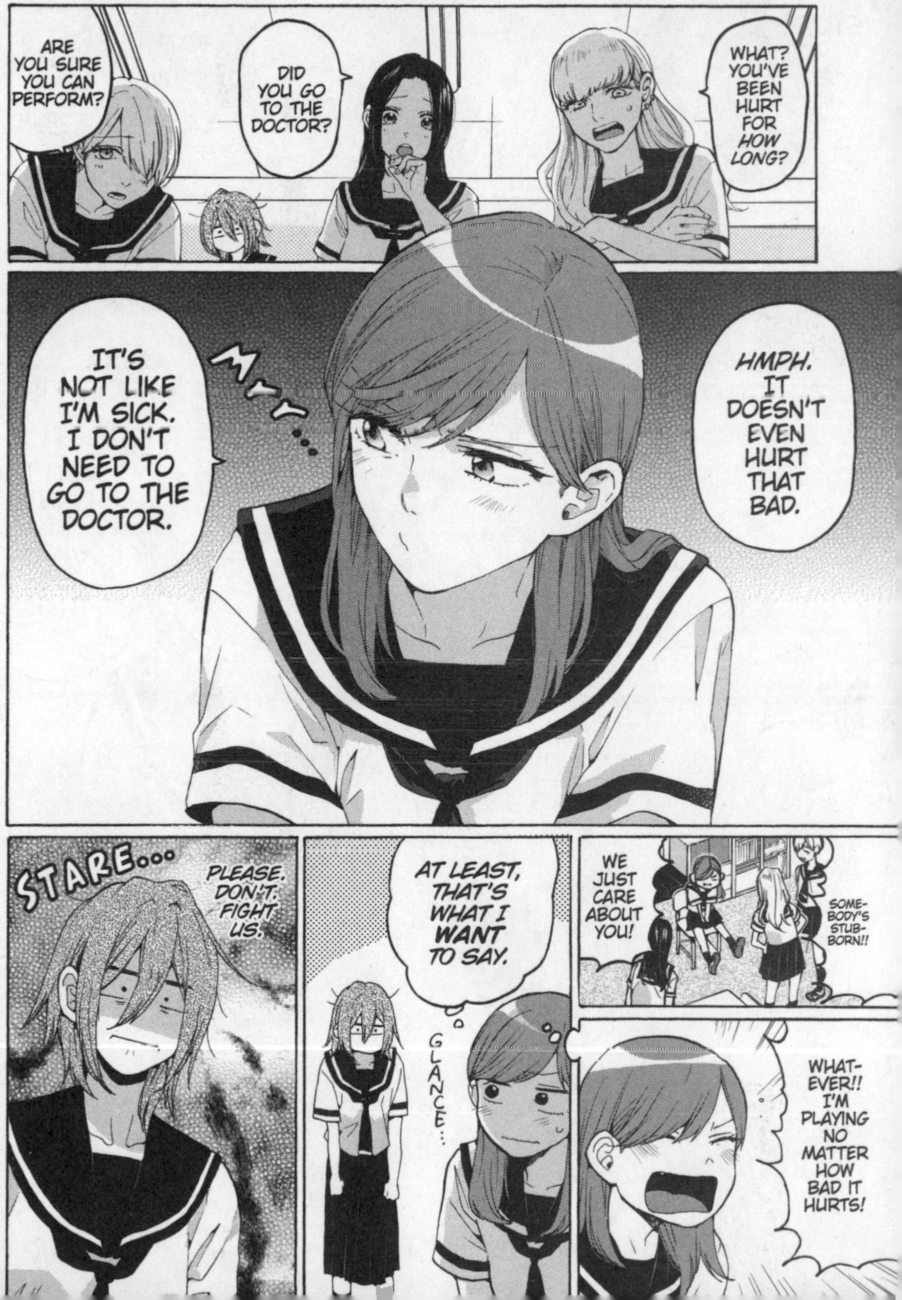
WHAT? YOU'VE BEEN HURT FOR HOW LONG?
DID YOU GO TO THE DOCTOR?
ARE YOU SURE YOU CAN PERFORM?
HMPH. IT DOESN'T EVEN HURT THAT BAD.
IT'S NOT LIKE I'M SICK. I DON'T NEED TO GO TO THE DOCTOR.
SOMEBODY'S STUBBORN!!
WE JUST CARE ABOUT YOU!
WHATEVER!! I'M PLAYING NO MATTER HOW BAD IT HURTS!
AT LEAST, THAT'S WHAT I WANT TO SAY.
GLANCE...
STARE...
PLEASE. DON'T. FIGHT US.

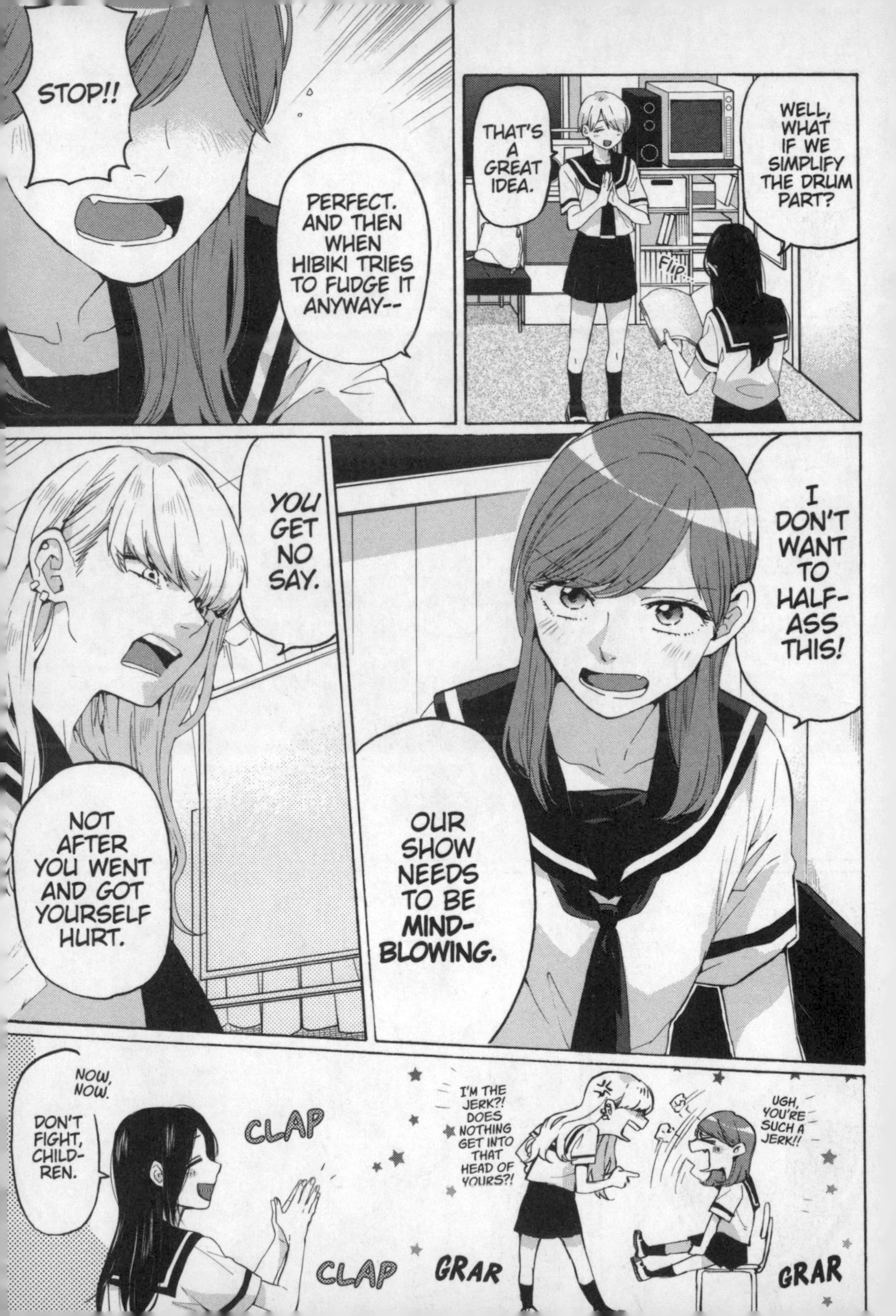
WELL, WHAT IF WE SIMPLIFY THE DRUM PART?
THAT'S A GREAT IDEA.
FLIP...
PERFECT. AND THEN WHEN HIBIKI TRIES TO FUDGE IT ANYWAY--
STOP!!
I DON'T WANT TO HALF-ASS THIS!
OUR SHOW NEEDS TO BE MIND-BLOWING.
YOU GET NO SAY.
NOT AFTER YOU WENT AND GOT YOURSELF HURT.
UGH, YOU'RE SUCH A JERK!!
I'M THE JERK?! DOES NOTHING GET INTO THAT HEAD OF YOURS?!
GRAR
GRAR
NOW, NOW.
DON'T FIGHT, CHILDREN.
CLAP
CLAP

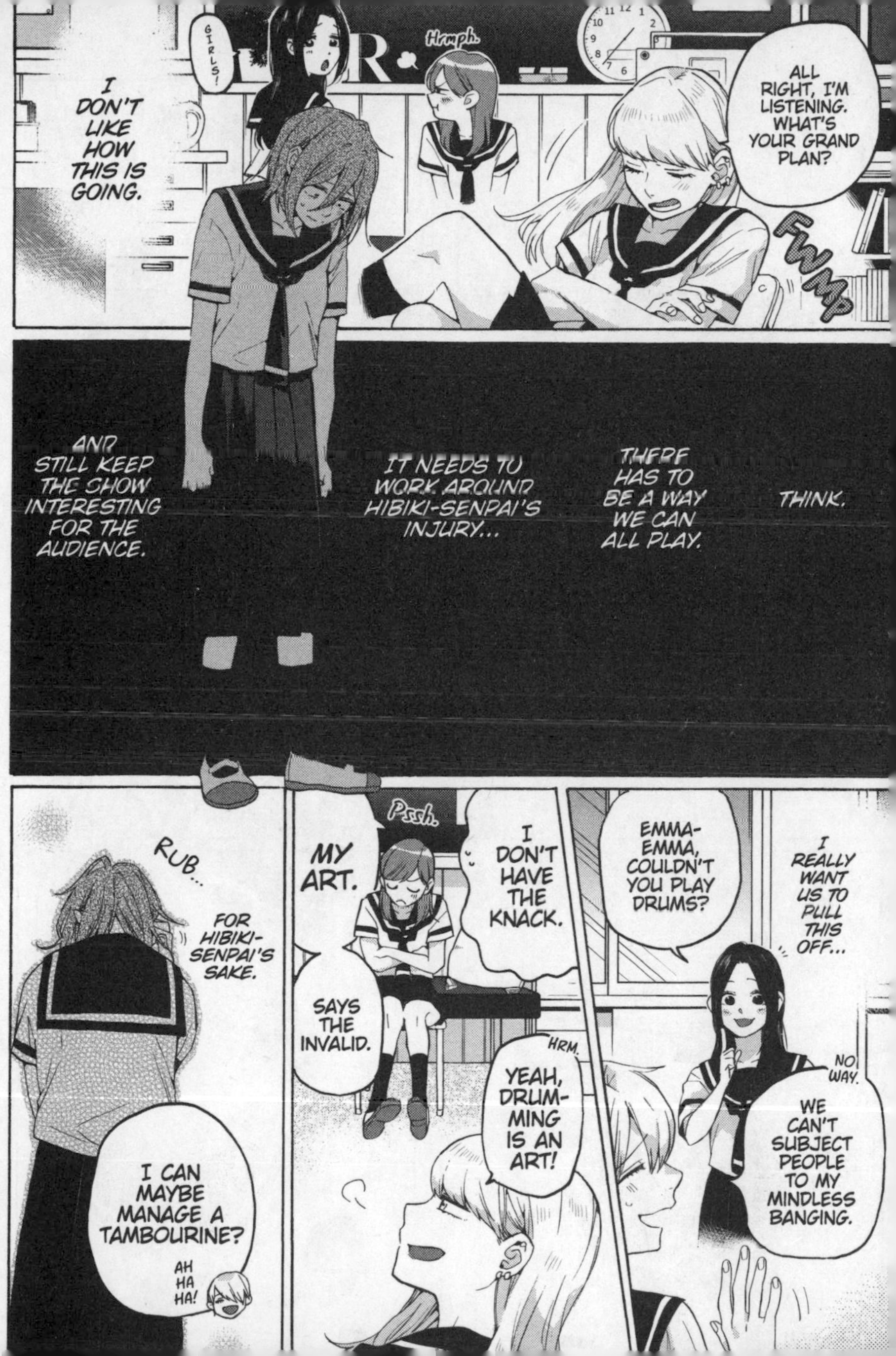
ALL RIGHT, I'M LISTENING. WHAT'S YOUR GRAND PLAN?
FWMP
Hrmph.
GIRLS!
I DON'T LIKE HOW THIS IS GOING.
THINK.
THERE HAS TO BE A WAY WE CAN ALL PLAY.
IT NEEDS TO WORK AROUND HIBIKI-SENPAI'S INJURY...
AND STILL KEEP THE SHOW INTERESTING FOR THE AUDIENCE.
I REALLY WANT US TO PULL THIS OFF...
EMMA-EMMA, COULDN'T YOU PLAY DRUMS?
NO WAY.
WE CAN'T SUBJECT PEOPLE TO MY MINDLESS BANGING.
HRM.
YEAH, DRUMMING IS AN ART!
I DON'T HAVE THE KNACK.
Pssh.
MY ART.
SAYS THE INVALID.
RUB...
FOR HIBIKI-SENPAI'S SAKE.
I CAN MAYBE MANAGE A TAMBOURINE?
AH HA HA!

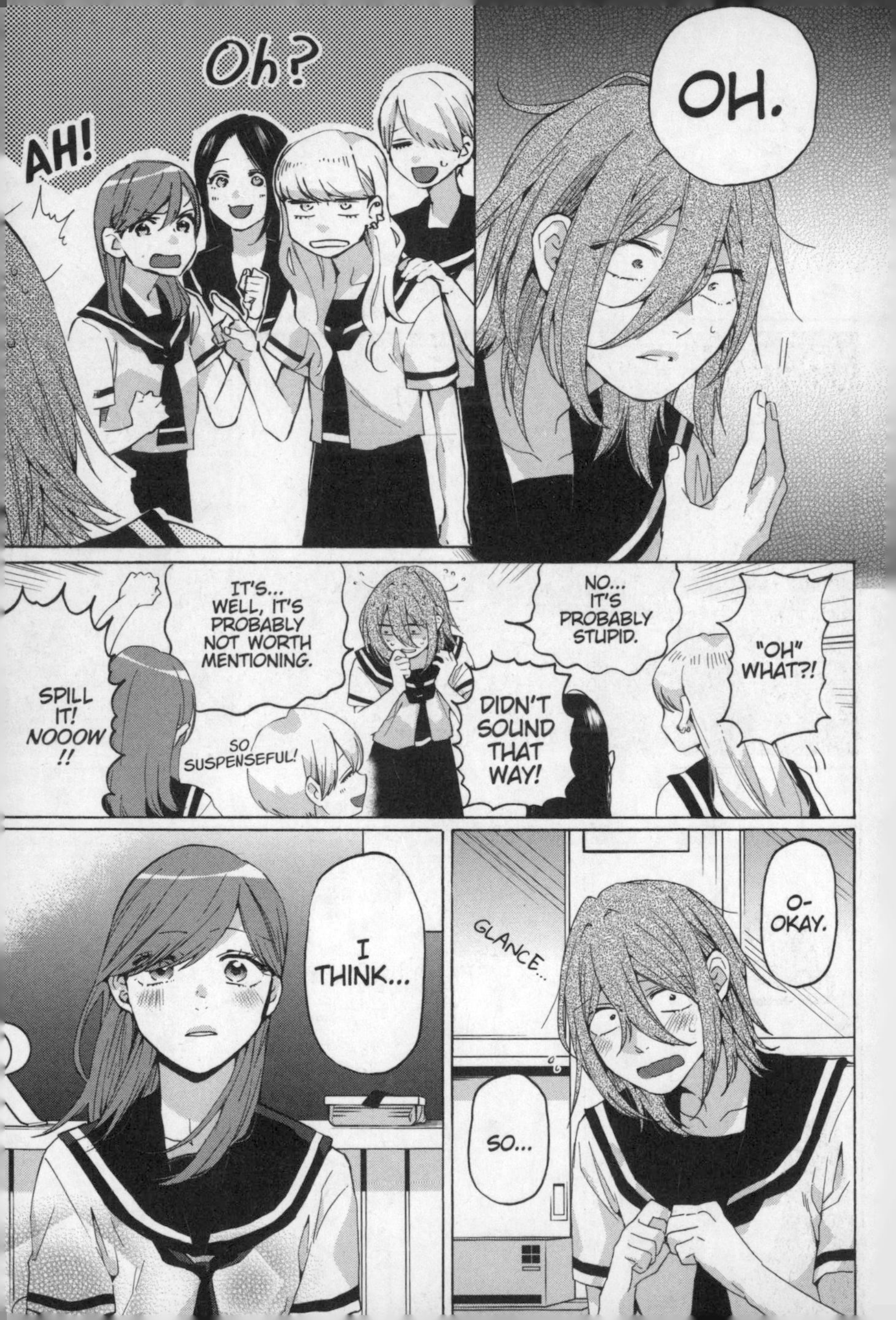
OH.
Oh?
AH!
"OH" WHAT?!
NO... IT'S PROBABLY STUPID.
DIDN'T SOUND THAT WAY!
IT'S... WELL, IT'S PROBABLY NOT WORTH MENTIONING.
SO SUSPENSEFUL!
SPILL IT! NOOOW!!
O-OKAY.
GLANCE...
SO...
I THINK...

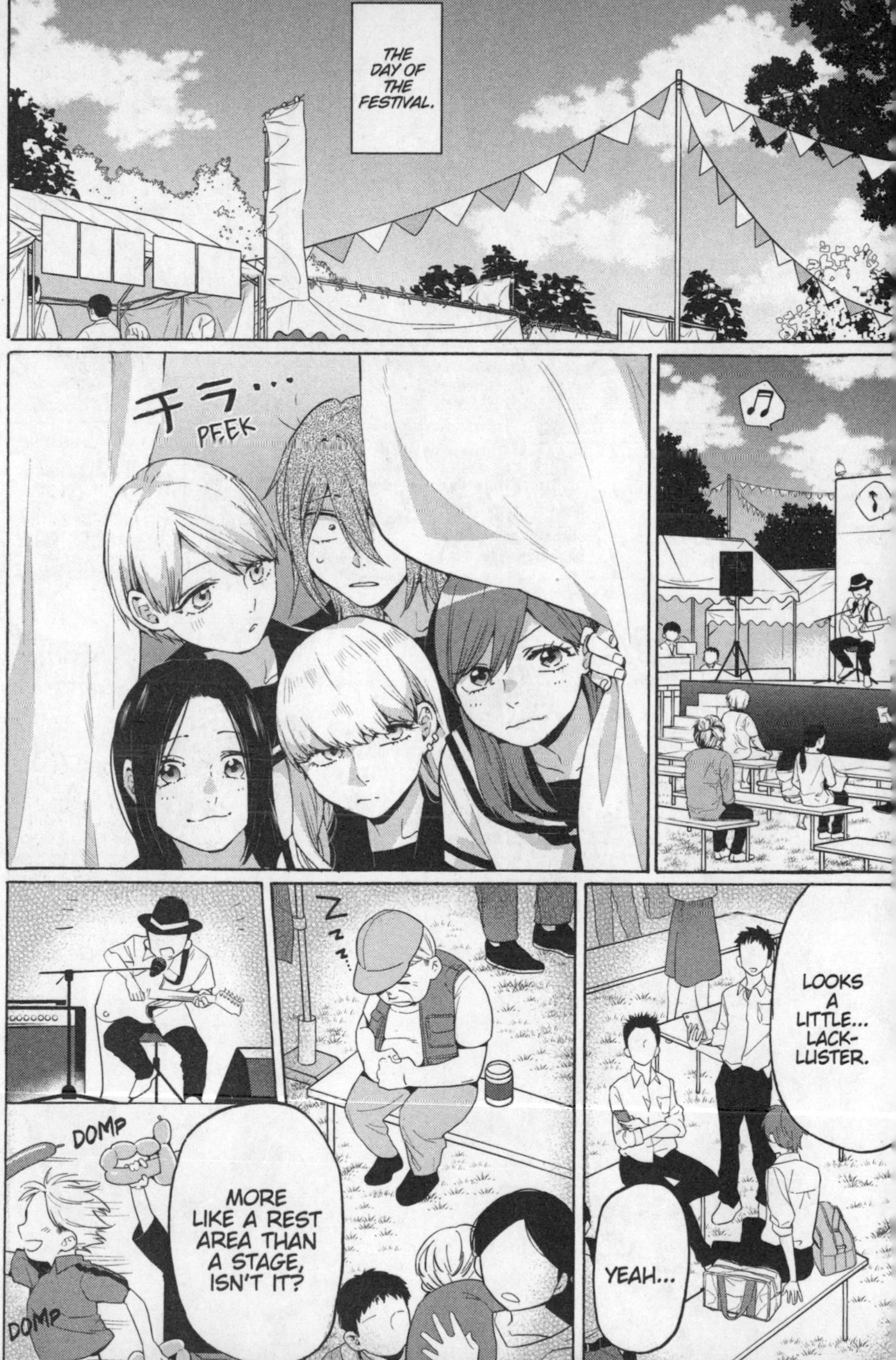
THE DAY OF THE FESTIVAL.
♪
チラ…
PEEK
LOOKS A LITTLE... LACK-LUSTER.
YEAH...
Z z z...
MORE LIKE A REST AREA THAN A STAGE, ISN'T IT?
DOMP
DOMP

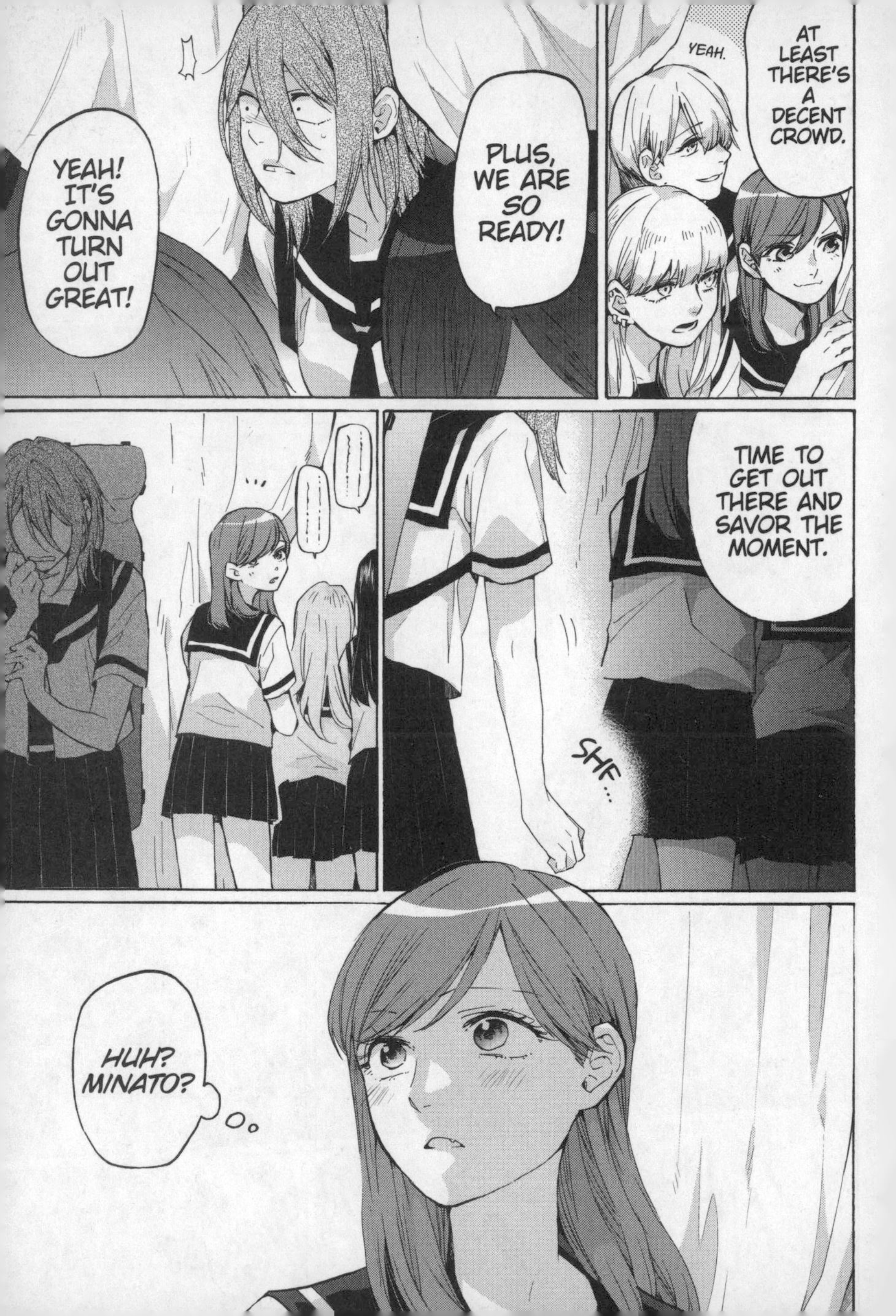
AT LEAST THERE'S A DECENT CROWD.
YEAH.
PLUS, WE ARE SO READY!
!
YEAH! IT'S GONNA TURN OUT GREAT!
TIME TO GET OUT THERE AND SAVOR THE MOMENT.
SHF...
......
......
...
HUH? MINATO?

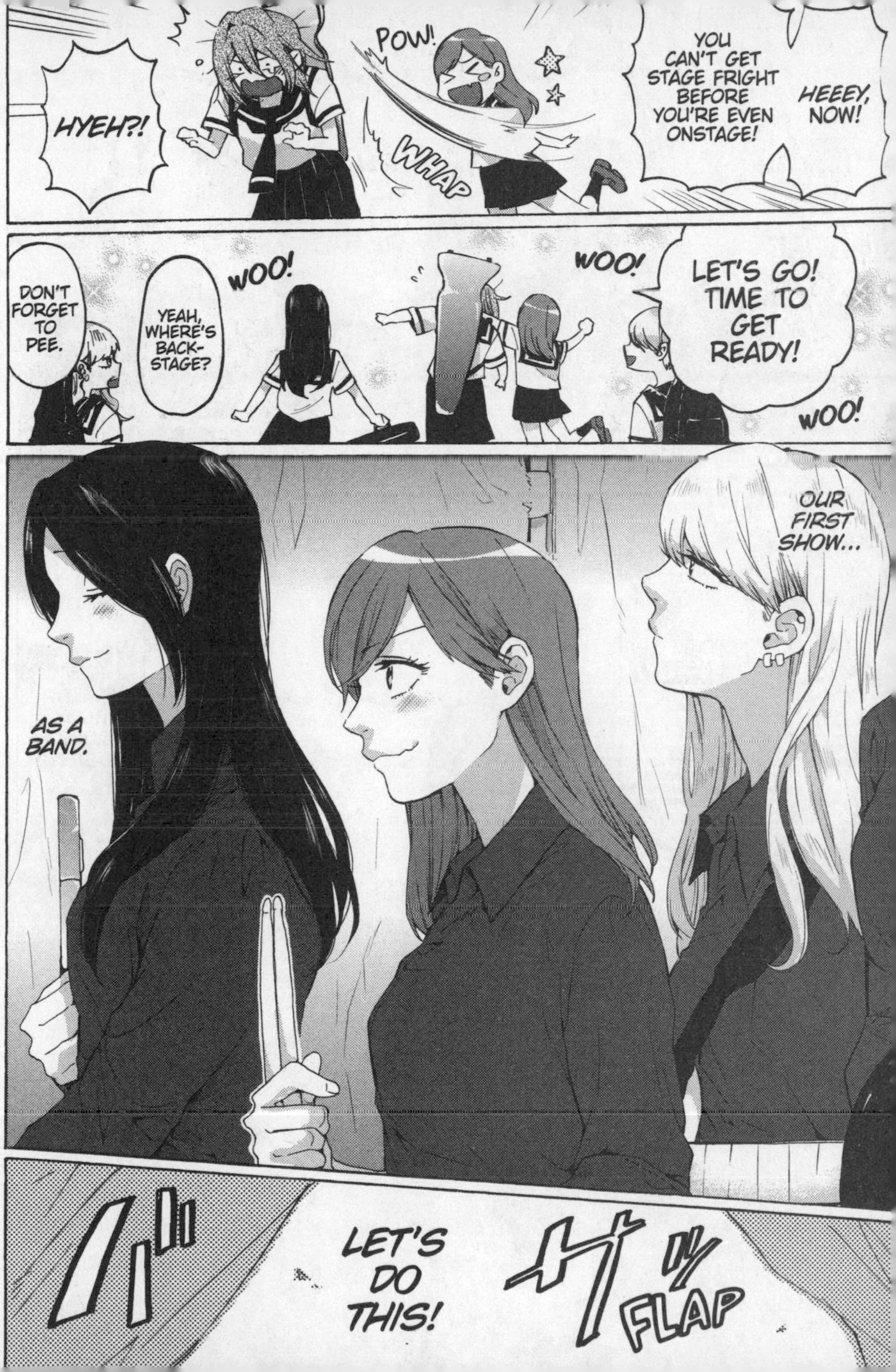
HEEEY, NOW!
YOU CAN'T GET STAGE FRIGHT BEFORE YOU'RE EVEN ONSTAGE!
POW!
WHAP
HYEH?!
LET'S GO! TIME TO GET READY!
WOO!
WOO!
WOO!
YEAH, WHERE'S BACK-STAGE?
DON'T FORGET TO PEE.
OUR FIRST SHOW...
AS A BAND.
FLAP
LET'S DO THIS!

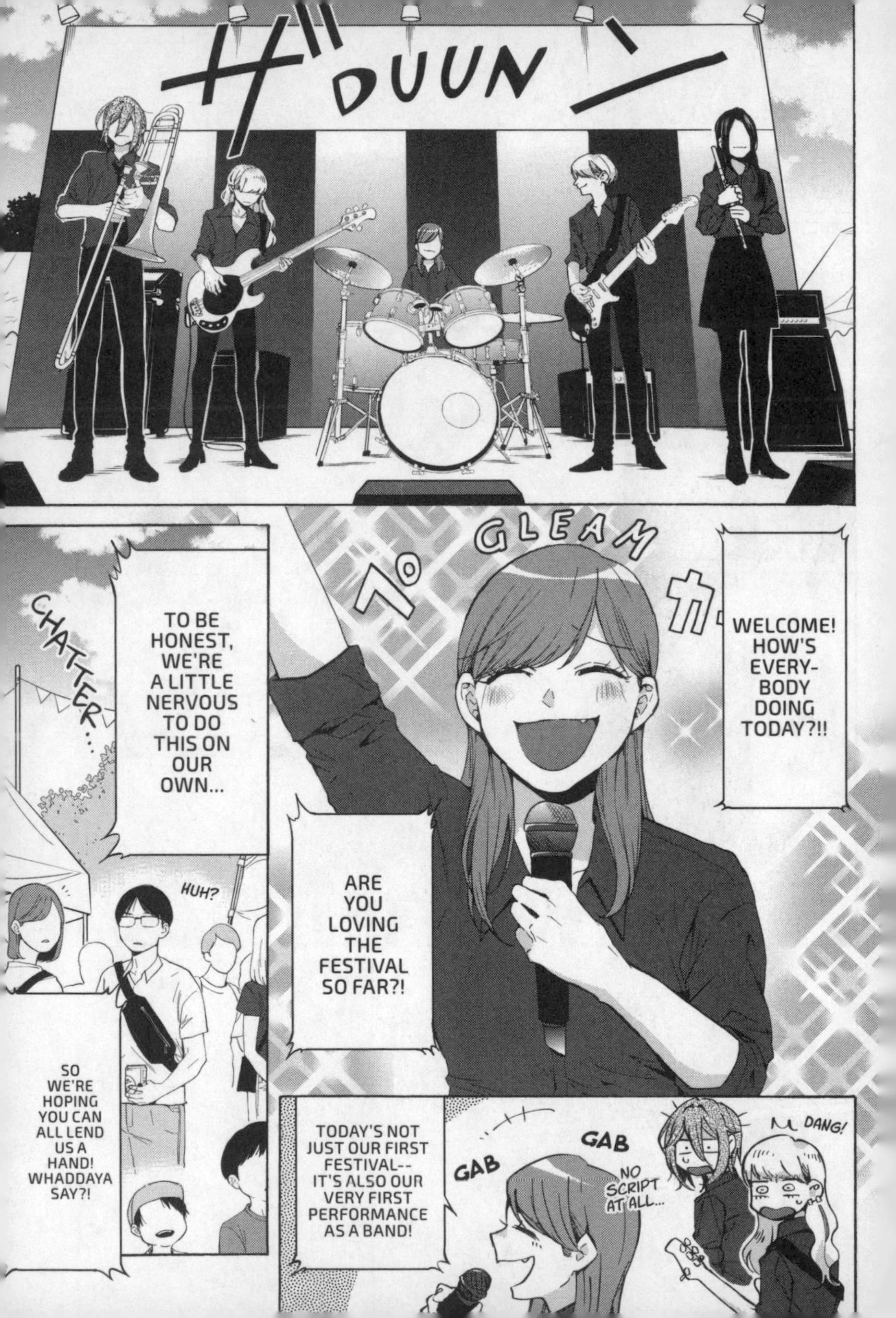
DUUN
GLEAM
WELCOME! HOW'S EVERYBODY DOING TODAY?!!
ARE YOU LOVING THE FESTIVAL SO FAR?!
DANG!
GAB
NO SCRIPT AT ALL...
TODAY'S NOT JUST OUR FIRST FESTIVAL-- IT'S ALSO OUR VERY FIRST PERFORMANCE AS A BAND!
GAB
TO BE HONEST, WE'RE A LITTLE NERVOUS TO DO THIS ON OUR OWN...
CHATTER...
HUH?
SO WE'RE HOPING YOU CAN ALL LEND US A HAND! WHADDAYA SAY?!

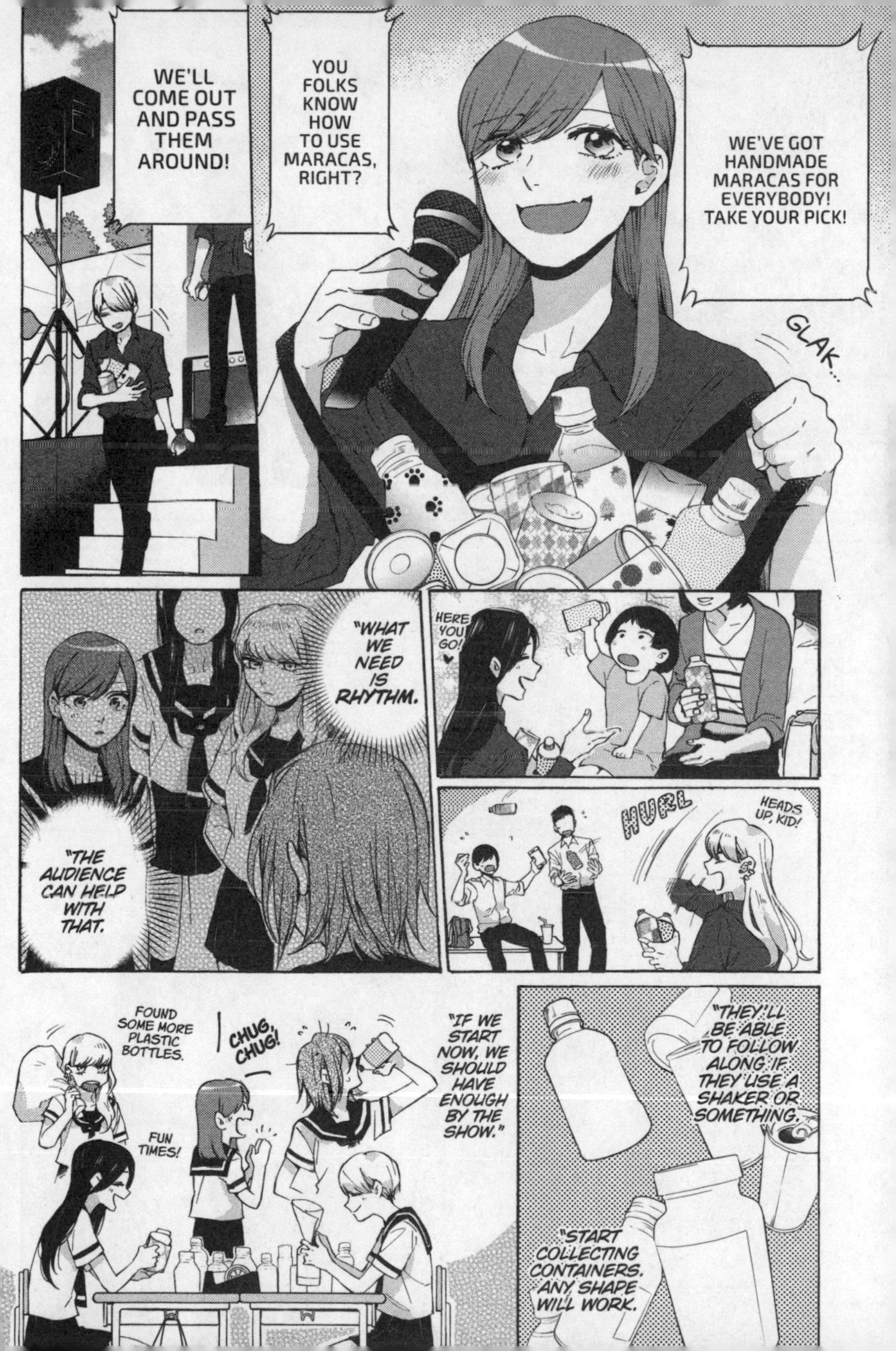
WE'VE GOT HANDMADE MARACAS FOR EVERYBODY! TAKE YOUR PICK!
GLAK...
YOU FOLKS KNOW HOW TO USE MARACAS, RIGHT?
WE'LL COME OUT AND PASS THEM AROUND!
HERE YOU GO!
HURL
HEADS UP, KID!
"WHAT WE NEED IS RHYTHM.
"THE AUDIENCE CAN HELP WITH THAT.
"THEY'LL BE ABLE TO FOLLOW ALONG IF THEY USE A SHAKER OR SOMETHING.
"START COLLECTING CONTAINERS. ANY SHAPE WILL WORK.
"IF WE START NOW, WE SHOULD HAVE ENOUGH BY THE SHOW."
CHUG, CHUG!
FOUND SOME MORE PLASTIC BOTTLES.
FUN TIMES!

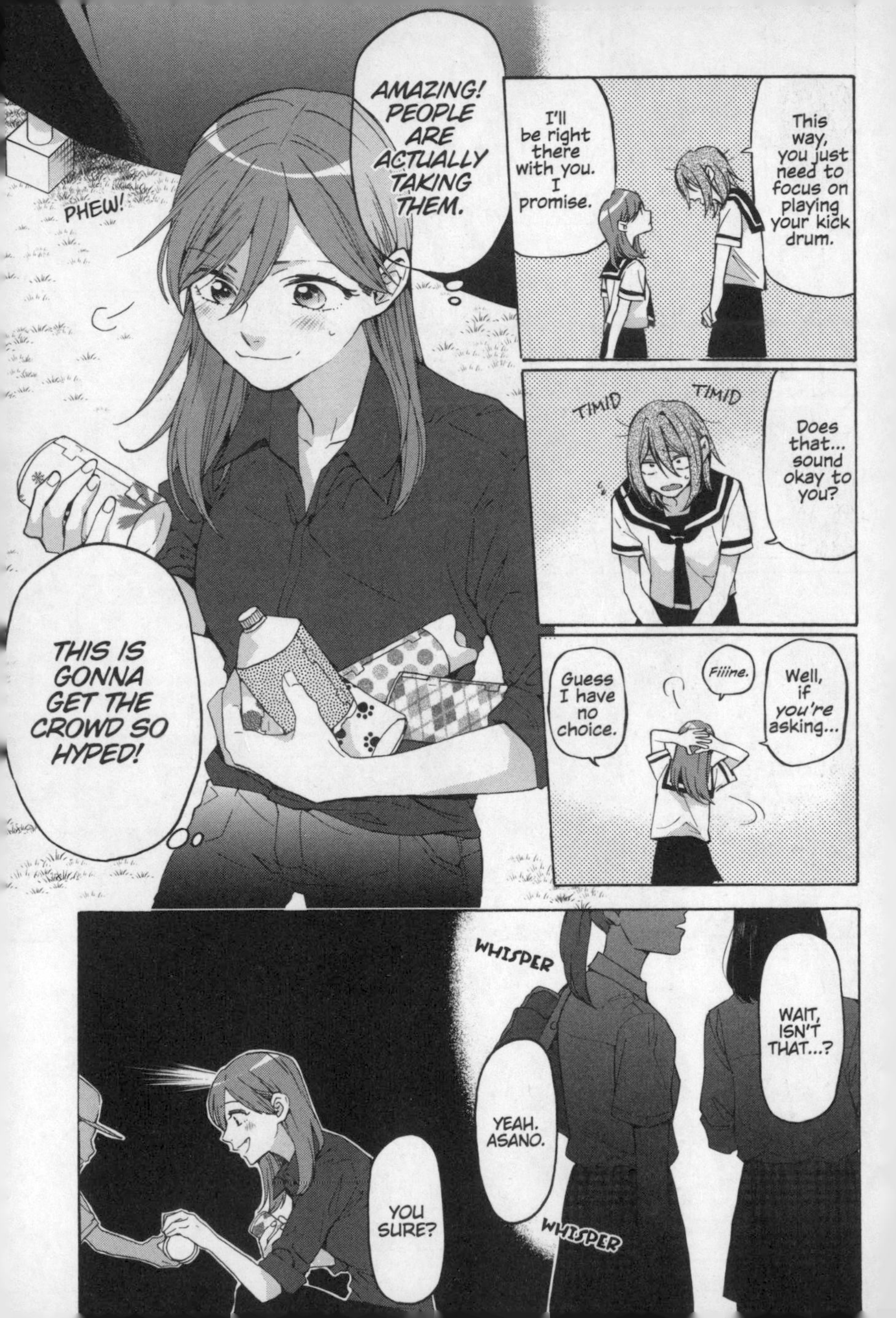
This way, you just need to focus on playing your kick drum.
I'll be right there with you. I promise.
TIMID
TIMID
Does that... sound okay to you?
Well, if *you're* asking...
Fiiine.
Guess I have no choice.
AMAZING! PEOPLE ARE ACTUALLY TAKING THEM.
PHEW!
THIS IS GONNA GET THE CROWD SO HYPED!
WHISPER
WAIT, ISN'T THAT...?
YEAH. ASANO.
WHISPER
YOU SURE?

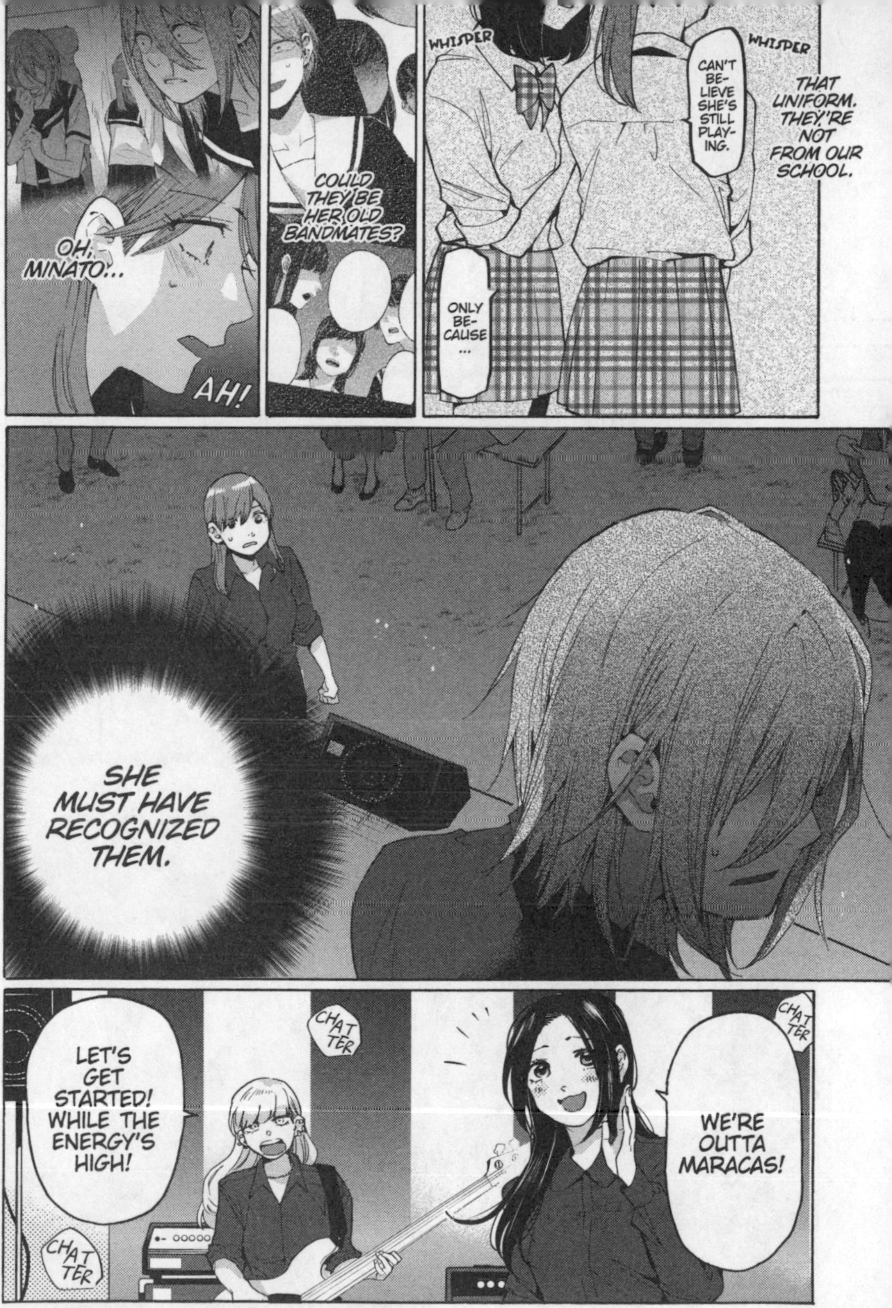
WHISPER
WHISPER
THAT UNIFORM. THEY'RE NOT FROM OUR SCHOOL.
CAN'T BELIEVE SHE'S STILL PLAYING.
ONLY BECAUSE...
COULD THEY BE HER OLD BANDMATES?
OH, MINATO...
AH!
SHE MUST HAVE RECOGNIZED THEM.
CHATTER
WE'RE OUTTA MARACAS!
CHATTER
LET'S GET STARTED! WHILE THE ENERGY'S HIGH!
CHATTER

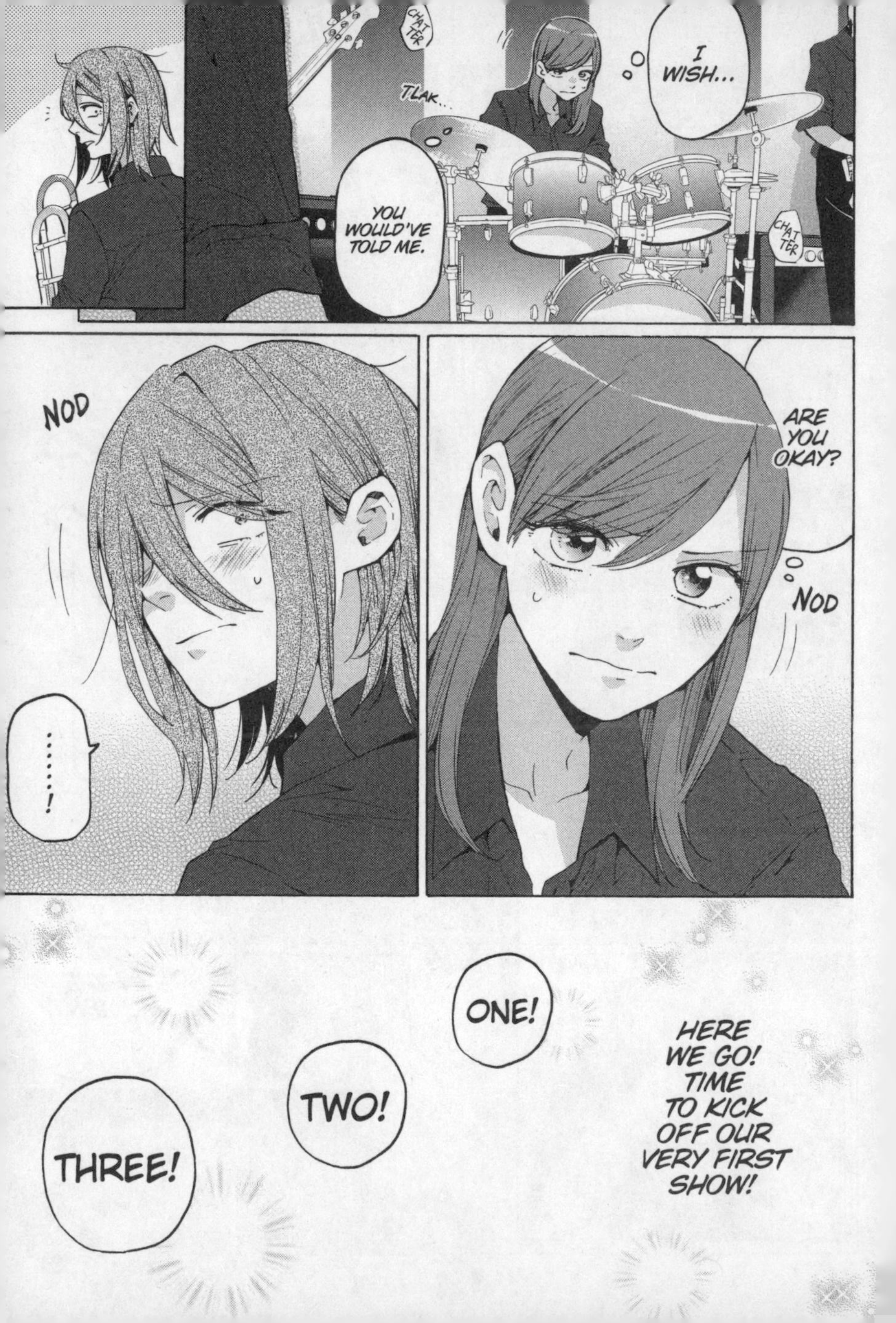
I WISH...
CHATTER
TLAK...
CHATTER
YOU WOULD'VE TOLD ME.
ARE YOU OKAY?
NOD
NOD
......!
HERE WE GO! TIME TO KICK OFF OUR VERY FIRST SHOW!
ONE!
TWO!
THREE!

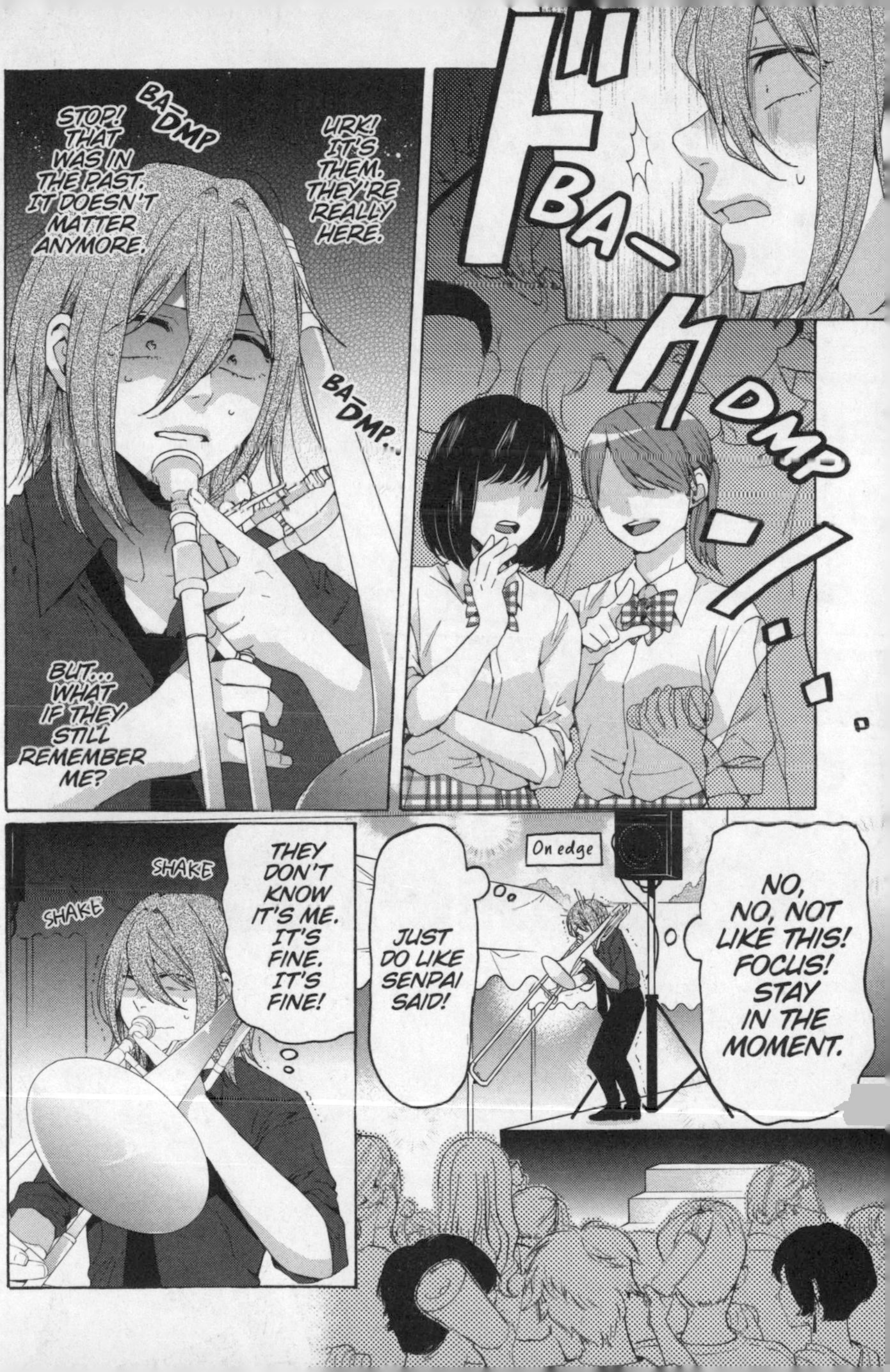
ド
BA–
ン
DMP
–!...
BA–DMP
URK! IT'S THEM. THEY'RE REALLY HERE.
STOP! THAT WAS IN THE PAST. IT DOESN'T MATTER ANYMORE.
BA–DMP...
BUT... WHAT IF THEY STILL REMEMBER ME?
NO, NO, NOT LIKE THIS! FOCUS! STAY IN THE MOMENT.
On edge
JUST DO LIKE SENPAI SAID!
THEY DON'T KNOW IT'S ME. IT'S FINE. IT'S FINE!
SHAKE
SHAKE

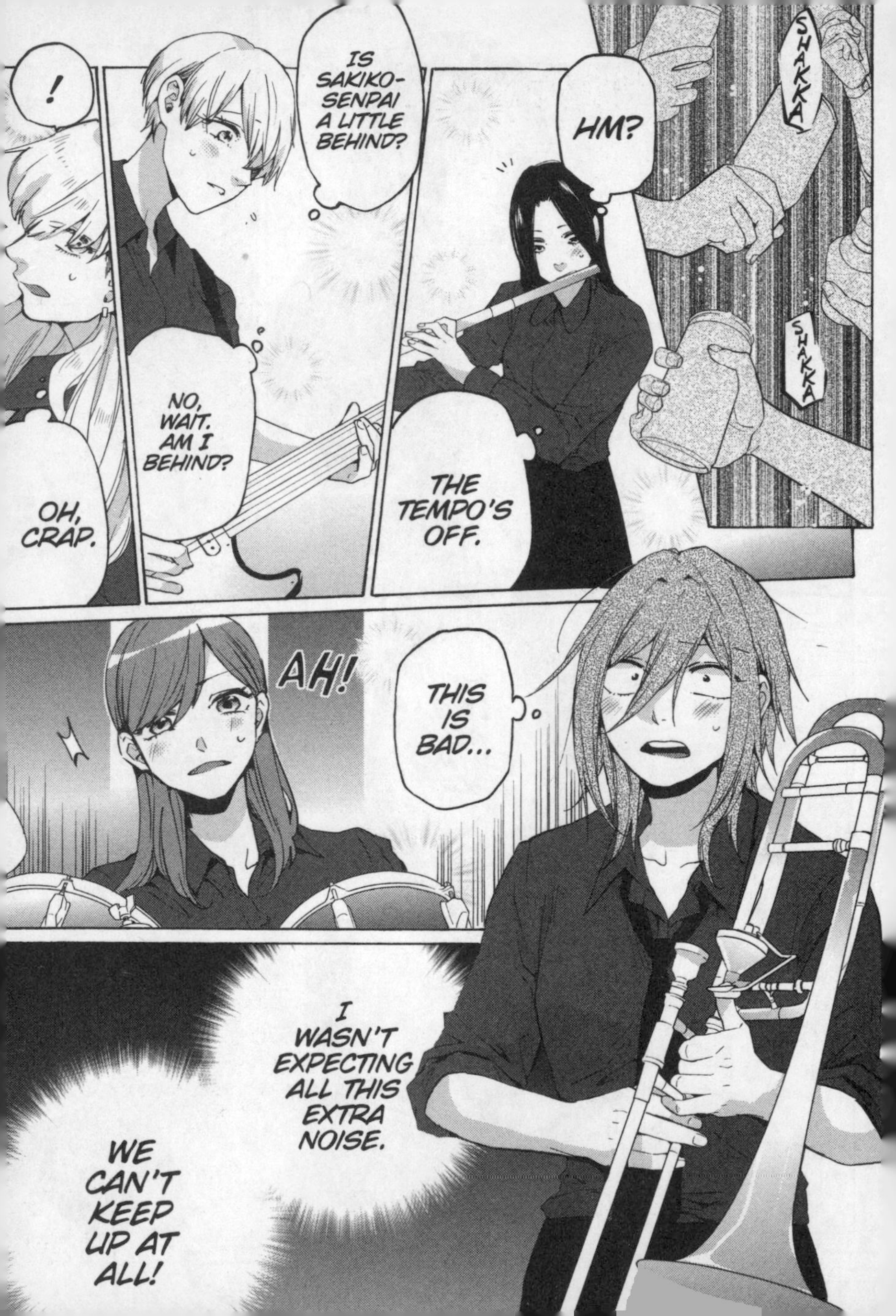
SHAKKA
SHAKKA
HM?
THE TEMPO'S OFF.
IS SAKIKO-SENPAI A LITTLE BEHIND?
NO, WAIT. AM I BEHIND?
!
OH, CRAP.
THIS IS BAD...
AH!
I WASN'T EXPECTING ALL THIS EXTRA NOISE.
WE CAN'T KEEP UP AT ALL!

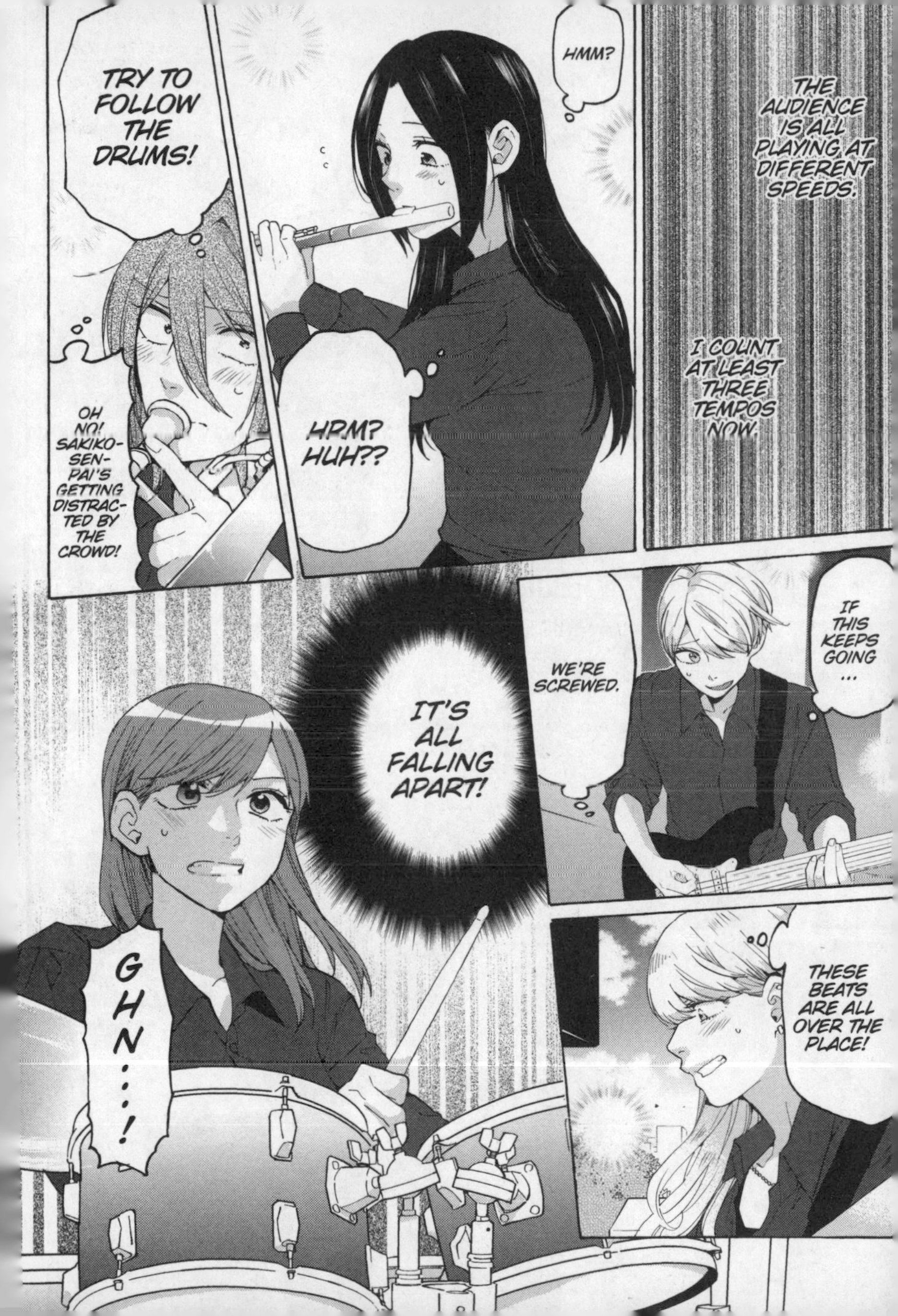
THE AUDIENCE IS ALL PLAYING AT DIFFERENT SPEEDS.
I COUNT AT LEAST THREE TEMPOS NOW.
HMM?
HRM? HUH??
TRY TO FOLLOW THE DRUMS!
OH NO! SAKIKO-SENPAI'S GETTING DISTRACTED BY THE CROWD!
IF THIS KEEPS GOING ...
WE'RE SCREWED.
THESE BEATS ARE ALL OVER THE PLACE!
IT'S ALL FALLING APART!
GHN...!

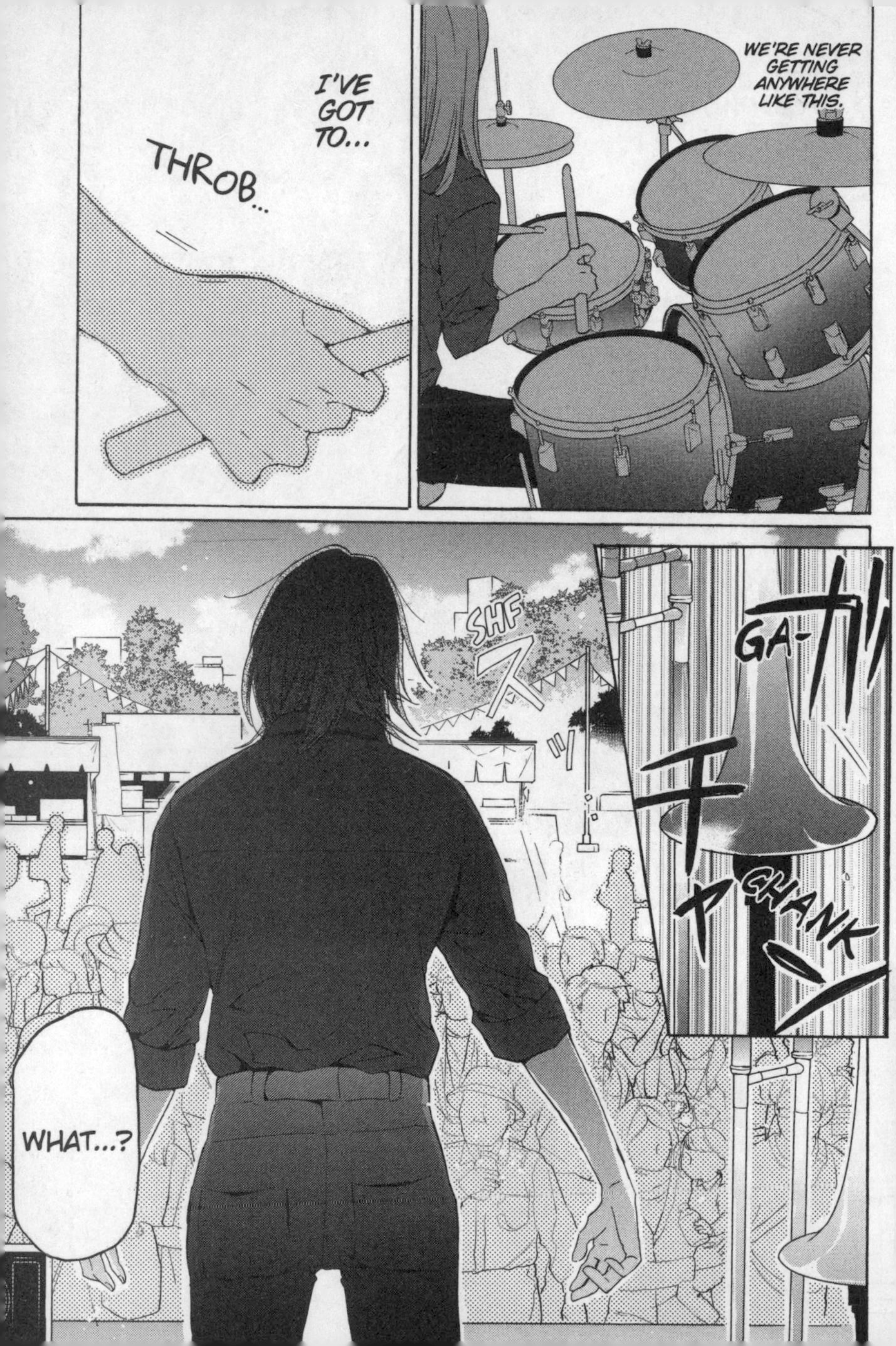
WE'RE NEVER GETTING ANYWHERE LIKE THIS.
I'VE GOT TO...
THROB...
GA-CHANK
SHF
WHAT...?

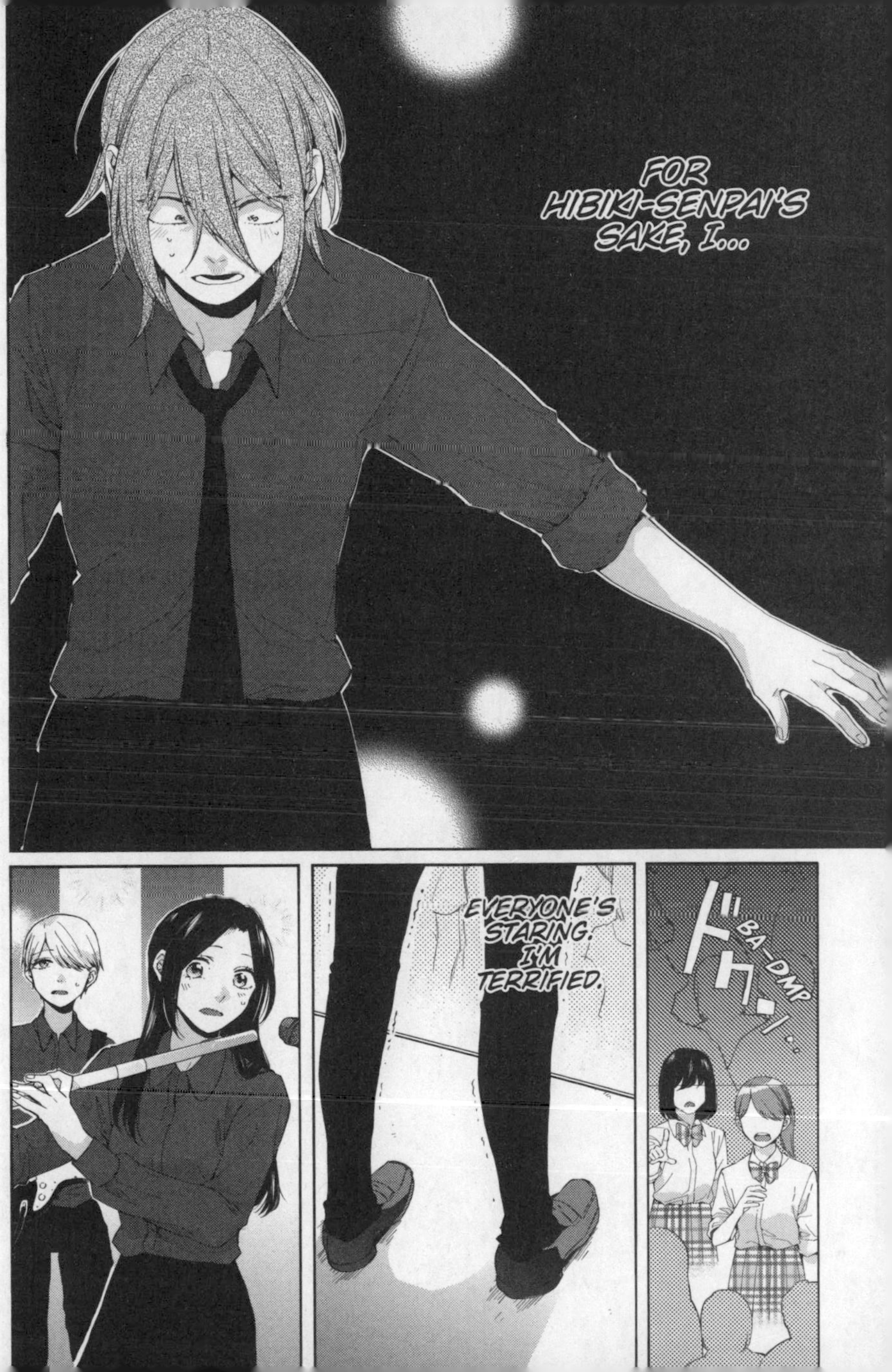
FOR HIBIKI-SENPAI'S SAKE, I...
BA-DMP
EVERYONE'S STARING. I'M TERRIFIED.

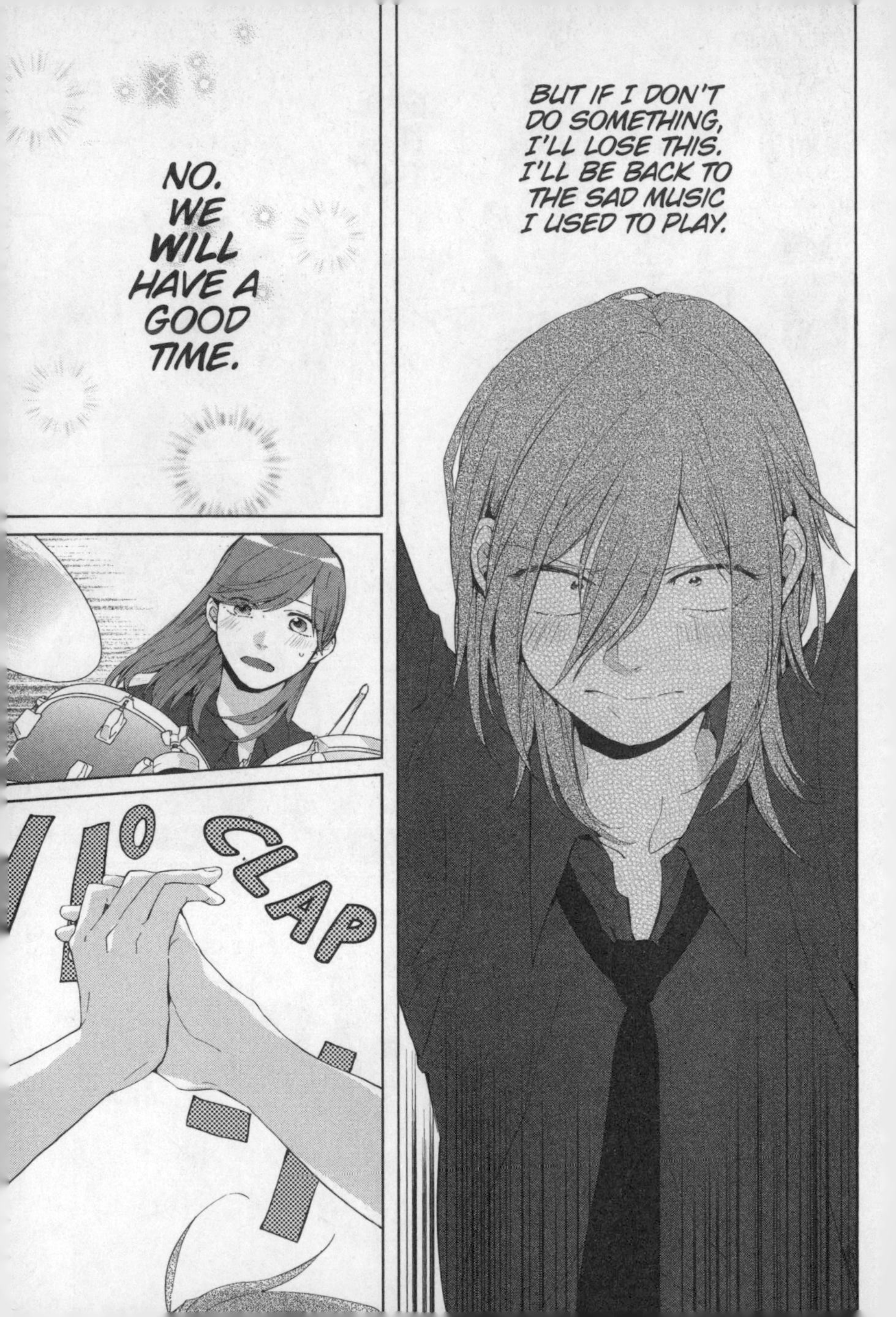
BUT IF I DON'T DO SOMETHING, I'LL LOSE THIS. I'LL BE BACK TO THE SAD MUSIC I USED TO PLAY.
NO. WE WILL HAVE A GOOD TIME.
CLAP

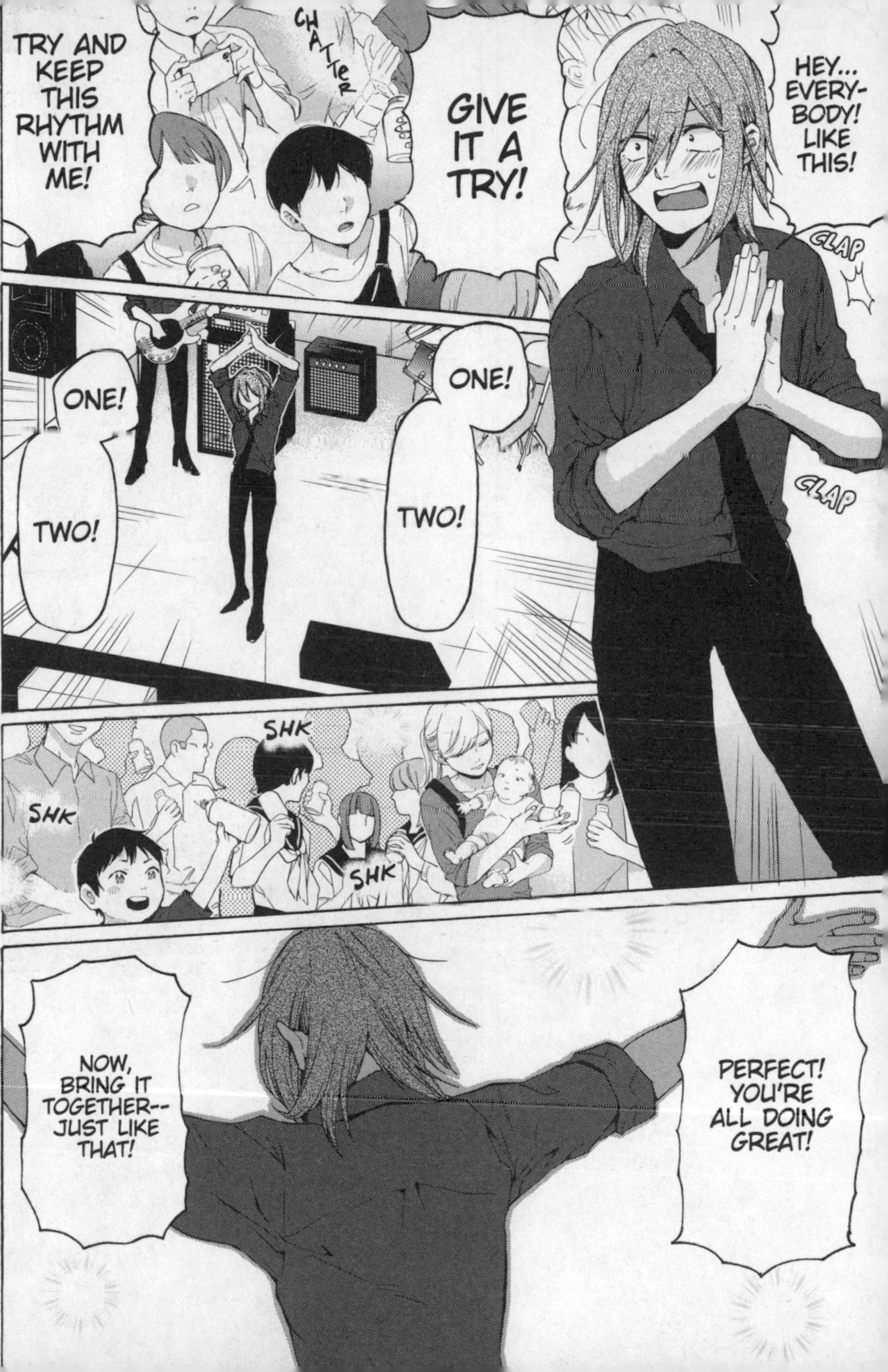
HEY... EVERYBODY! LIKE THIS!
CLAP
GIVE IT A TRY!
CHATTER
TRY AND KEEP THIS RHYTHM WITH ME!
CLAP
ONE!
TWO!
ONE!
TWO!
SHK
SHK
SHK
PERFECT! YOU'RE ALL DOING GREAT!
NOW, BRING IT TOGETHER-- JUST LIKE THAT!

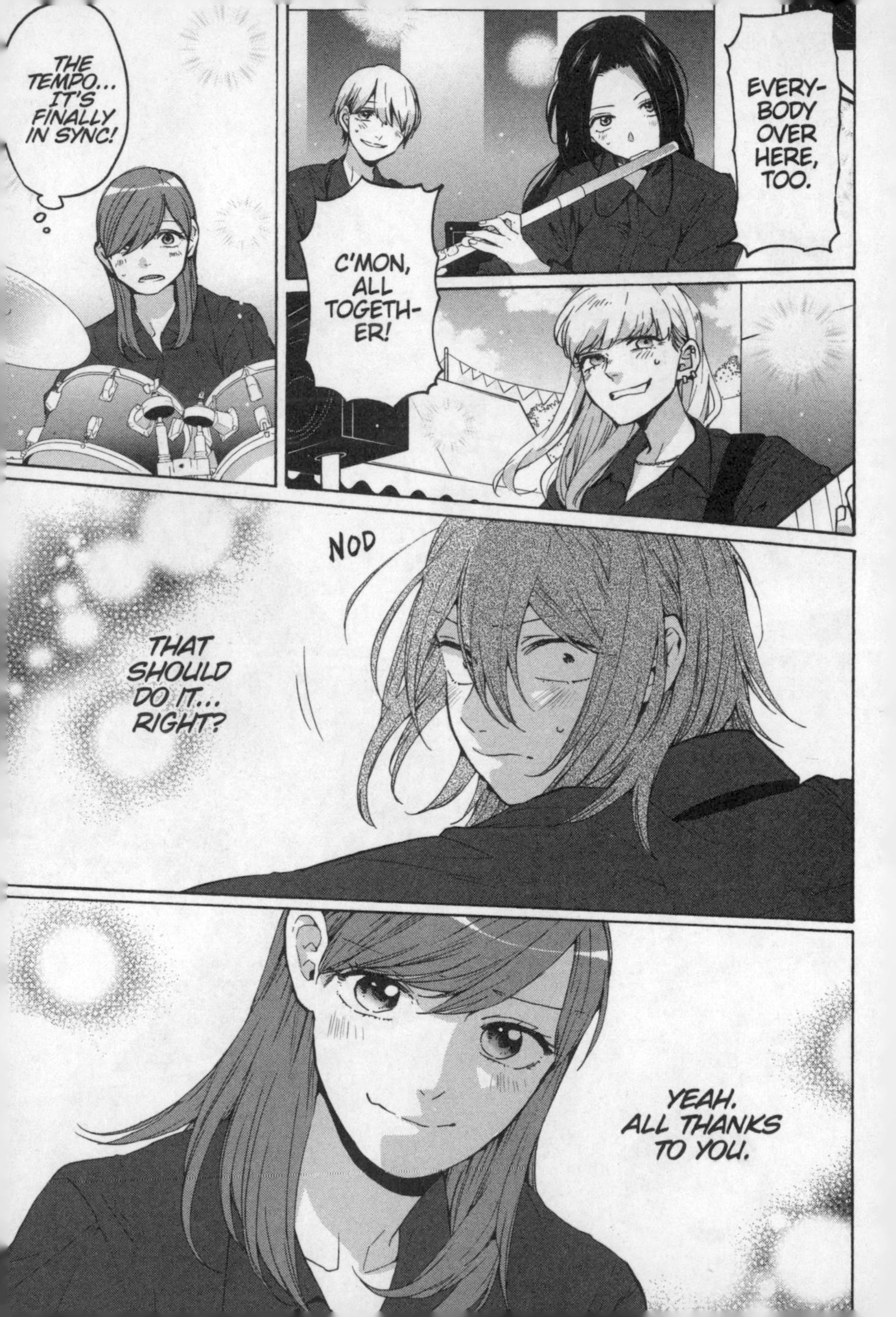
EVERY-BODY OVER HERE, TOO.
C'MON, ALL TOGETH-ER!
THE TEMPO... IT'S FINALLY IN SYNC!
NOD
THAT SHOULD DO IT... RIGHT?
YEAH. ALL THANKS TO YOU.

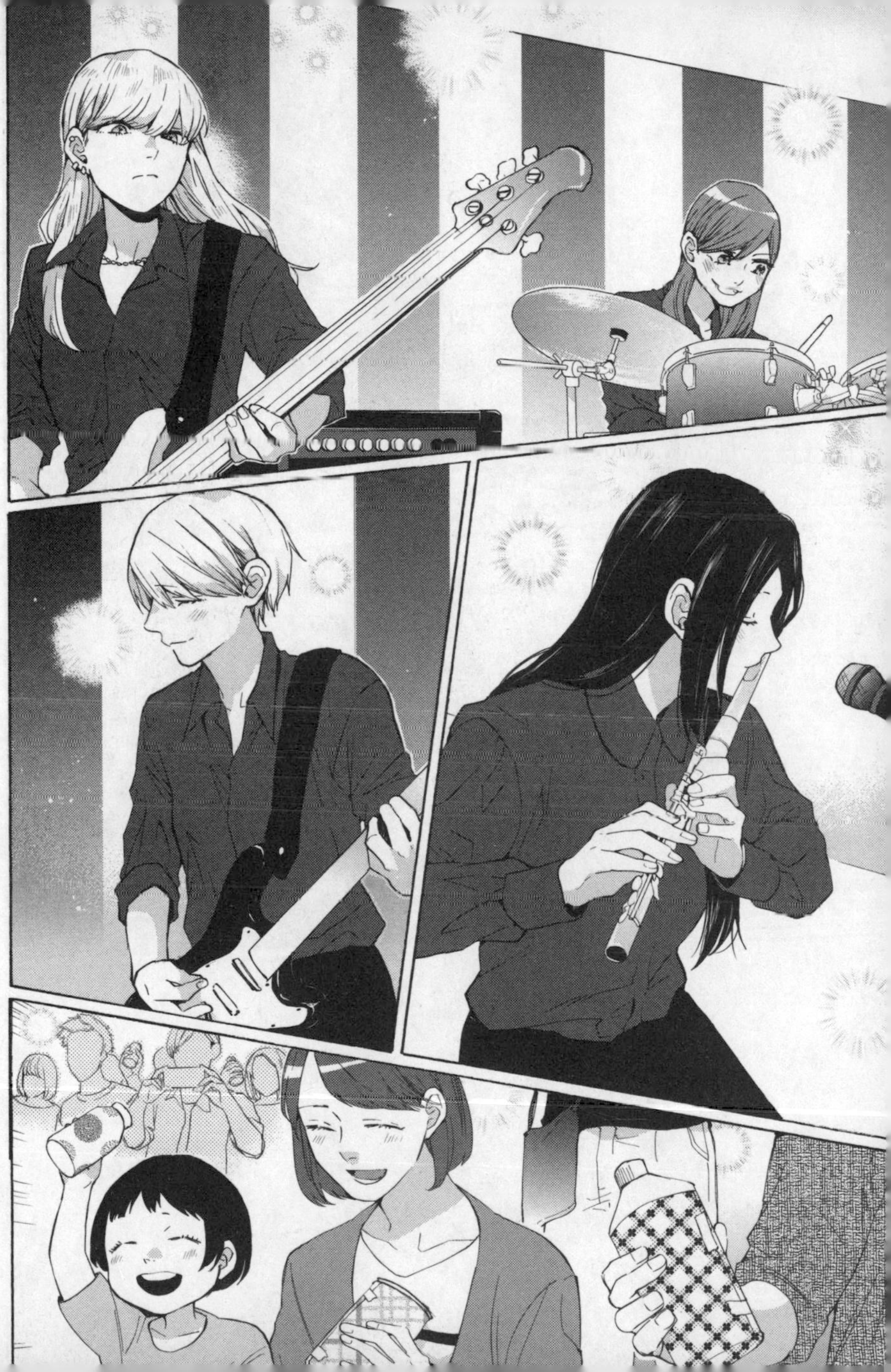

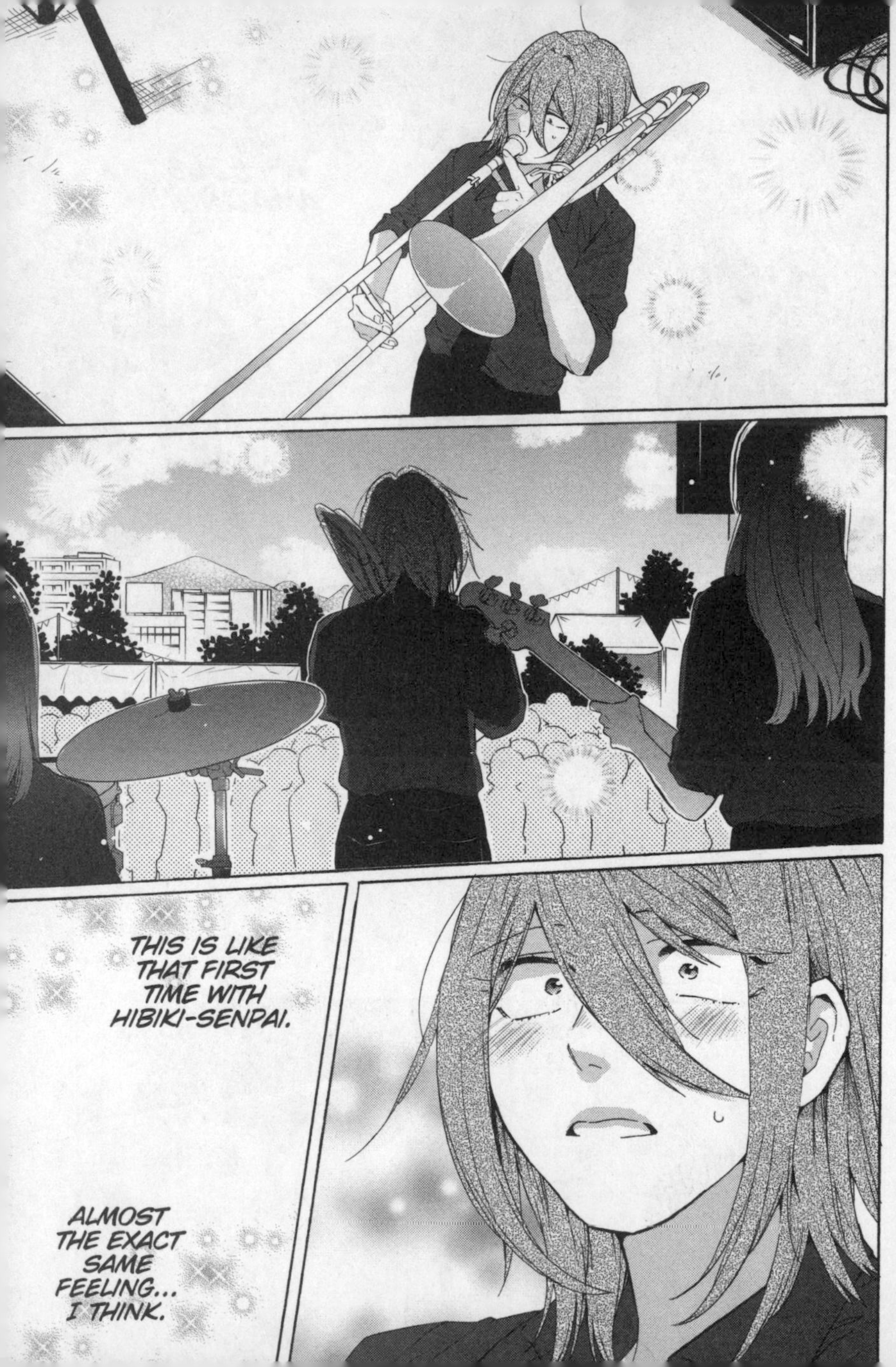
THIS IS LIKE THAT FIRST TIME WITH HIBIKI-SENPAI.
ALMOST THE EXACT SAME FEELING... I THINK.

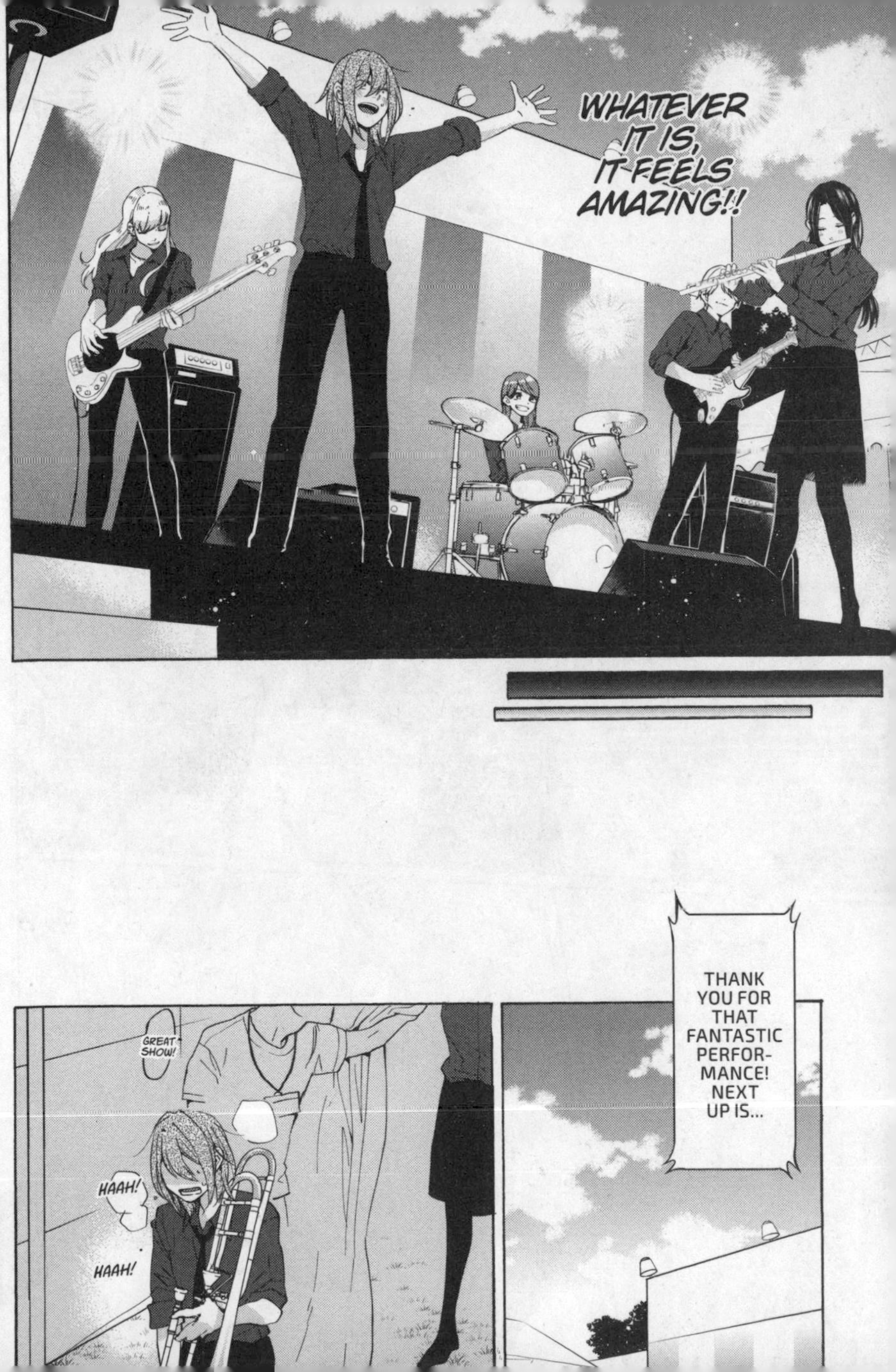
WHATEVER IT IS, IT FEELS AMAZING!!
THANK YOU FOR THAT FANTASTIC PERFOR-MANCE! NEXT UP IS...
GREAT SHOW!
HAAH!
HAAH!

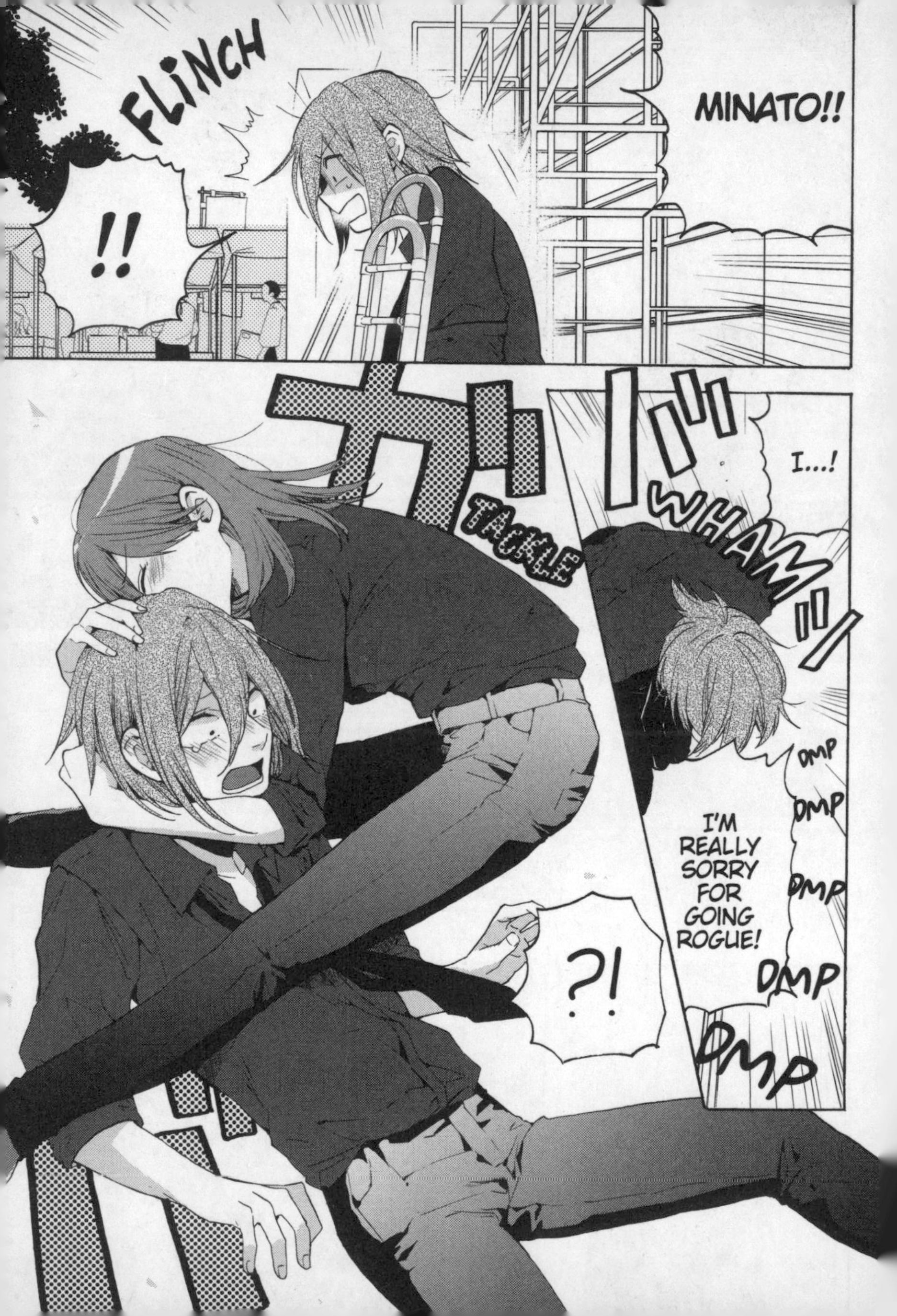
MINATO!!
FLINCH
!!
I...!
WHAM!!
DMP
DMP
DMP
DMP
DMP
I'M REALLY SORRY FOR GOING ROGUE!
TACKLE
?!

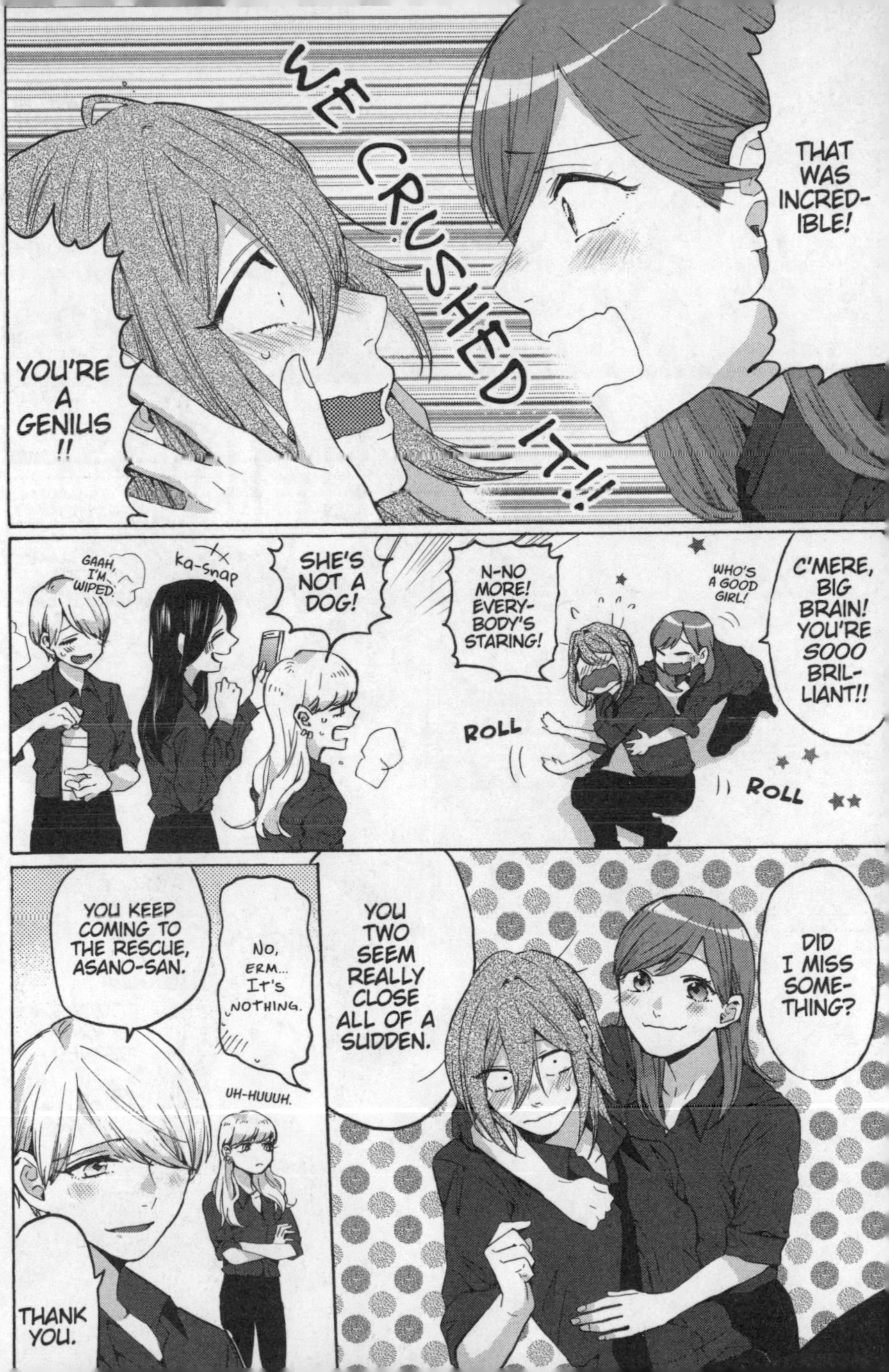
THAT WAS INCREDIBLE!
WE CRUSHED IT!!
YOU'RE A GENIUS!!
C'MERE, BIG BRAIN! YOU'RE SOOO BRILLIANT!!
WHO'S A GOOD GIRL!
N-NO MORE! EVERYBODY'S STARING!
ROLL
ROLL
SHE'S NOT A DOG!
ka-snap
GAAH, I'M WIPED.
DID I MISS SOMETHING?
YOU TWO SEEM REALLY CLOSE ALL OF A SUDDEN.
YOU KEEP COMING TO THE RESCUE, ASANO-SAN.
No, erm... It's NOTHING.
UH-HUUUH.
THANK YOU.

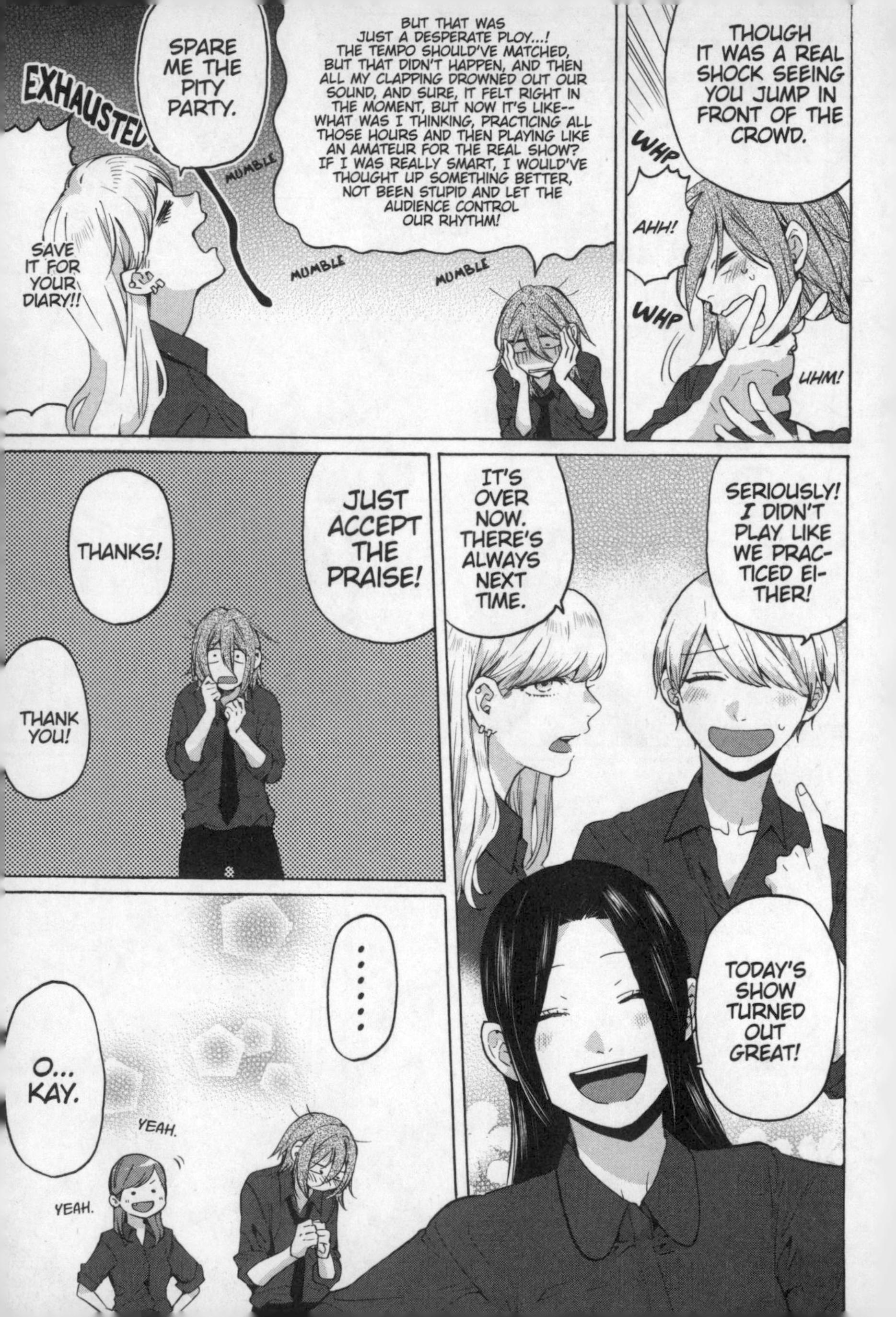
THOUGH IT WAS A REAL SHOCK SEEING YOU JUMP IN FRONT OF THE CROWD.
WHP
AHH!
WHP
UHM!
BUT THAT WAS JUST A DESPERATE PLOY...! THE TEMPO SHOULD'VE MATCHED, BUT THAT DIDN'T HAPPEN, AND THEN ALL MY CLAPPING DROWNED OUT OUR SOUND, AND SURE, IT FELT RIGHT IN THE MOMENT, BUT NOW IT'S LIKE-- WHAT WAS I THINKING, PRACTICING ALL THOSE HOURS AND THEN PLAYING LIKE AN AMATEUR FOR THE REAL SHOW? IF I WAS REALLY SMART, I WOULD'VE THOUGHT UP SOMETHING BETTER, NOT BEEN STUPID AND LET THE AUDIENCE CONTROL OUR RHYTHM!
MUMBLE
SPARE ME THE PITY PARTY.
EXHAUSTED
MUMBLE
MUMBLE
SAVE IT FOR YOUR DIARY!!
SERIOUSLY! I DIDN'T PLAY LIKE WE PRAC- TICED EI- THER!
IT'S OVER NOW. THERE'S ALWAYS NEXT TIME.
TODAY'S SHOW TURNED OUT GREAT!
JUST ACCEPT THE PRAISE!
THANKS!
THANK YOU!
......
O... KAY.
YEAH.
YEAH.

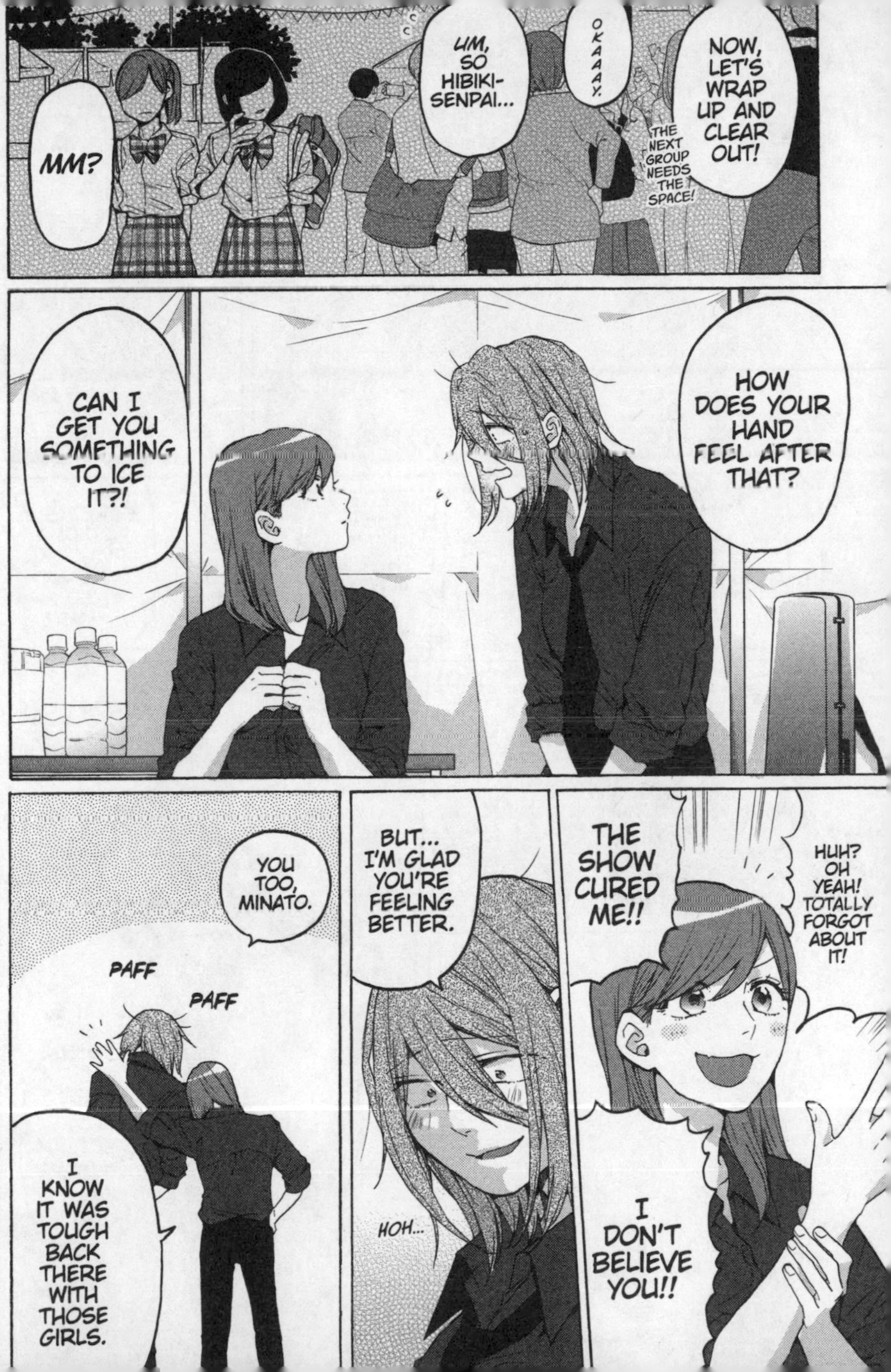
NOW, LET'S WRAP UP AND CLEAR OUT!
THE NEXT GROUP NEEDS THE SPACE!
OKAAAY.
UM, SO HIBIKI-SENPAI...
MM?
HOW DOES YOUR HAND FEEL AFTER THAT?
CAN I GET YOU SOMETHING TO ICE IT?!
HUH? OH YEAH! TOTALLY FORGOT ABOUT IT!
THE SHOW CURED ME!!
I DON'T BELIEVE YOU!!
BUT... I'M GLAD YOU'RE FEELING BETTER.
HOH...
YOU TOO, MINATO.
PAFF
PAFF
I KNOW IT WAS TOUGH BACK THERE WITH THOSE GIRLS.

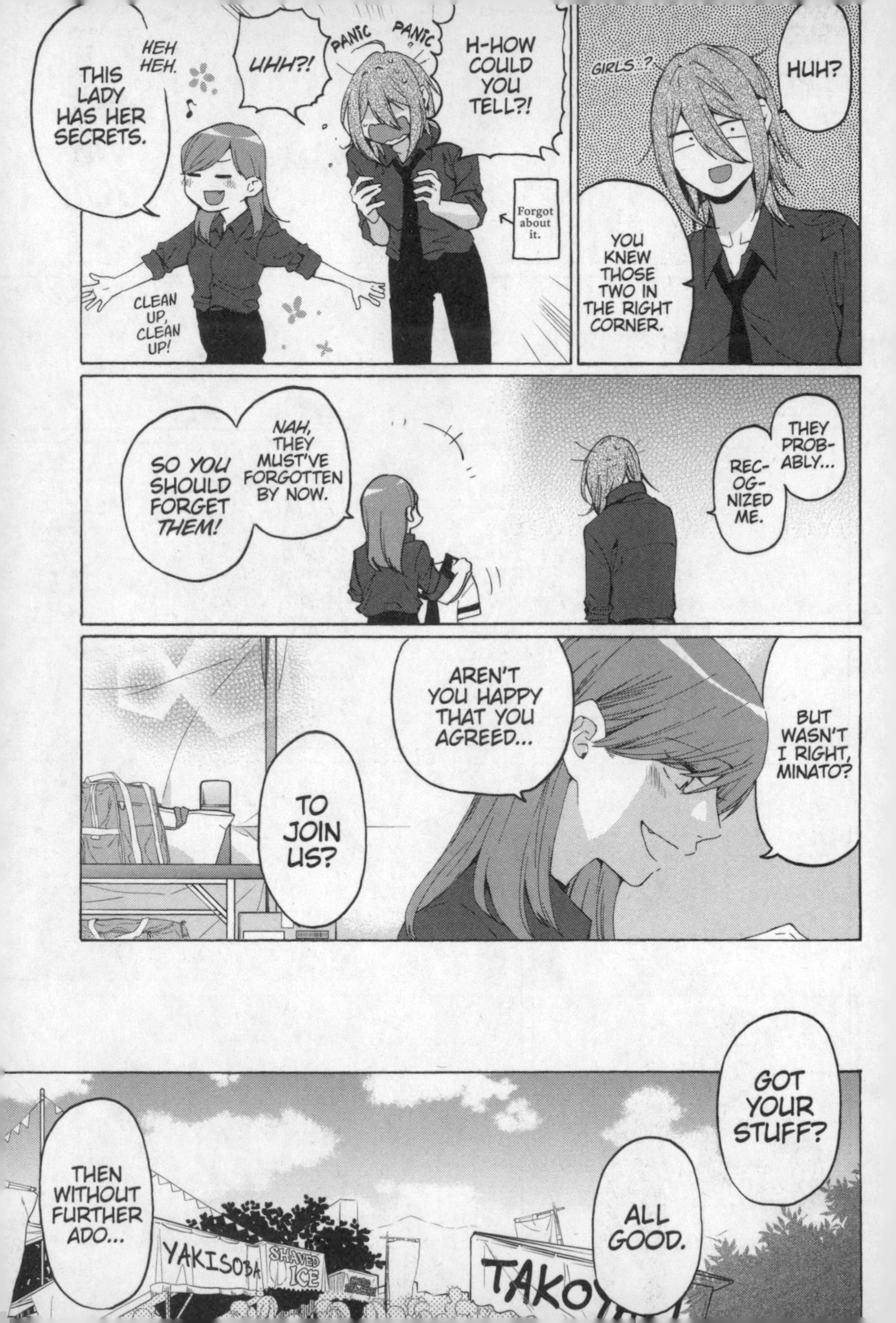
GIRLS...?
HUH?
YOU KNEW THOSE TWO IN THE RIGHT CORNER.
H-HOW COULD YOU TELL?!
PANIC
PANIC
UHH?!
Forgot about it.
HEH HEH.
THIS LADY HAS HER SECRETS.
CLEAN UP, CLEAN UP!
THEY PROBABLY...
RECOGNIZED ME.
NAH, THEY MUST'VE FORGOTTEN BY NOW.
SO YOU SHOULD FORGET THEM!
BUT WASN'T I RIGHT, MINATO?
AREN'T YOU HAPPY THAT YOU AGREED...
TO JOIN US?
GOT YOUR STUFF?
ALL GOOD.
THEN WITHOUT FURTHER ADO...
YAKISOBA
SHAVED ICE

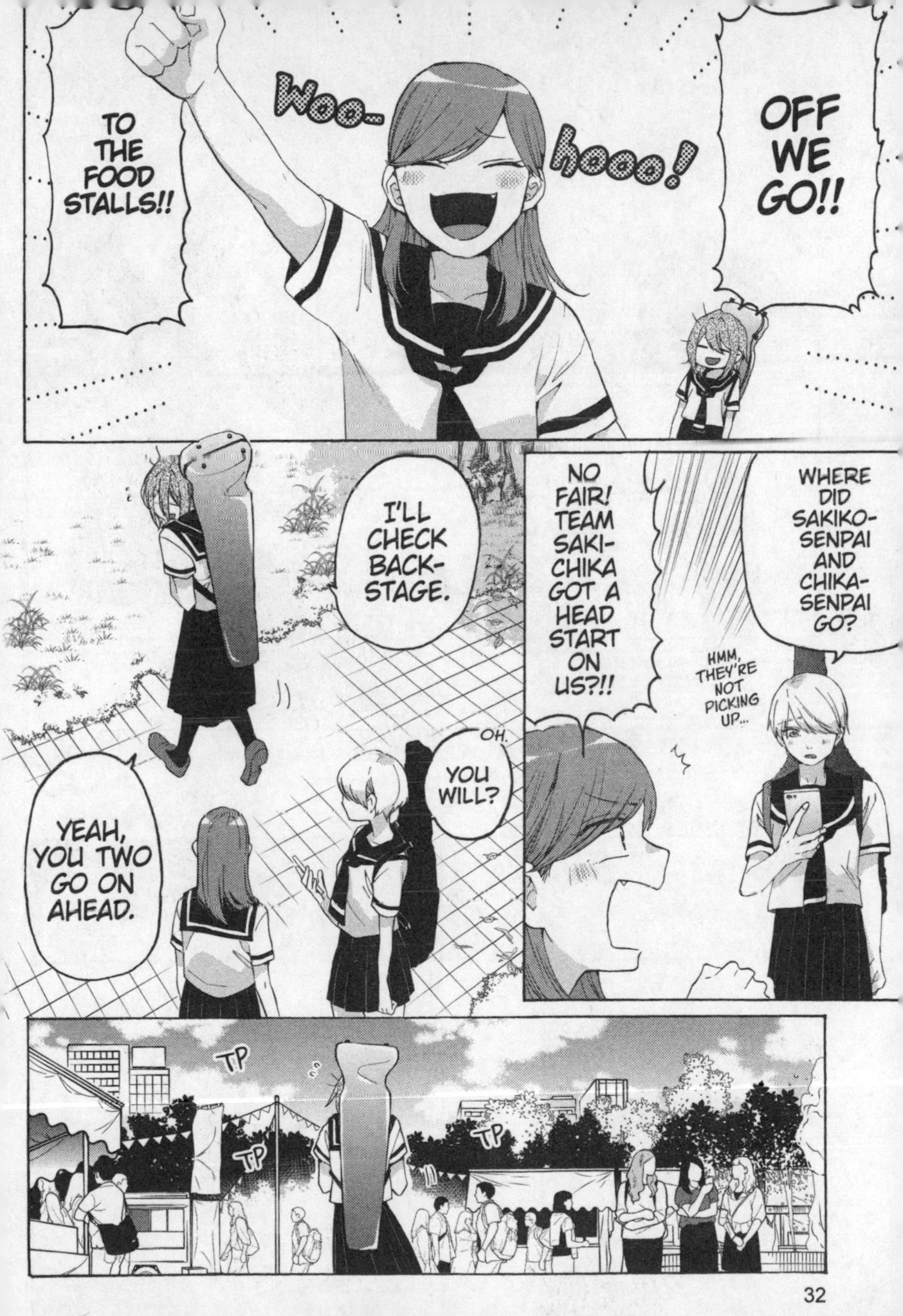
OFF WE GO!!
Woo-hooo!
TO THE FOOD STALLS!!
WHERE DID SAKIKO-SENPAI AND CHIKA-SENPAI GO?
HMM, THEY'RE NOT PICKING UP...
NO FAIR! TEAM SAKI-CHIKA GOT A HEAD START ON US?!!
I'LL CHECK BACK-STAGE.
OH.
YOU WILL?
YEAH, YOU TWO GO ON AHEAD.
TP
TP
TP

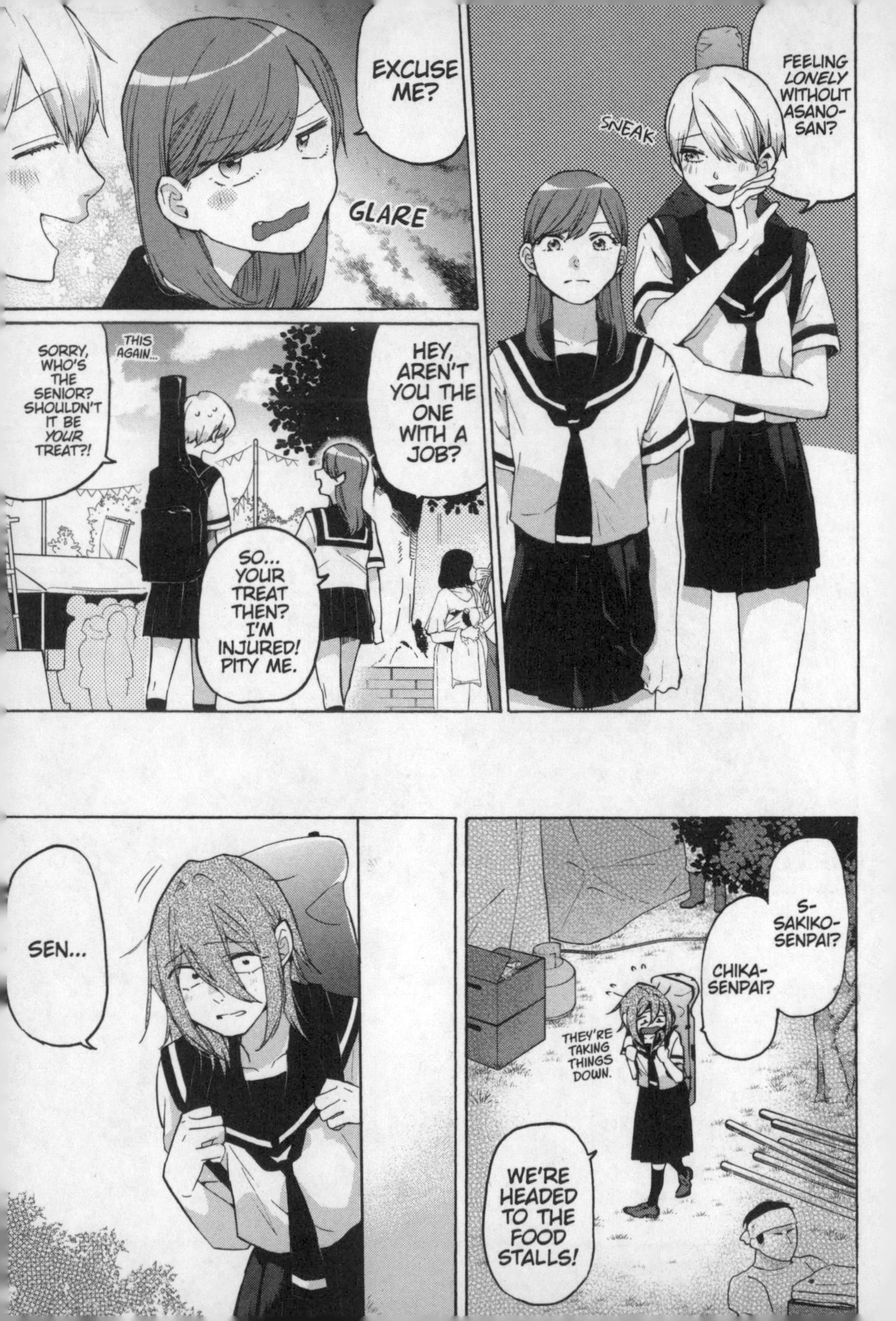
SNEAK
FEELING LONELY WITHOUT ASANO-SAN?
EXCUSE ME?
GLARE
HEY, AREN'T YOU THE ONE WITH A JOB?
SO... YOUR TREAT THEN? I'M INJURED! PITY ME.
THIS AGAIN...
SORRY, WHO'S THE SENIOR? SHOULDN'T IT BE YOUR TREAT?!
S-SAKIKO-SENPAI?
CHIKA-SENPAI?
THEY'RE TAKING THINGS DOWN.
WE'RE HEADED TO THE FOOD STALLS!
SEN...

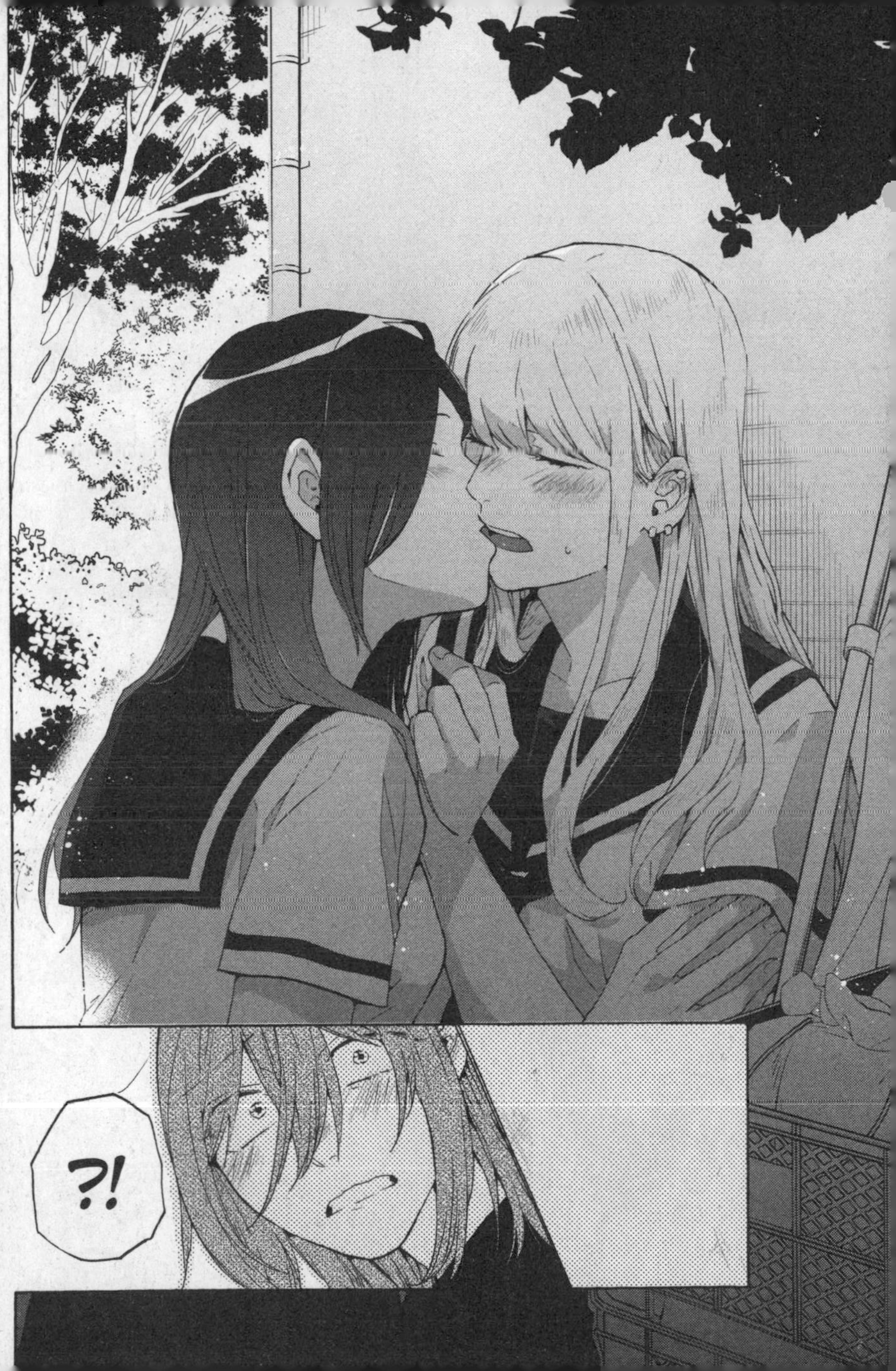
?!

Hello, Melancholic!

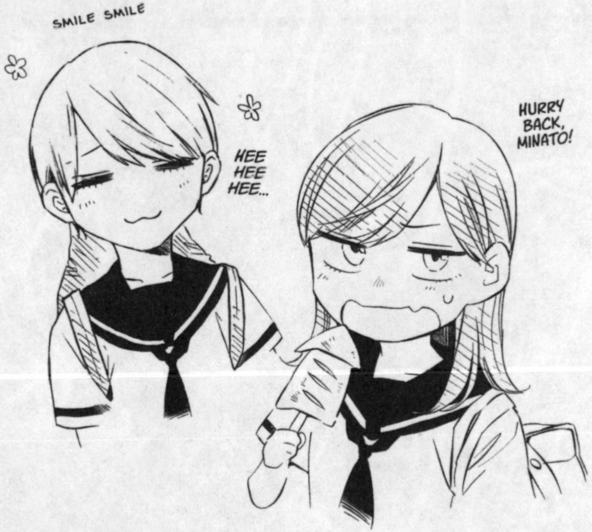
HURRY BACK, MINATO!
HEE HEE HEE...
SMILE SMILE

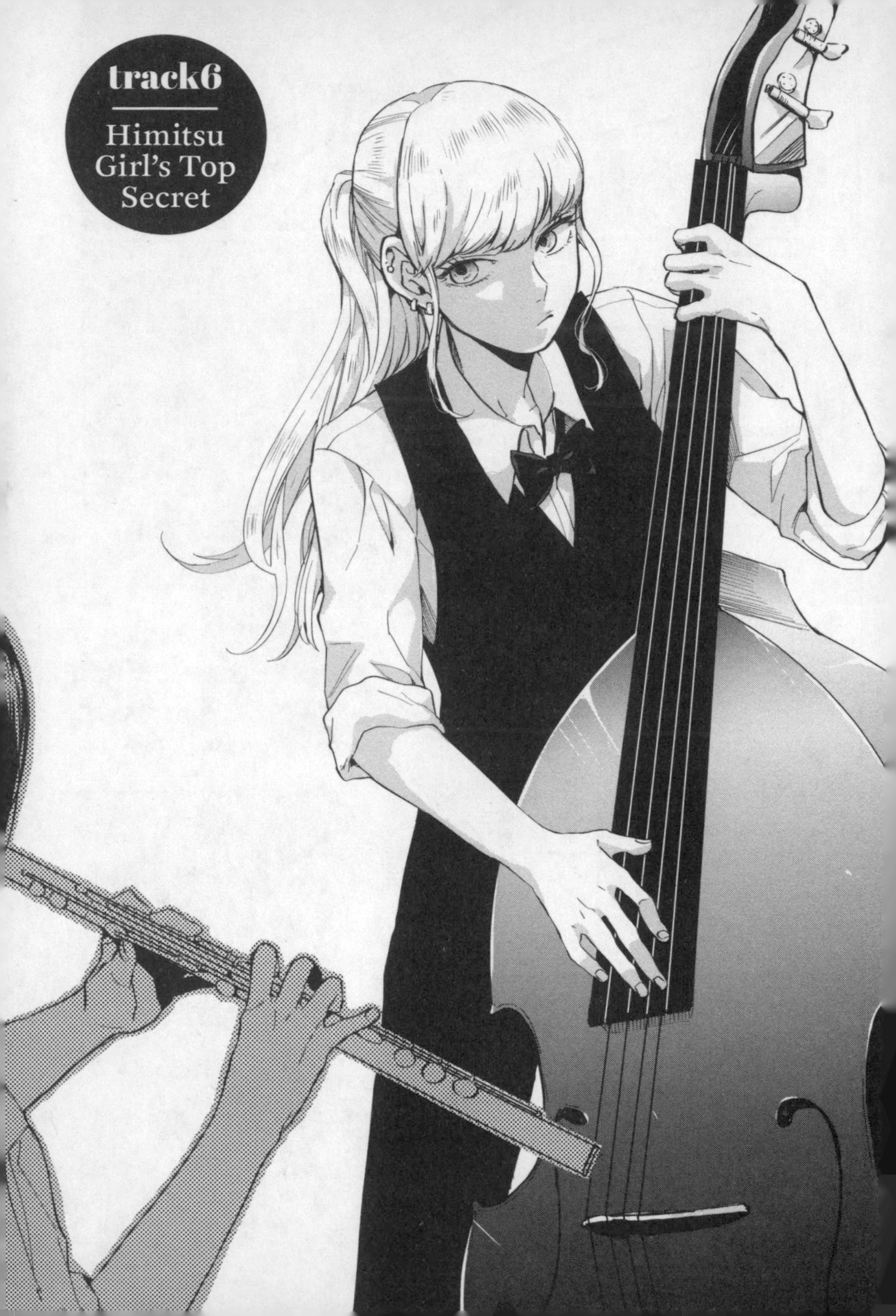
track6
Himitsu Girl's Top Secret

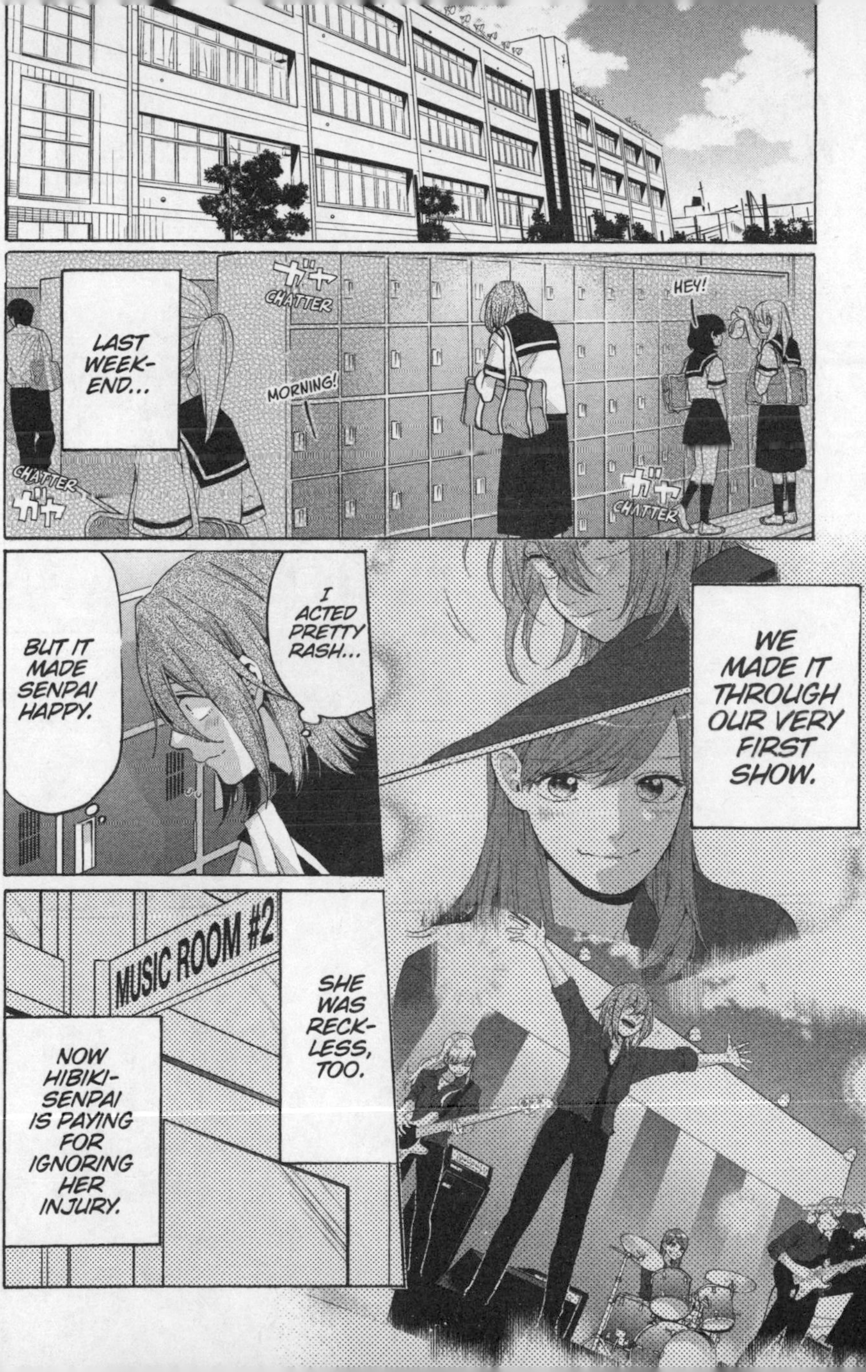
HEY!
ガヤ
CHATTER
MORNING!
ガヤ
CHATTER
LAST WEEKEND...
CHATTER
ガヤ
WE MADE IT THROUGH OUR VERY FIRST SHOW.
I ACTED PRETTY RASH...
BUT IT MADE SENPAI HAPPY.
SHE WAS RECKLESS, TOO.
MUSIC ROOM #2
NOW HIBIKI-SENPAI IS PAYING FOR IGNORING HER INJURY.

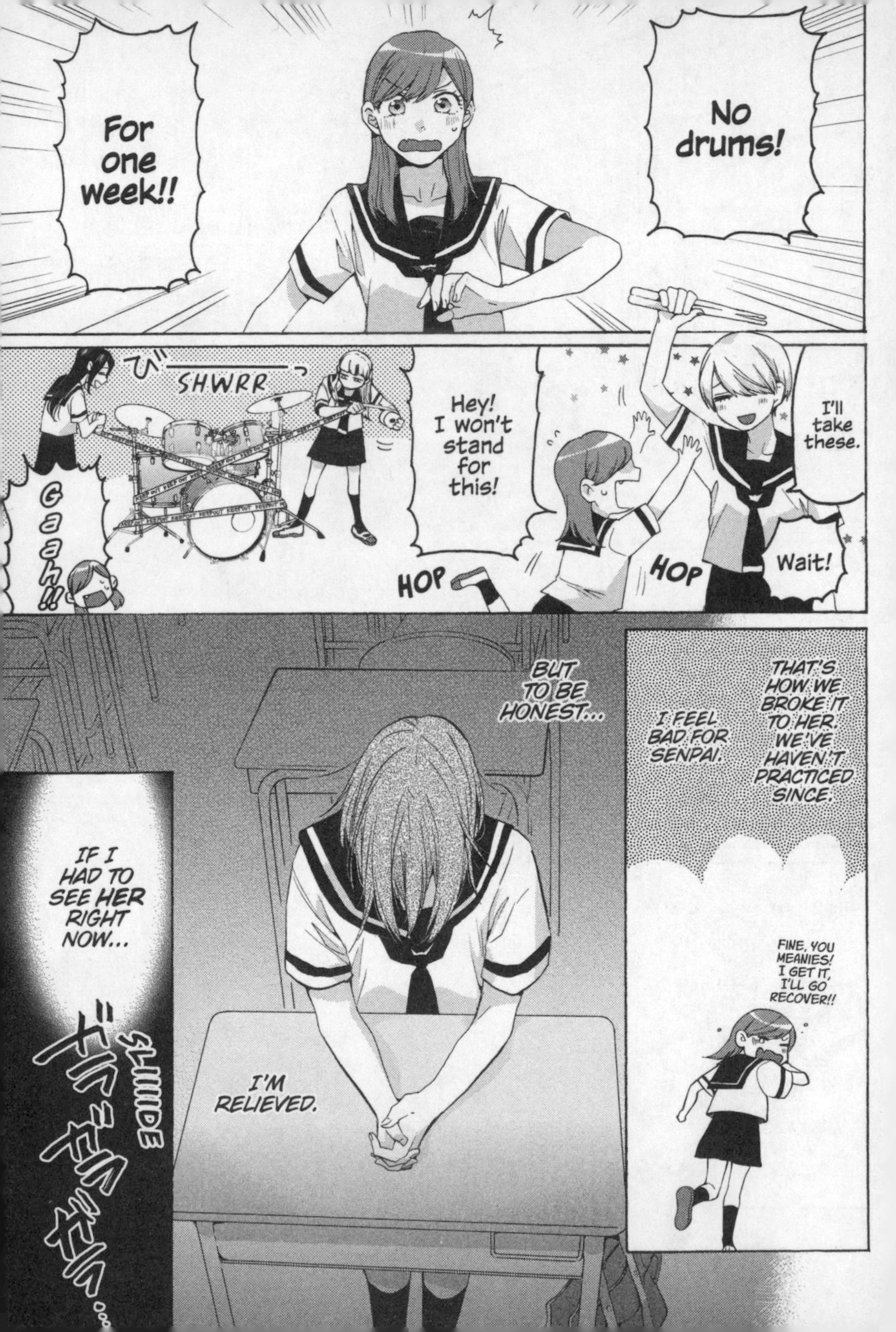
No drums!
For one week!!
I'll take these.
Hey! I won't stand for this!
Wait!
HOP
HOP
び
SHWRR
Gaah!!
THAT'S HOW WE BROKE IT TO HER. WE'VE HAVEN'T PRACTICED SINCE.
I FEEL BAD FOR SENPAI.
FINE, YOU MEANIES! I GET IT, I'LL GO RECOVER!!
BUT TO BE HONEST...
I'M RELIEVED.
IF I HAD TO SEE HER RIGHT NOW...
SLIIIDE

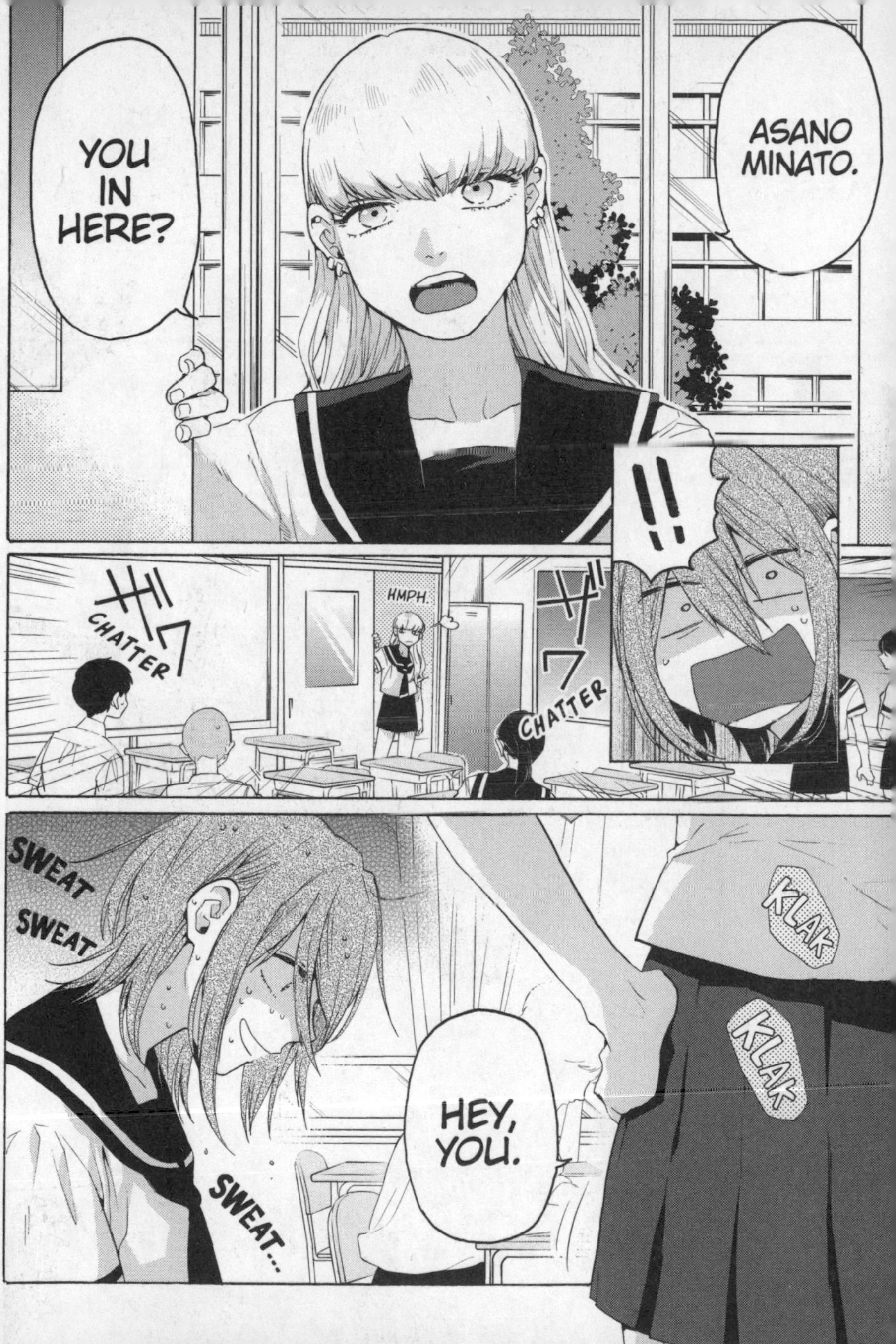
ASANO MINATO.
YOU IN HERE?
!!
CHATTER
HMPH.
CHATTER
KLAK
KLAK
HEY, YOU.
SWEAT
SWEAT
SWEAT...

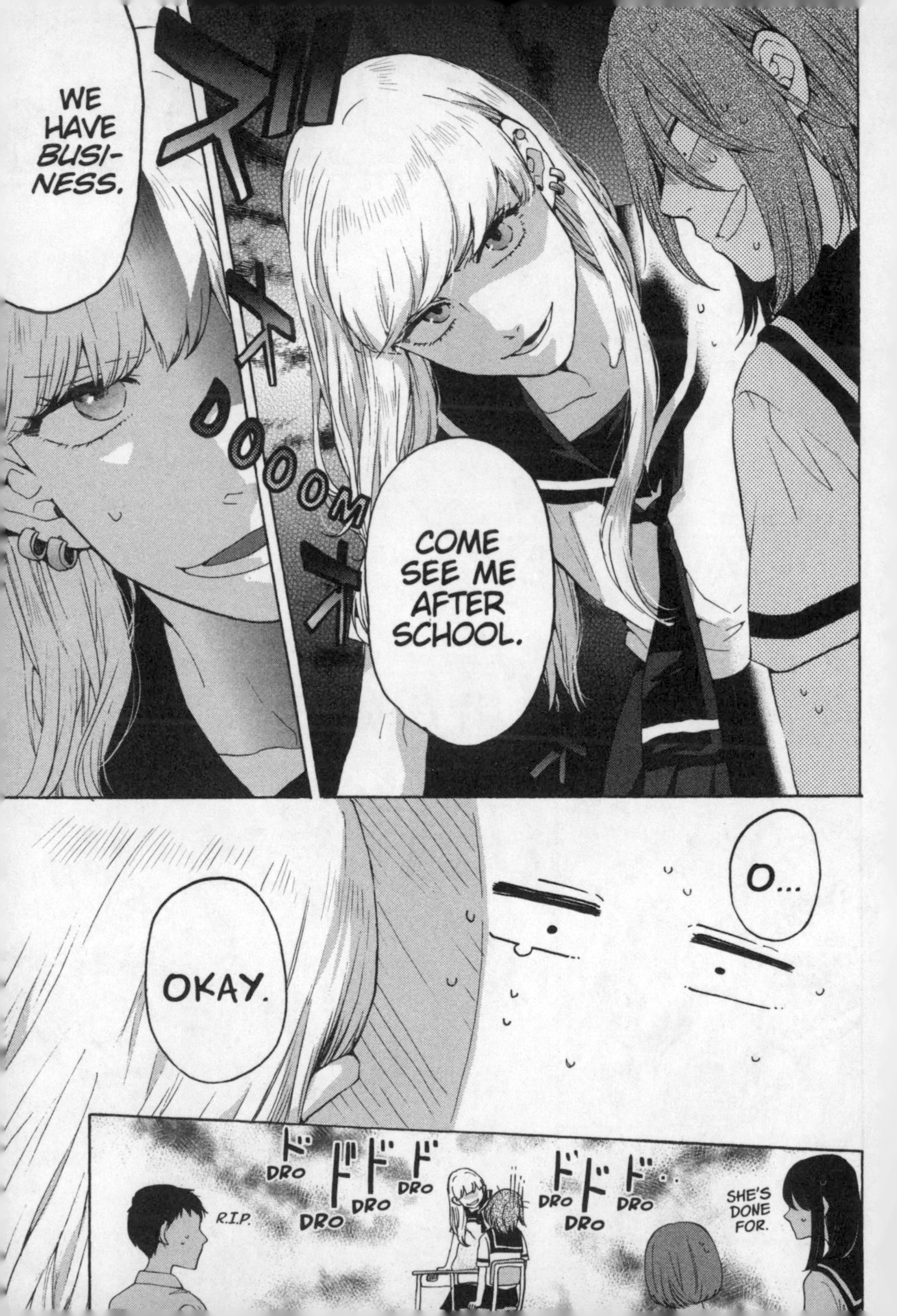
COME SEE ME AFTER SCHOOL.
DOOOOM
WE HAVE BUSI-NESS.
O...
OKAY.
SHE'S DONE FOR.
DRO DRO DRO DRO DRO DRO DRO DRO
R.I.P.

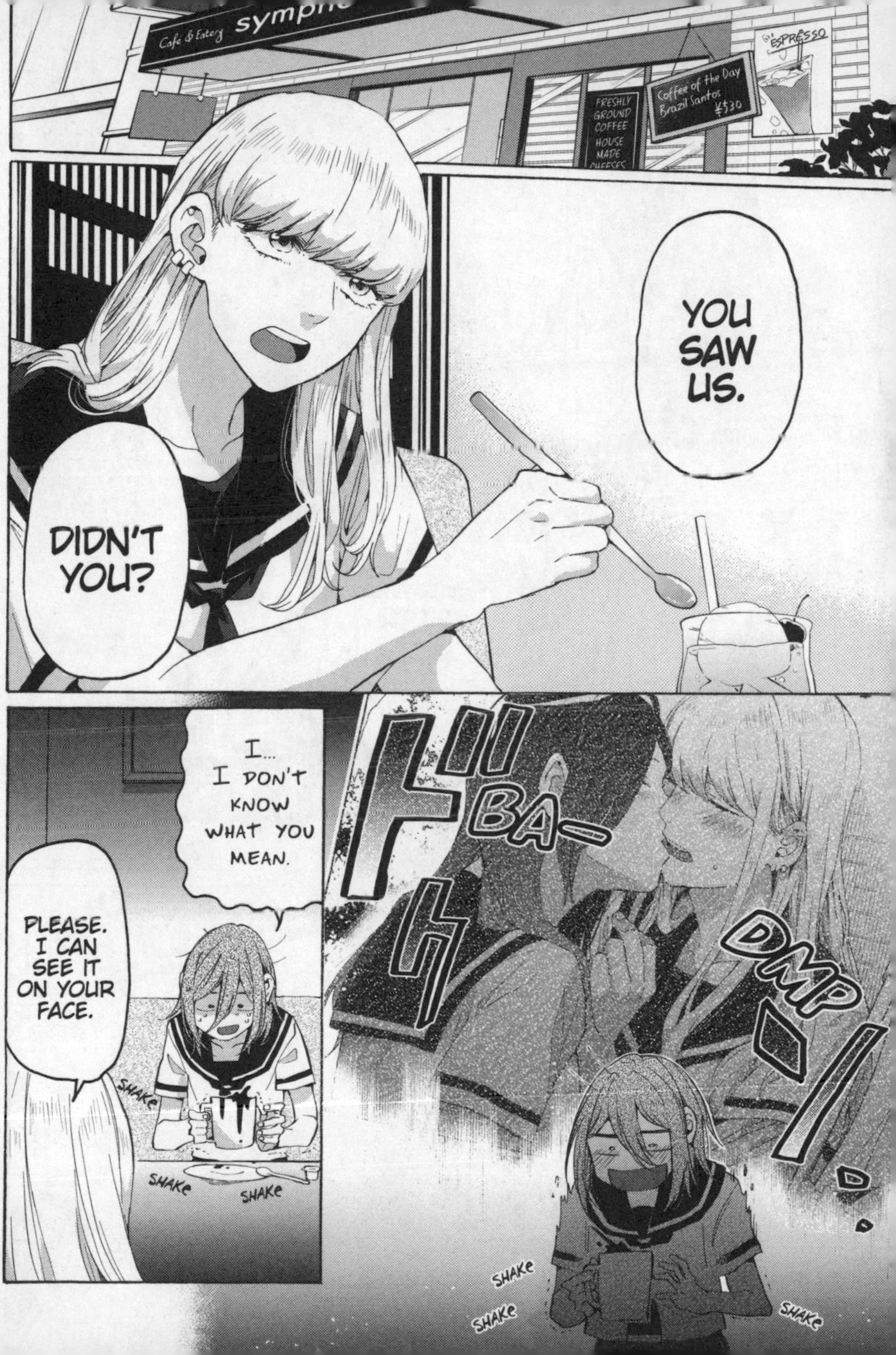
Cafe & Eatery
ESPRESSO
Coffee of the Day Brazil Santos ¥530
FRESHLY GROUND COFFEE HOUSE MADE
YOU SAW US.
DIDN'T YOU?
BA-DMP
SHAKE
SHAKE
SHAKE
I... I DON'T KNOW WHAT YOU MEAN.
PLEASE. I CAN SEE IT ON YOUR FACE.
SHAKE
SHAKE
SHAKE

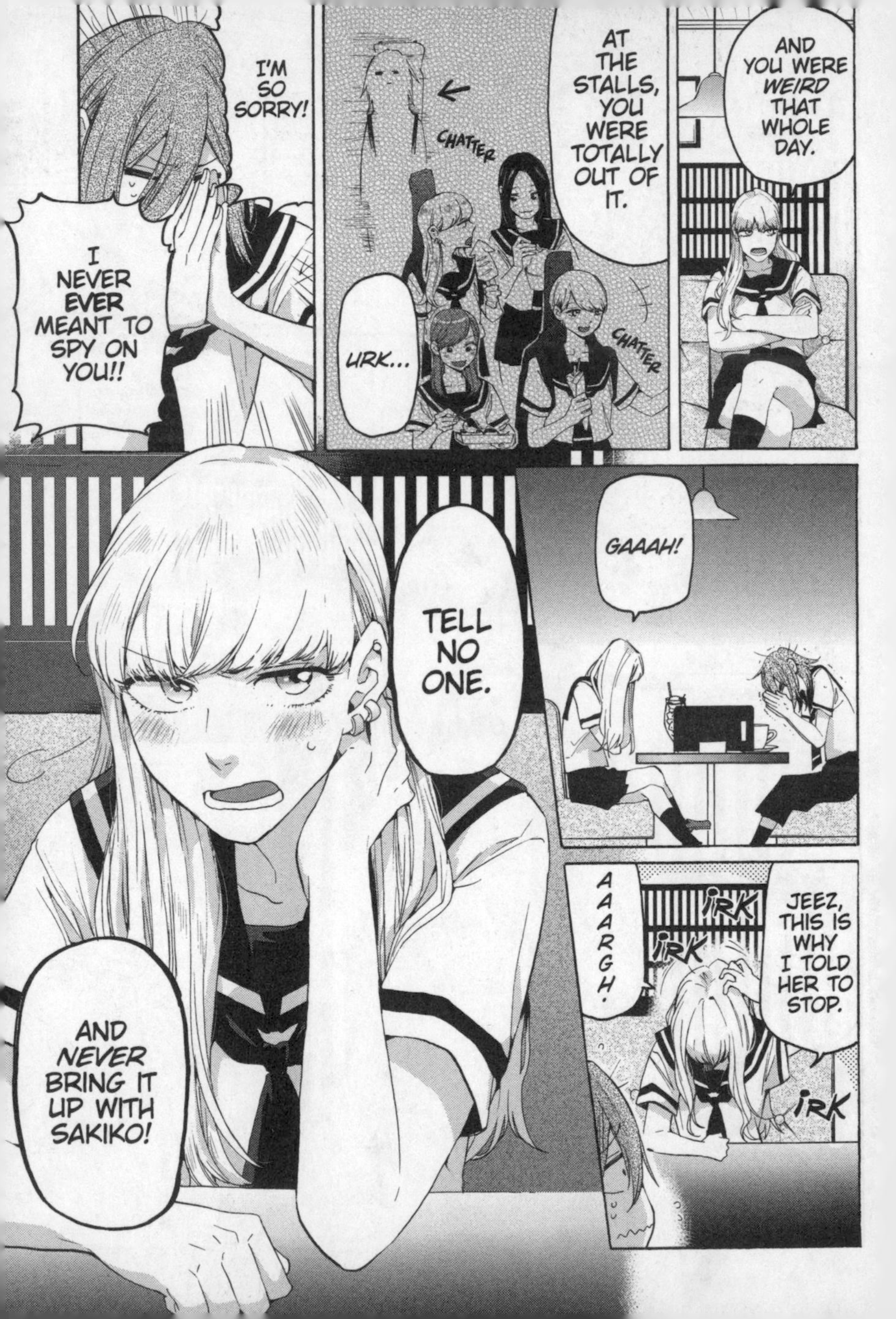
AND YOU WERE *WEIRD* THAT WHOLE DAY.
AT THE STALLS, YOU WERE TOTALLY OUT OF IT.
CHATTER
URK...
CHATTER
I'M SO SORRY!
I NEVER *EVER* MEANT TO SPY ON YOU!!
GAAAH!
JEEZ, THIS IS WHY I TOLD HER TO STOP.
IRK
IRK
IRK
AAAARGH.
TELL NO ONE.
AND *NEVER* BRING IT UP WITH SAKIKO!

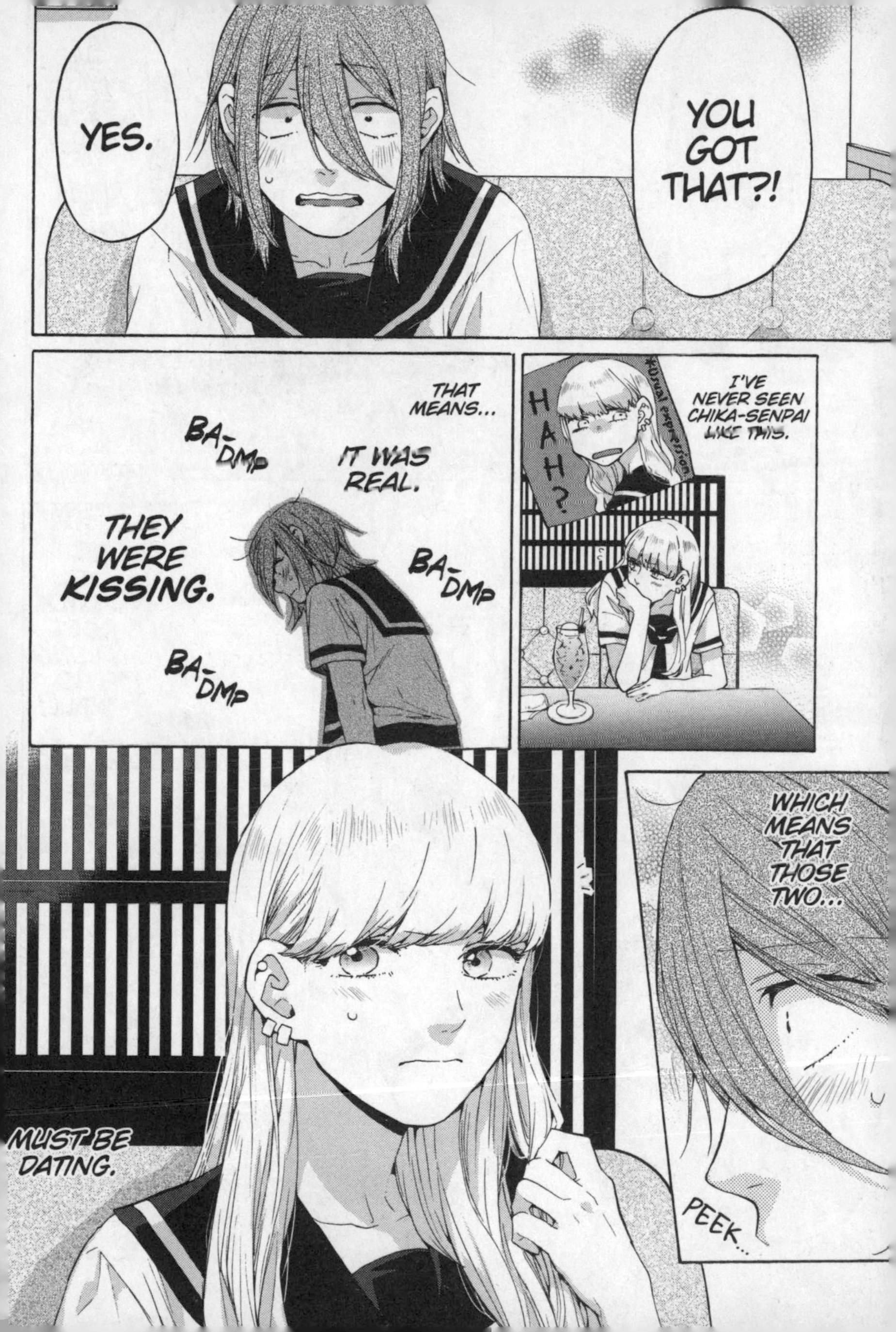
YOU GOT THAT?!
YES.
I'VE NEVER SEEN CHIKA-SENPAI LIKE THIS.
HAH?
*Usual expression
THAT MEANS...
IT WAS REAL.
BA-DMP
THEY WERE KISSING.
BA-DMP
BA-DMP
WHICH MEANS THAT THOSE TWO...
PEEK...
MUST BE DATING.

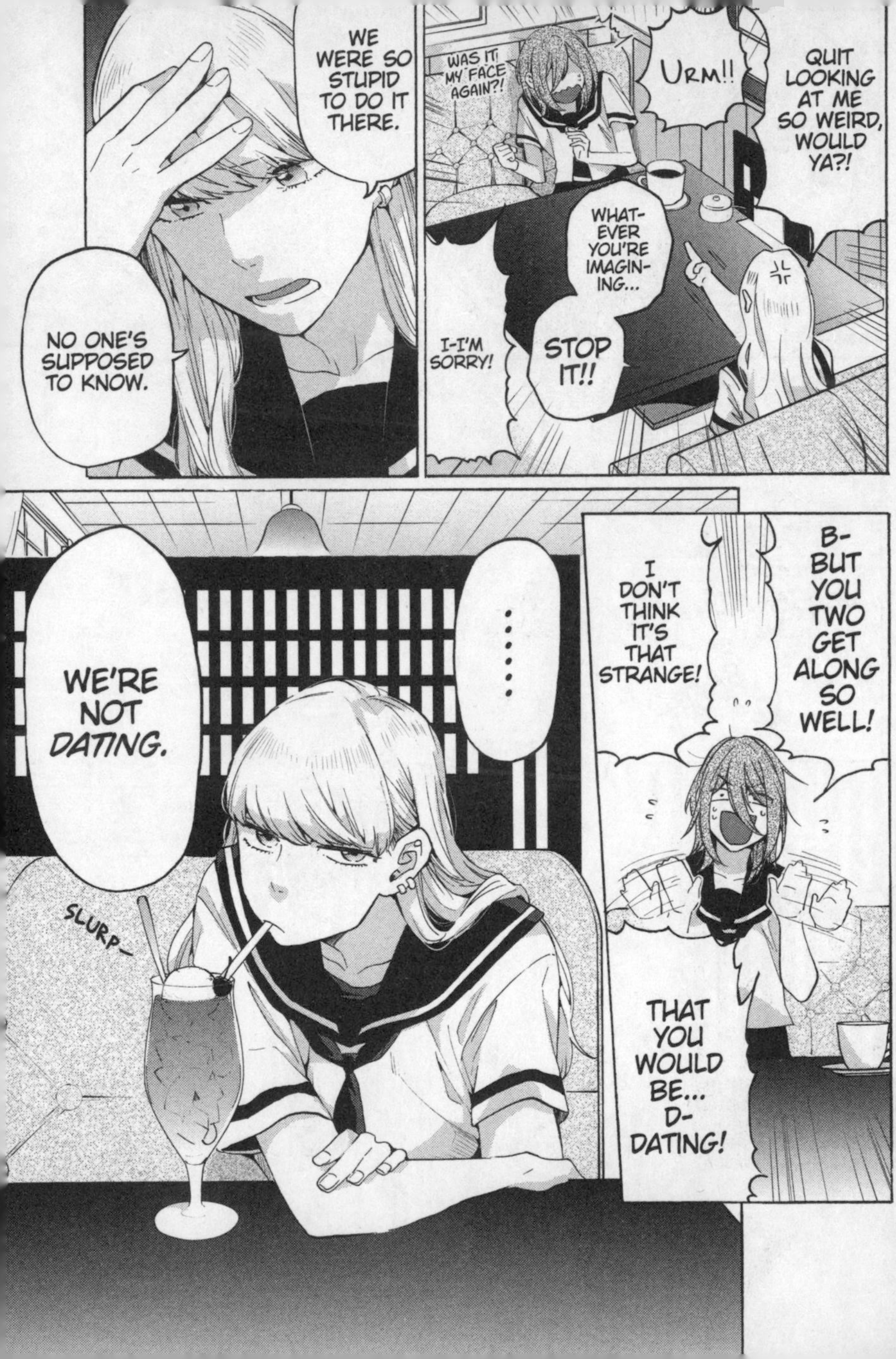
QUIT LOOKING AT ME SO WEIRD, WOULD YA?!
URM!!
WAS IT MY FACE AGAIN?!
WHATEVER YOU'RE IMAGINING...
STOP IT!!
I-I'M SORRY!
WE WERE SO STUPID TO DO IT THERE.
NO ONE'S SUPPOSED TO KNOW.
B-BUT YOU TWO GET ALONG SO WELL!
I DON'T THINK IT'S THAT STRANGE!
THAT YOU WOULD BE... D-DATING!
......
WE'RE NOT DATING.
SLURP-

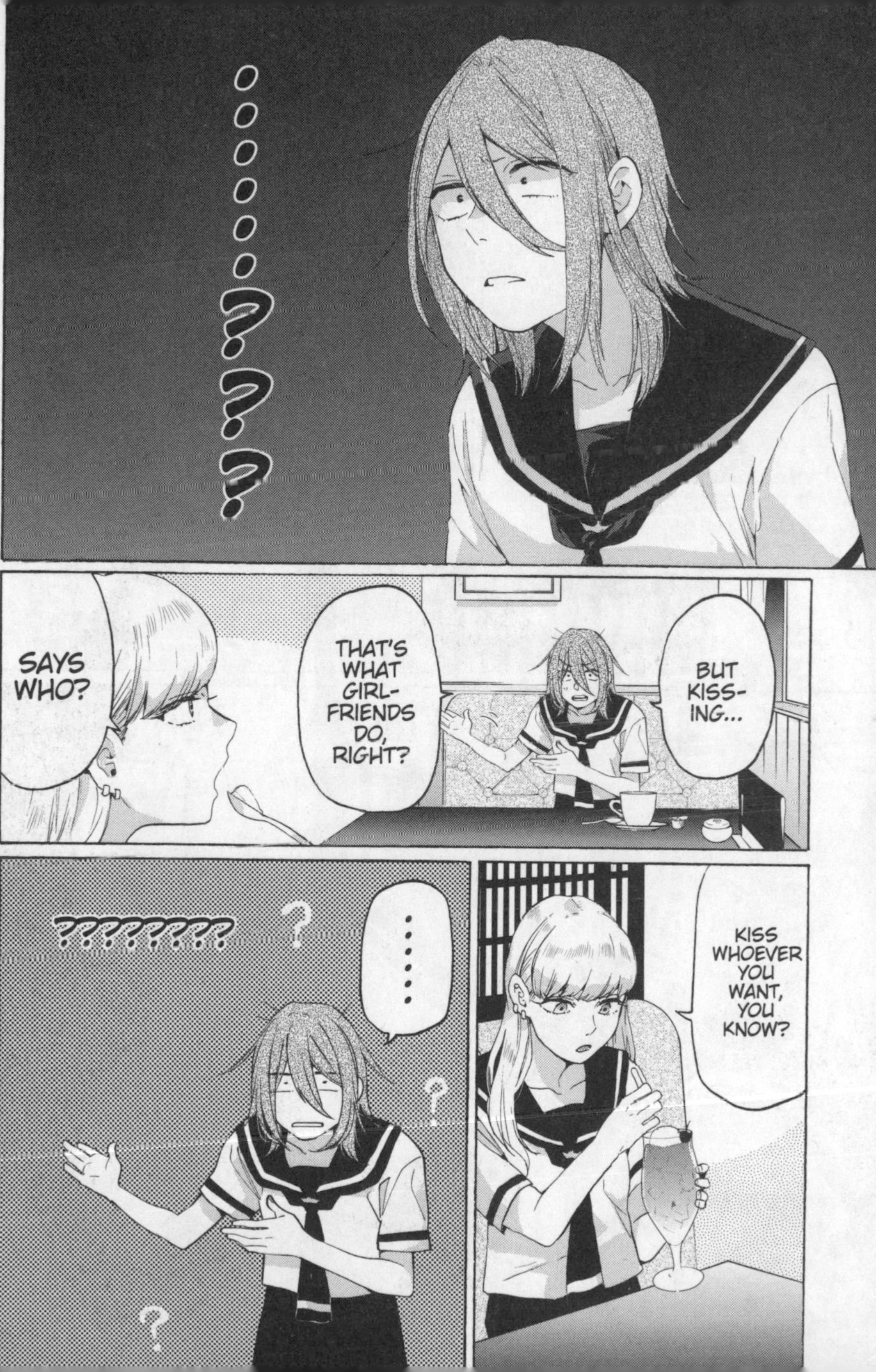
oooooo???
BUT KISSING...
THAT'S WHAT GIRLFRIENDS DO, RIGHT?
SAYS WHO?
KISS WHOEVER YOU WANT, YOU KNOW?
......
?????????
?
?
?

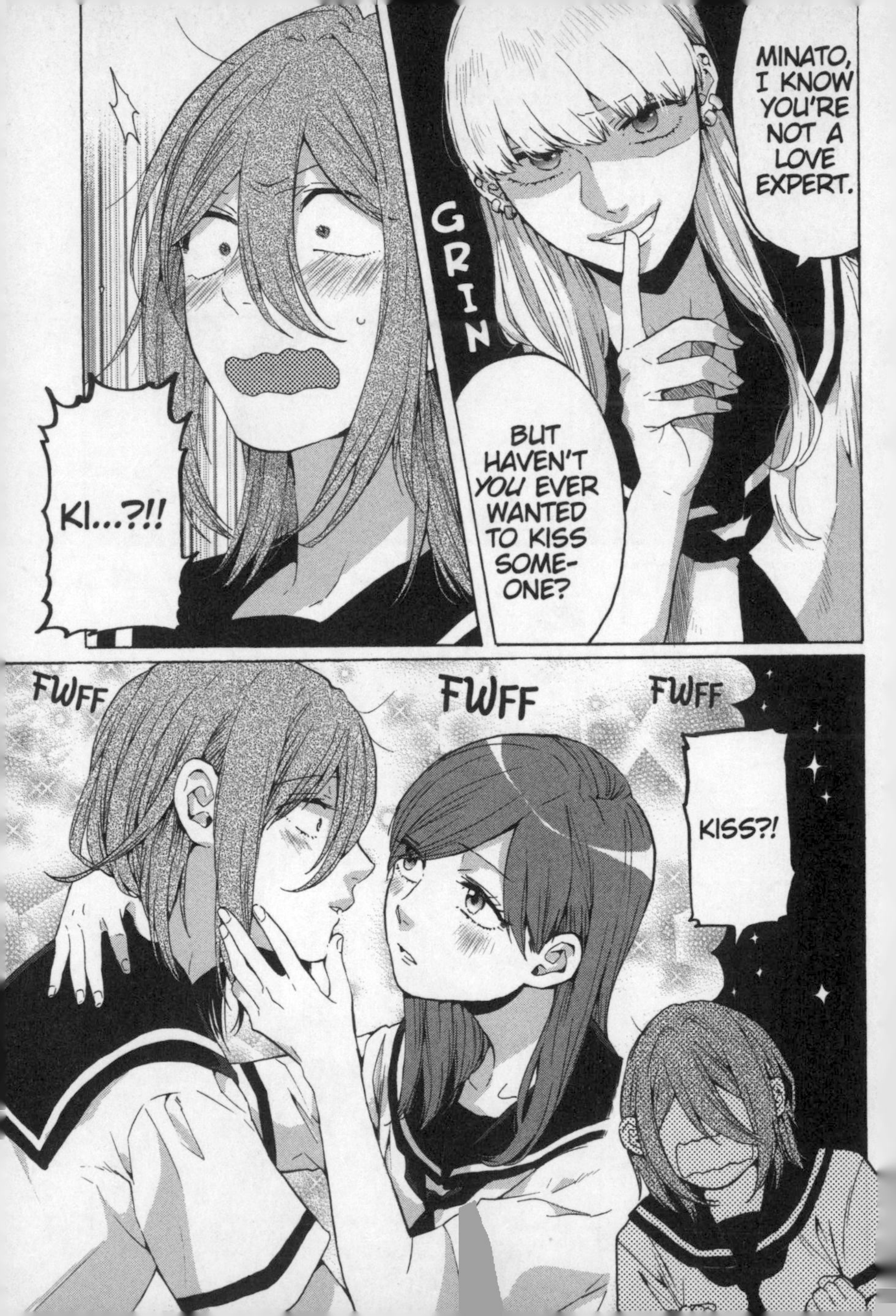
MINATO, I KNOW YOU'RE NOT A LOVE EXPERT.
GRIN
BUT HAVEN'T *YOU* EVER WANTED TO KISS SOME-ONE?
KI...?!!
FWFF
FWFF
FWFF
KISS?!

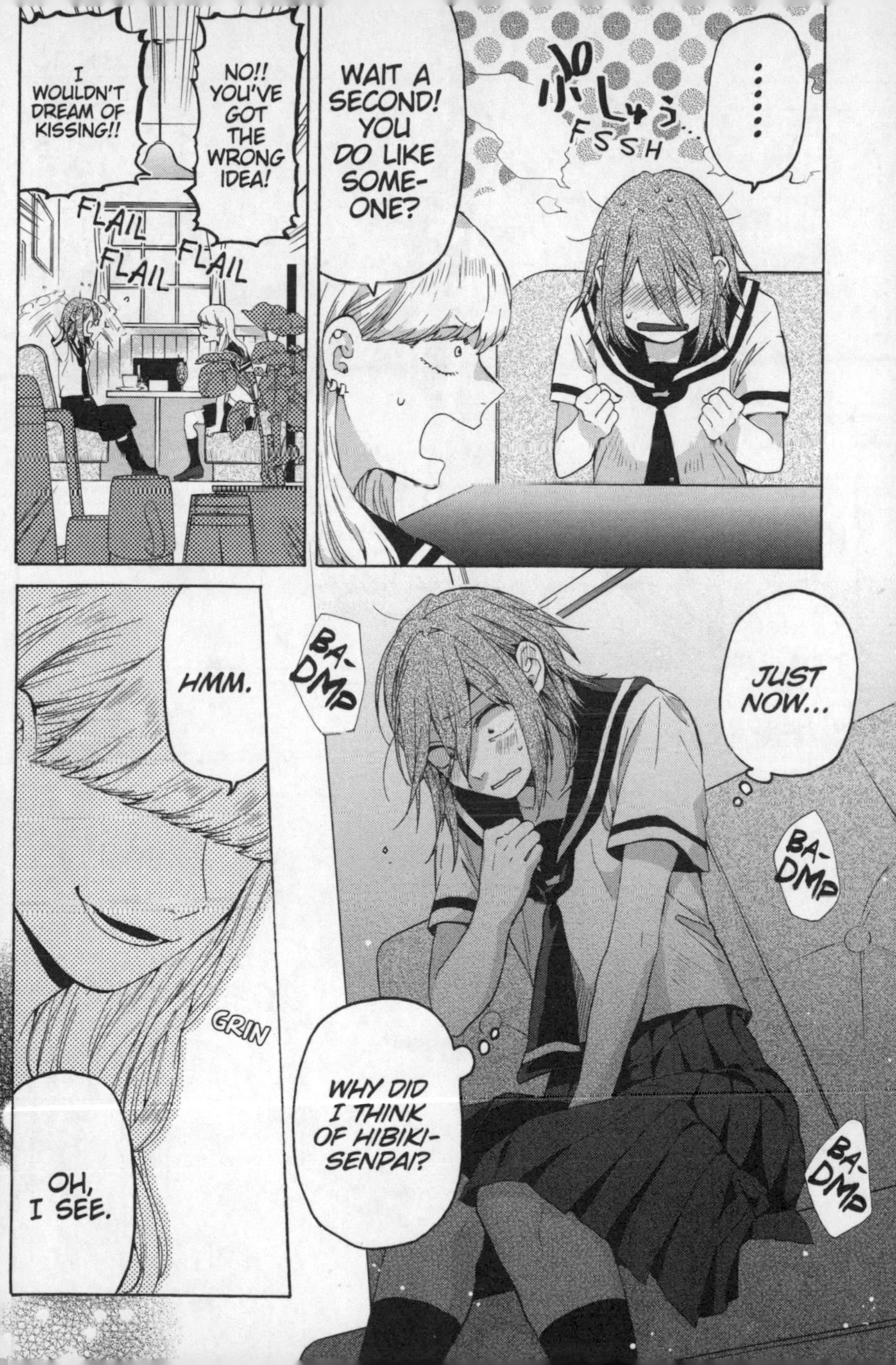
......
ぷしゅう…
FSSH
WAIT A SECOND! YOU DO LIKE SOME-ONE?
NO!! YOU'VE GOT THE WRONG IDEA!
I WOULDN'T DREAM OF KISSING!!
FLAIL
FLAIL
FLAIL
BA-DMP
JUST NOW...
BA-DMP
WHY DID I THINK OF HIBIKI-SENPAI?
BA-DMP
HMM.
GRIN
OH, I SEE.

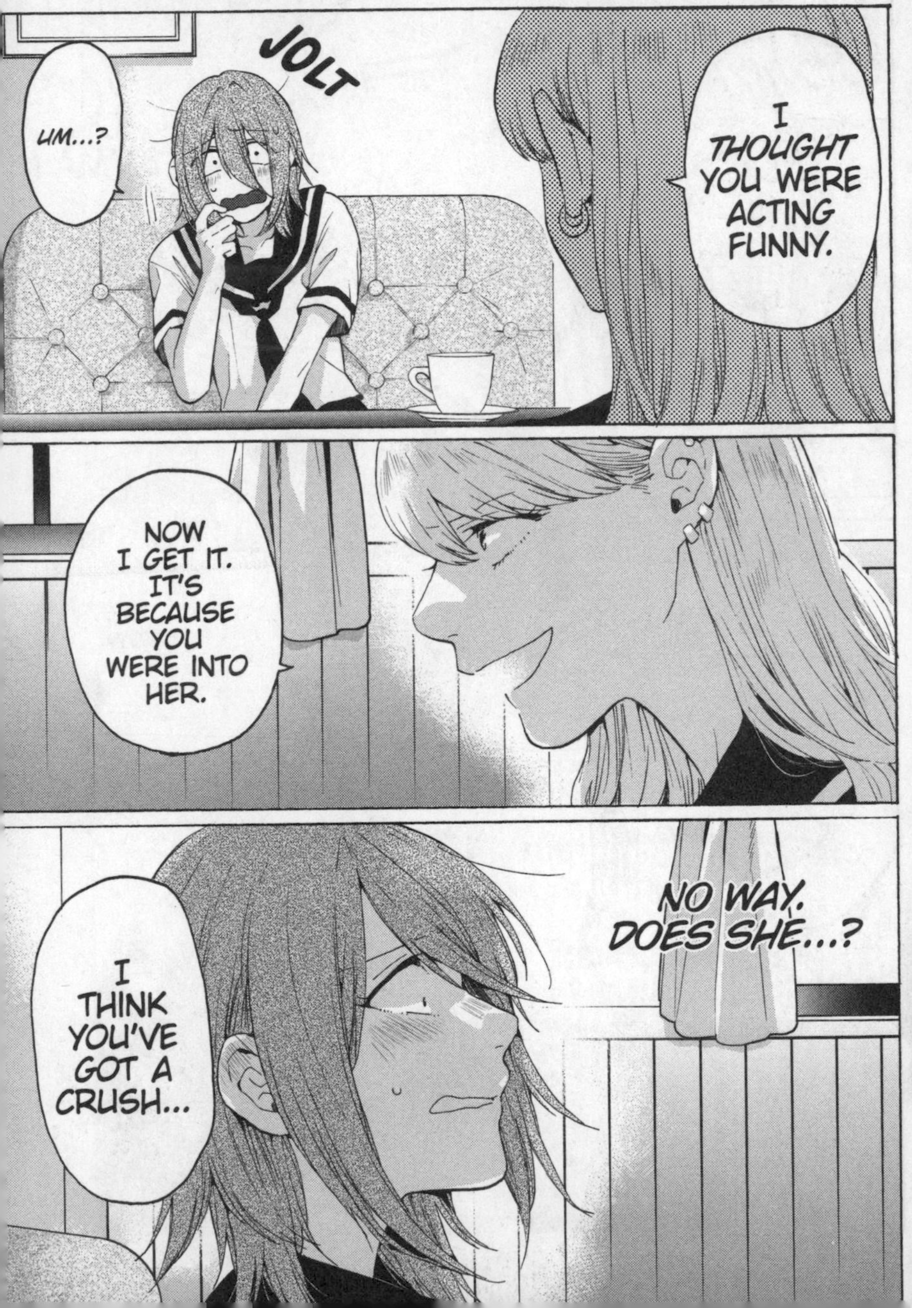
I THOUGHT YOU WERE ACTING FUNNY.
JOLT
UM...?
NOW I GET IT. IT'S BECAUSE YOU WERE INTO HER.
NO WAY. DOES SHE...?
I THINK YOU'VE GOT A CRUSH...

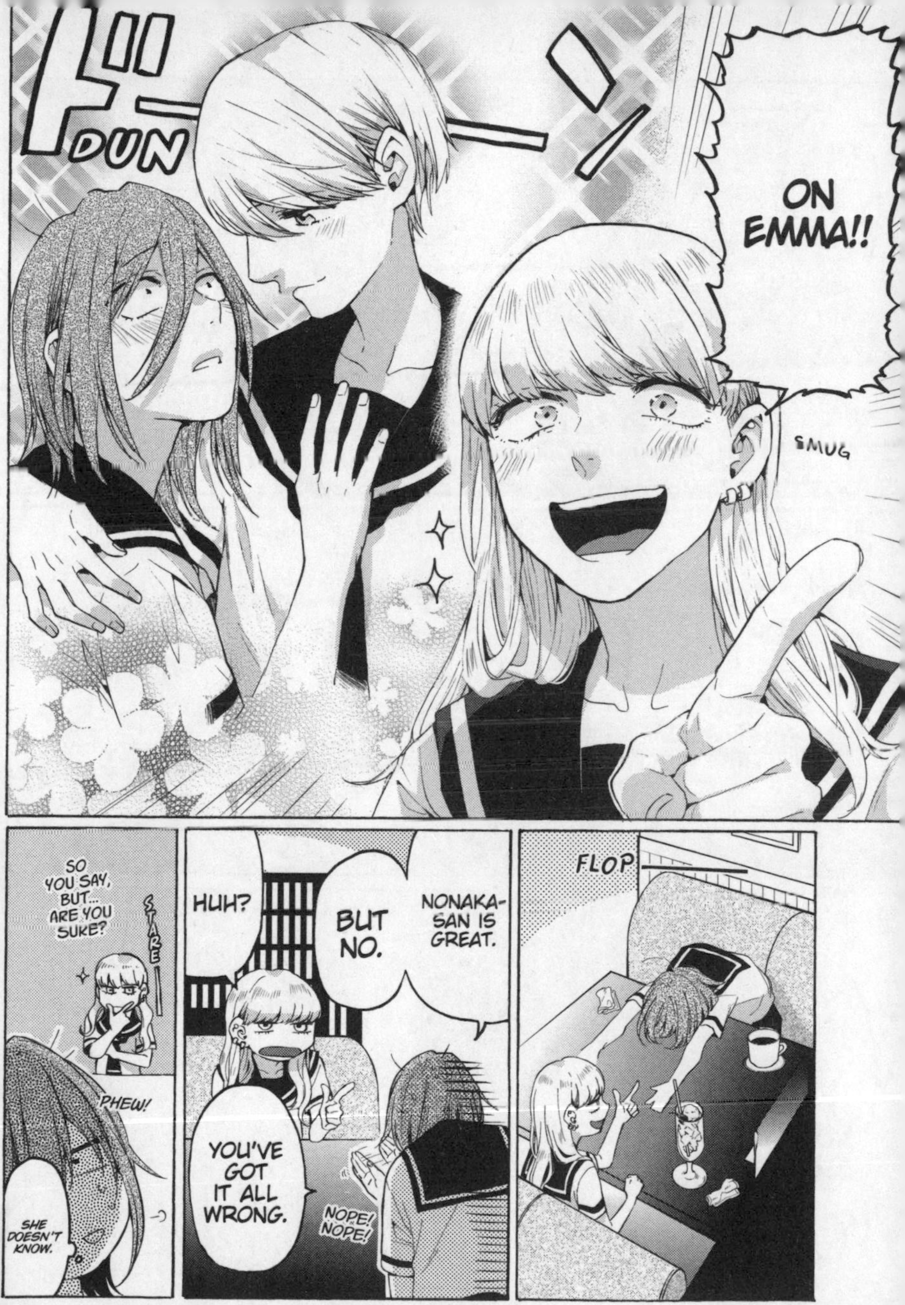
ON EMMA!!
SMUG
DUN
FLOP
NONAKA-SAN IS GREAT.
BUT NO.
HUH?
YOU'VE GOT IT ALL WRONG.
NOPE! NOPE!
SO YOU SAY, BUT... ARE YOU SUKE?
STARE
PHEW!
SHE DOESN'T KNOW.

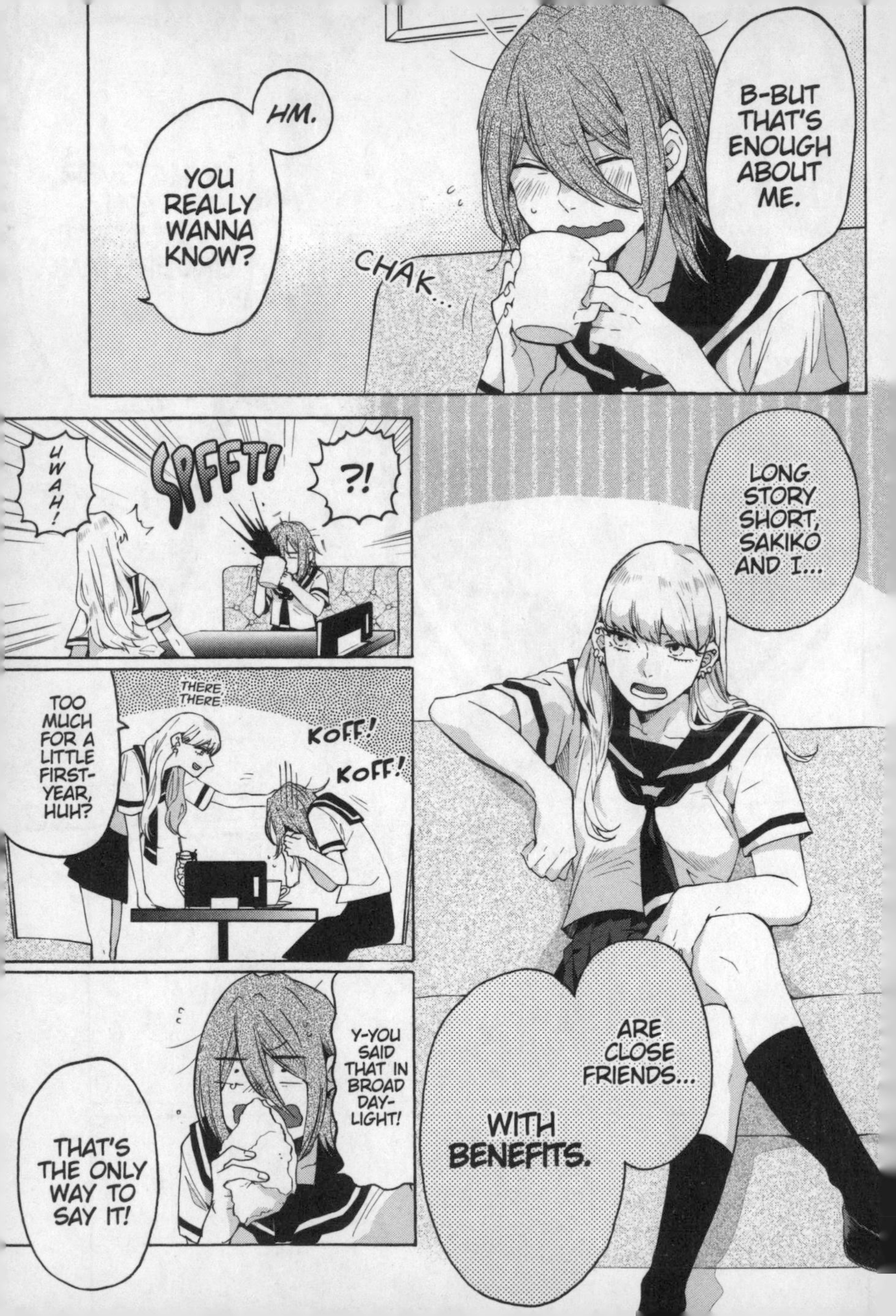
B-BUT THAT'S ENOUGH ABOUT ME.
CHAK...
HM.
YOU REALLY WANNA KNOW?
LONG STORY SHORT, SAKIKO AND I...
ARE CLOSE FRIENDS...
WITH BENEFITS.
?!
SPFFT!
UWAH!
KOFF!
KOFF!
THERE, THERE.
TOO MUCH FOR A LITTLE FIRST-YEAR, HUH?
Y-YOU SAID THAT IN BROAD DAY-LIGHT!
THAT'S THE ONLY WAY TO SAY IT!

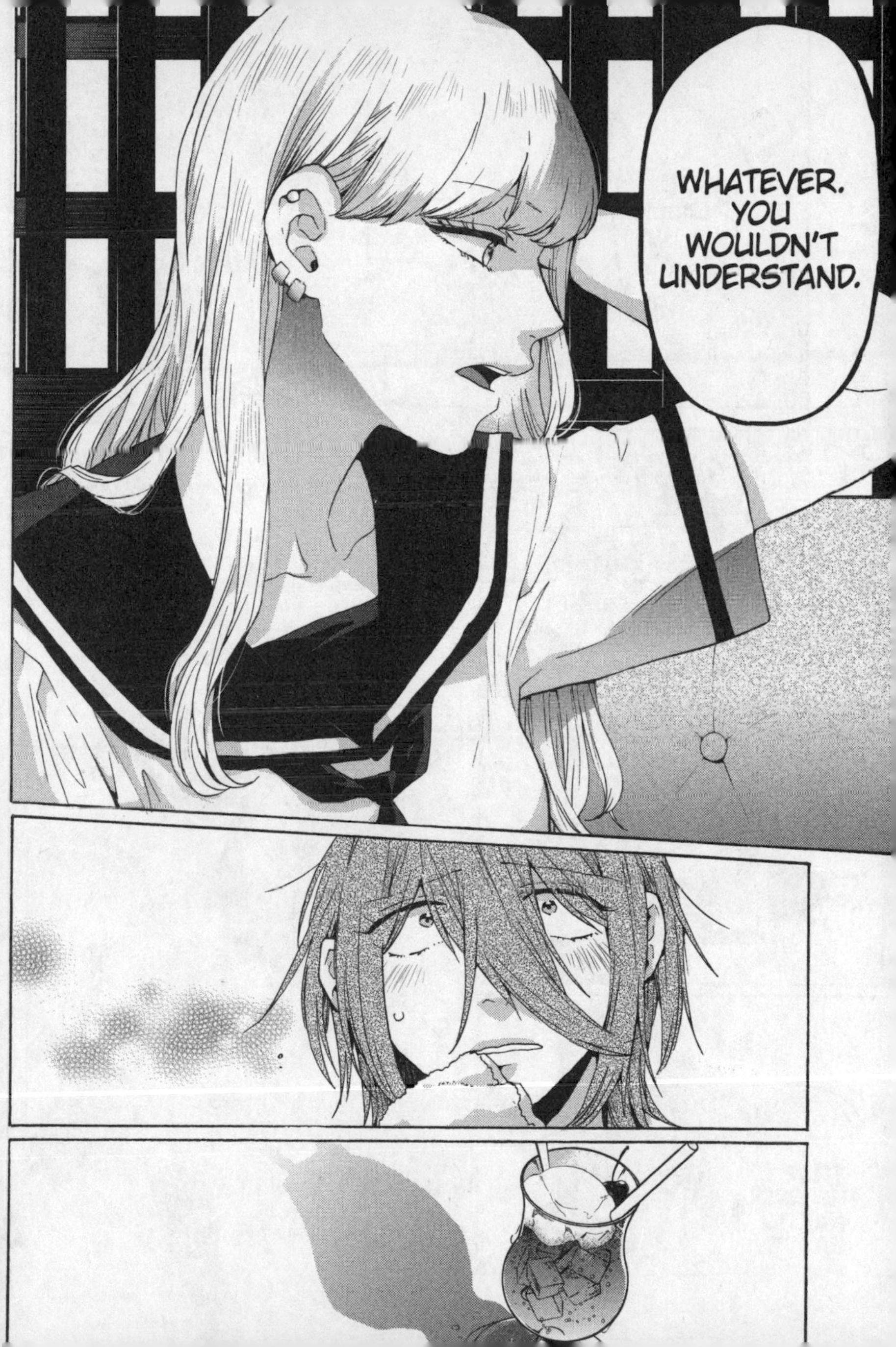
WHATEVER. YOU WOULDN'T UNDERSTAND.

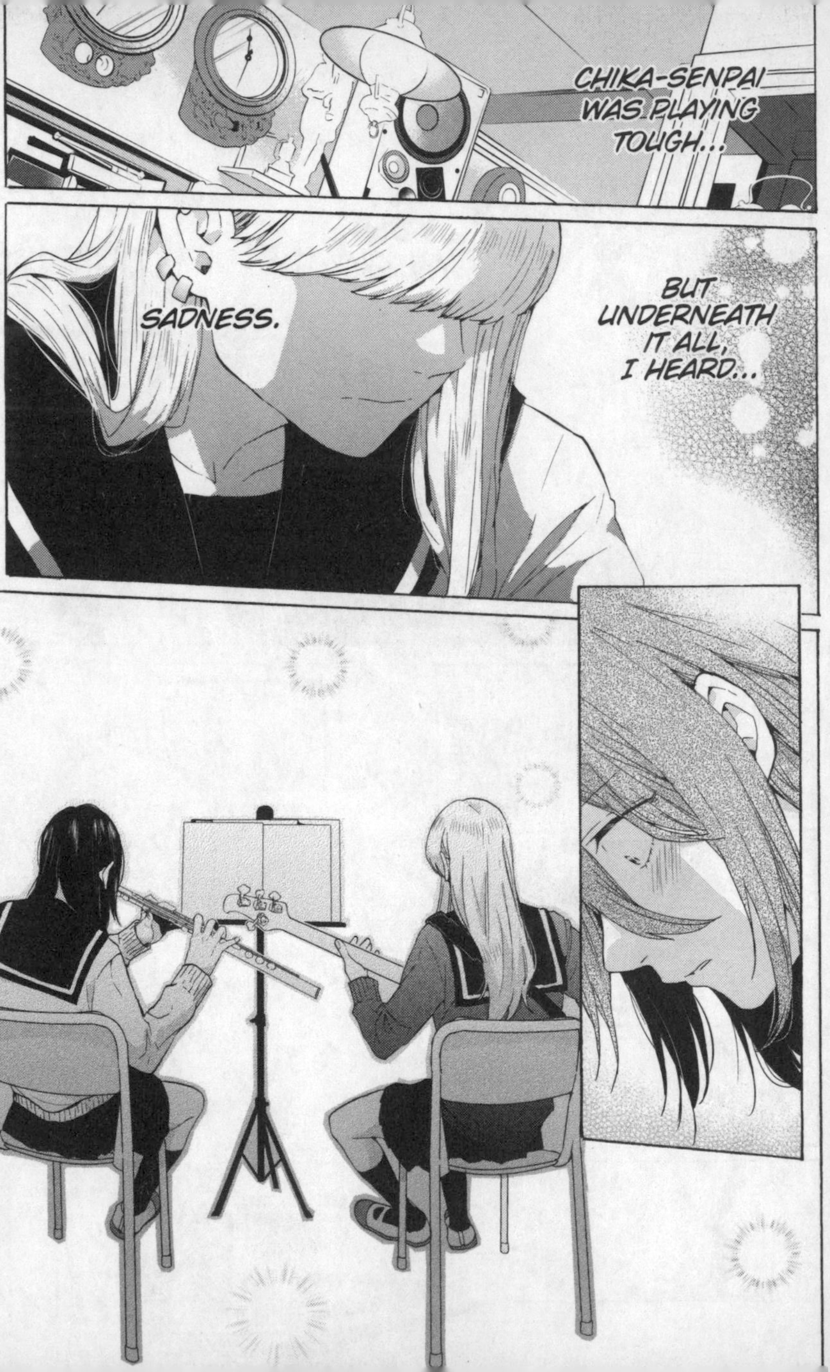
CHIKA-SENPAI WAS PLAYING TOUGH...
BUT UNDERNEATH IT ALL, I HEARD...
SADNESS.

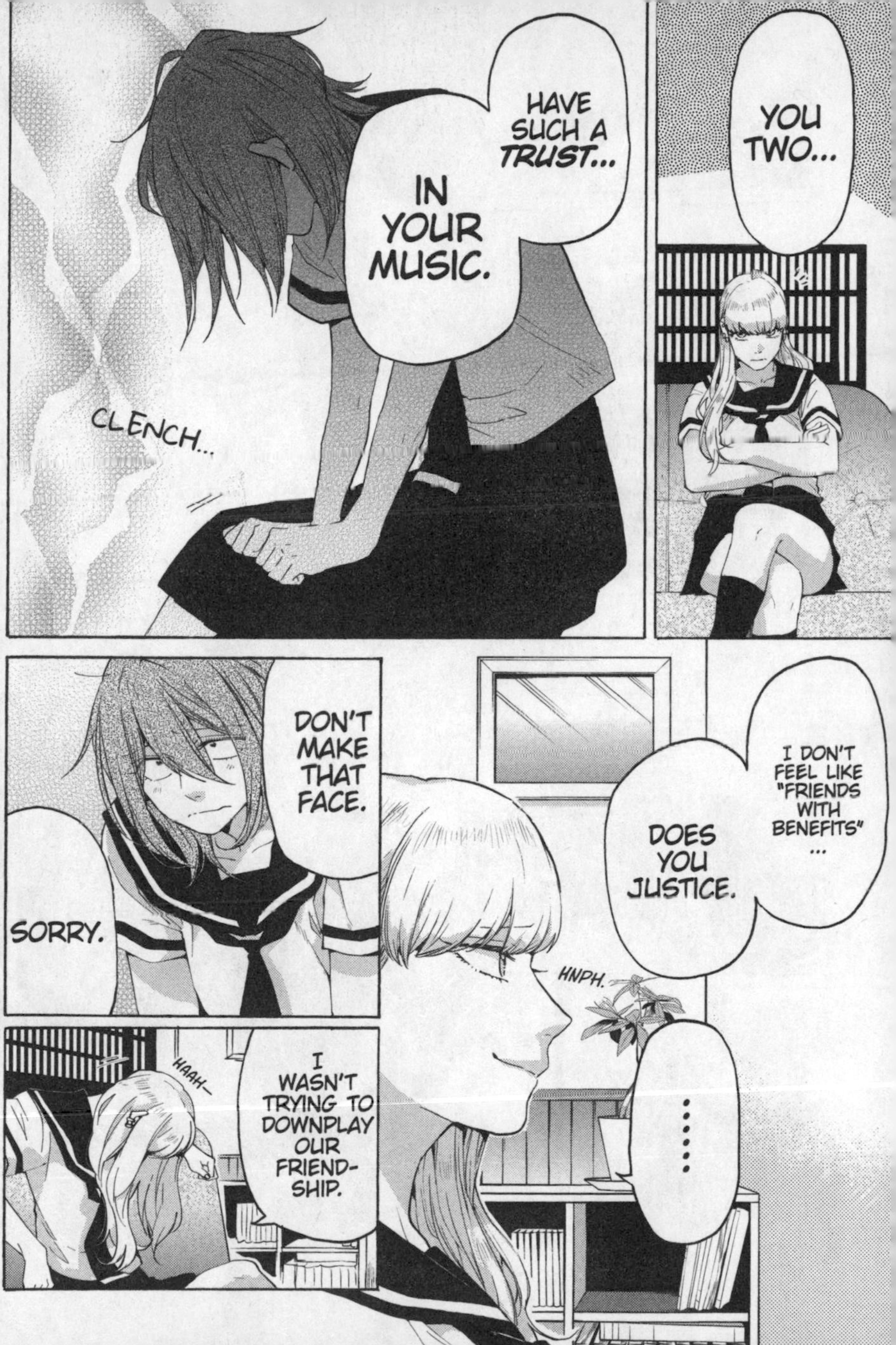
YOU TWO...
HAVE SUCH A TRUST...
IN YOUR MUSIC.
CLENCH...
I DON'T FEEL LIKE "FRIENDS WITH BENEFITS"...
DOES YOU JUSTICE.
HNPH.
......
DON'T MAKE THAT FACE.
SORRY.
HAAH—
I WASN'T TRYING TO DOWNPLAY OUR FRIEND-SHIP.

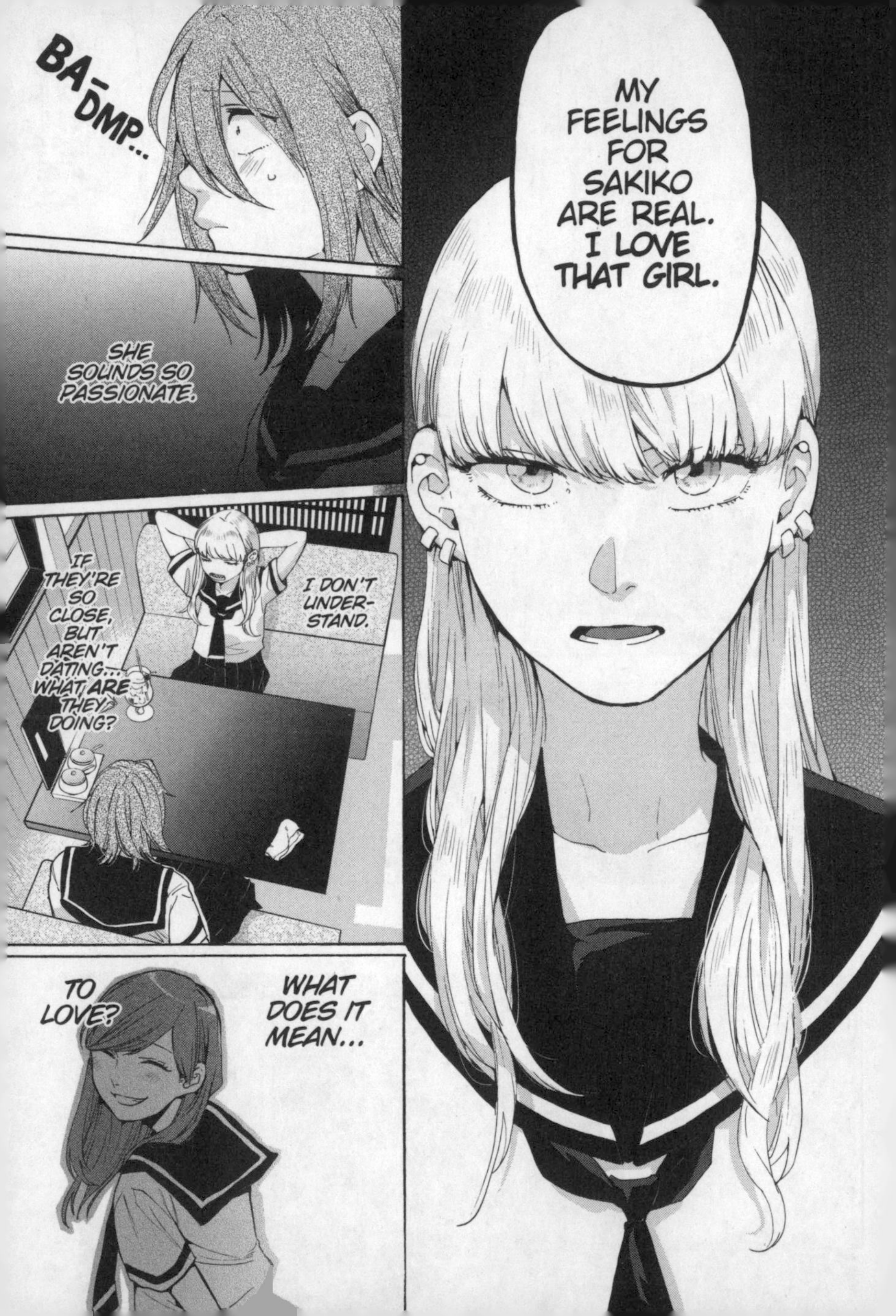
MY FEELINGS FOR SAKIKO ARE REAL. I LOVE THAT GIRL.
BA-DMP...
SHE SOUNDS SO PASSIONATE.
I DON'T UNDER-STAND.
IF THEY'RE SO CLOSE, BUT AREN'T DATING... WHAT ARE THEY DOING?
WHAT DOES IT MEAN...
TO LOVE?

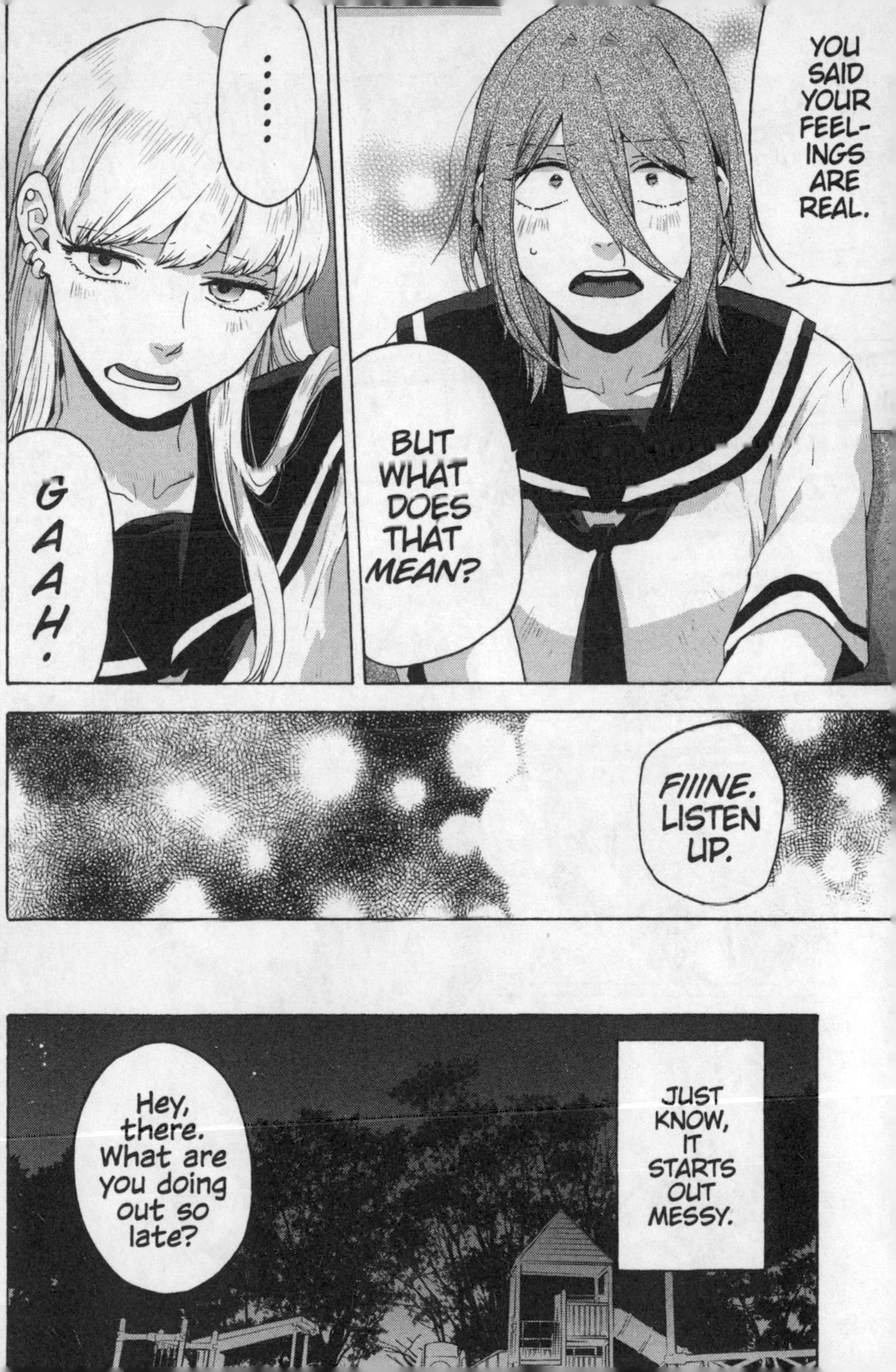
YOU SAID YOUR FEEL-INGS ARE REAL.
BUT WHAT DOES THAT MEAN?
......
GAAH.
FIIINE. LISTEN UP.
JUST KNOW, IT STARTS OUT MESSY.
Hey, there. What are you doing out so late?

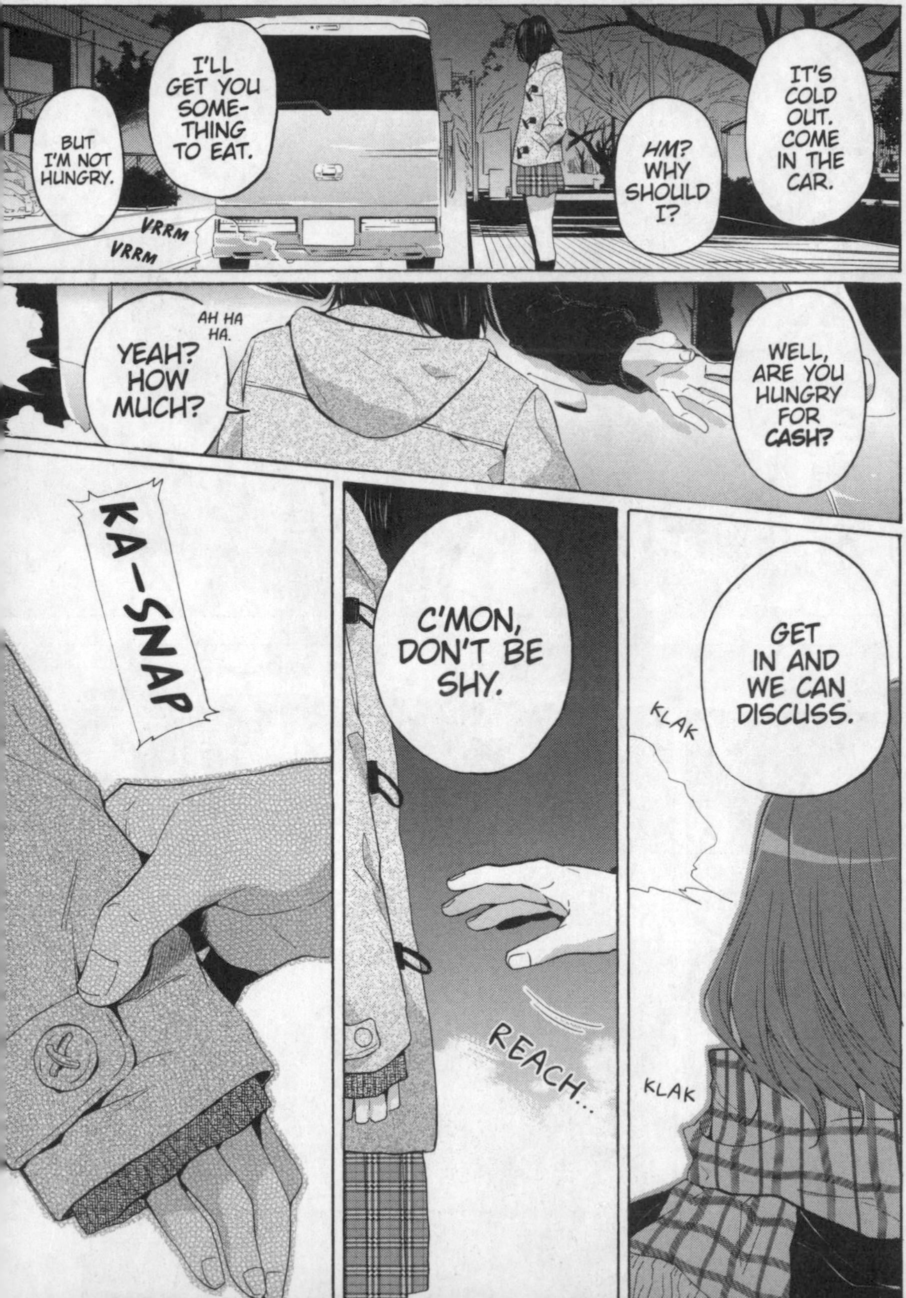
IT'S COLD OUT. COME IN THE CAR.
HM? WHY SHOULD I?
I'LL GET YOU SOME-THING TO EAT.
BUT I'M NOT HUNGRY.
VRRM
VRRM
WELL, ARE YOU HUNGRY FOR CASH?
AH HA HA.
YEAH? HOW MUCH?
GET IN AND WE CAN DISCUSS.
KLAK
KLAK
C'MON, DON'T BE SHY.
REACH...
KA-SNAP

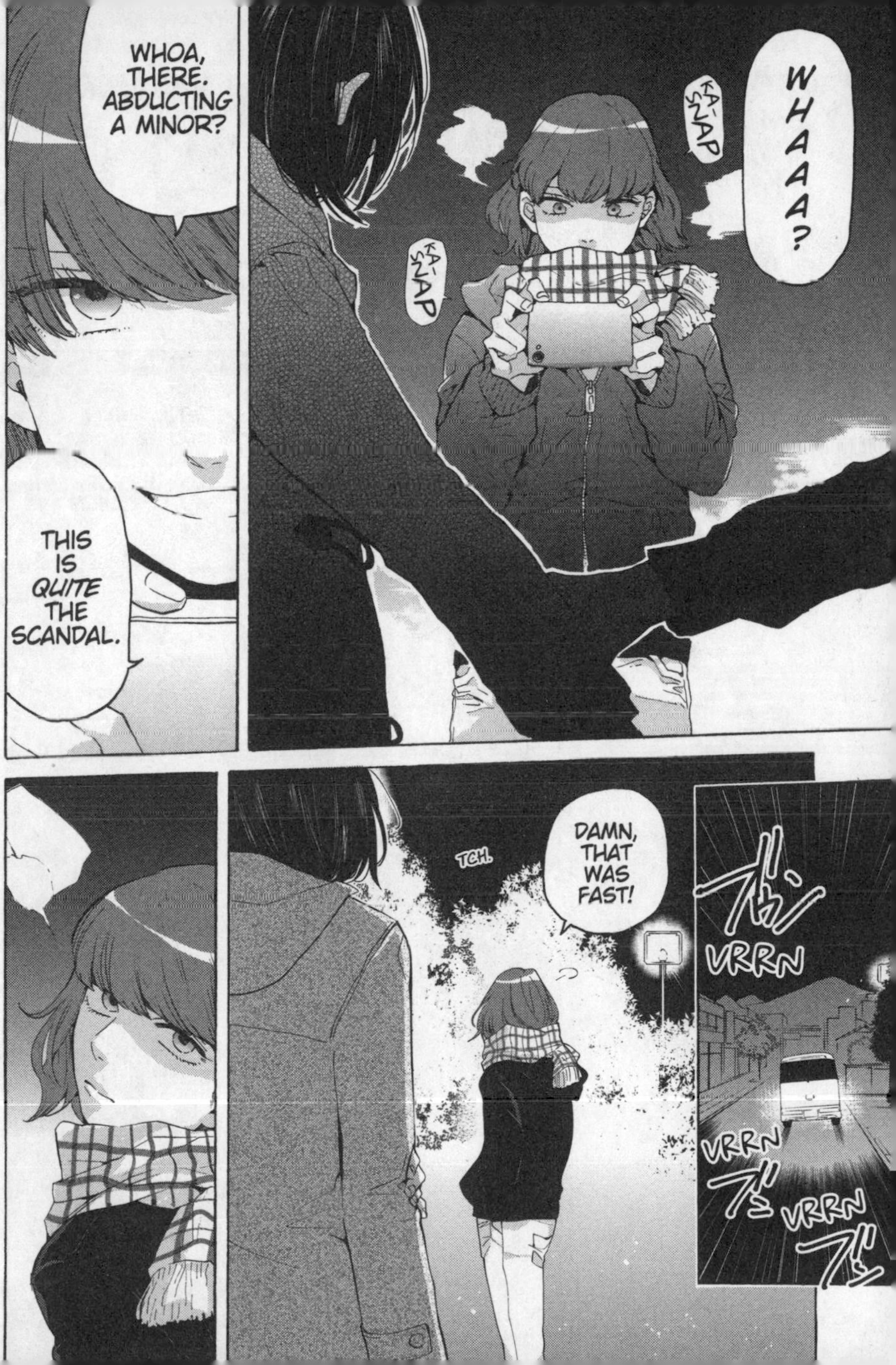
WHAAAA?
KA-SNAP
KA-SNAP
WHOA, THERE. ABDUCTING A MINOR?
THIS IS *QUITE* THE SCANDAL.
VRRN
VRRN
VRRN
TCH.
DAMN, THAT WAS FAST!

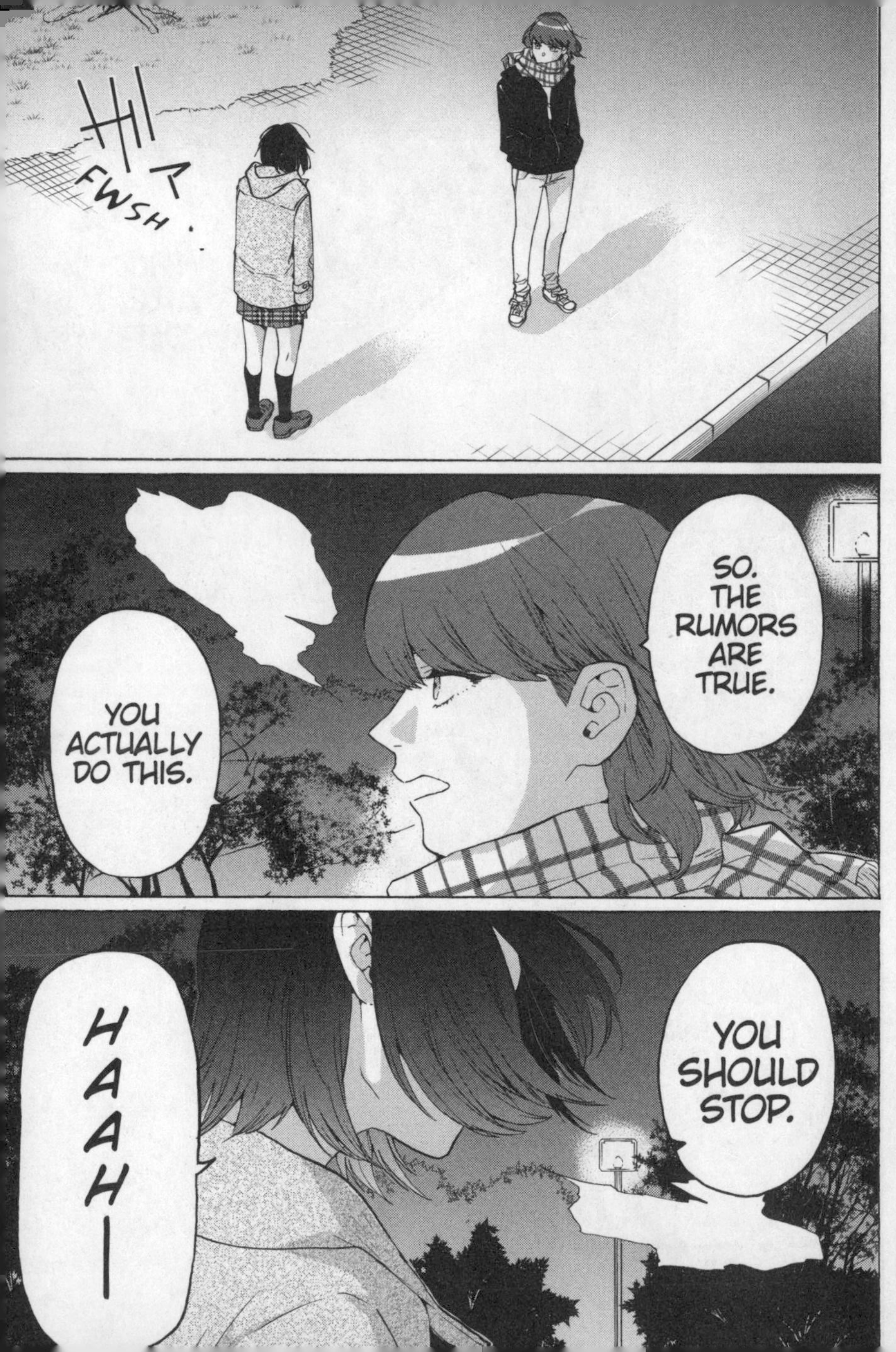
FWSH
SO. THE RUMORS ARE TRUE.
YOU ACTUALLY DO THIS.
YOU SHOULD STOP.
HAAH—

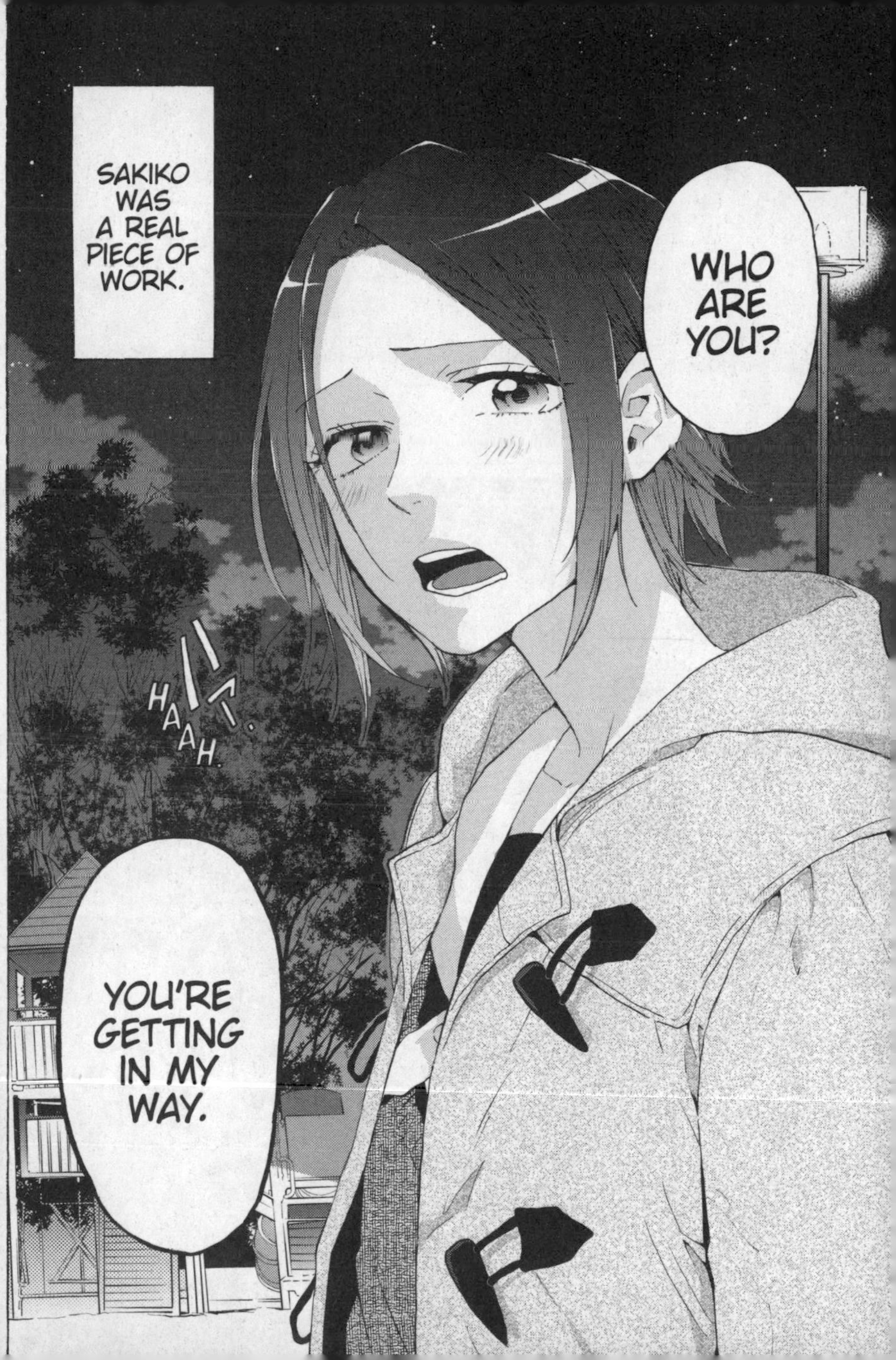
WHO ARE YOU?
SAKIKO WAS A REAL PIECE OF WORK.
HAAAH.
YOU'RE GETTING IN MY WAY.

Hello, Melancholic!

CHIKA-CHAN
HAS A
SWEET TOOTH.

KA-SNAP

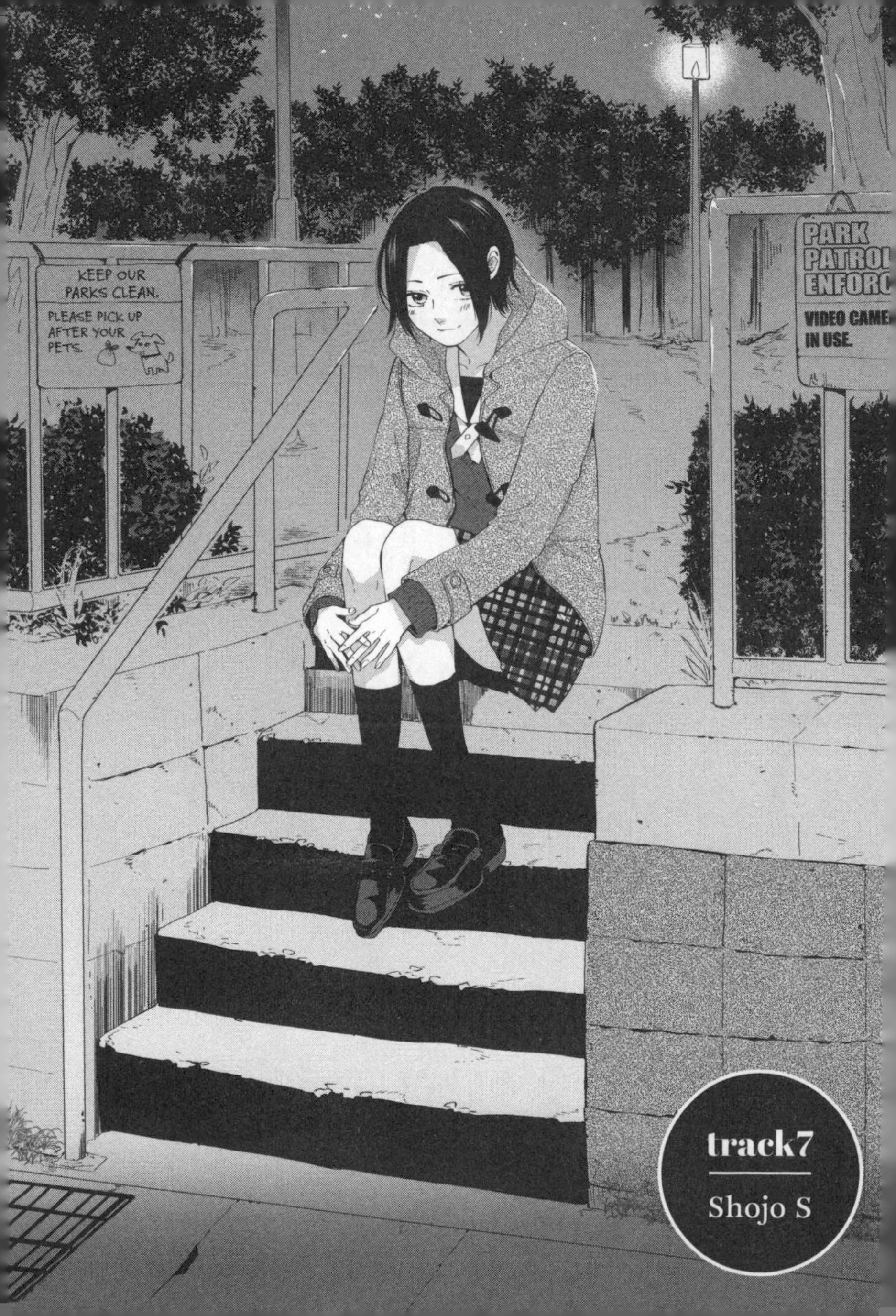
KEEP OUR PARKS CLEAN.
PLEASE PICK UP AFTER YOUR PETS.
track7
Shojo S

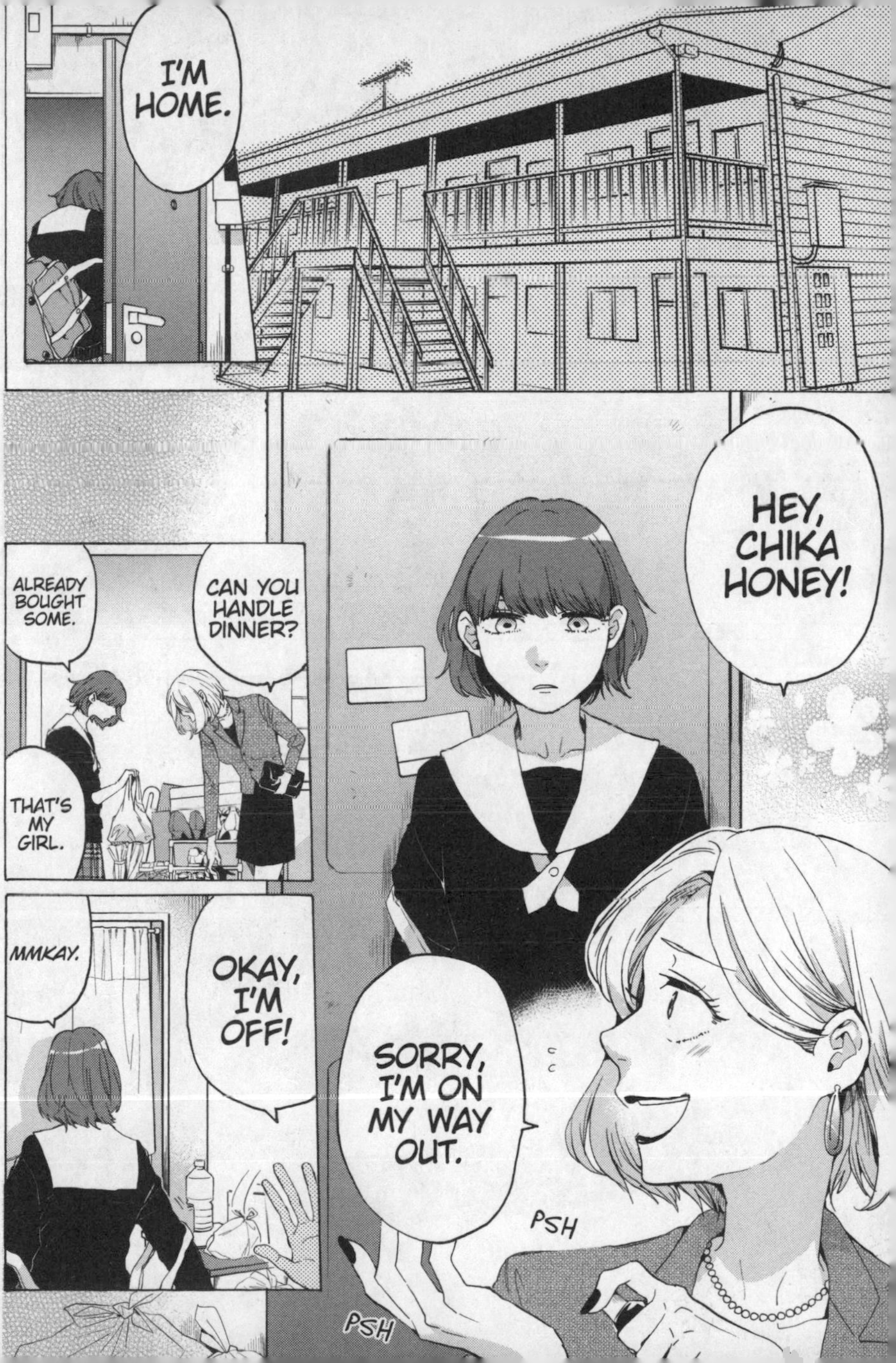
I'M HOME.
HEY, CHIKA HONEY!
SORRY, I'M ON MY WAY OUT.
PSH
PSH
CAN YOU HANDLE DINNER?
ALREADY BOUGHT SOME.
THAT'S MY GIRL.
OKAY, I'M OFF!
MMKAY.

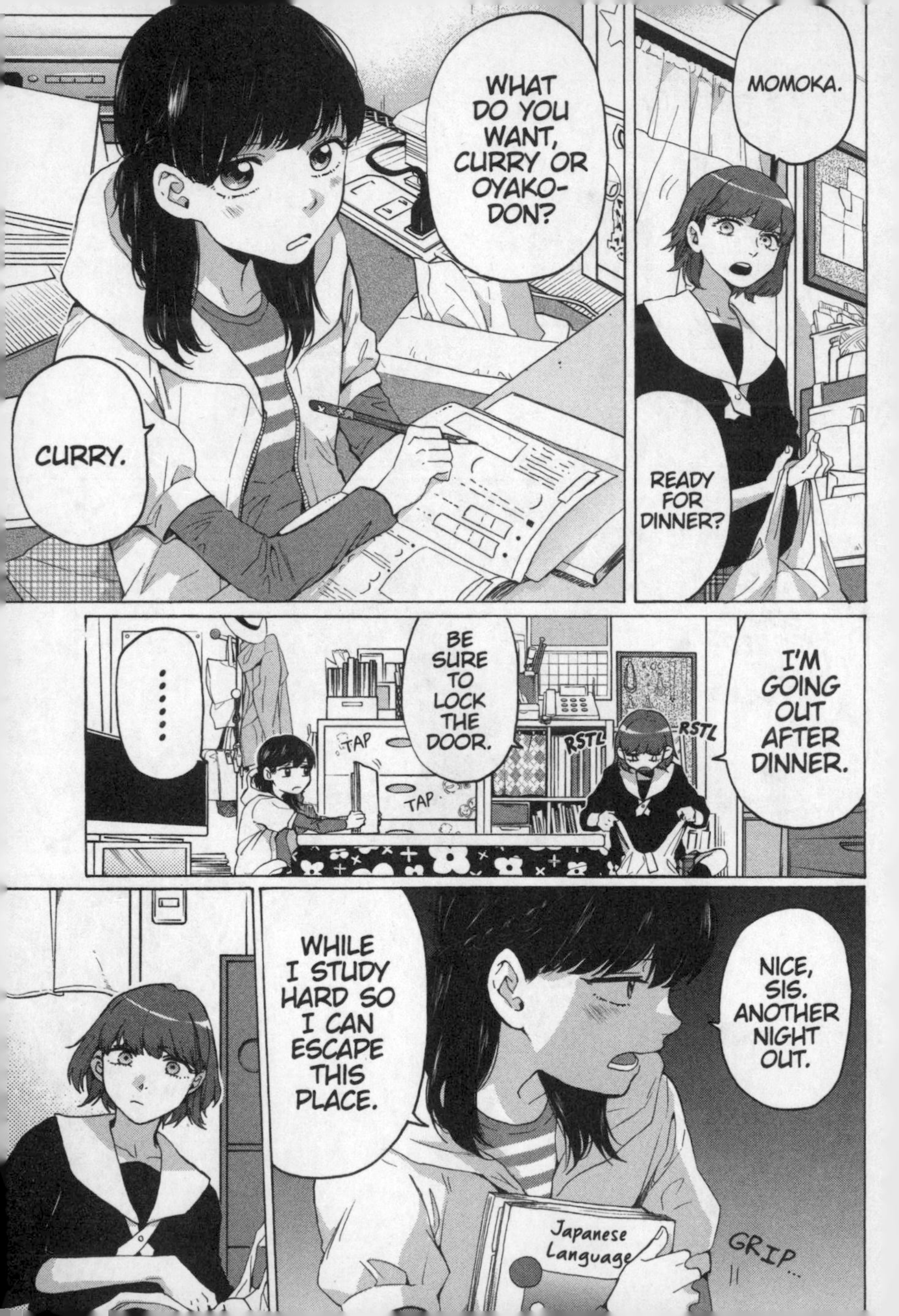
MOMOKA.
READY FOR DINNER?
WHAT DO YOU WANT, CURRY OR OYAKO-DON?
CURRY.
I'M GOING OUT AFTER DINNER.
RSTL
BE SURE TO LOCK THE DOOR.
TAP
TAP
......
NICE, SIS. ANOTHER NIGHT OUT.
WHILE I STUDY HARD SO I CAN ESCAPE THIS PLACE.
Japanese Language
GRIP...

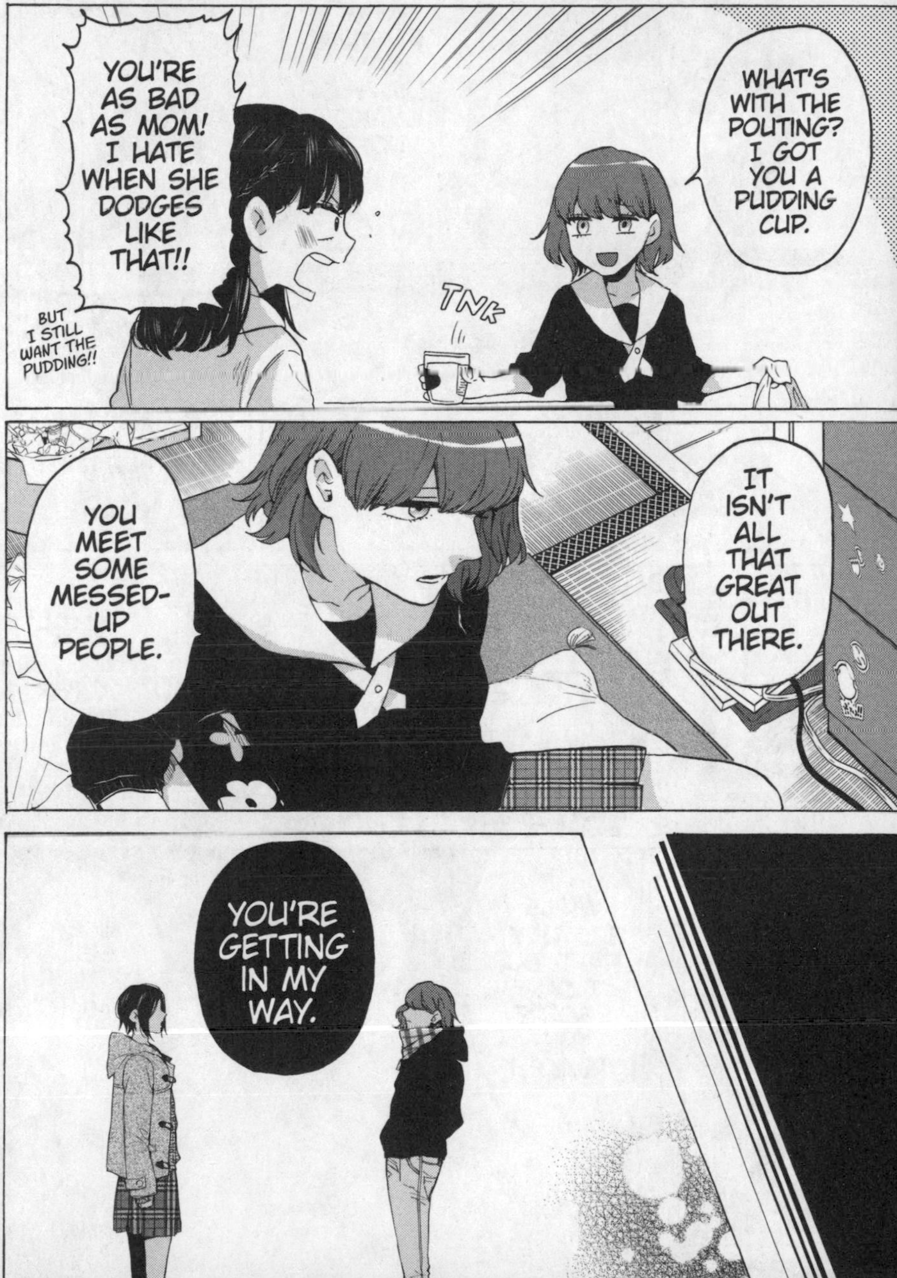
WHAT'S WITH THE POUTING? I GOT YOU A PUDDING CUP.
TNK
YOU'RE AS BAD AS MOM! I HATE WHEN SHE DODGES LIKE THAT!!
BUT I STILL WANT THE PUDDING!!
IT ISN'T ALL THAT GREAT OUT THERE.
YOU MEET SOME MESSED-UP PEOPLE.
YOU'RE GETTING IN MY WAY.

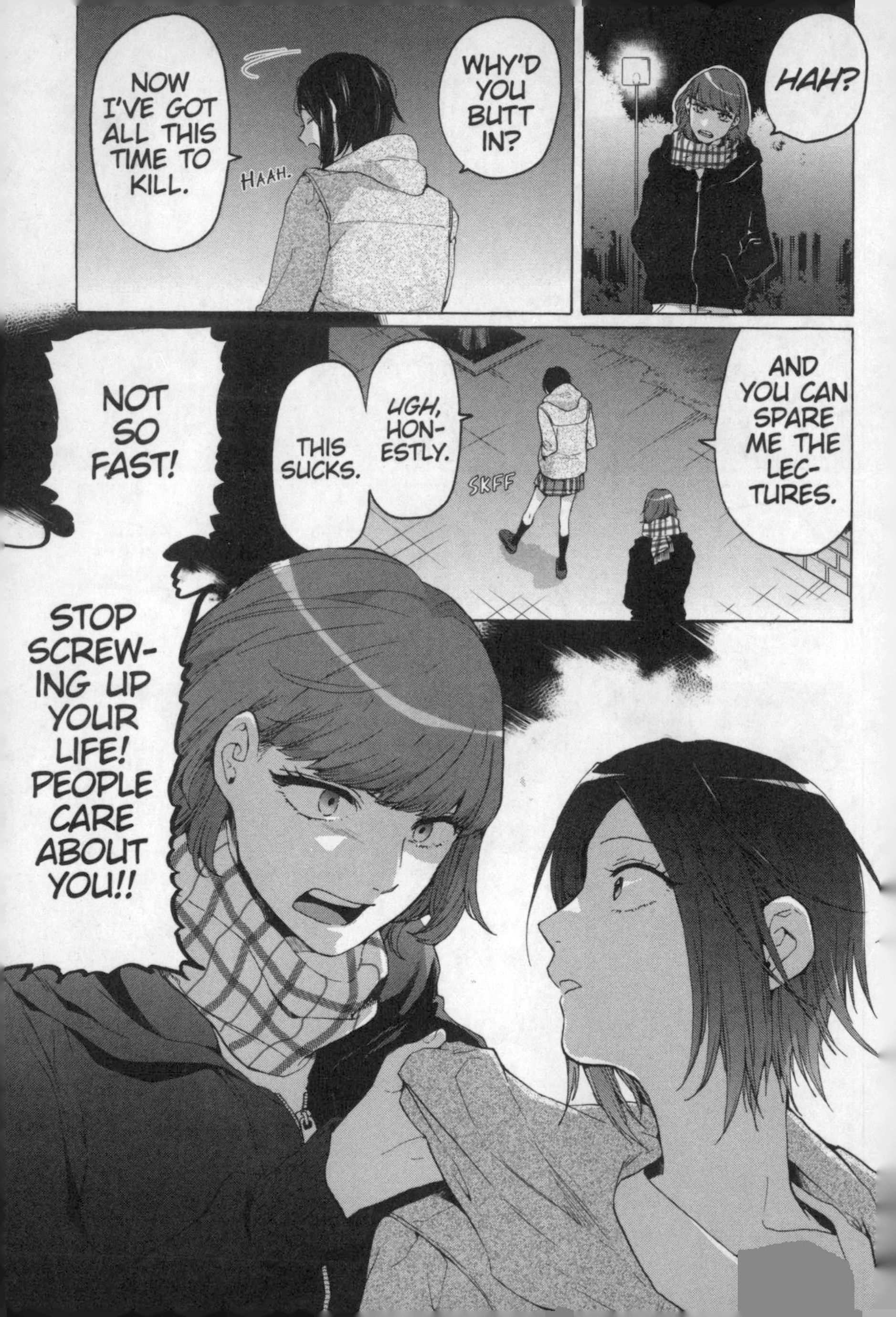
HAH?
WHY'D YOU BUTT IN?
HAAH.
NOW I'VE GOT ALL THIS TIME TO KILL.
AND YOU CAN SPARE ME THE LEC-TURES.
UGH, HON-ESTLY.
THIS SUCKS.
SKFF
NOT SO FAST!
STOP SCREW-ING UP YOUR LIFE! PEOPLE CARE ABOUT YOU!!

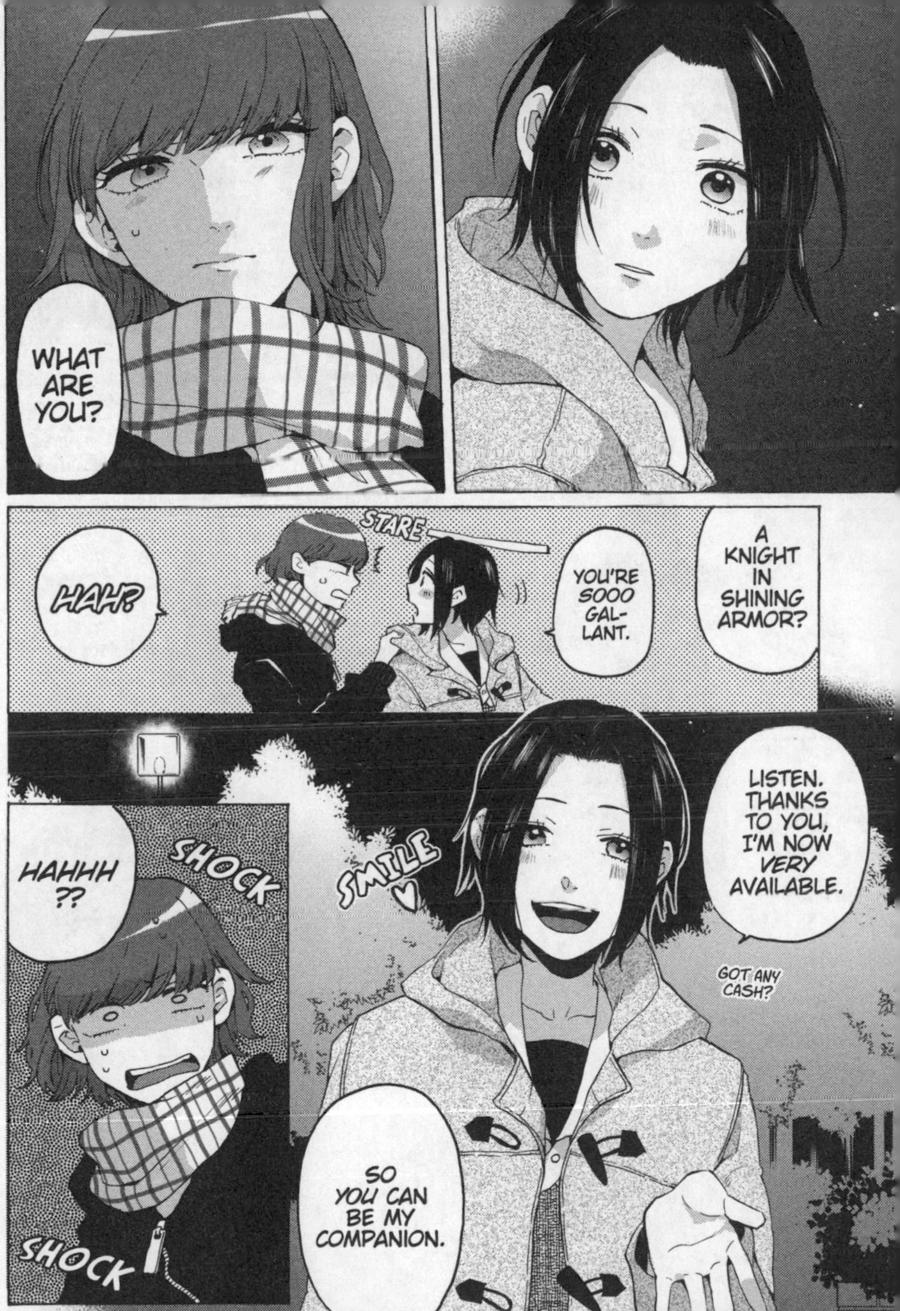
WHAT ARE YOU?
A KNIGHT IN SHINING ARMOR?
YOU'RE SOOO GAL-LANT.
STARE
HAH?
LISTEN. THANKS TO YOU, I'M NOW VERY AVAILABLE.
SMILE
GOT ANY CASH?
SO YOU CAN BE MY COMPANION.
HAHHH ??
SHOCK
SHOCK

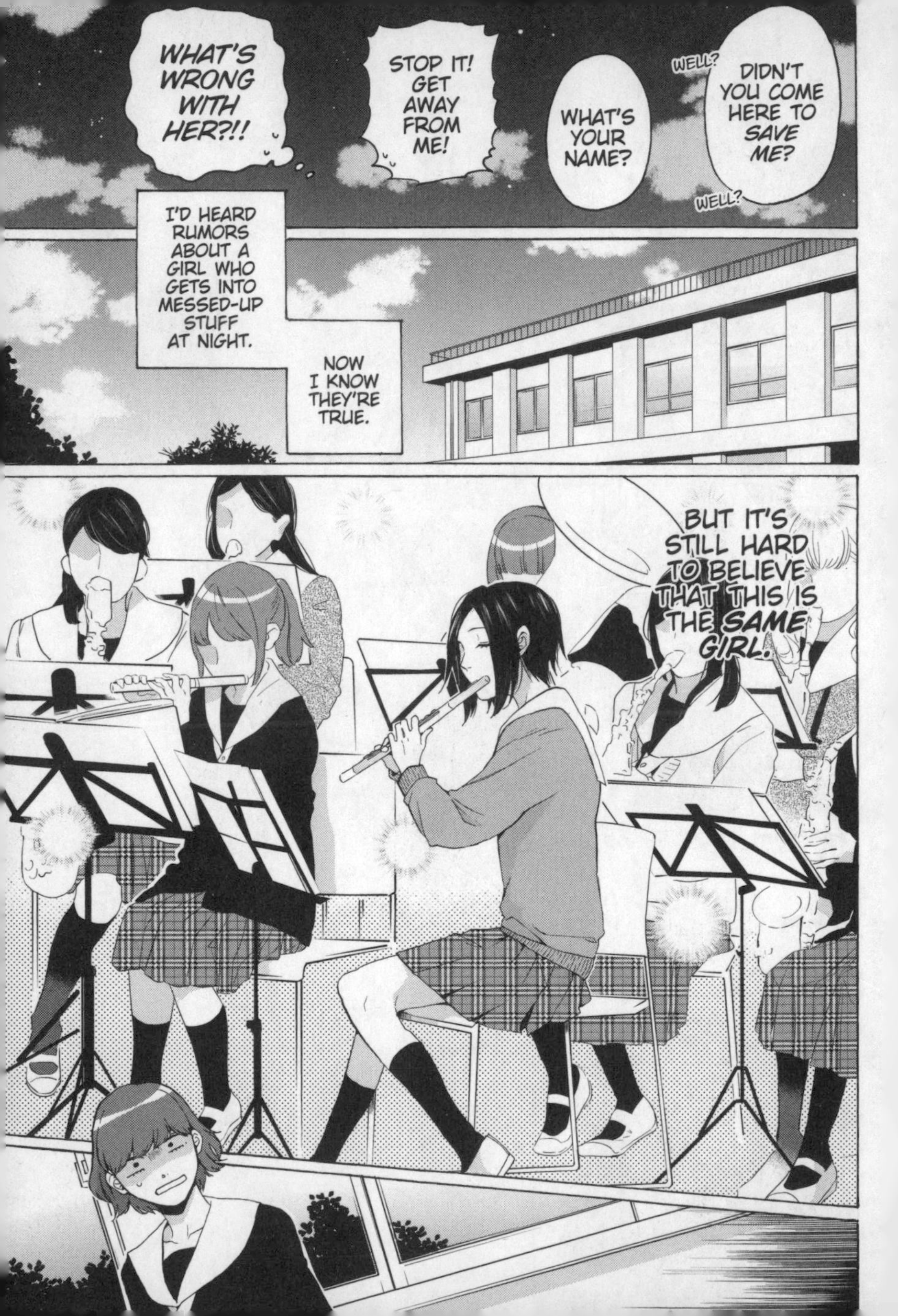
WELL?
DIDN'T YOU COME HERE TO SAVE ME?
WELL?
WHAT'S YOUR NAME?
STOP IT! GET AWAY FROM ME!
WHAT'S WRONG WITH HER?!!
I'D HEARD RUMORS ABOUT A GIRL WHO GETS INTO MESSED-UP STUFF AT NIGHT.
NOW I KNOW THEY'RE TRUE.
BUT IT'S STILL HARD TO BELIEVE THAT THIS IS THE SAME GIRL.

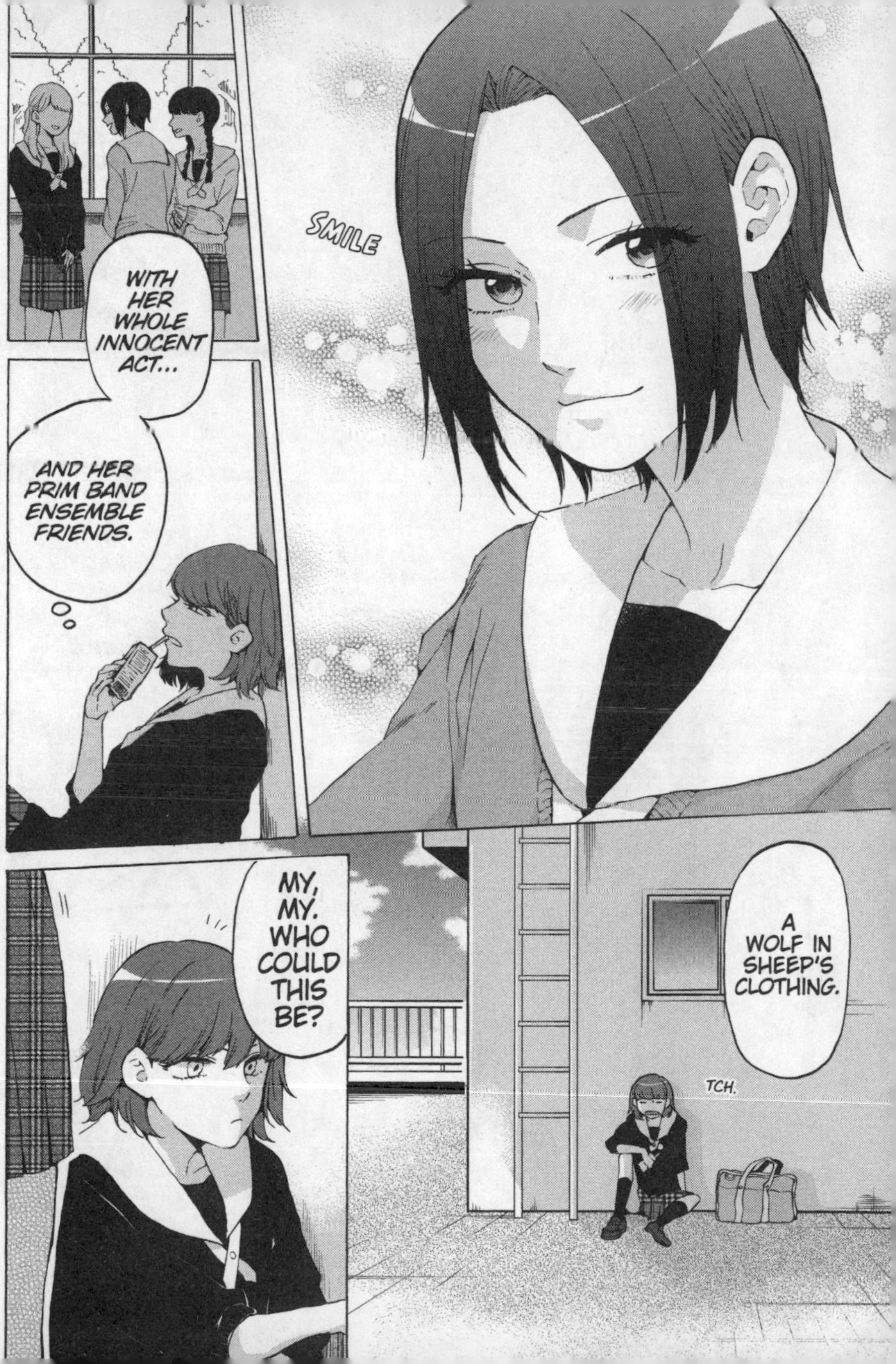
SMILE
WITH HER WHOLE INNOCENT ACT...
AND HER PRIM BAND ENSEMBLE FRIENDS.
A WOLF IN SHEEP'S CLOTHING.
TCH.
MY, MY. WHO COULD THIS BE?

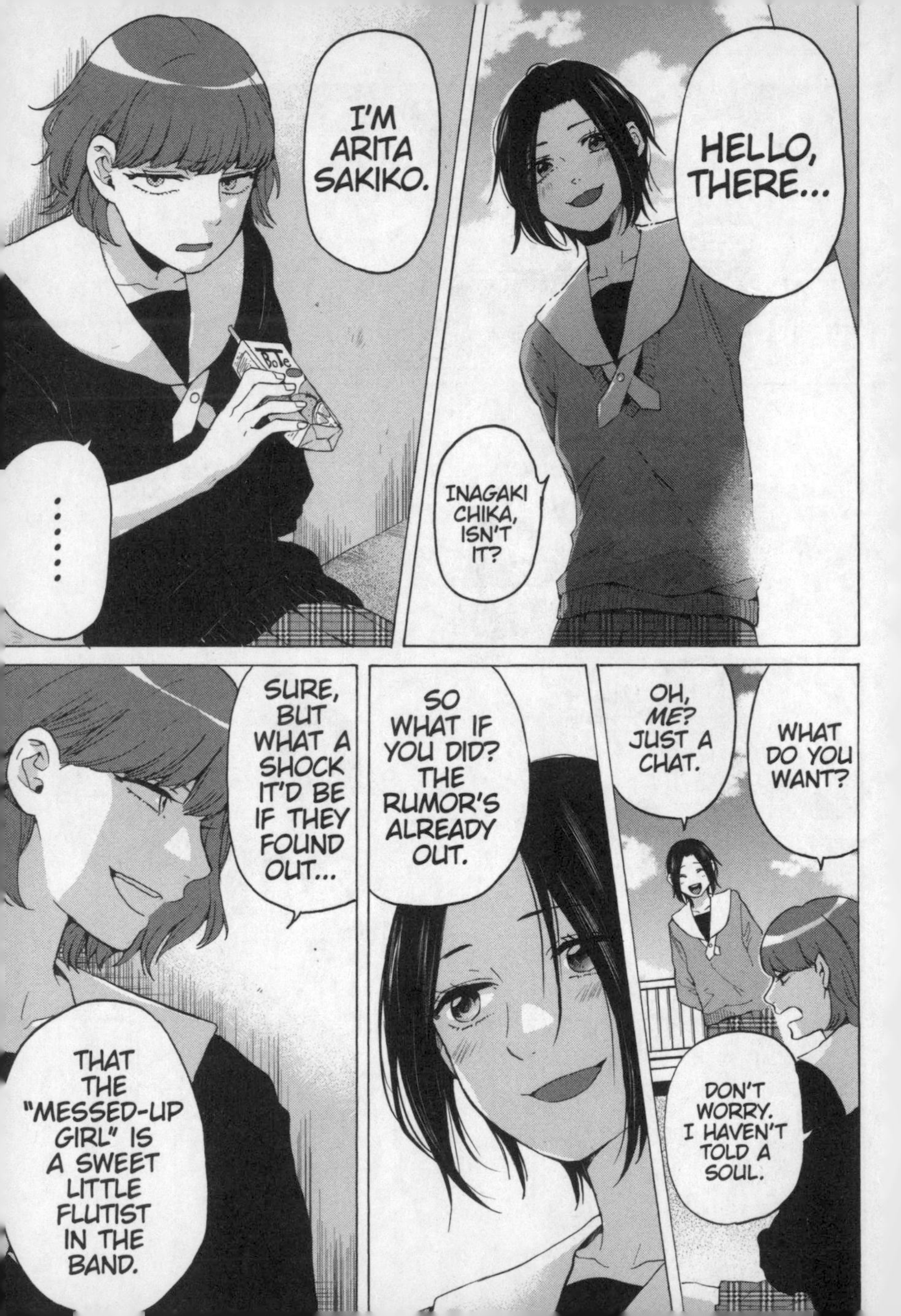
HELLO, THERE...
INAGAKI CHIKA, ISN'T IT?
I'M ARITA SAKIKO.
......
WHAT DO YOU WANT?
OH, *ME*? JUST A CHAT.
DON'T WORRY. I HAVEN'T TOLD A SOUL.
SO WHAT IF YOU DID? THE RUMOR'S ALREADY OUT.
SURE, BUT WHAT A SHOCK IT'D BE IF THEY FOUND OUT...
THAT THE "MESSED-UP GIRL" IS A SWEET LITTLE FLUTIST IN THE BAND.

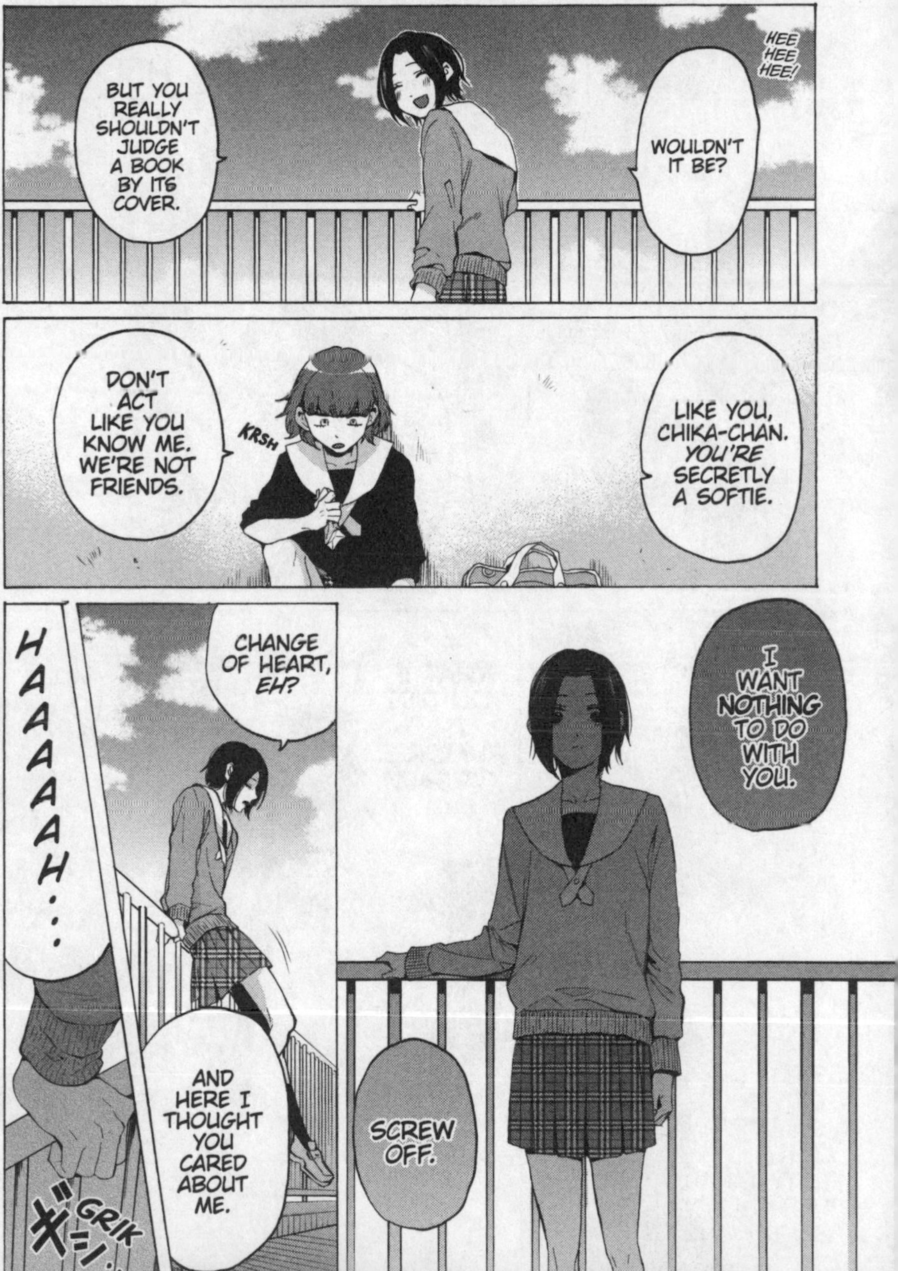
HEE HEE HEE!
WOULDN'T IT BE?
BUT YOU REALLY SHOULDN'T JUDGE A BOOK BY ITS COVER.
LIKE YOU, CHIKA-CHAN. YOU'RE SECRETLY A SOFTIE.
KRSH
DON'T ACT LIKE YOU KNOW ME. WE'RE NOT FRIENDS.
I WANT NOTHING TO DO WITH YOU.
SCREW OFF.
CHANGE OF HEART, EH?
HAAAAAAH...
AND HERE I THOUGHT YOU CARED ABOUT ME.
GRIK

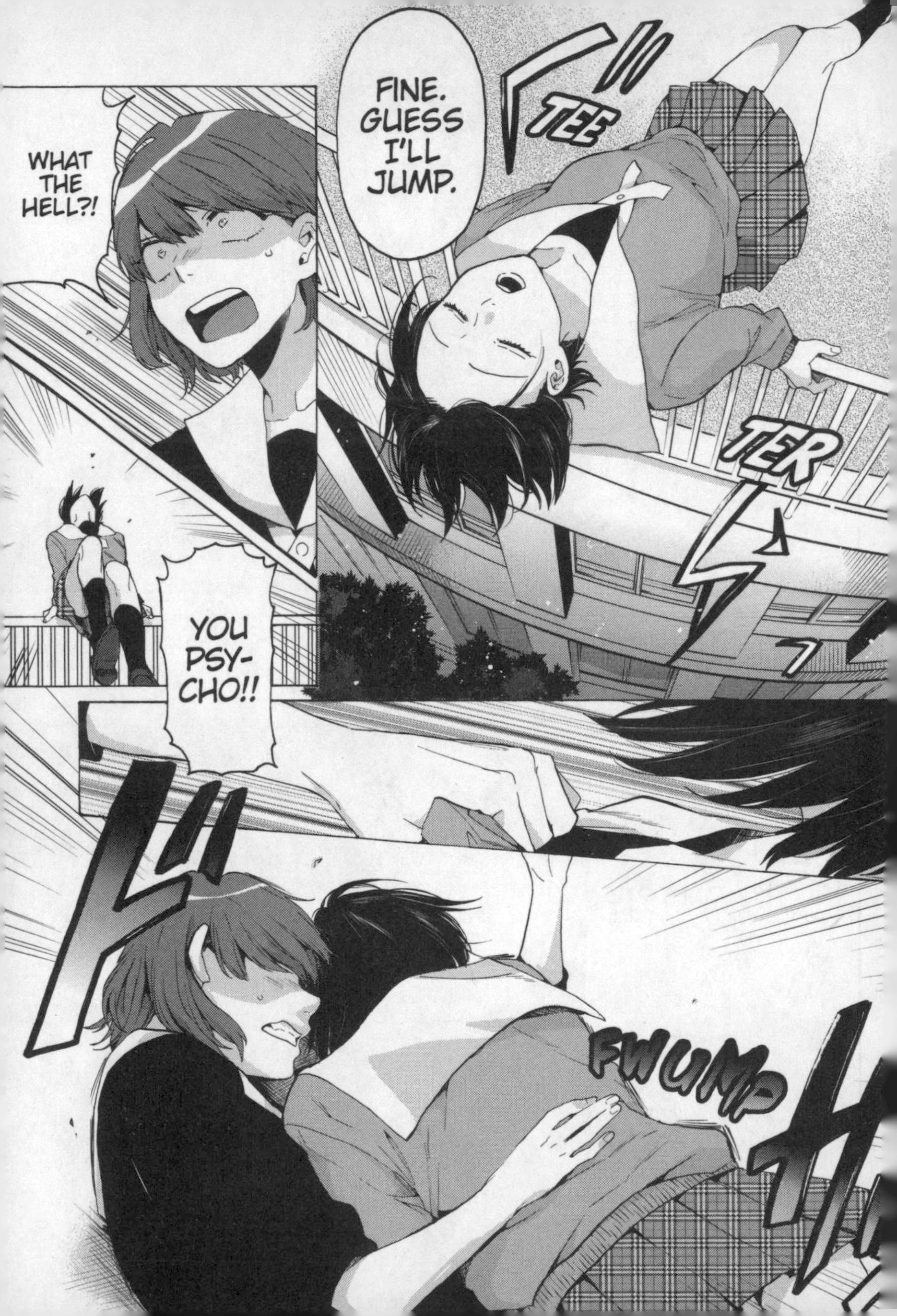
FINE. GUESS I'LL JUMP.
TEE
TER
WHAT THE HELL?!
YOU PSY-CHO!!
FWUMP

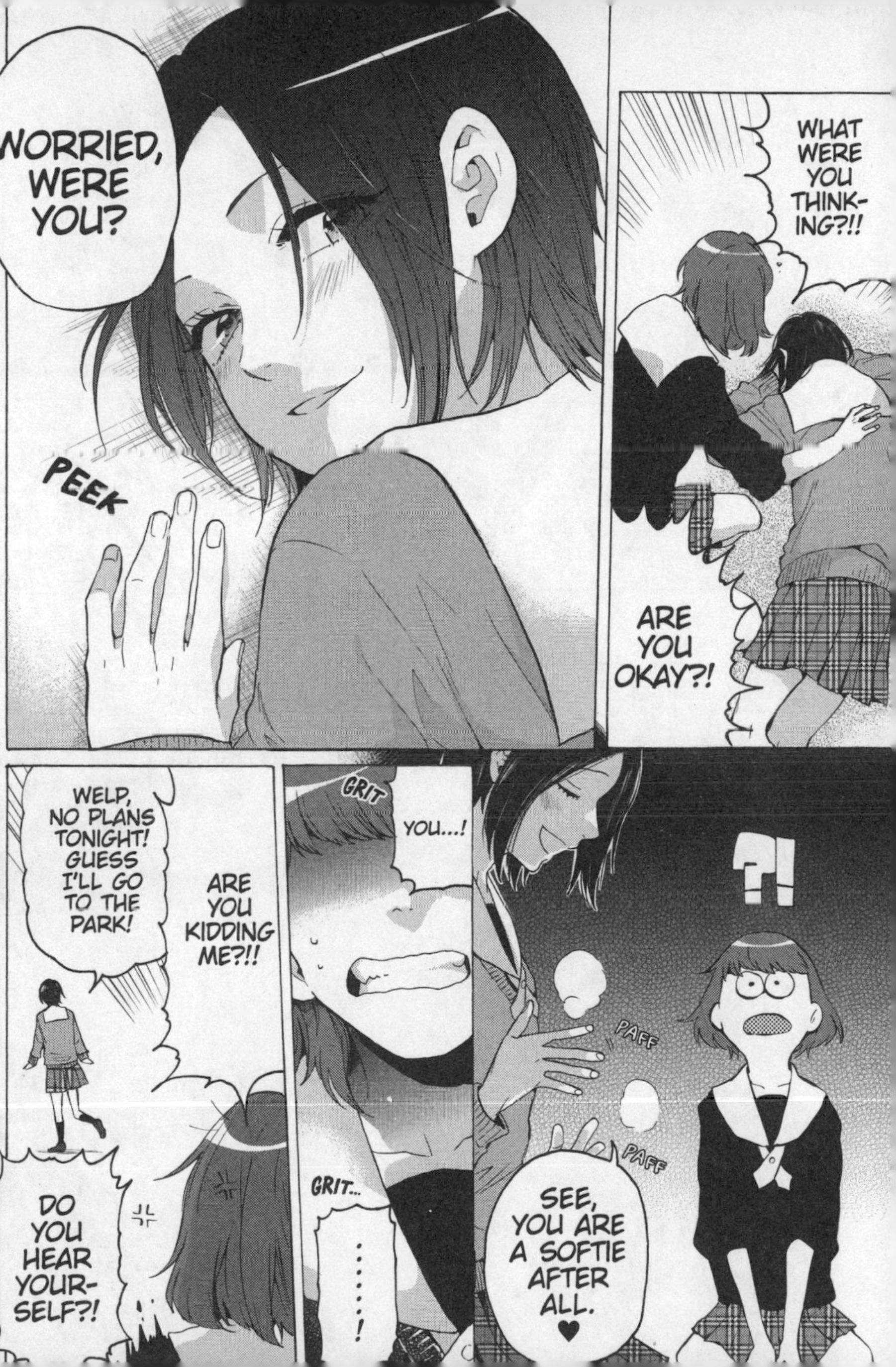
WHAT WERE YOU THINKING?!!
ARE YOU OKAY?!
WORRIED, WERE YOU?
PEEK
?!
PAFF
PAFF
SEE, YOU ARE A SOFTIE AFTER ALL. ♥
GRIT
YOU...!
GRIT...
......!
WELP, NO PLANS TONIGHT! GUESS I'LL GO TO THE PARK!
ARE YOU KIDDING ME?!!
DO YOU HEAR YOURSELF?!

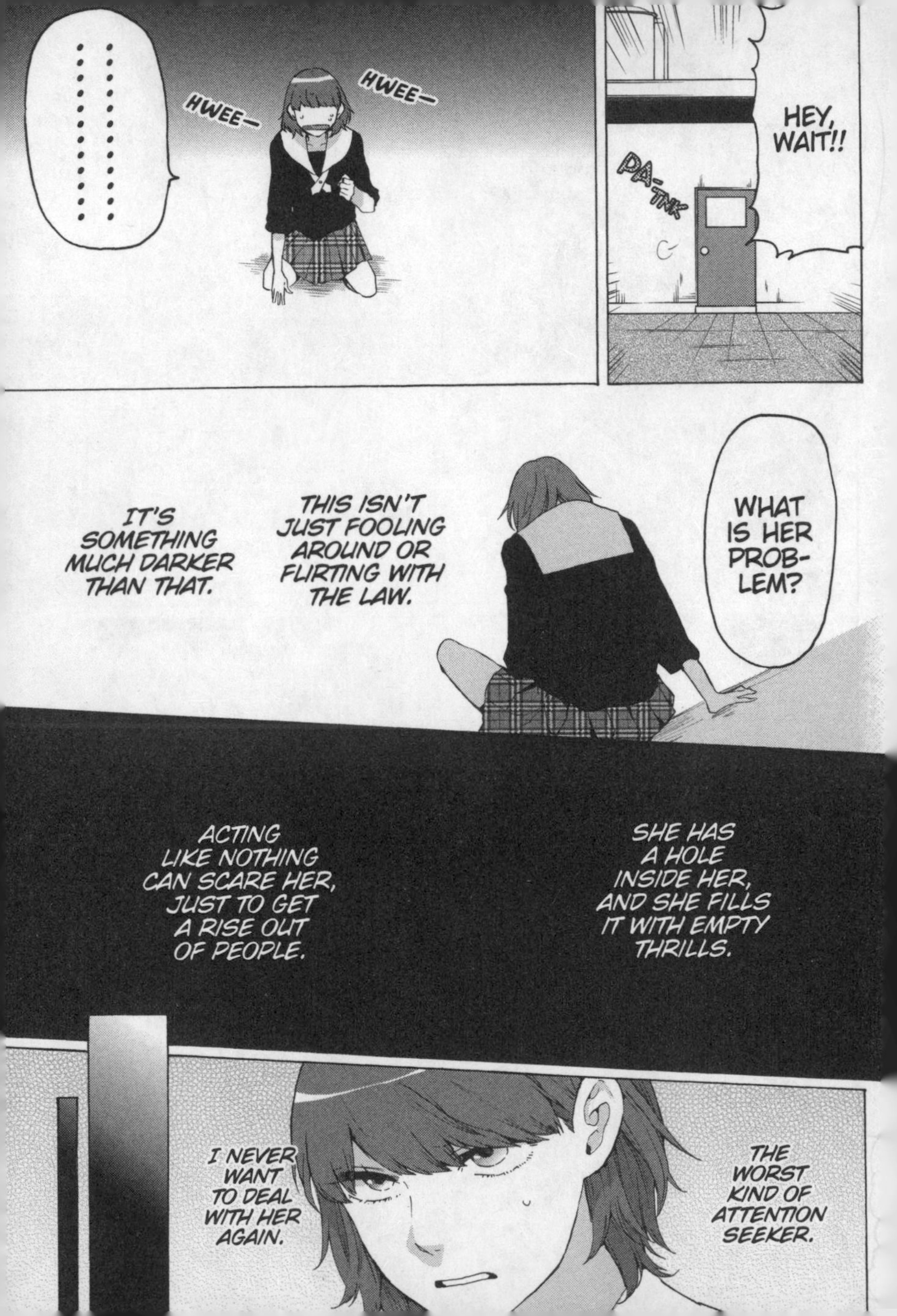
HEY, WAIT!!
PA-TNK
HWEE–
HWEE–
......
WHAT IS HER PROBLEM?
THIS ISN'T JUST FOOLING AROUND OR FLIRTING WITH THE LAW.
IT'S SOMETHING MUCH DARKER THAN THAT.
SHE HAS A HOLE INSIDE HER, AND SHE FILLS IT WITH EMPTY THRILLS.
ACTING LIKE NOTHING CAN SCARE HER, JUST TO GET A RISE OUT OF PEOPLE.
THE WORST KIND OF ATTENTION SEEKER.
I NEVER WANT TO DEAL WITH HER AGAIN.

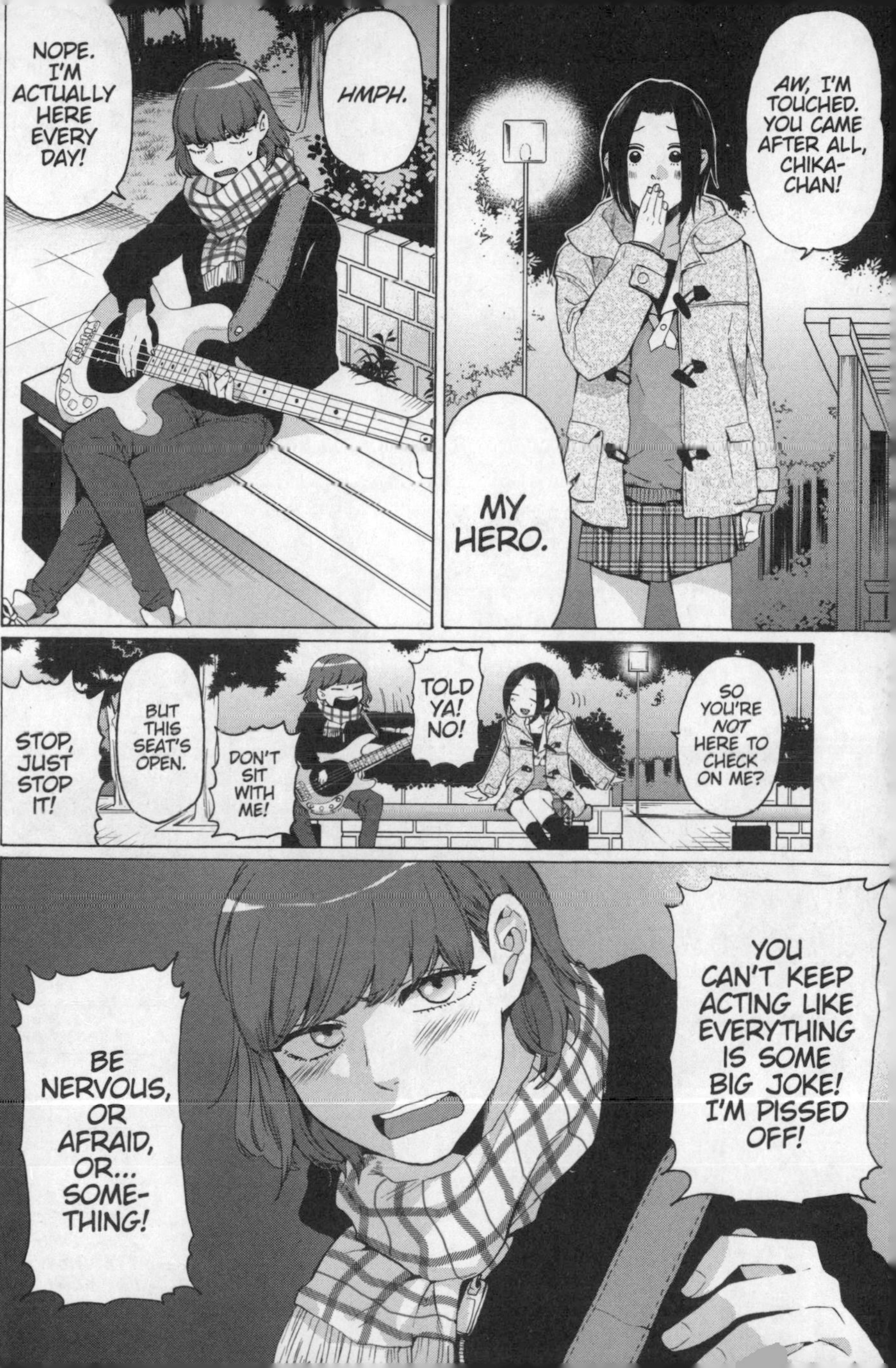
AW, I'M TOUCHED. YOU CAME AFTER ALL, CHIKA-CHAN!
MY HERO.
HMPH.
NOPE. I'M ACTUALLY HERE EVERY DAY!
SO YOU'RE *NOT* HERE TO CHECK ON ME?
TOLD YA! NO!
DON'T SIT WITH ME!
BUT THIS SEAT'S OPEN.
STOP, JUST STOP IT!
YOU CAN'T KEEP ACTING LIKE EVERYTHING IS SOME BIG JOKE! I'M PISSED OFF!
BE NERVOUS, OR AFRAID, OR... SOME-THING!

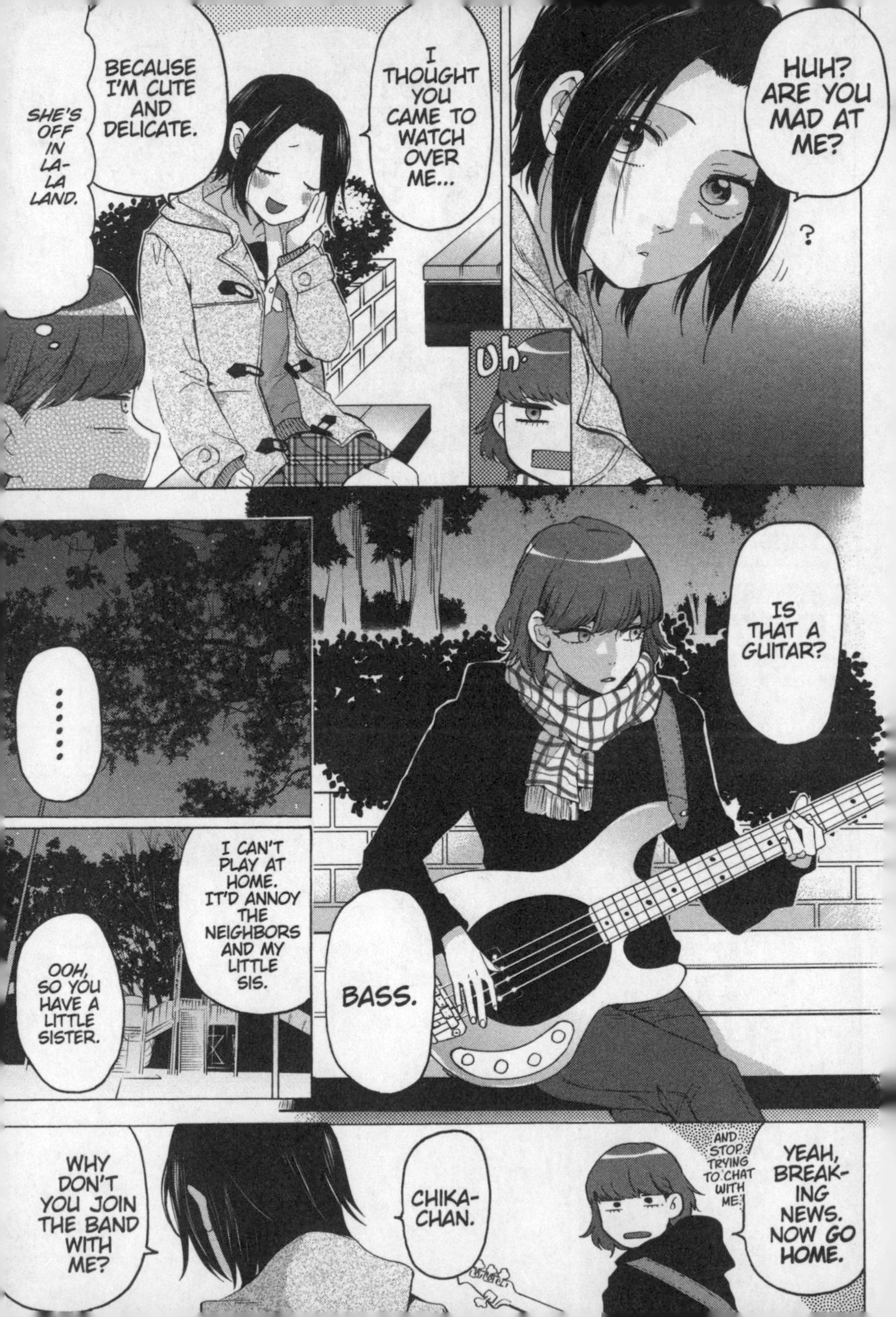
HUH? ARE YOU MAD AT ME?
?
Uh.
I THOUGHT YOU CAME TO WATCH OVER ME...
BECAUSE I'M CUTE AND DELICATE.
SHE'S OFF IN LA-LA LAND.
IS THAT A GUITAR?
BASS.
......
I CAN'T PLAY AT HOME. IT'D ANNOY THE NEIGHBORS AND MY LITTLE SIS.
OOH, SO YOU HAVE A LITTLE SISTER.
YEAH, BREAKING NEWS. NOW GO HOME.
AND STOP TRYING TO CHAT WITH ME.
CHIKA-CHAN.
WHY DON'T YOU JOIN THE BAND WITH ME?

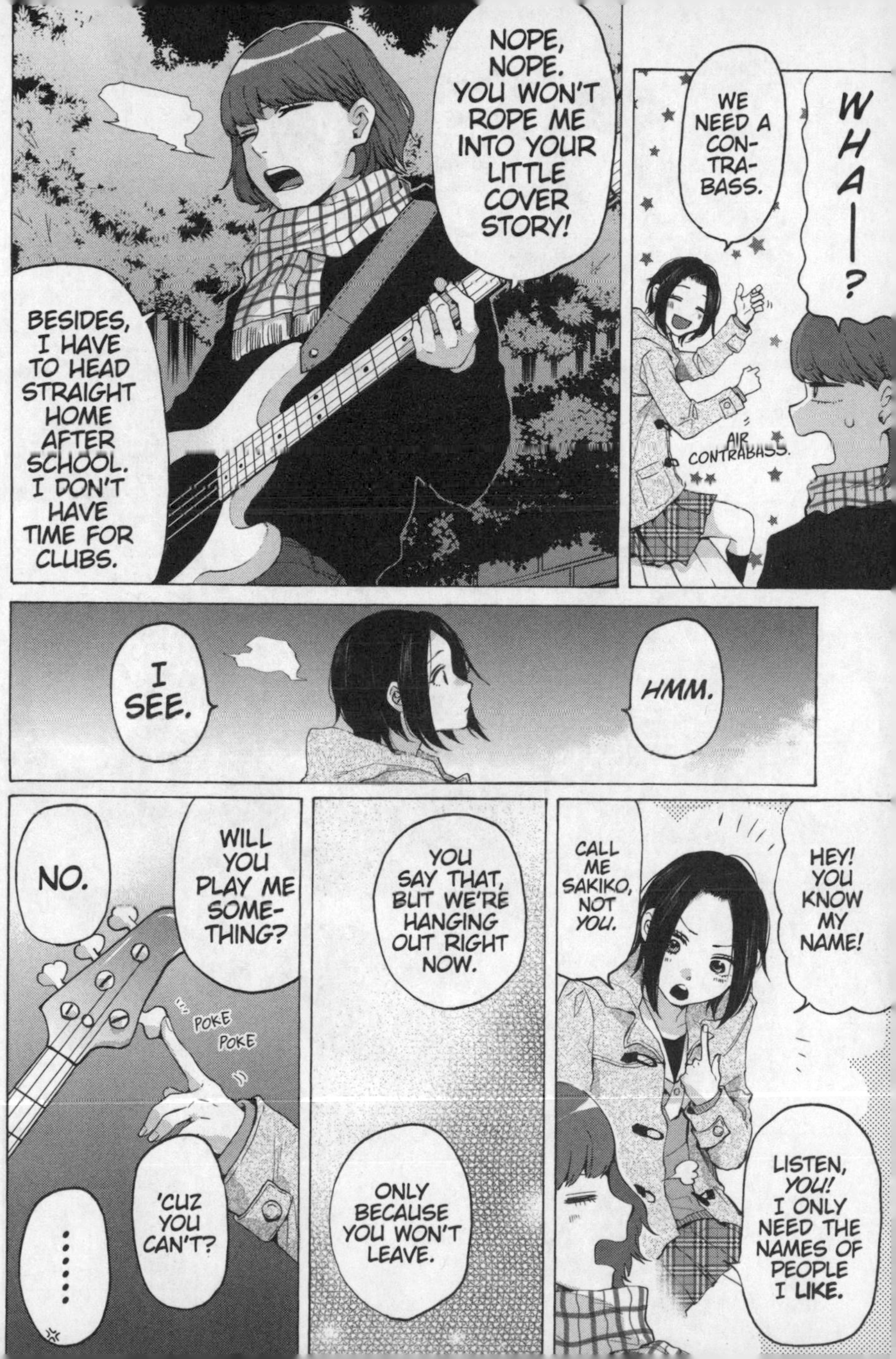
WHA—?
WE NEED A CONTRA-BASS.
AIR CONTRABASS.
NOPE, NOPE. YOU WON'T ROPE ME INTO YOUR LITTLE COVER STORY!
BESIDES, I HAVE TO HEAD STRAIGHT HOME AFTER SCHOOL. I DON'T HAVE TIME FOR CLUBS.
HMM.
I SEE.
HEY! YOU KNOW MY NAME!
CALL ME SAKIKO, NOT YOU.
LISTEN, YOU! I ONLY NEED THE NAMES OF PEOPLE I LIKE.
YOU SAY THAT, BUT WE'RE HANGING OUT RIGHT NOW.
ONLY BECAUSE YOU WON'T LEAVE.
WILL YOU PLAY ME SOMETHING?
NO.
POKE
POKE
'CUZ YOU CAN'T?
......

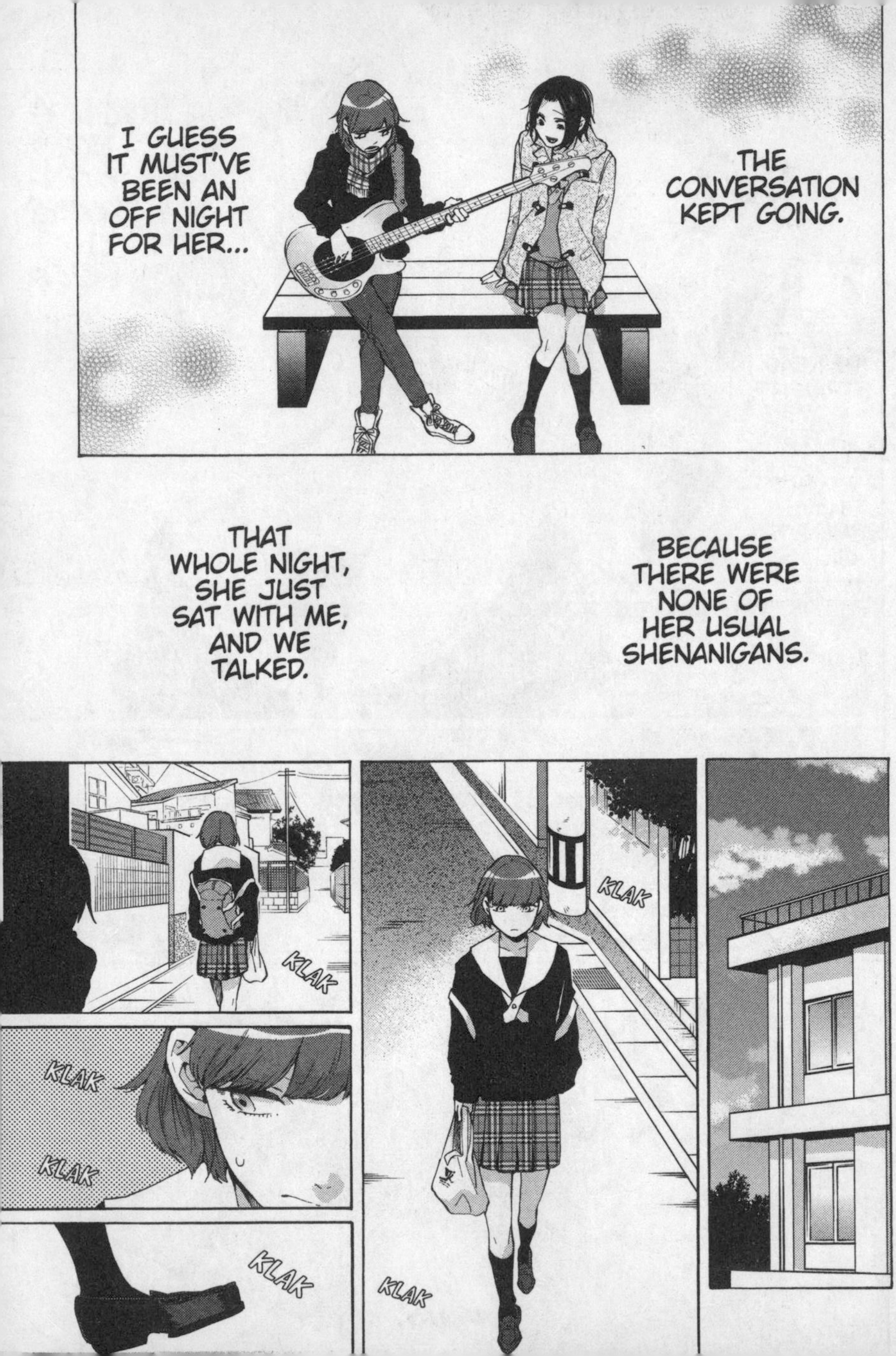
THE CONVERSATION KEPT GOING.
I GUESS IT MUST'VE BEEN AN OFF NIGHT FOR HER...
BECAUSE THERE WERE NONE OF HER USUAL SHENANIGANS.
THAT WHOLE NIGHT, SHE JUST SAT WITH ME, AND WE TALKED.
KLAK
KLAK
KLAK
KLAK
KLAK
KLAK

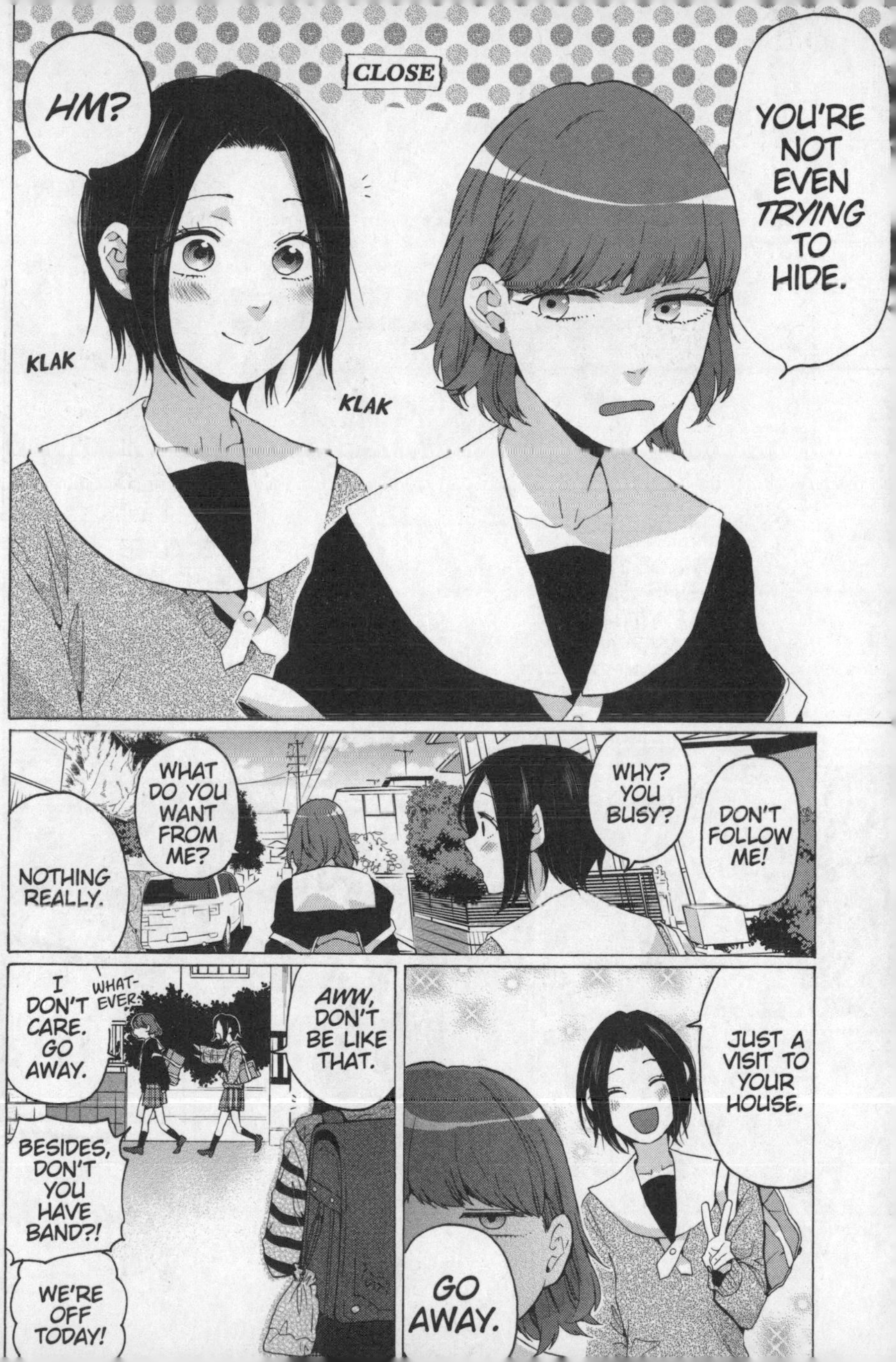
YOU'RE NOT EVEN TRYING TO HIDE.
CLOSE
HM?
KLAK
KLAK
DON'T FOLLOW ME!
WHY? YOU BUSY?
WHAT DO YOU WANT FROM ME?
NOTHING REALLY.
JUST A VISIT TO YOUR HOUSE.
GO AWAY.
AWW, DON'T BE LIKE THAT.
I DON'T CARE. GO AWAY.
WHAT-EVER.
BESIDES, DON'T YOU HAVE BAND?!
WE'RE OFF TODAY!

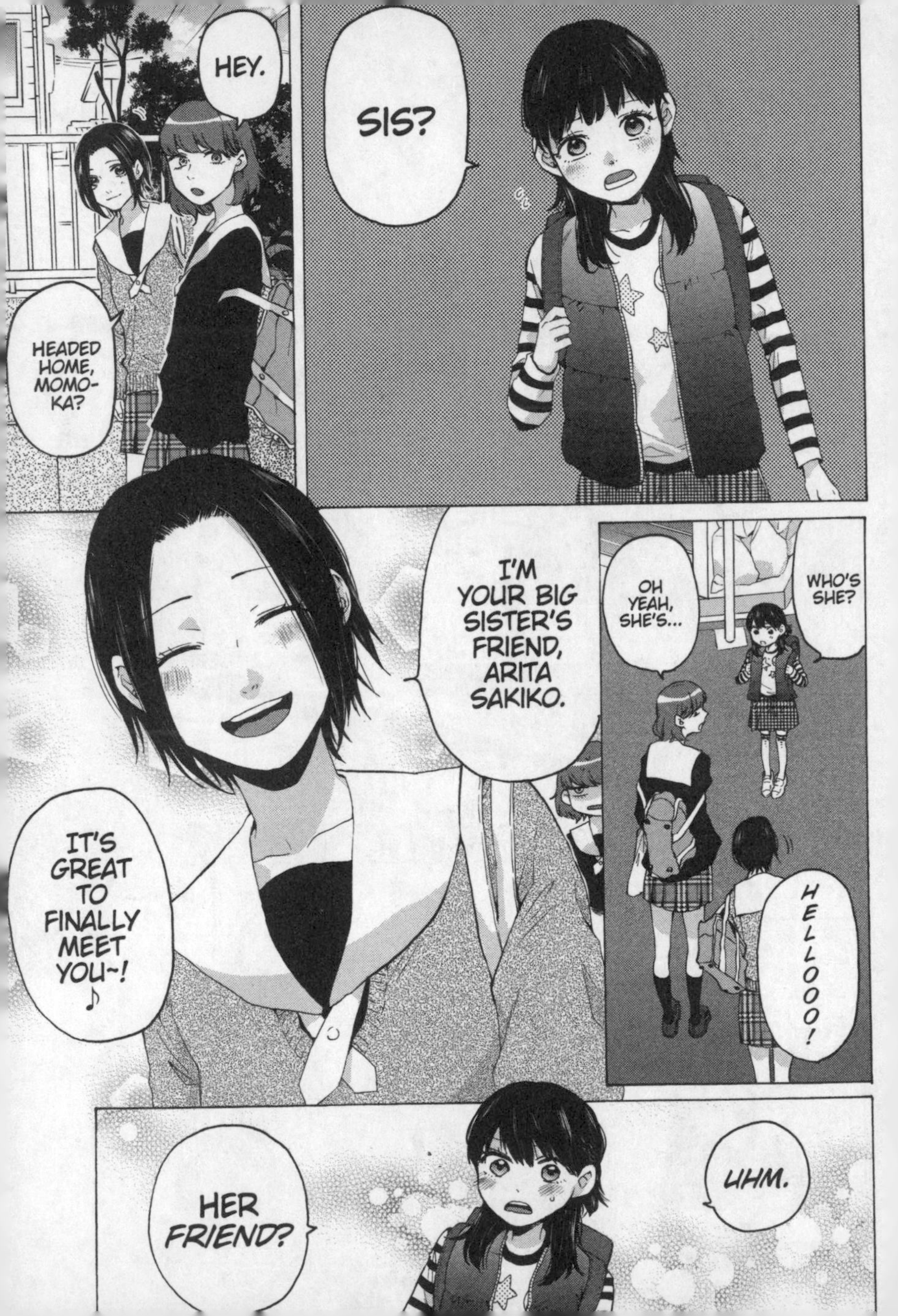
SIS?
HEY.
HEADED HOME, MOMOKA?
WHO'S SHE?
OH YEAH, SHE'S...
HELLOOO!
I'M YOUR BIG SISTER'S FRIEND, ARITA SAKIKO.
IT'S GREAT TO FINALLY MEET YOU~! ♪
UHM.
HER FRIEND?

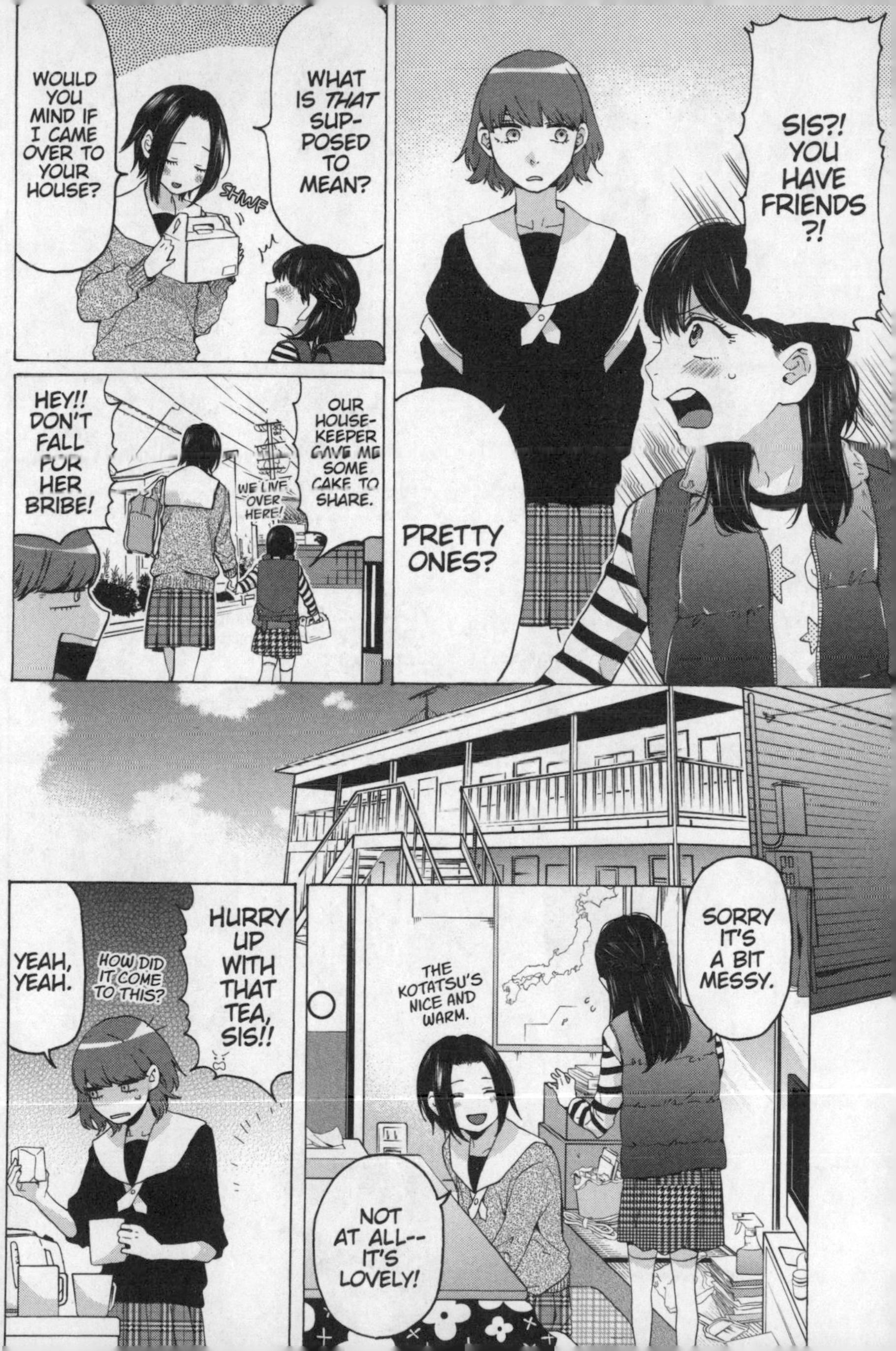
SIS?! YOU HAVE FRIENDS ?!
PRETTY ONES?
WHAT IS THAT SUP-POSED TO MEAN?
WOULD YOU MIND IF I CAME OVER TO YOUR HOUSE?
SHWF
OUR HOUSE-KEEPER GAVE ME SOME CAKE TO SHARE.
WE LIVE OVER HERE!
HEY!! DON'T FALL FOR HER BRIBE!
SORRY IT'S A BIT MESSY.
THE KOTATSU'S NICE AND WARM.
NOT AT ALL-- IT'S LOVELY!
HURRY UP WITH THAT TEA, SIS!!
YEAH, YEAH.
HOW DID IT COME TO THIS?

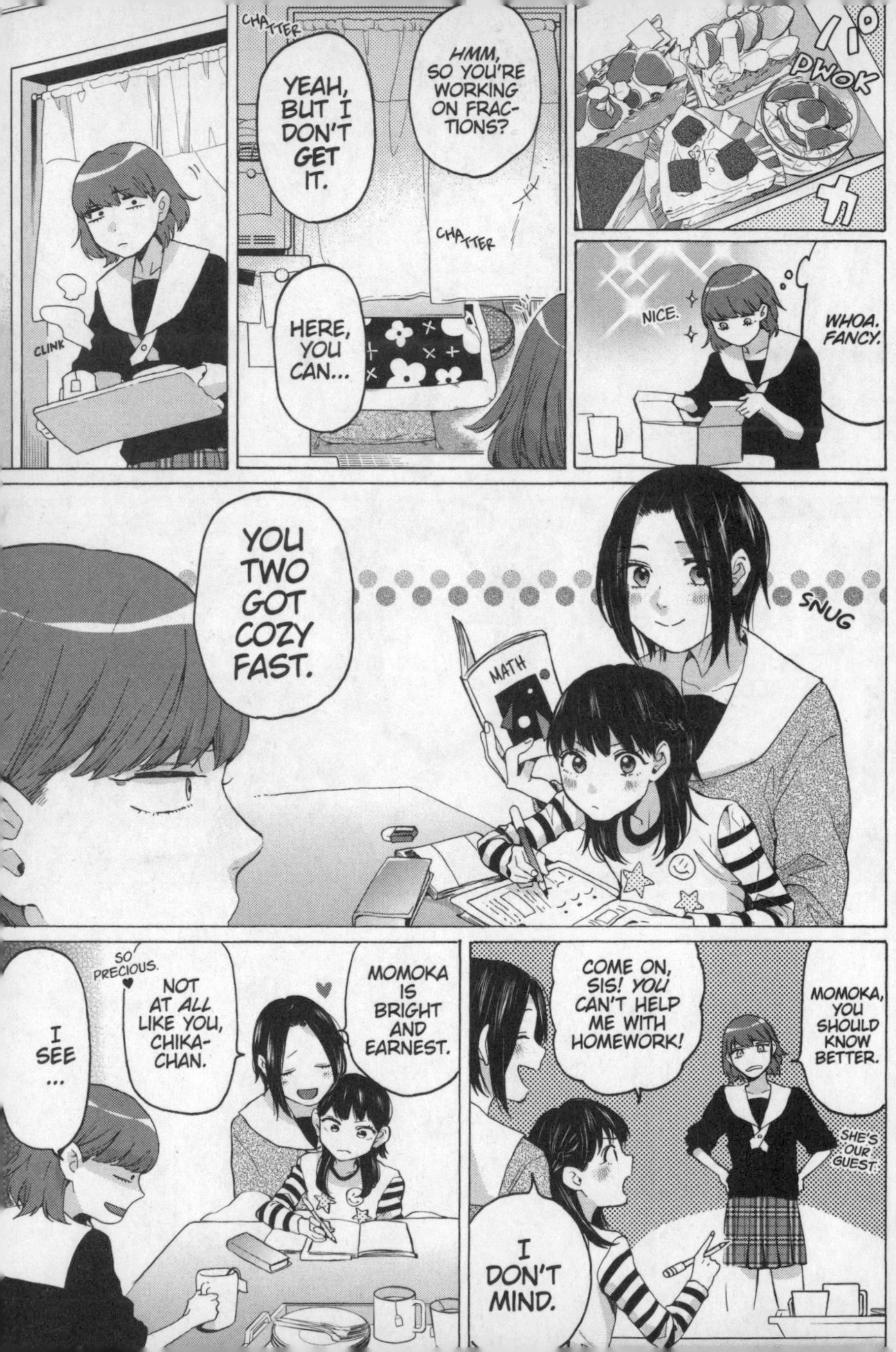
パ
PWOK
カ
WHOA. FANCY.
NICE.
HMM, SO YOU'RE WORKING ON FRAC-TIONS?
CHATTER
YEAH, BUT I DON'T GET IT.
CHATTER
HERE, YOU CAN...
CLINK
SNUG
YOU TWO GOT COZY FAST.
MOMOKA, YOU SHOULD KNOW BETTER.
SHE'S OUR GUEST.
COME ON, SIS! YOU CAN'T HELP ME WITH HOMEWORK!
I DON'T MIND.
MOMOKA IS BRIGHT AND EARNEST.
NOT AT ALL LIKE YOU, CHIKA-CHAN.
SO PRECIOUS.
I SEE...
MATH

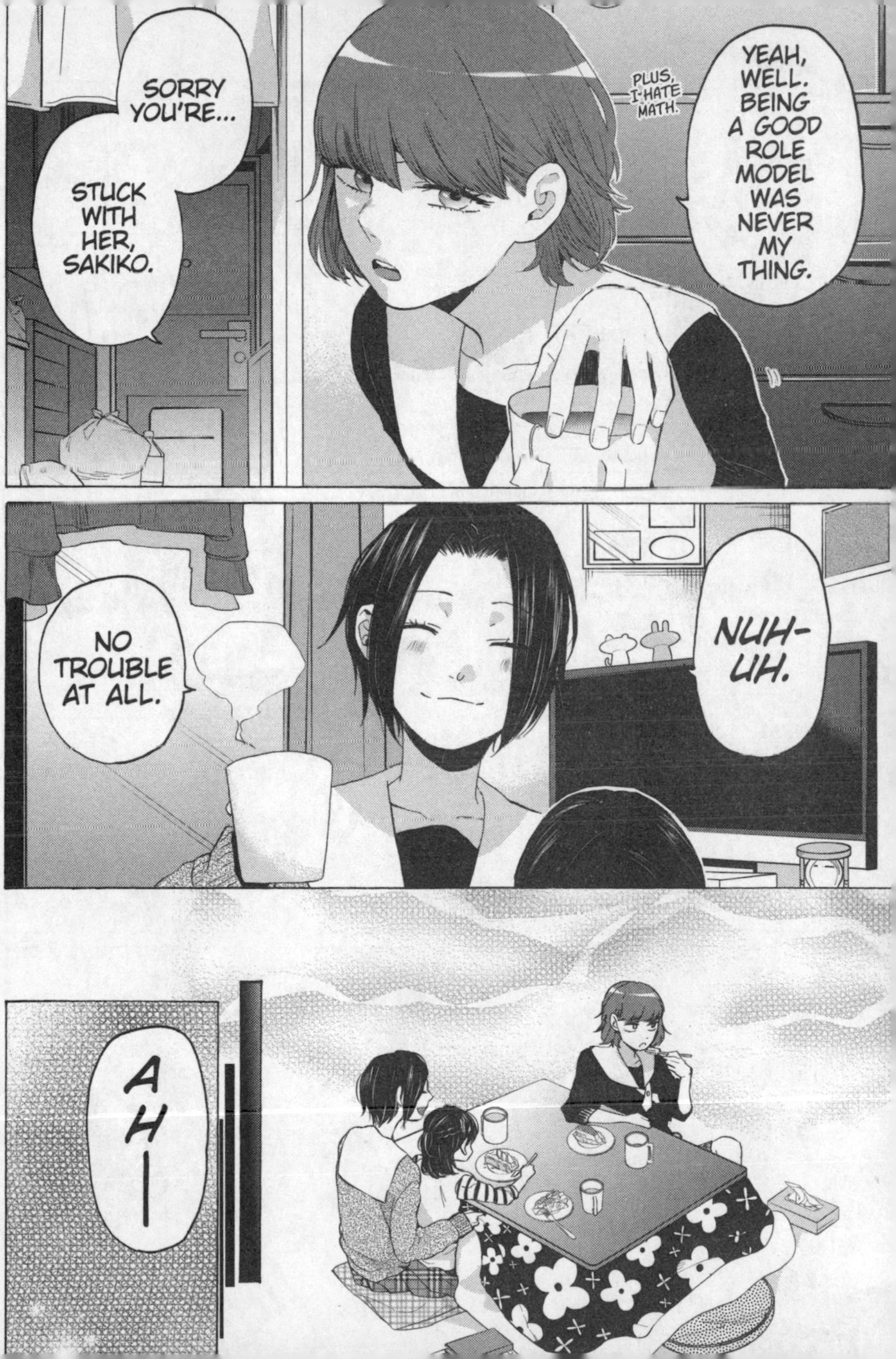
YEAH, WELL. BEING A GOOD ROLE MODEL WAS NEVER MY THING.
PLUS, I HATE MATH.
SORRY YOU'RE...
STUCK WITH HER, SAKIKO.
NUH-UH.
NO TROUBLE AT ALL.
AH!

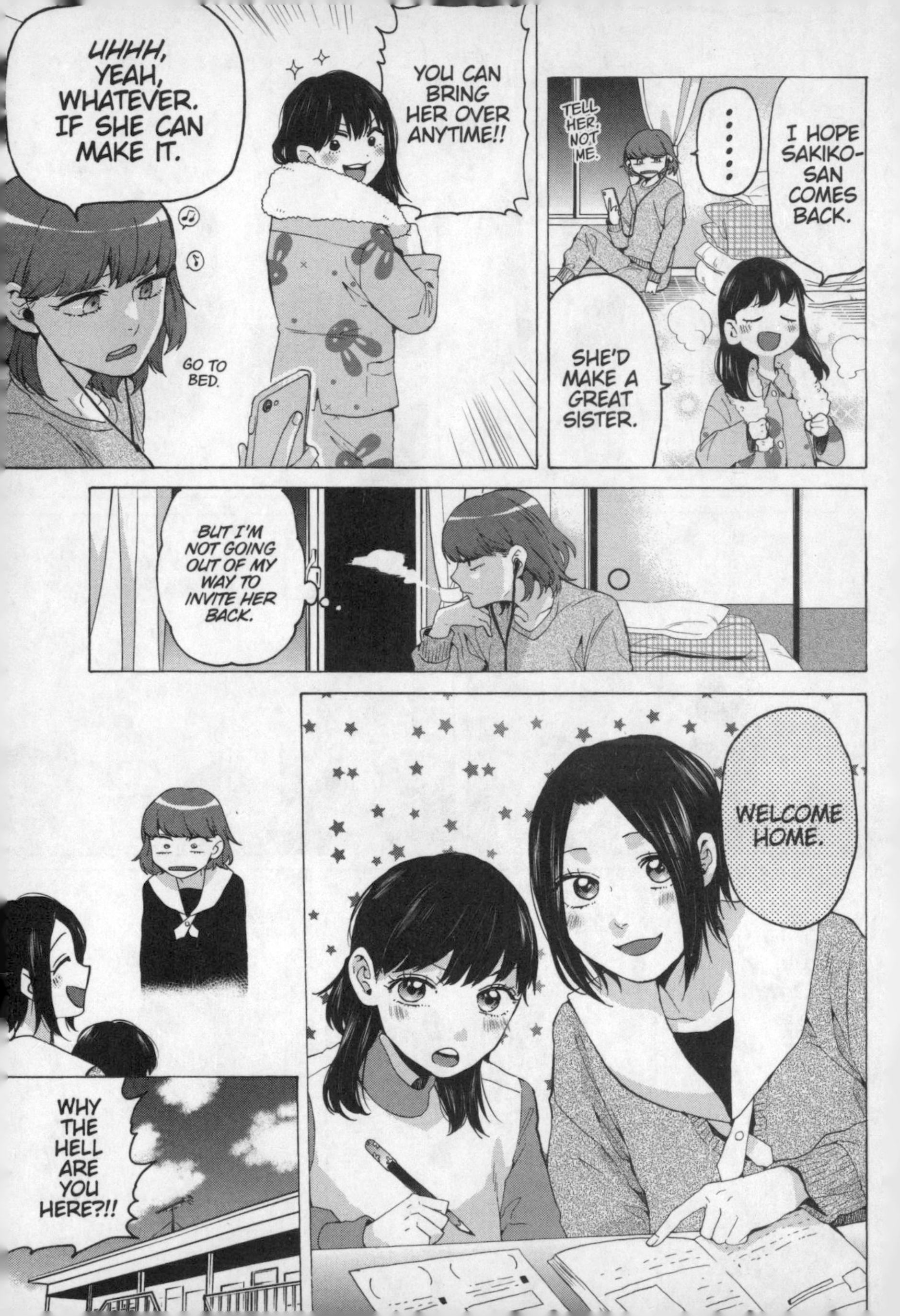
I HOPE SAKIKO-SAN COMES BACK.
......
TELL HER, NOT ME.
SHE'D MAKE A GREAT SISTER.
YOU CAN BRING HER OVER ANYTIME!!
UHHH, YEAH, WHATEVER. IF SHE CAN MAKE IT.
GO TO BED.
BUT I'M NOT GOING OUT OF MY WAY TO INVITE HER BACK.
WELCOME HOME.
WHY THE HELL ARE YOU HERE?!!

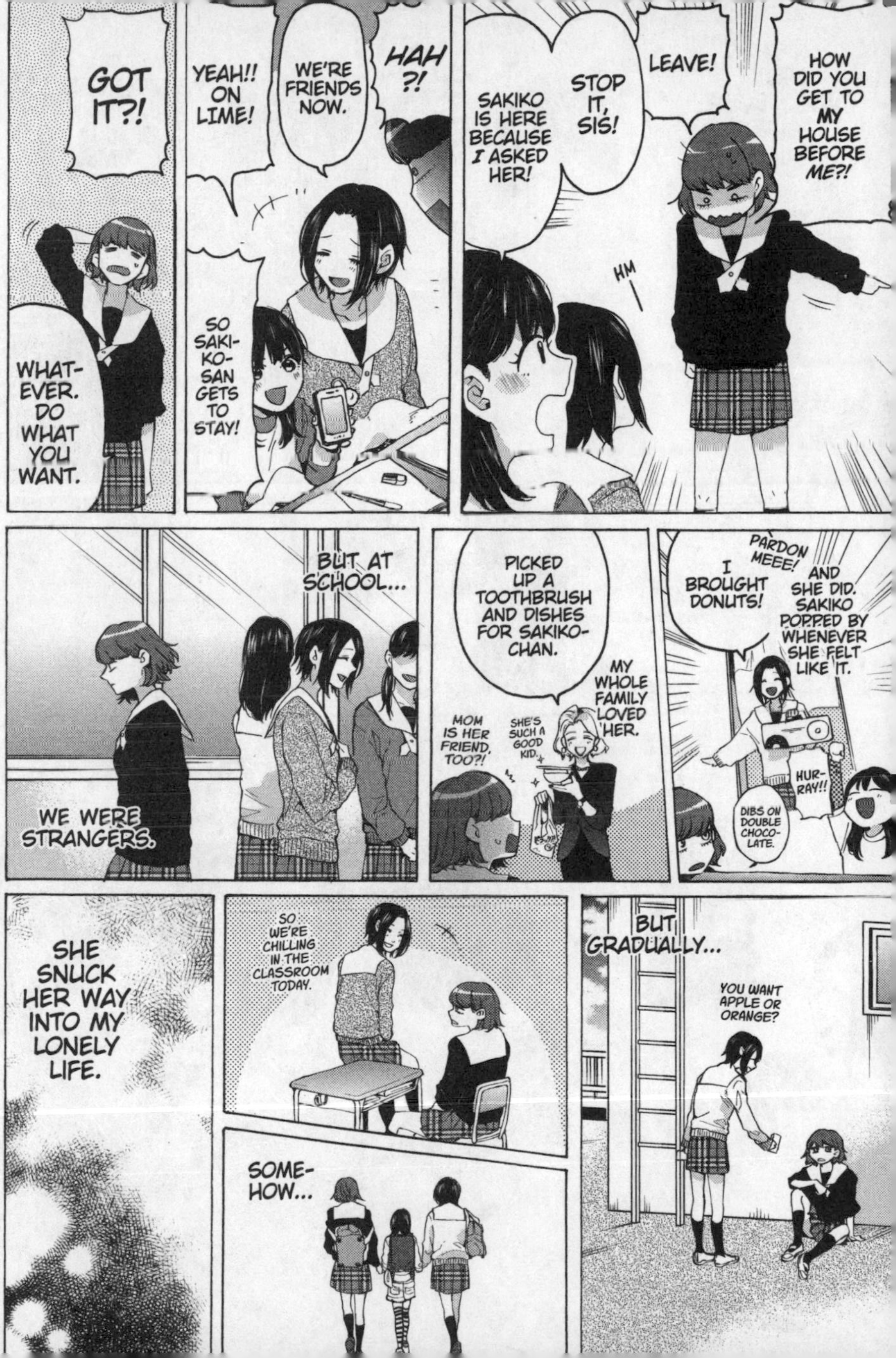
LEAVE!
HOW DID YOU GET TO MY HOUSE BEFORE ME?!
STOP IT, SIS!
SAKIKO IS HERE BECAUSE I ASKED HER!
HM
HAH ?!
WE'RE FRIENDS NOW.
YEAH!! ON LIME!
SO SAKI-KO-SAN GETS TO STAY!
GOT IT?!
WHAT-EVER. DO WHAT YOU WANT.
PARDON MEEE!
I BROUGHT DONUTS!
AND SHE DID. SAKIKO POPPED BY WHENEVER SHE FELT LIKE IT.
HUR-RAY!!
DIBS ON DOUBLE CHOCO-LATE.
PICKED UP A TOOTHBRUSH AND DISHES FOR SAKIKO-CHAN.
MY WHOLE FAMILY LOVED HER.
SHE'S SUCH A GOOD KID.
MOM IS HER FRIEND, TOO?!
BUT AT SCHOOL...
WE WERE STRANGERS.
BUT GRADUALLY...
YOU WANT APPLE OR ORANGE?
SO WE'RE CHILLING IN THE CLASSROOM TODAY.
SOME-HOW...
SHE SNUCK HER WAY INTO MY LONELY LIFE.

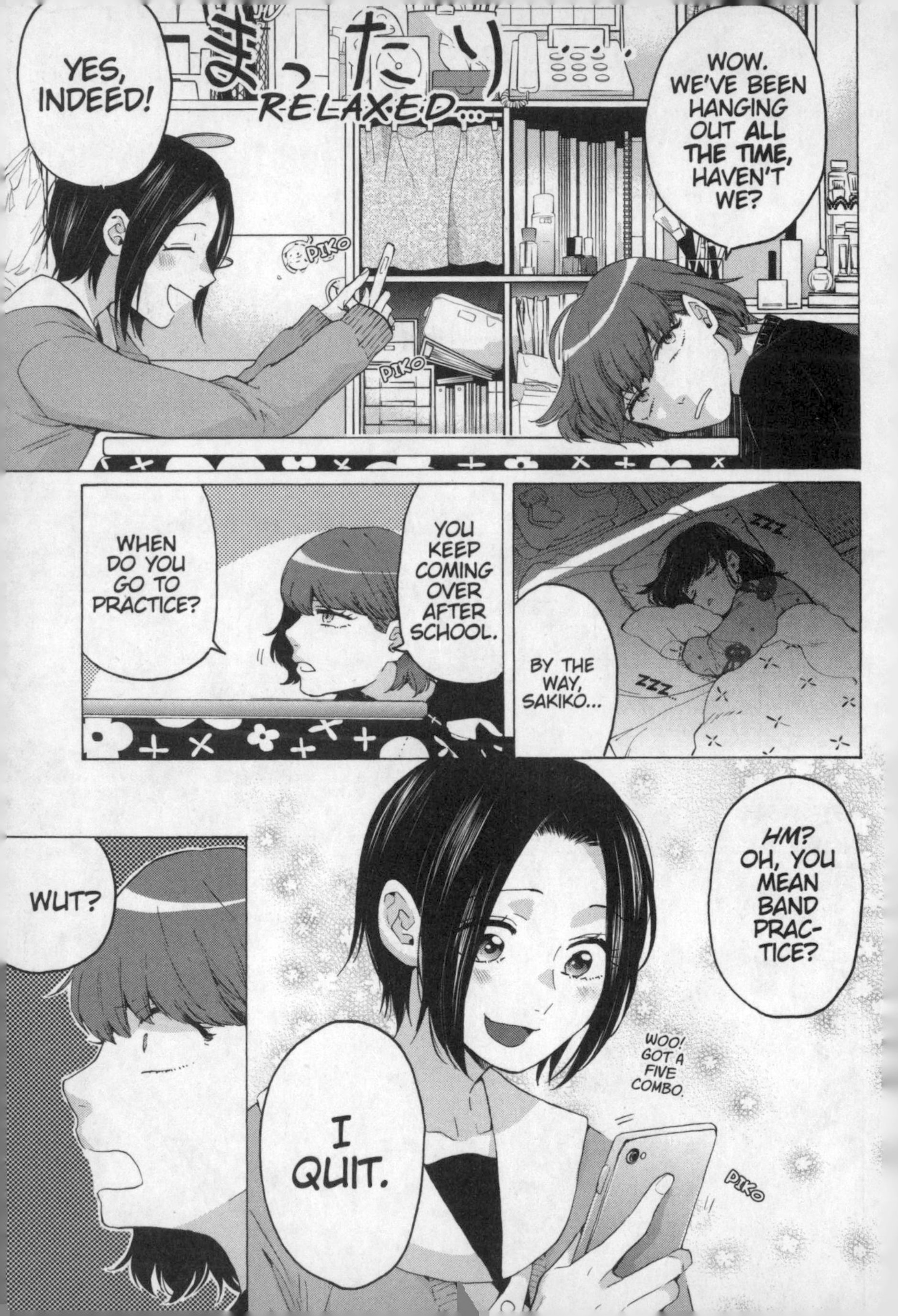
WOW. WE'VE BEEN HANGING OUT ALL THE TIME, HAVEN'T WE?
まったり...
RELAXED...
YES, INDEED!
PIKO
PIKO
ZZZ
BY THE WAY, SAKIKO...
ZZZ
YOU KEEP COMING OVER AFTER SCHOOL.
WHEN DO YOU GO TO PRACTICE?
HM? OH, YOU MEAN BAND PRAC-TICE?
WOO! GOT A FIVE COMBO.
I QUIT.
PIKO
WUT?

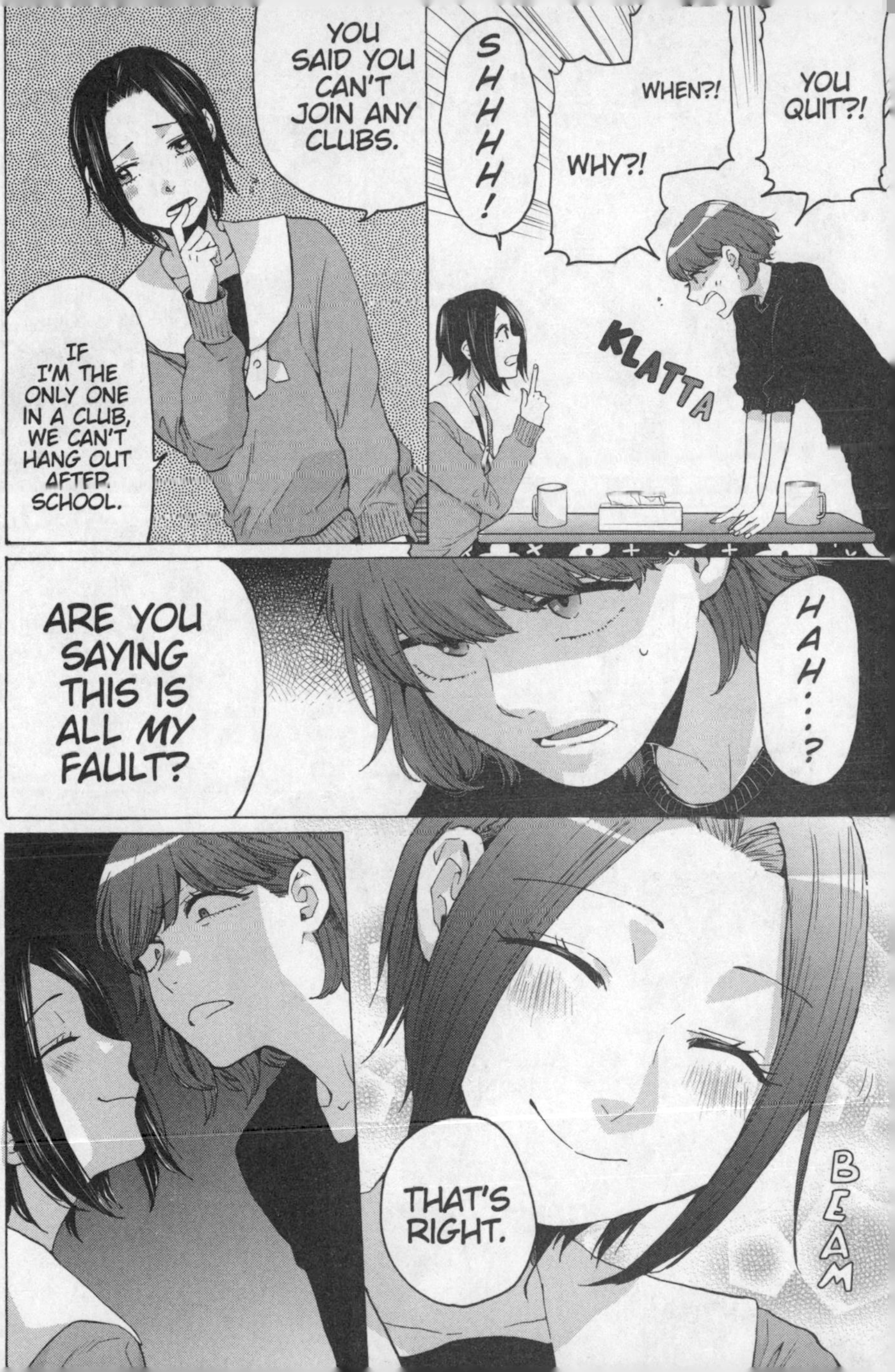
YOU QUIT?!
WHEN?!
WHY?!
SHHHHH!
KLATTA
YOU SAID YOU CAN'T JOIN ANY CLUBS.
IF I'M THE ONLY ONE IN A CLUB, WE CAN'T HANG OUT AFTER SCHOOL.
HAH...?
ARE YOU SAYING THIS IS ALL *MY* FAULT?
BEAM
THAT'S RIGHT.

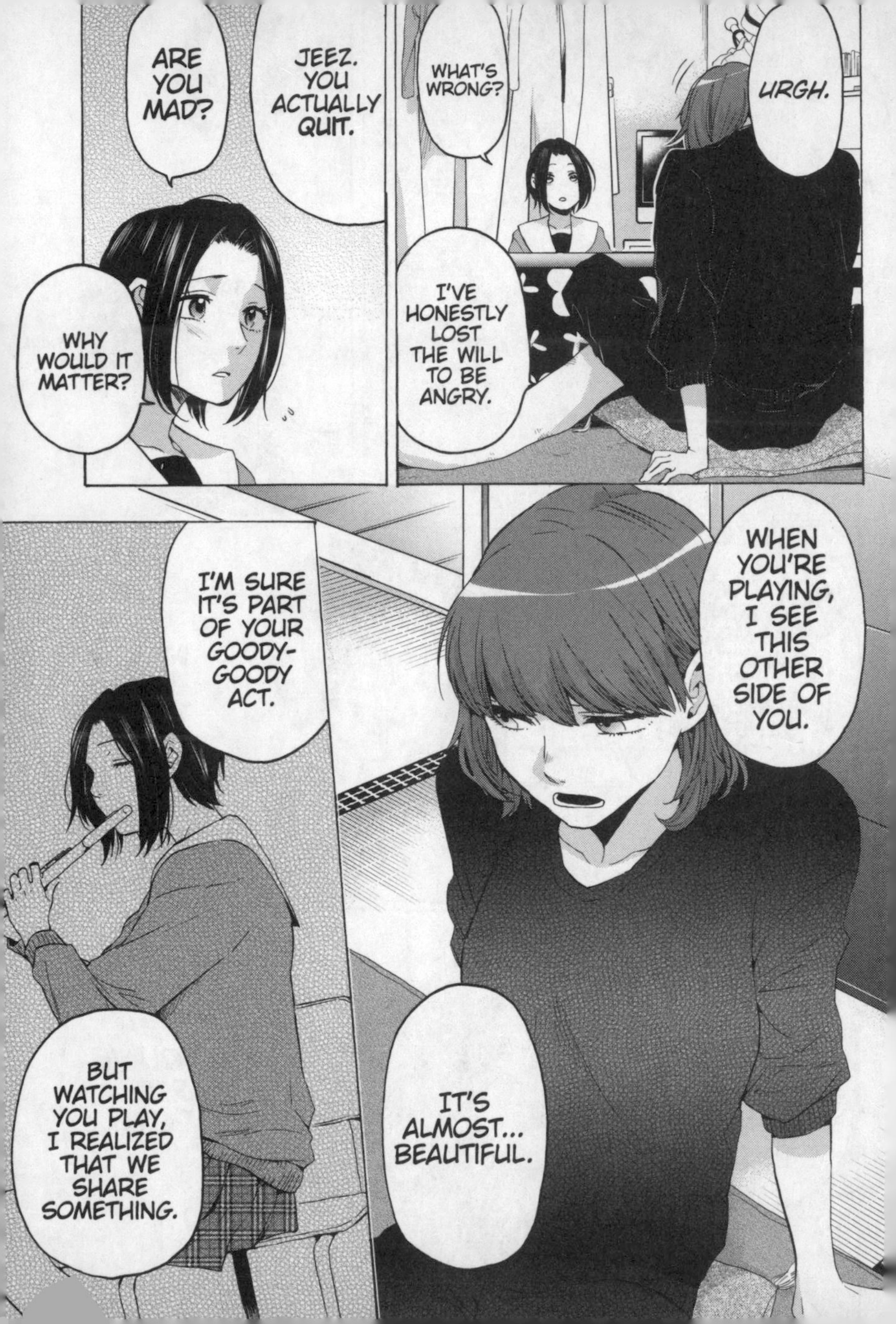
URGH.
WHAT'S WRONG?
I'VE HONESTLY LOST THE WILL TO BE ANGRY.
JEEZ. YOU ACTUALLY QUIT.
ARE YOU MAD?
WHY WOULD IT MATTER?
WHEN YOU'RE PLAYING, I SEE THIS OTHER SIDE OF YOU.
IT'S ALMOST... BEAUTIFUL.
I'M SURE IT'S PART OF YOUR GOODY-GOODY ACT.
BUT WATCHING YOU PLAY, I REALIZED THAT WE SHARE SOMETHING.

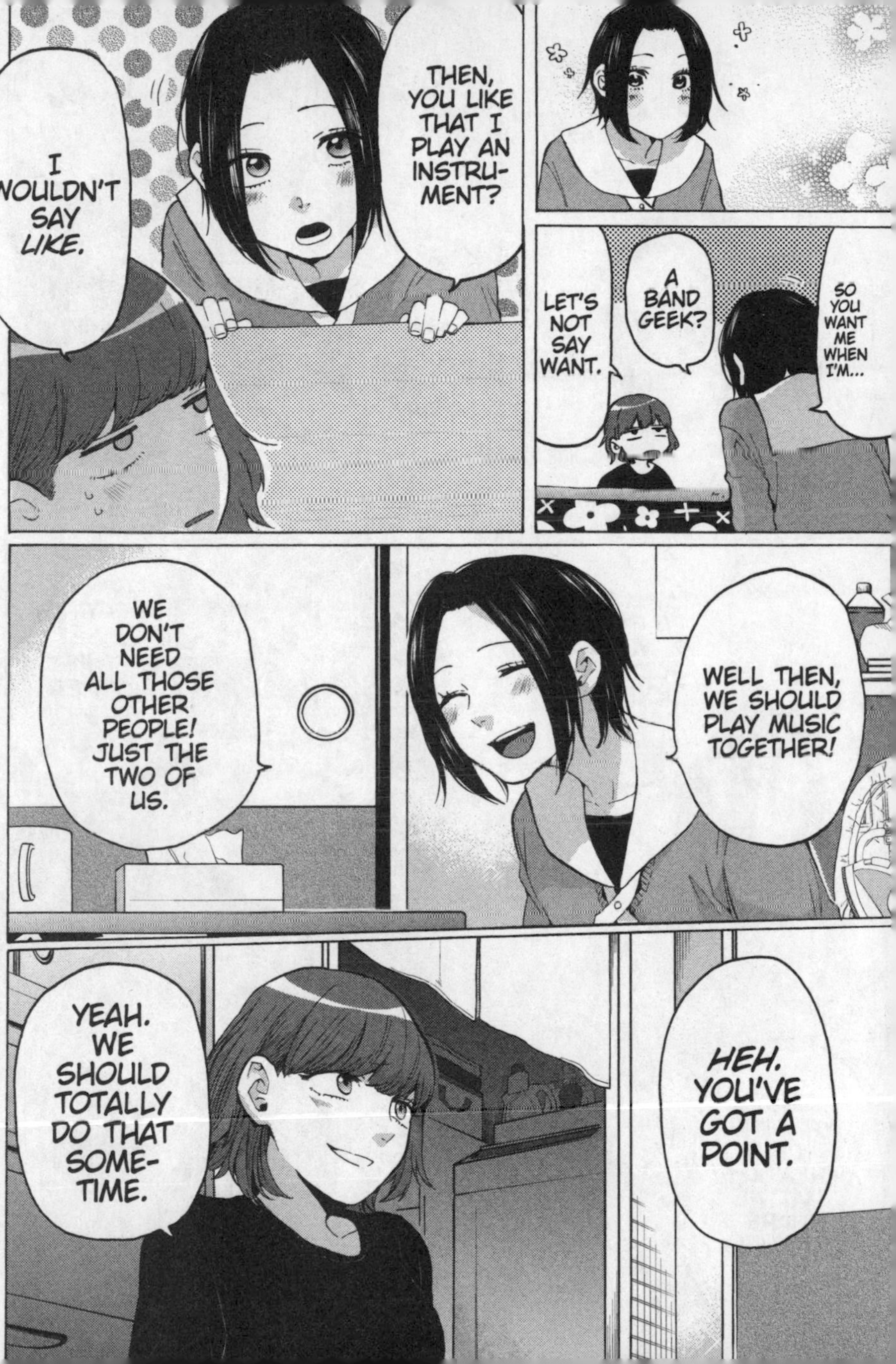
SO YOU WANT ME WHEN I'M...
A BAND GEEK?
LET'S NOT SAY WANT.
THEN, YOU LIKE THAT I PLAY AN INSTRUMENT?
I WOULDN'T SAY LIKE.
WELL THEN, WE SHOULD PLAY MUSIC TOGETHER!
WE DON'T NEED ALL THOSE OTHER PEOPLE! JUST THE TWO OF US.
HEH. YOU'VE GOT A POINT.
YEAH. WE SHOULD TOTALLY DO THAT SOMETIME.

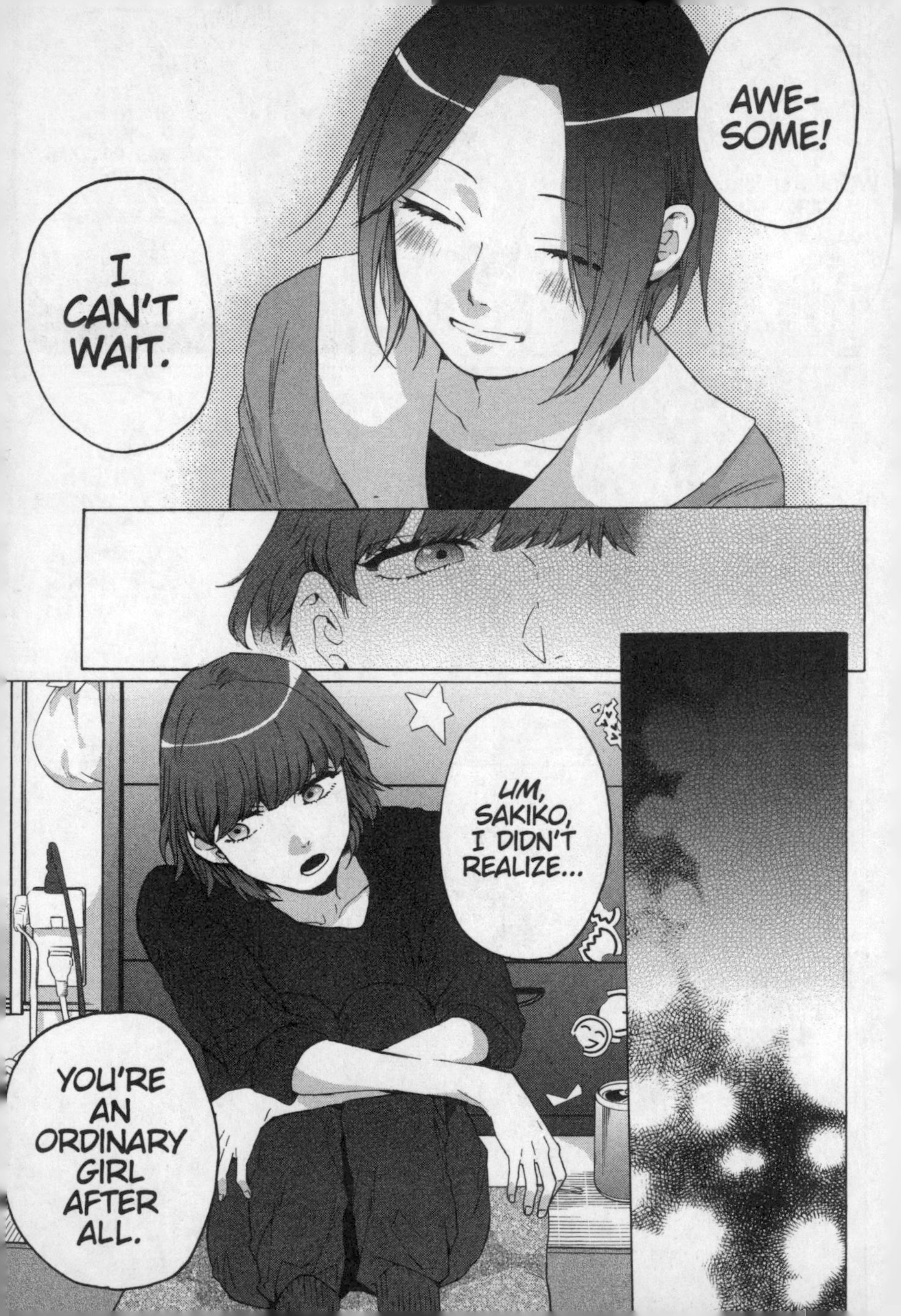
AWE-SOME!
I CAN'T WAIT.
UM, SAKIKO, I DIDN'T REALIZE...
YOU'RE AN ORDINARY GIRL AFTER ALL.

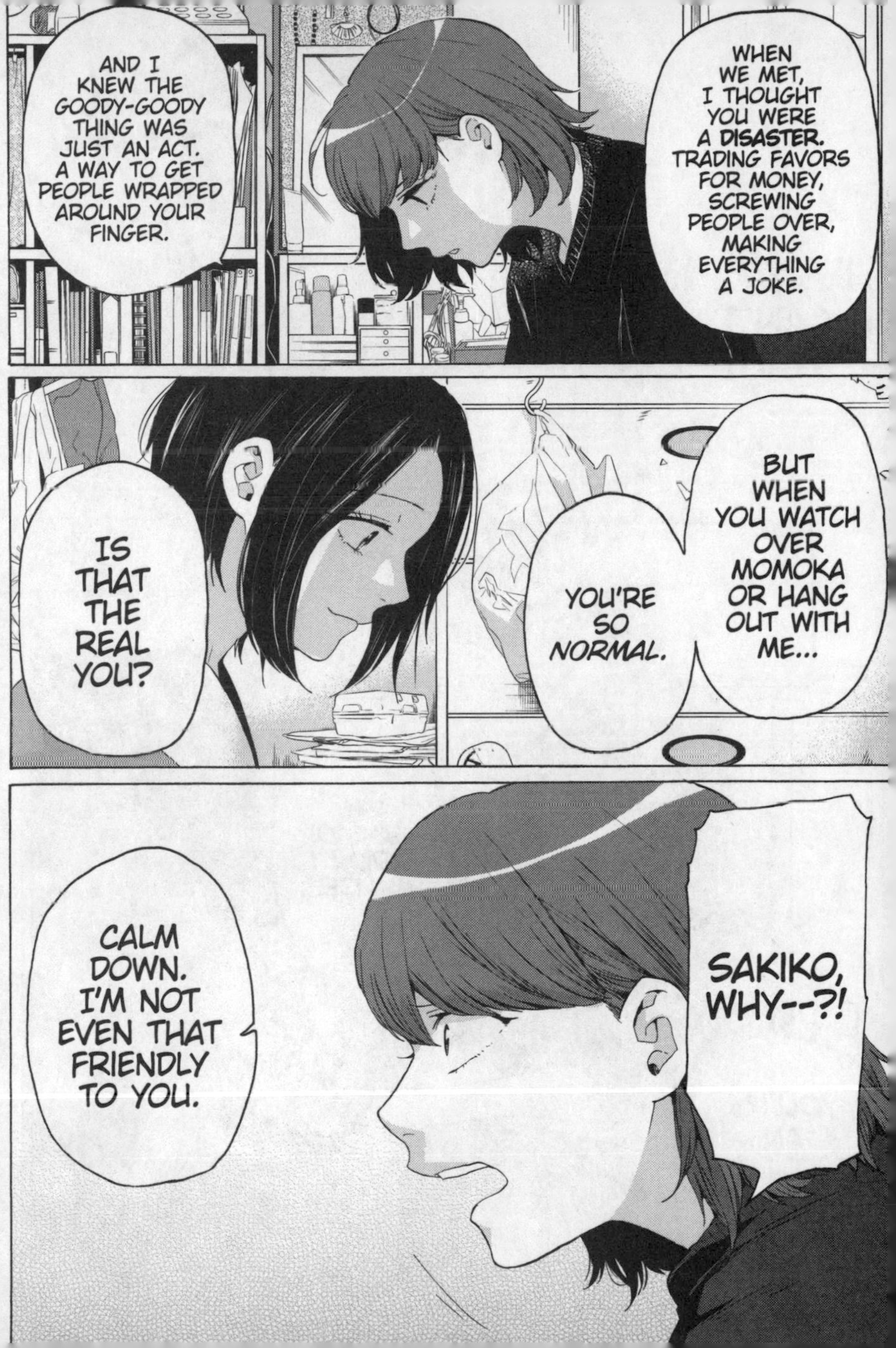
WHEN WE MET, I THOUGHT YOU WERE A **DISASTER.** TRADING FAVORS FOR MONEY, SCREWING PEOPLE OVER, MAKING EVERYTHING A JOKE.
AND I KNEW THE GOODY-GOODY THING WAS JUST AN ACT. A WAY TO GET PEOPLE WRAPPED AROUND YOUR FINGER.
BUT WHEN YOU WATCH OVER MOMOKA OR HANG OUT WITH ME...
YOU'RE SO *NORMAL.*
IS THAT THE REAL YOU?
SAKIKO, WHY--?!
CALM DOWN. I'M NOT EVEN THAT FRIENDLY TO YOU.

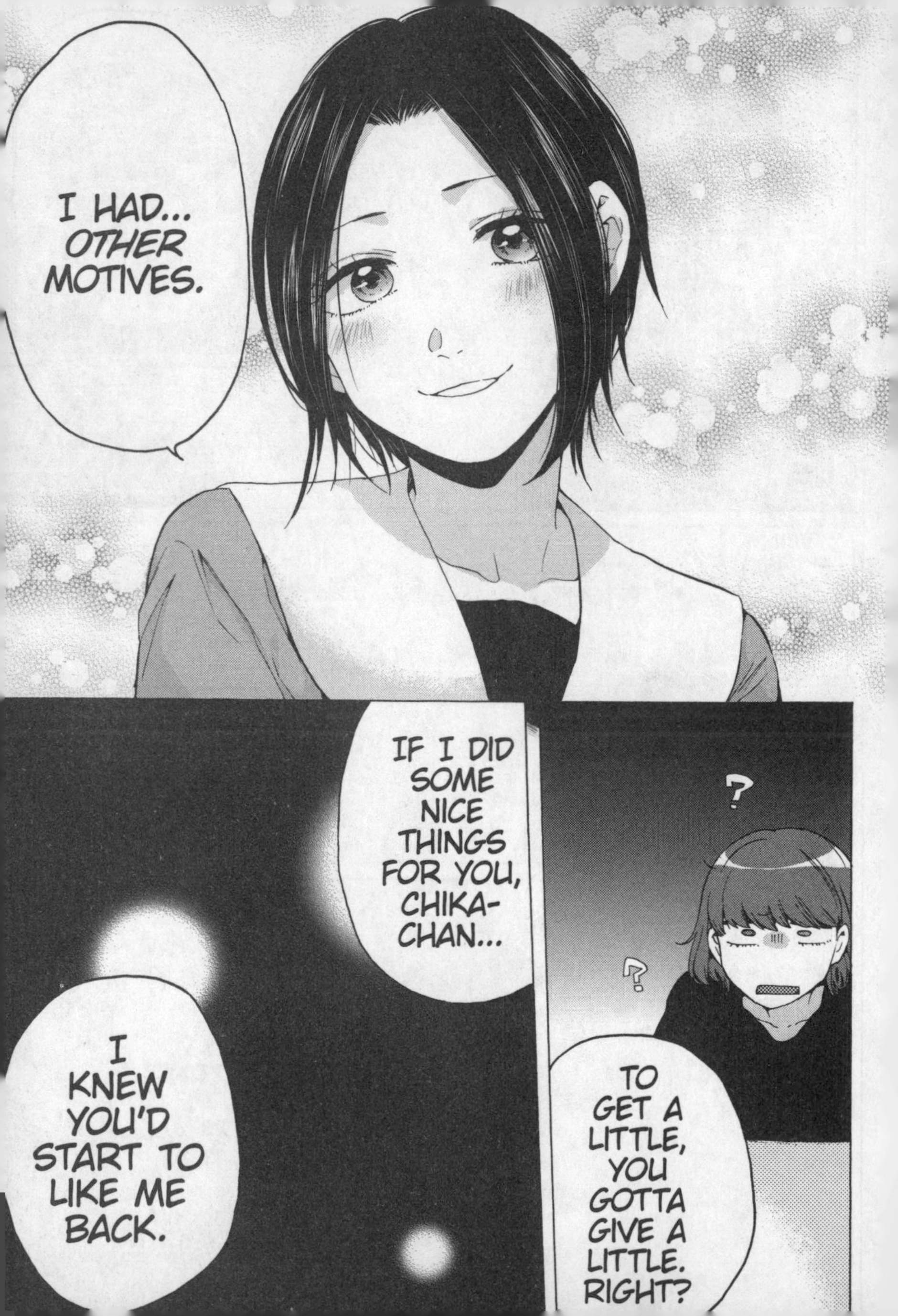
I HAD... *OTHER* MOTIVES.
?
?
TO GET A LITTLE, YOU GOTTA GIVE A LITTLE. RIGHT?
IF I DID SOME NICE THINGS FOR YOU, CHIKA-CHAN...
I KNEW YOU'D START TO LIKE ME BACK.

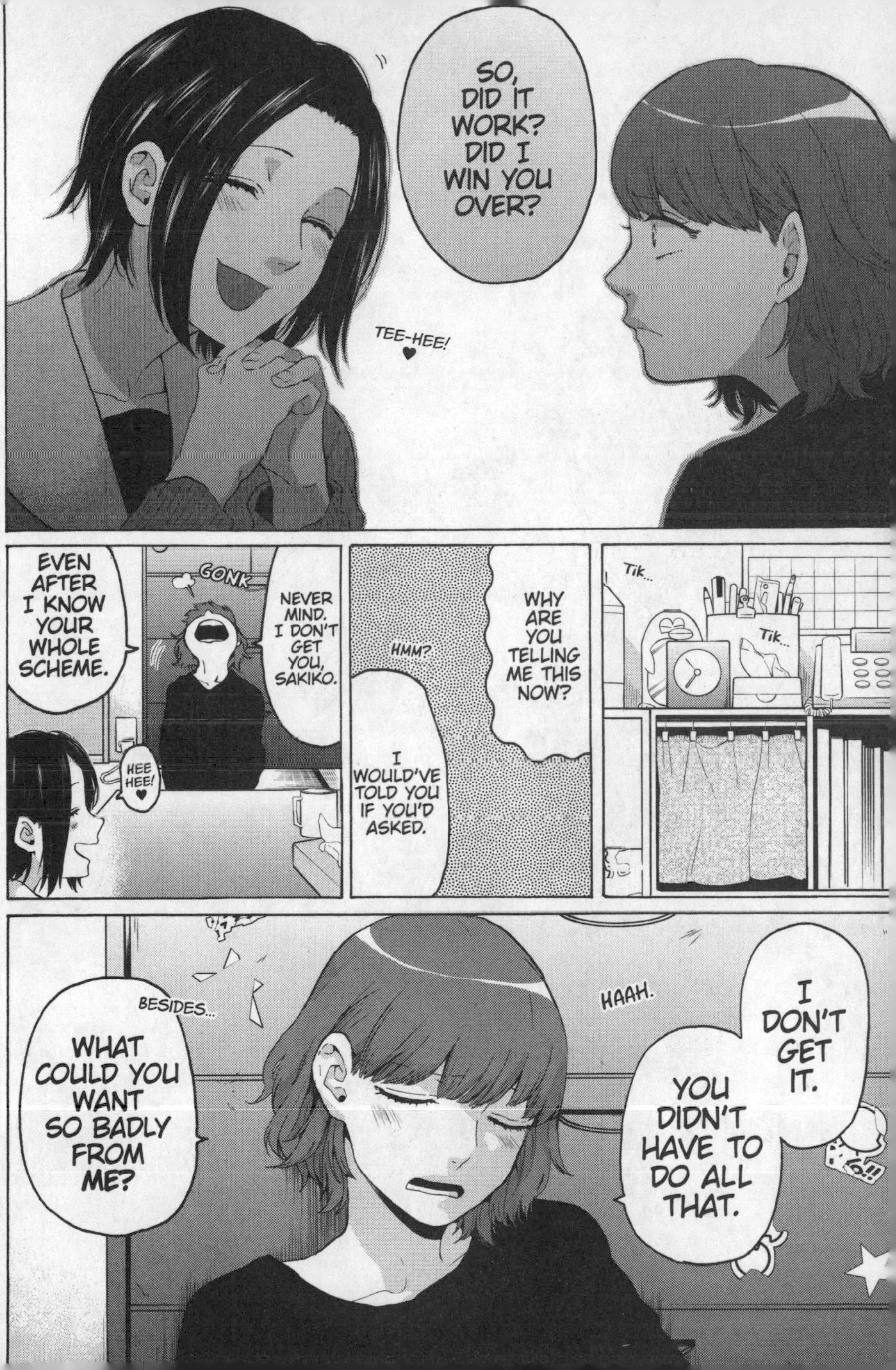
SO, DID IT WORK? DID I WIN YOU OVER?
TEE-HEE! ♥
Tik...
Tik...
WHY ARE YOU TELLING ME THIS NOW?
HMM?
I WOULD'VE TOLD YOU IF YOU'D ASKED.
NEVER MIND. I DON'T GET YOU, SAKIKO.
GONK
EVEN AFTER I KNOW YOUR WHOLE SCHEME.
HEE HEE! ♥
I DON'T GET IT.
YOU DIDN'T HAVE TO DO ALL THAT.
HAAH.
BESIDES...
WHAT COULD YOU WANT SO BADLY FROM ME?

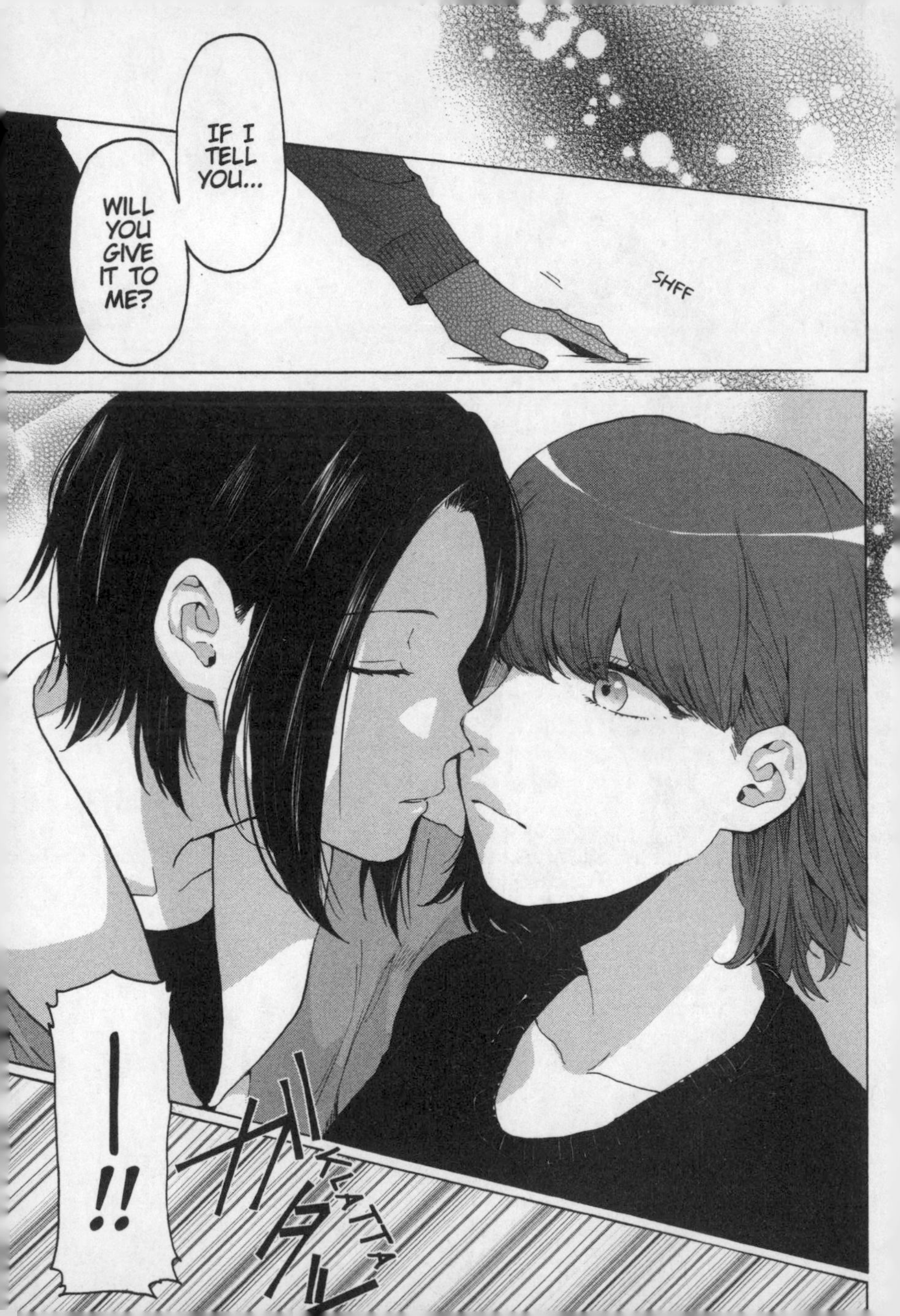
IF I TELL YOU...
WILL YOU GIVE IT TO ME?
SHFF
KATTA
—!!

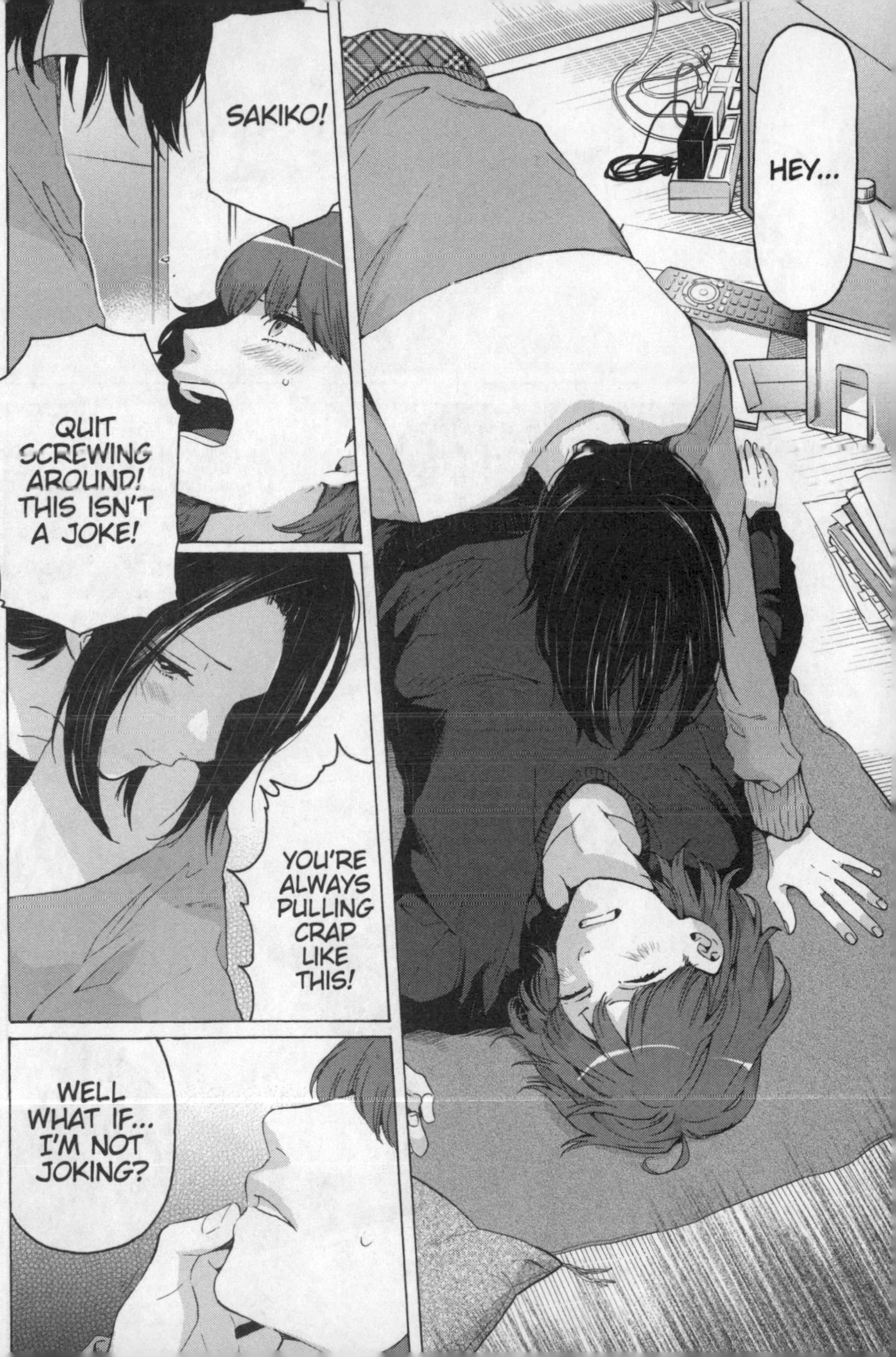
HEY...
SAKIKO!
QUIT SCREWING AROUND! THIS ISN'T A JOKE!
YOU'RE ALWAYS PULLING CRAP LIKE THIS!
WELL WHAT IF... I'M NOT JOKING?

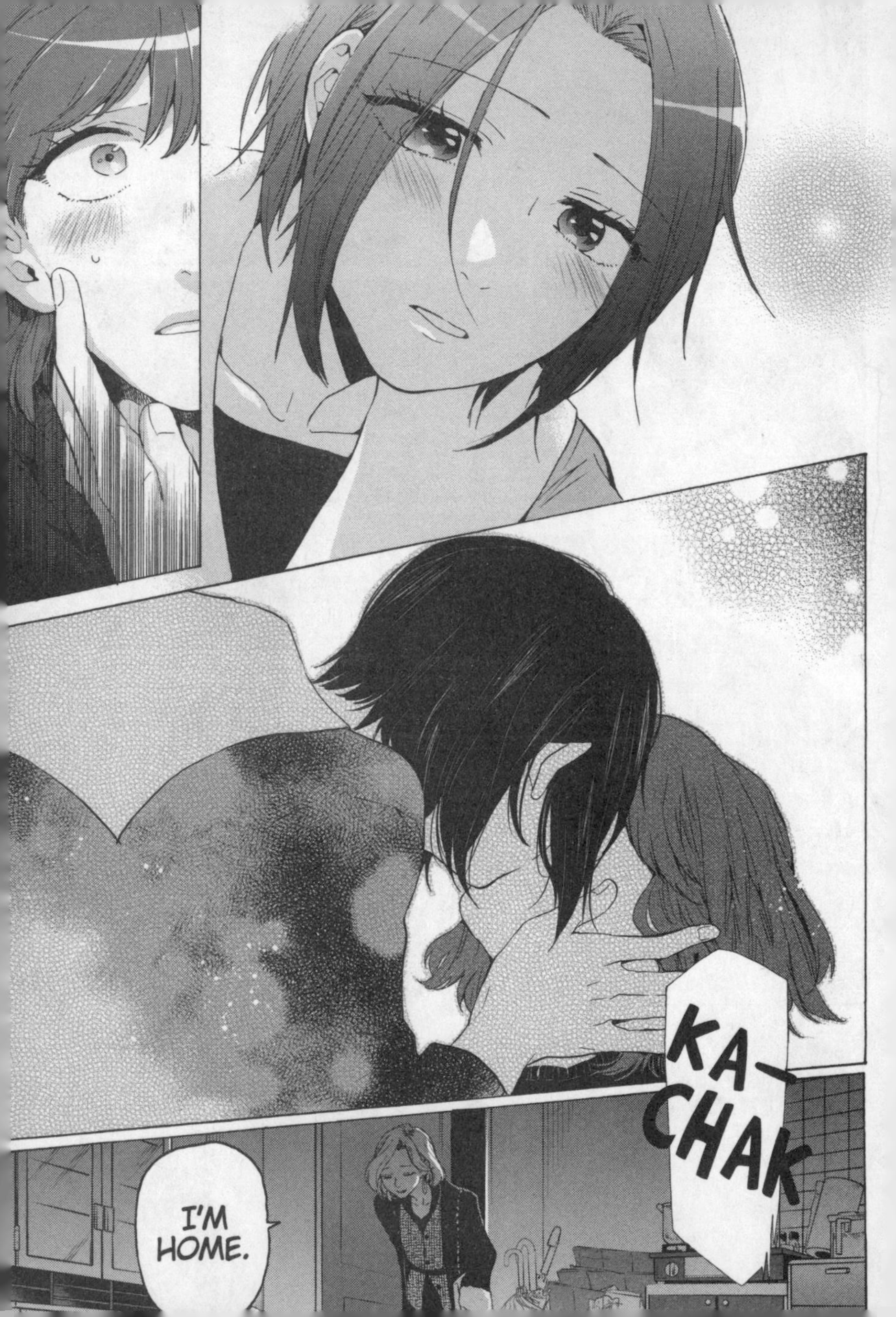
KA-CHAK
I'M HOME.

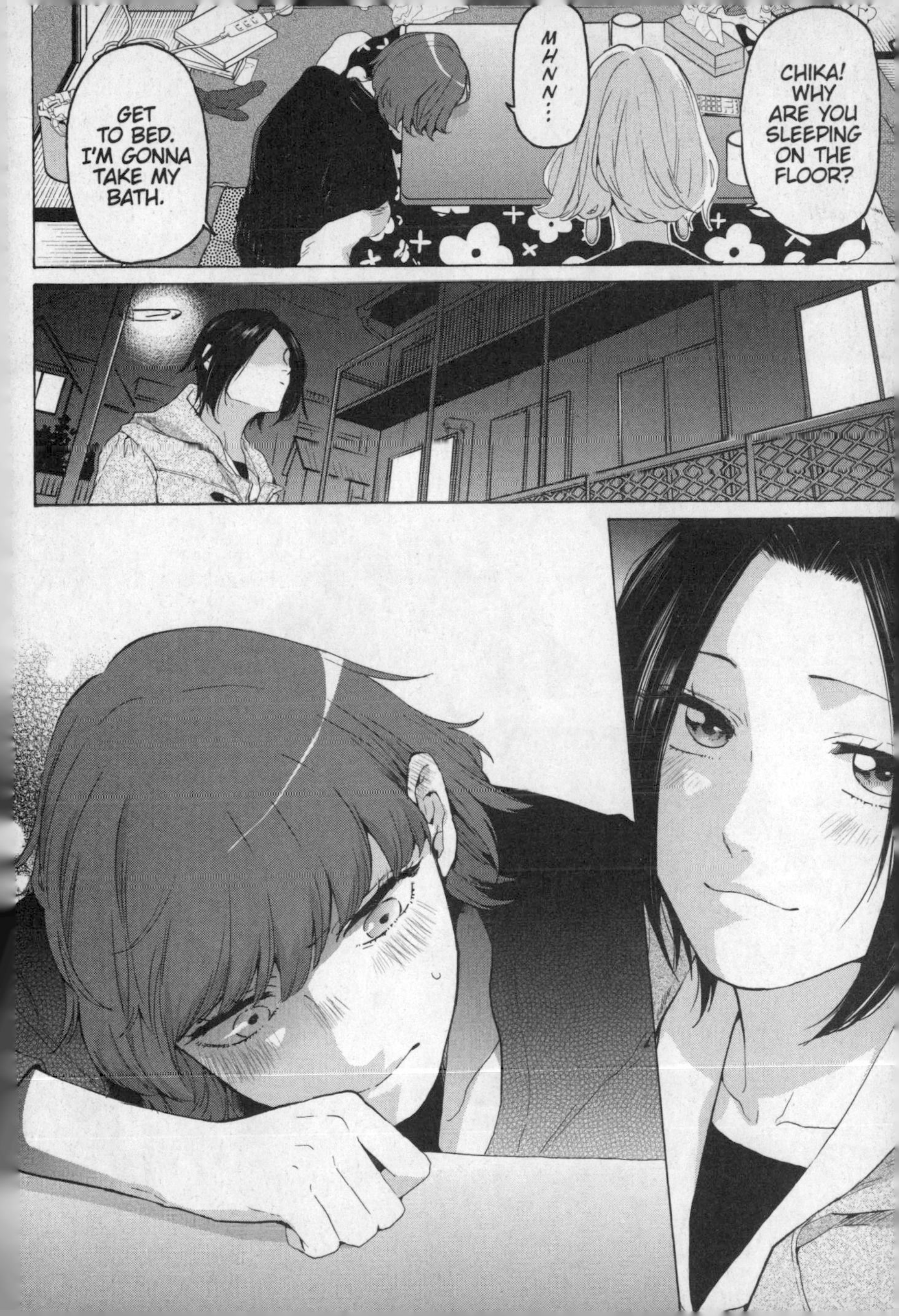
CHIKA! WHY ARE YOU SLEEPING ON THE FLOOR?
MHNN...
GET TO BED. I'M GONNA TAKE MY BATH.

Hello, Melancholic!

STRAY CAT
APPROVED.

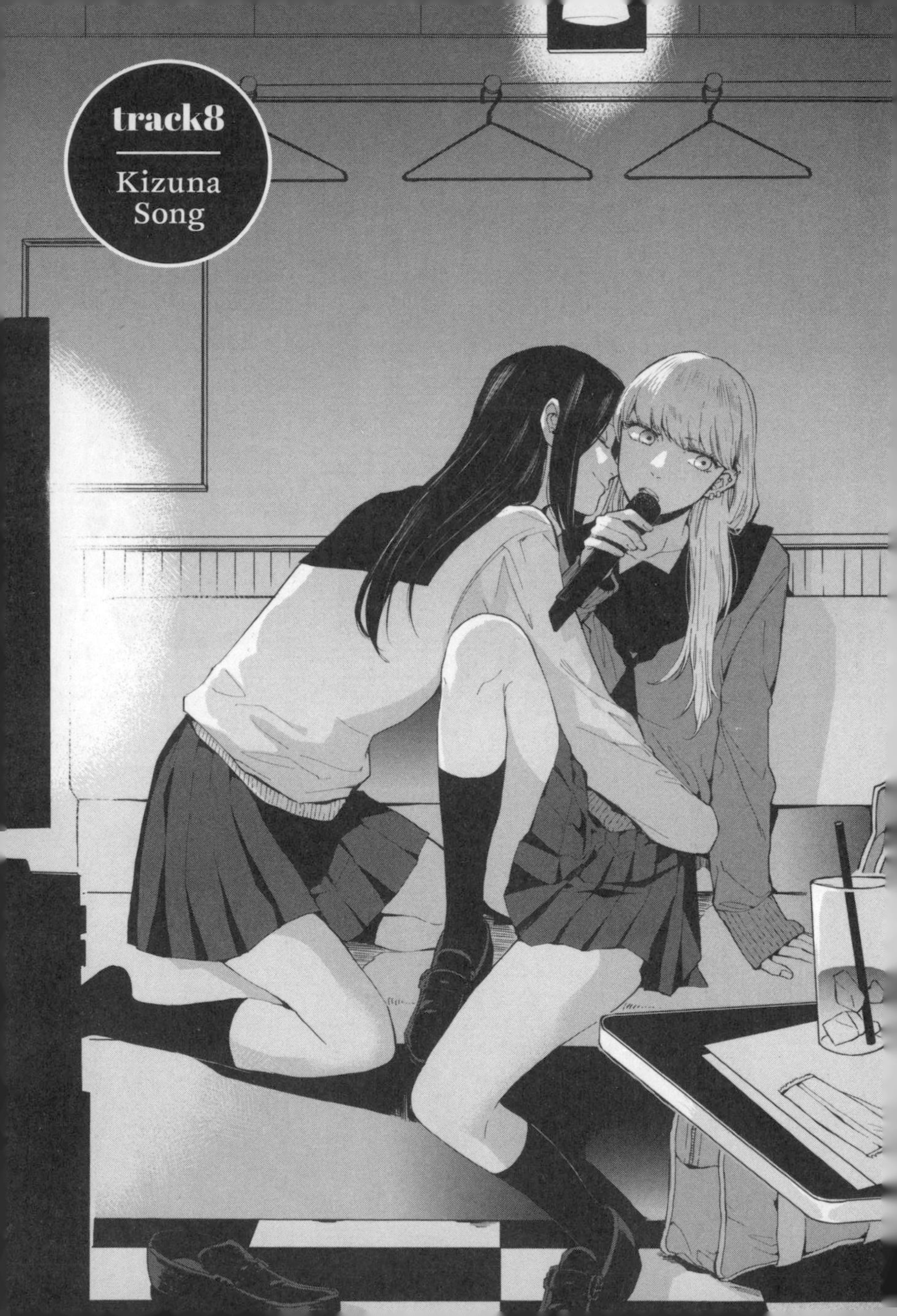
track8
Kizuna Song

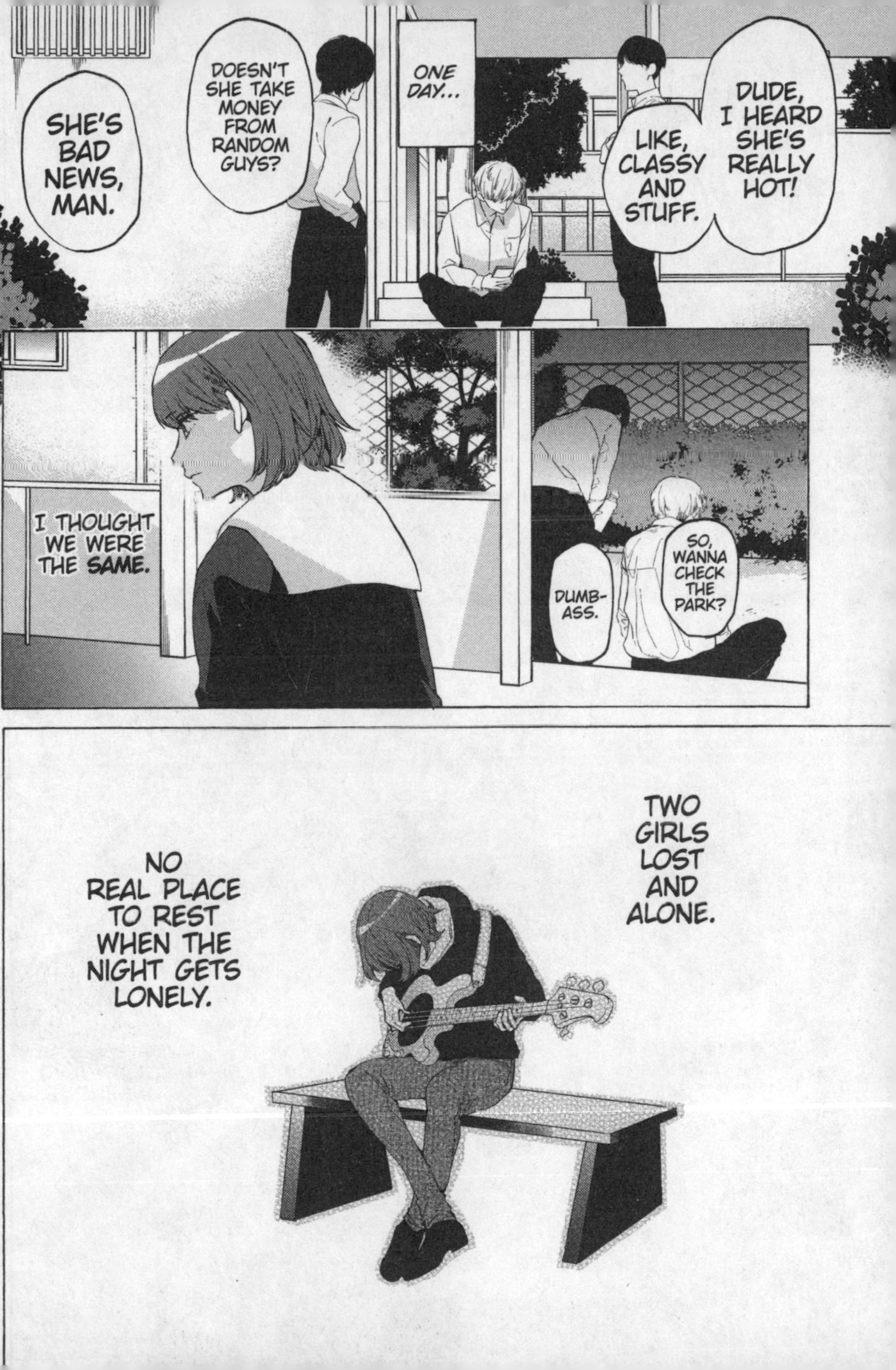
DUDE, I HEARD SHE'S REALLY HOT!
LIKE, CLASSY AND STUFF.
ONE DAY...
DOESN'T SHE TAKE MONEY FROM RANDOM GUYS?
SHE'S BAD NEWS, MAN.
SO, WANNA CHECK THE PARK?
DUMB-ASS.
I THOUGHT WE WERE THE SAME.
TWO GIRLS LOST AND ALONE.
NO REAL PLACE TO REST WHEN THE NIGHT GETS LONELY.

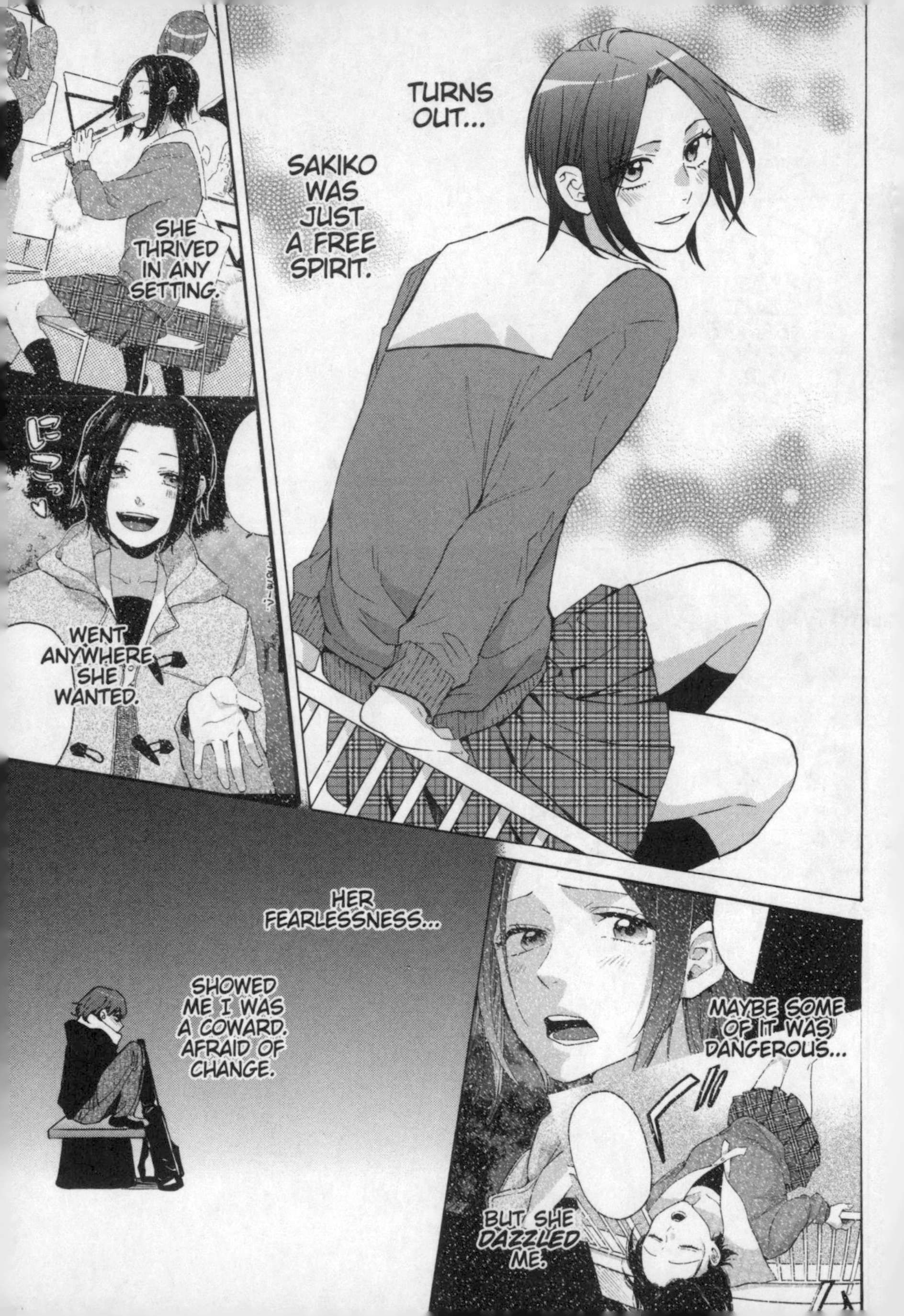
TURNS OUT...
SAKIKO WAS JUST A FREE SPIRIT.
SHE THRIVED IN ANY SETTING.
にこっ
WENT ANYWHERE SHE WANTED.
MAYBE SOME OF IT WAS DANGEROUS...
BUT SHE DAZZLED ME.
HER FEARLESSNESS...
SHOWED ME I WAS A COWARD. AFRAID OF CHANGE.

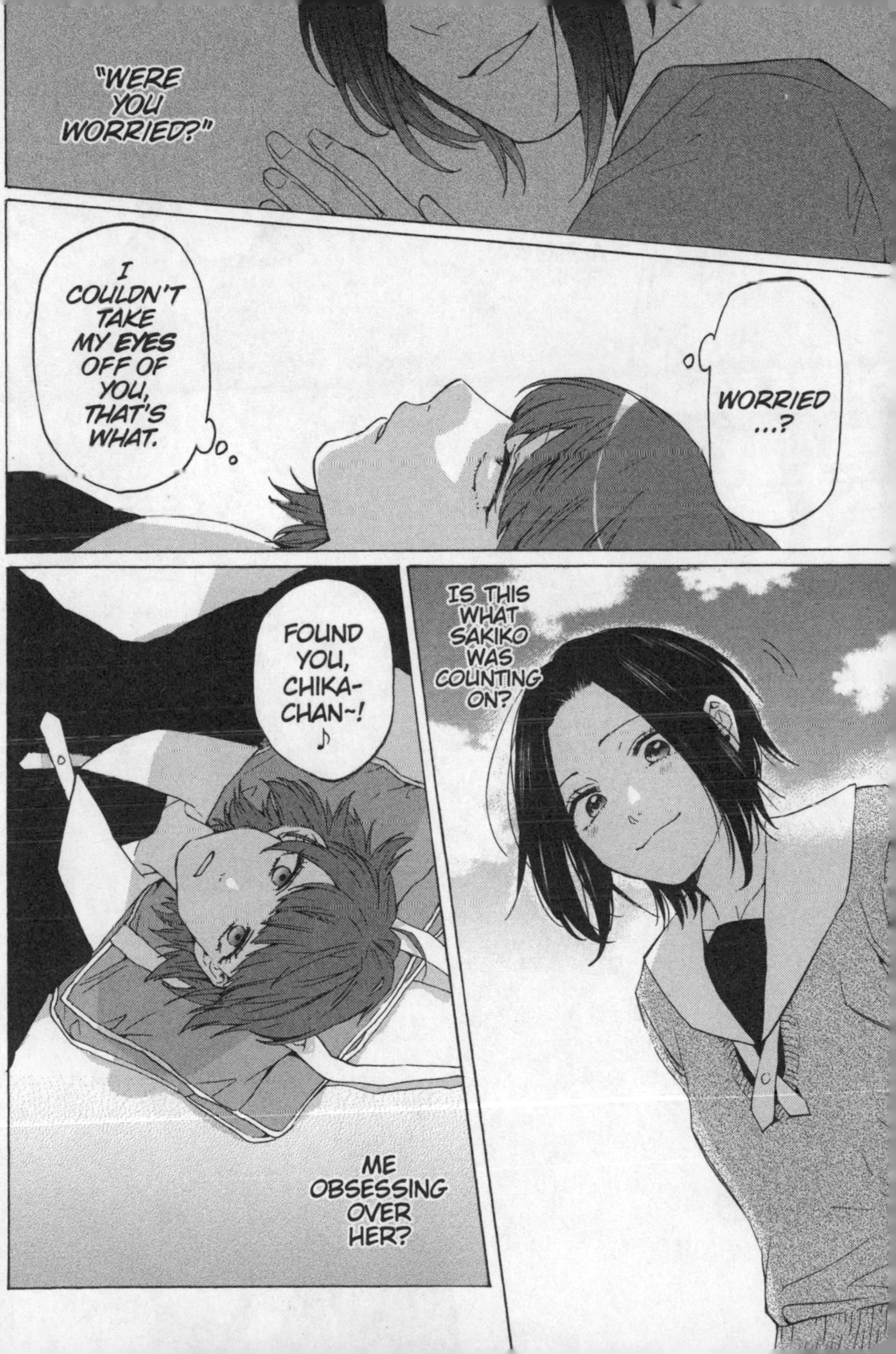
"WERE YOU WORRIED?"
WORRIED ...?
I COULDN'T TAKE MY EYES OFF OF YOU, THAT'S WHAT.
IS THIS WHAT SAKIKO WAS COUNTING ON?
FOUND YOU, CHIKA-CHAN~! ♪
ME OBSESSING OVER HER?

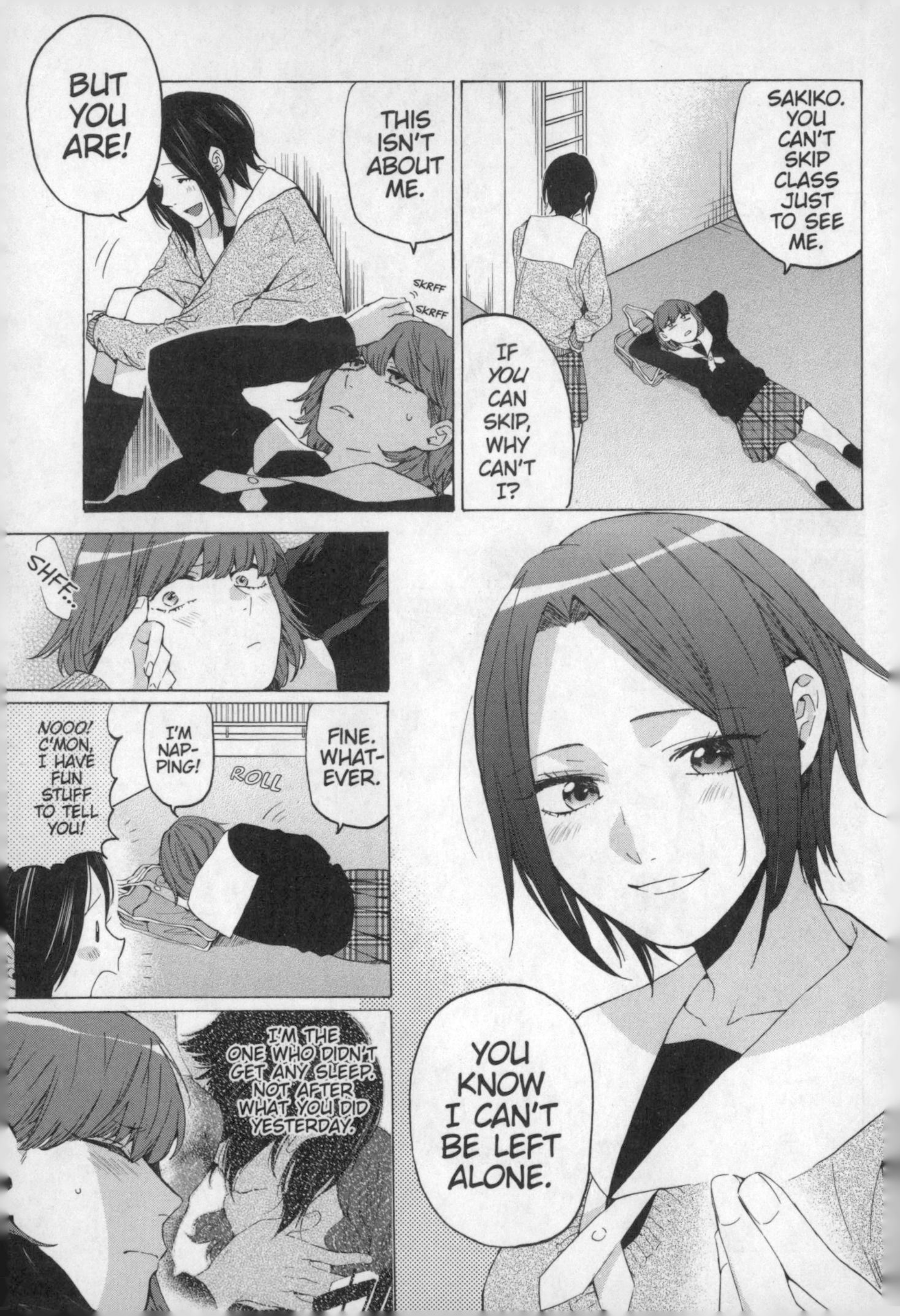
SAKIKO. YOU CAN'T SKIP CLASS JUST TO SEE ME.
IF YOU CAN SKIP, WHY CAN'T I?
THIS ISN'T ABOUT ME.
BUT YOU ARE!
SKRFF
SKRFF
YOU KNOW I CAN'T BE LEFT ALONE.
SHFF...
FINE. WHATEVER.
ROLL
I'M NAPPING!
NOOO! C'MON, I HAVE FUN STUFF TO TELL YOU!
I'M THE ONE WHO DIDN'T GET ANY SLEEP. NOT AFTER WHAT YOU DID YESTERDAY.

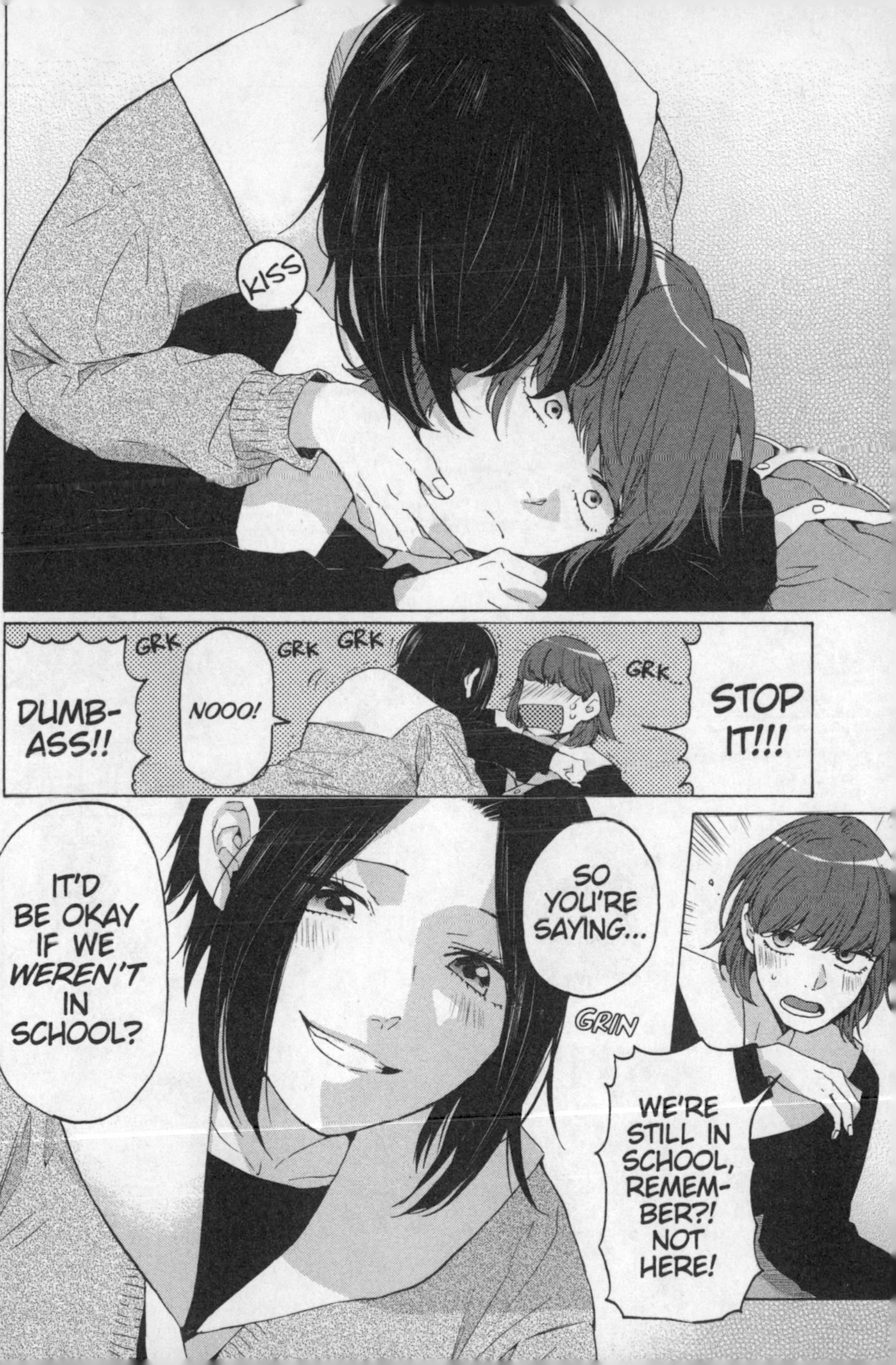
KISS
STOP IT!!!
GRK...
GRK
GRK
NOOO!
GRK
DUMB-ASS!!
WE'RE STILL IN SCHOOL, REMEMBER?! NOT HERE!
GRIN
SO YOU'RE SAYING...
IT'D BE OKAY IF WE WEREN'T IN SCHOOL?

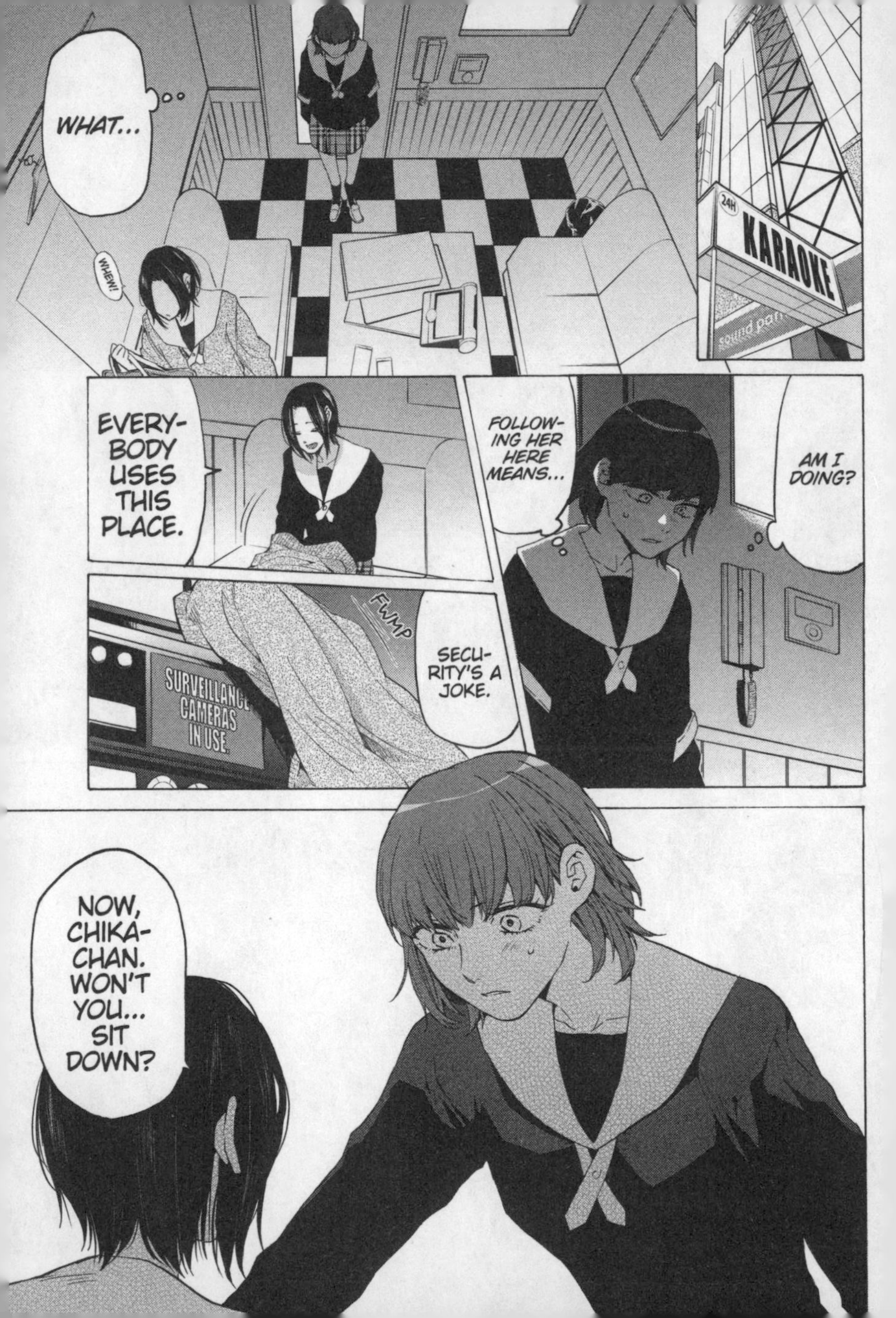
24H
KARAOKE
WHAT...
WHEW!
AM I DOING?
FOLLOWING HER HERE MEANS...
EVERYBODY USES THIS PLACE.
FWMP
SECURITY'S A JOKE.
SURVEILLANCE CAMERAS IN USE.
NOW, CHIKA-CHAN. WON'T YOU... SIT DOWN?

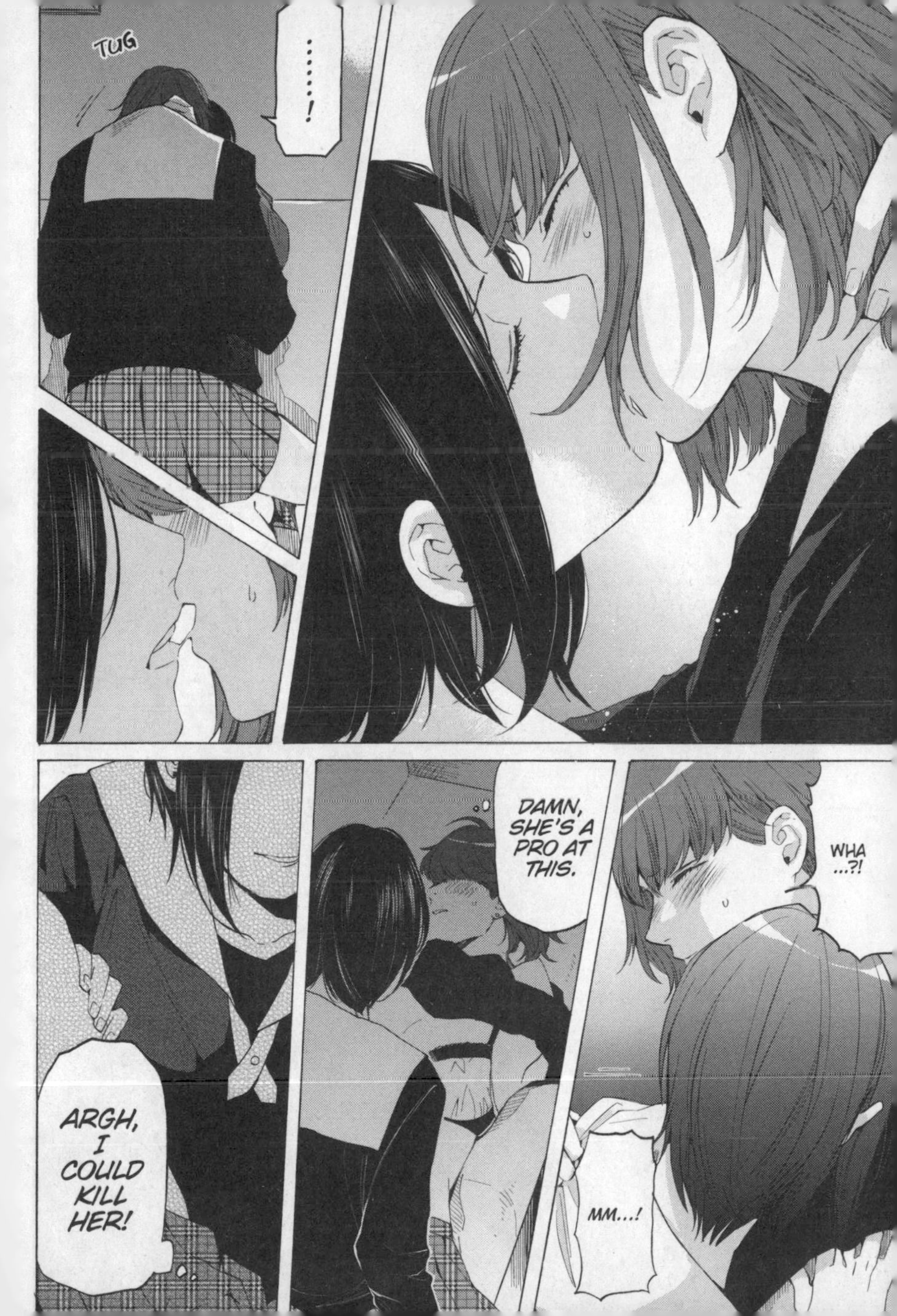
......!
TUG
WHA ...?!
MM...!
DAMN, SHE'S A PRO AT THIS.
ARGH, I COULD KILL HER!

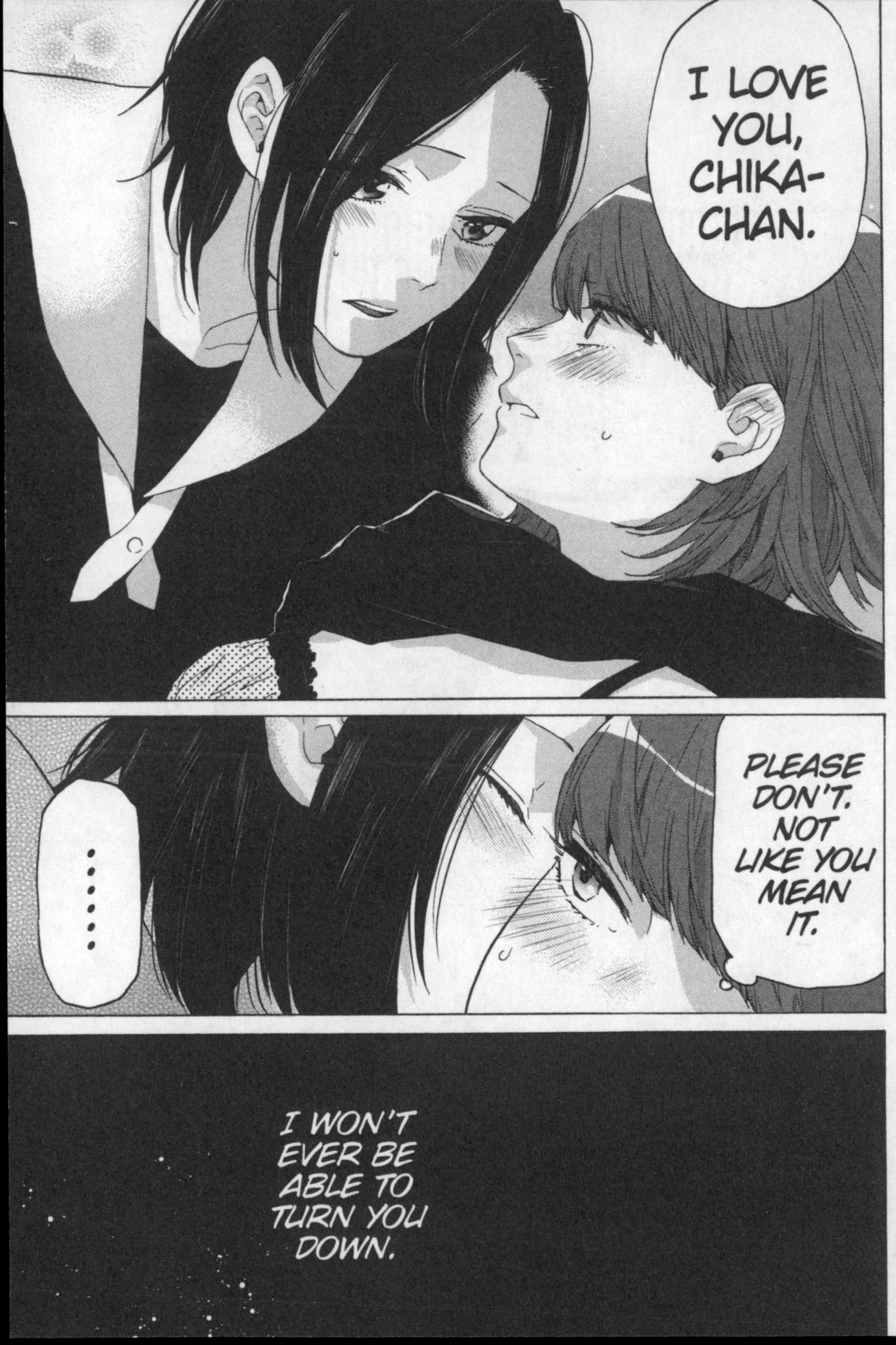
I LOVE YOU, CHIKA-CHAN.
PLEASE DON'T. NOT LIKE YOU MEAN IT.
......
I WON'T EVER BE ABLE TO TURN YOU DOWN.

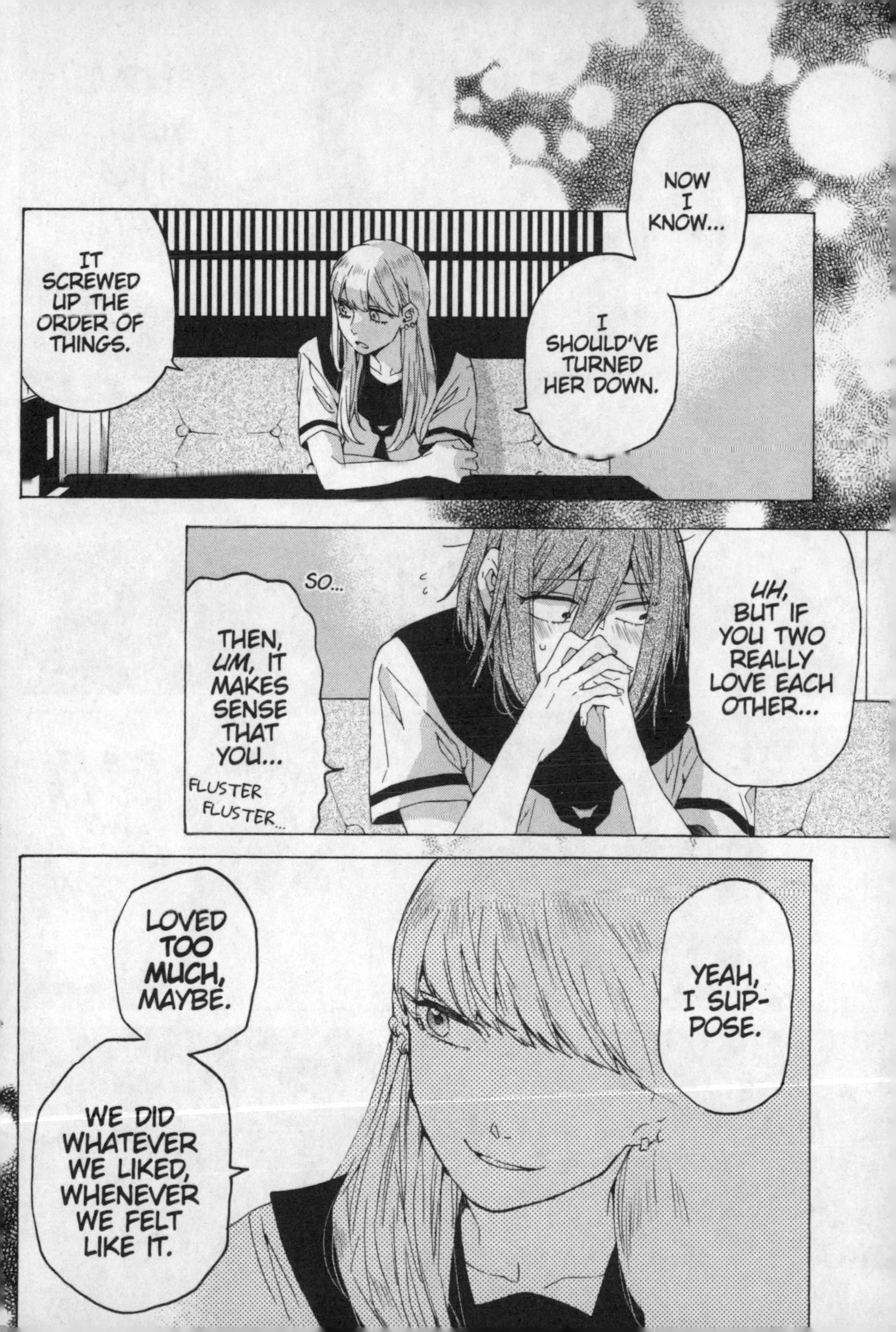
NOW I KNOW...
I SHOULD'VE TURNED HER DOWN.
IT SCREWED UP THE ORDER OF THINGS.
UH, BUT IF YOU TWO REALLY LOVE EACH OTHER...
SO...
THEN, UM, IT MAKES SENSE THAT YOU...
FLUSTER FLUSTER...
YEAH, I SUPPOSE.
LOVED TOO MUCH, MAYBE.
WE DID WHATEVER WE LIKED, WHENEVER WE FELT LIKE IT.

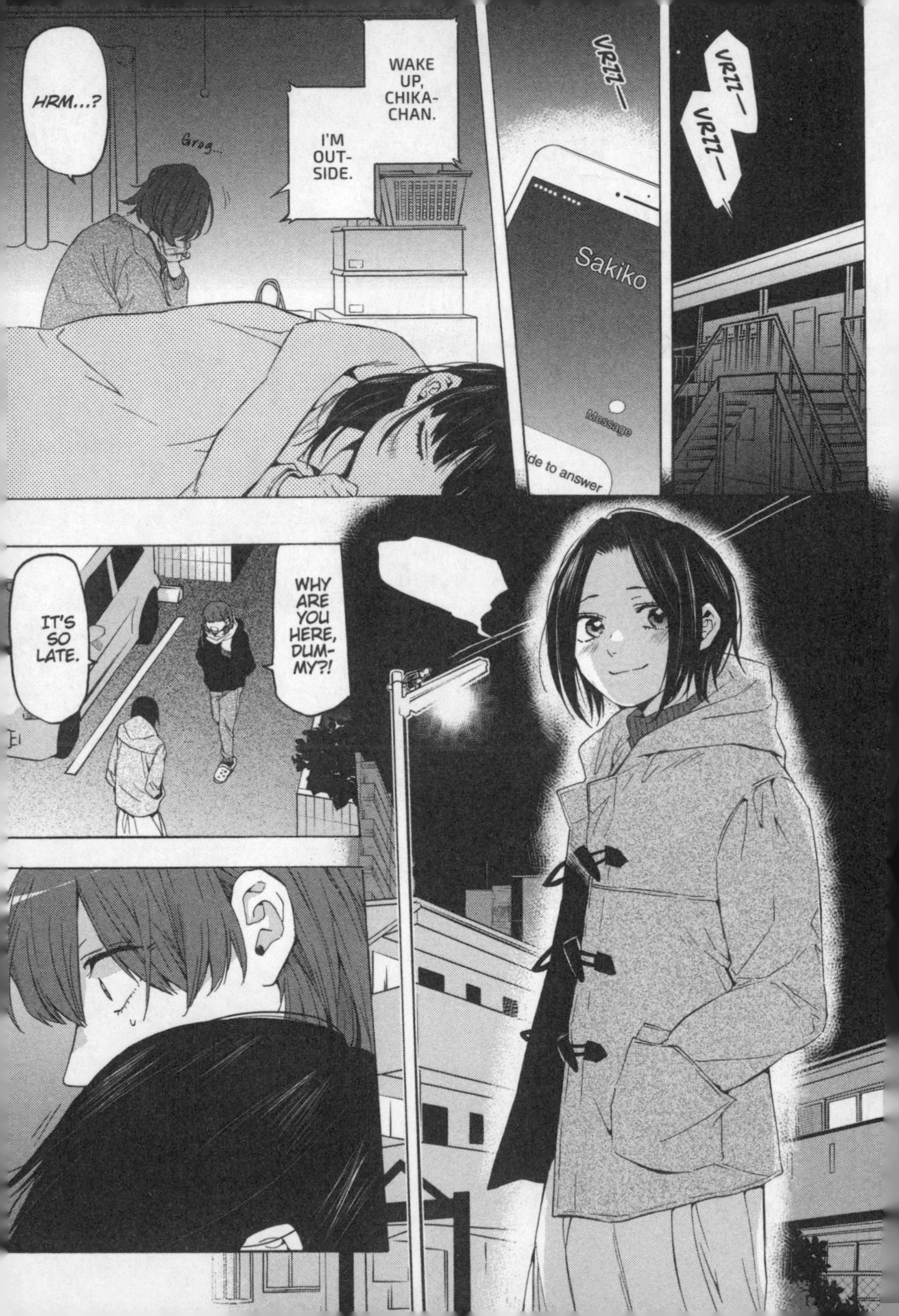
VRII— VRII—
VRII—
Sakiko
Message
ide to answer
WAKE UP, CHIKA-CHAN.
I'M OUTSIDE.
HRM...?
Grog...
WHY ARE YOU HERE, DUMMY?!
IT'S SO LATE.

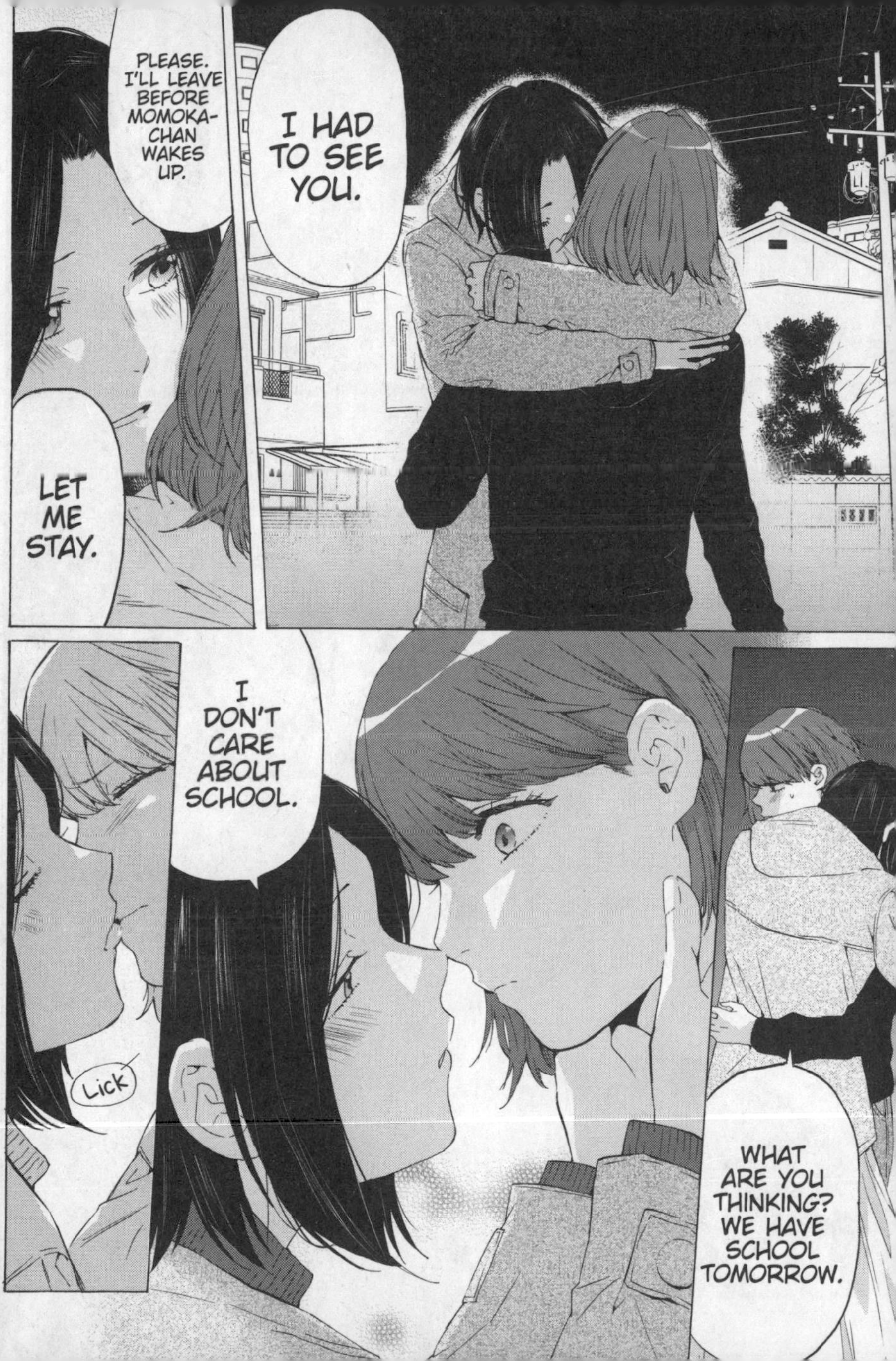
I HAD TO SEE YOU.
PLEASE. I'LL LEAVE BEFORE MOMOKA-CHAN WAKES UP.
LET ME STAY.
WHAT ARE YOU THINKING? WE HAVE SCHOOL TOMORROW.
I DON'T CARE ABOUT SCHOOL.
Lick

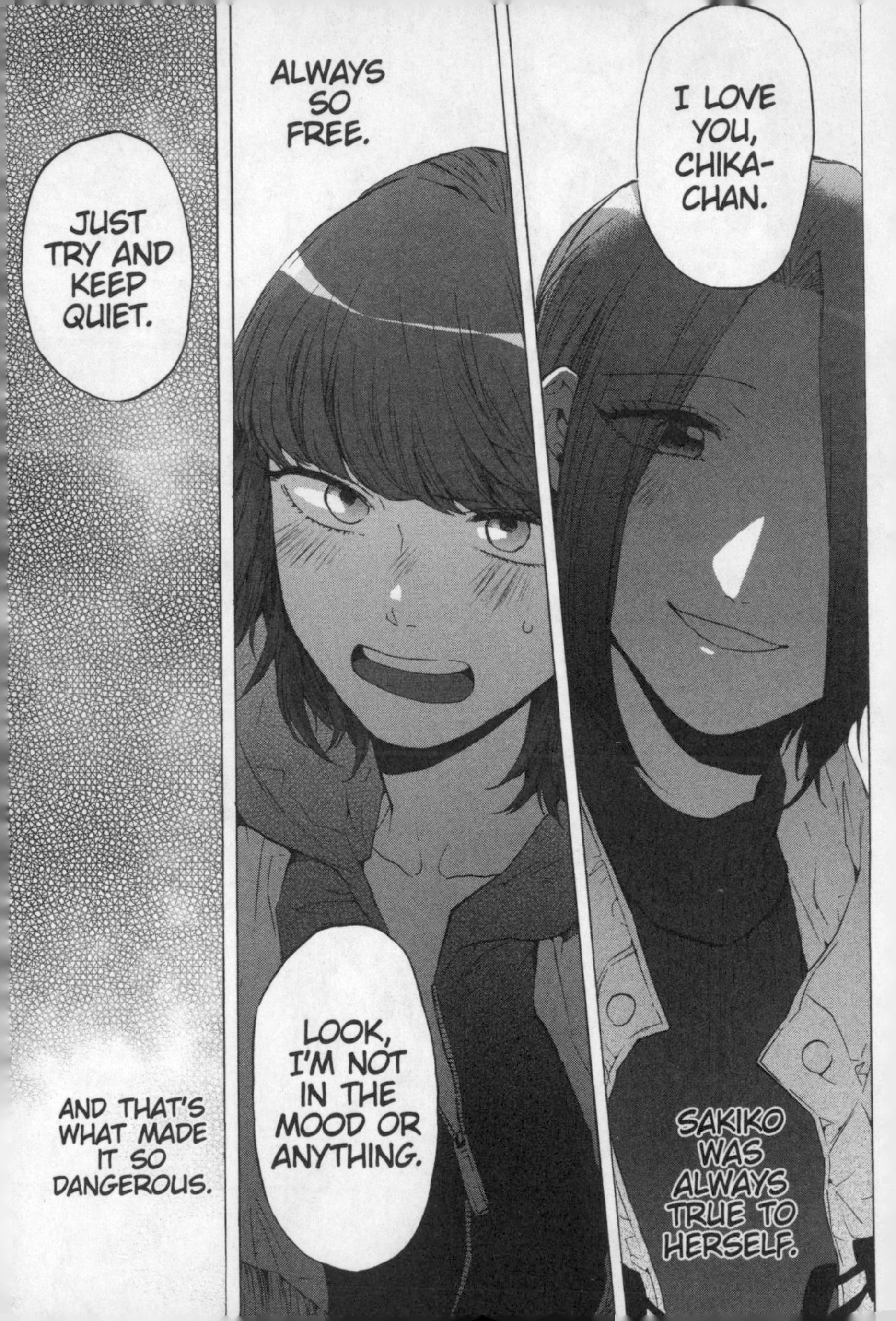
I LOVE YOU, CHIKA-CHAN.
SAKIKO WAS ALWAYS TRUE TO HERSELF.
ALWAYS SO FREE.
LOOK, I'M NOT IN THE MOOD OR ANYTHING.
JUST TRY AND KEEP QUIET.
AND THAT'S WHAT MADE IT SO DANGEROUS.

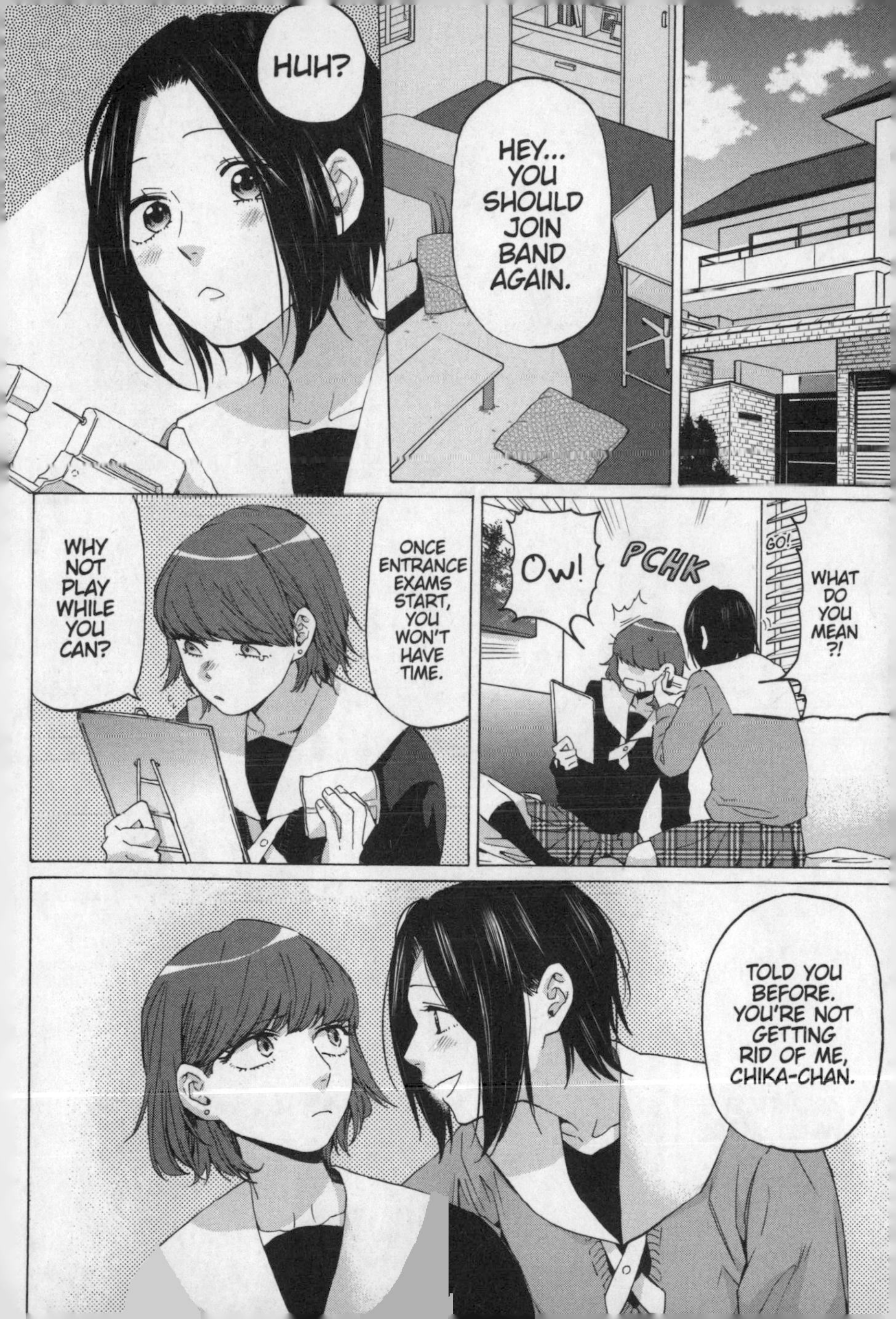
HEY... YOU SHOULD JOIN BAND AGAIN.
HUH?
GO!
WHAT DO YOU MEAN ?!
PCHK
Ow!
ONCE ENTRANCE EXAMS START, YOU WON'T HAVE TIME.
WHY NOT PLAY WHILE YOU CAN?
TOLD YOU BEFORE. YOU'RE NOT GETTING RID OF ME, CHIKA-CHAN.

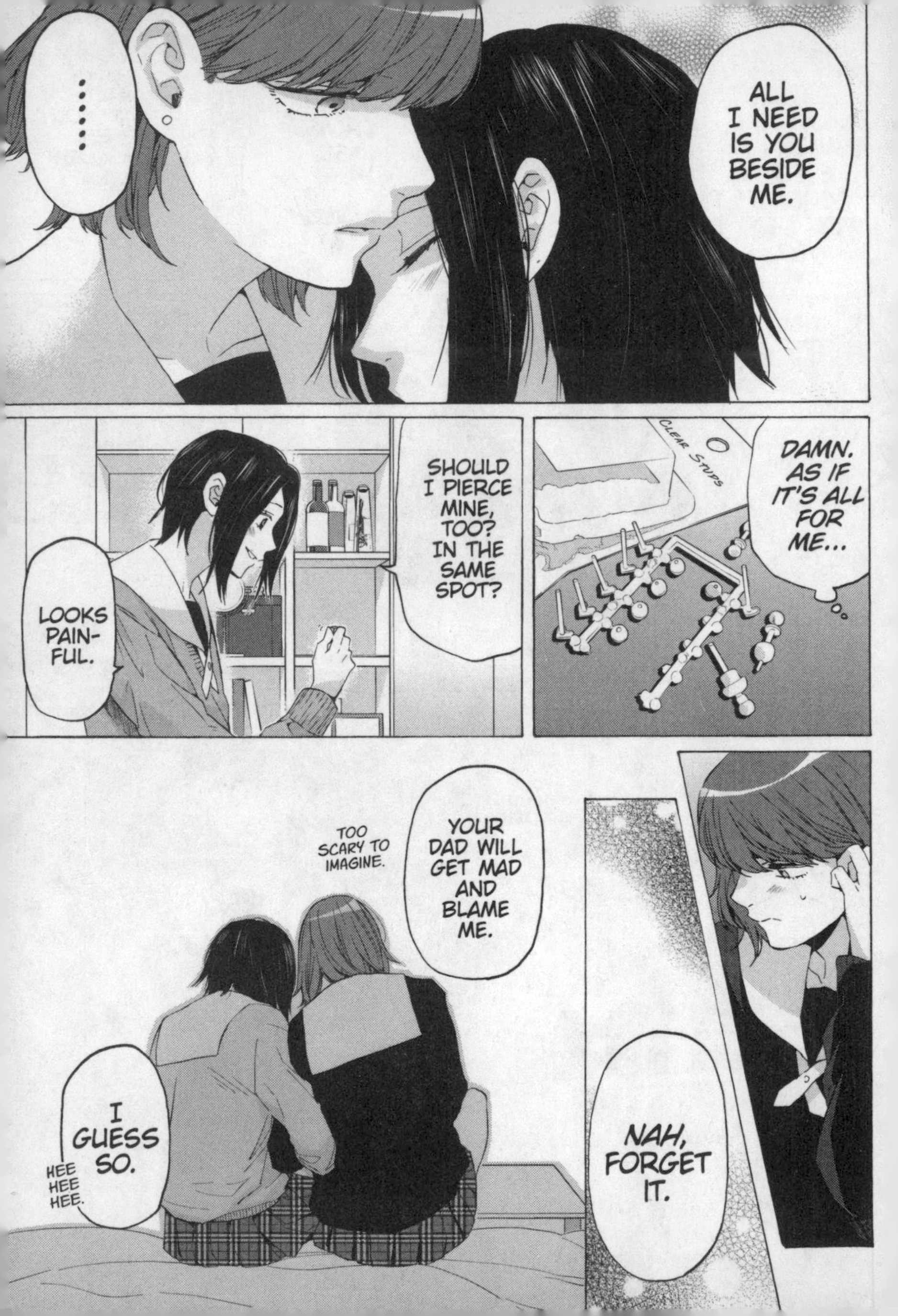
ALL I NEED IS YOU BESIDE ME.
……
CLEAR STUDS
DAMN. AS IF IT'S ALL FOR ME...
SHOULD I PIERCE MINE, TOO? IN THE SAME SPOT?
LOOKS PAINFUL.
NAH, FORGET IT.
YOUR DAD WILL GET MAD AND BLAME ME.
TOO SCARY TO IMAGINE.
I GUESS SO.
HEE HEE HEE.

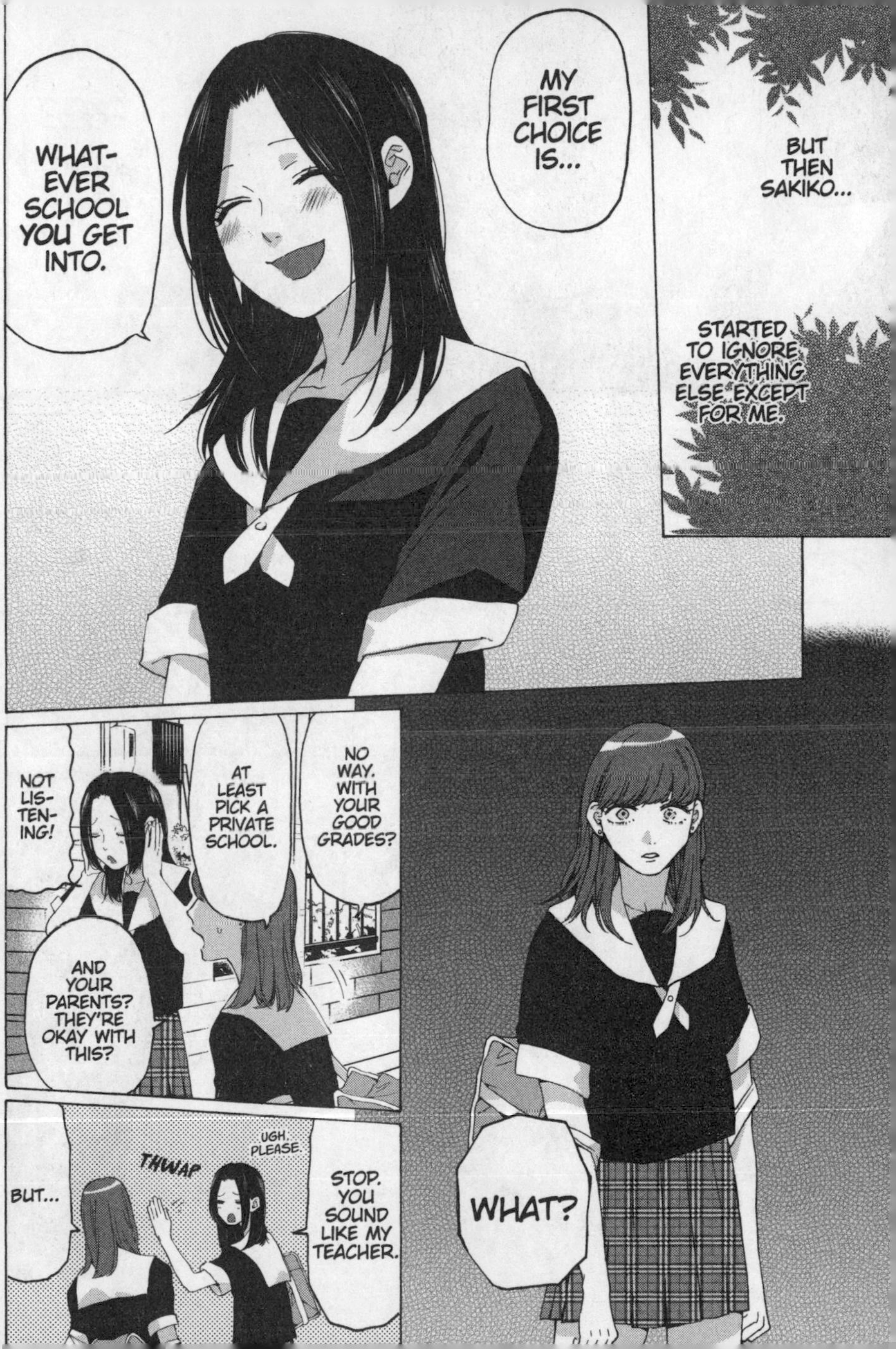
BUT THEN SAKIKO...
STARTED TO IGNORE EVERYTHING ELSE EXCEPT FOR ME.
MY FIRST CHOICE IS...
WHAT-EVER SCHOOL YOU GET INTO.
WHAT?
NO WAY. WITH YOUR GOOD GRADES?
AT LEAST PICK A PRIVATE SCHOOL.
NOT LIS-TEN-ING!
AND YOUR PARENTS? THEY'RE OKAY WITH THIS?
UGH. PLEASE.
STOP. YOU SOUND LIKE MY TEACHER.
THWAP
BUT...

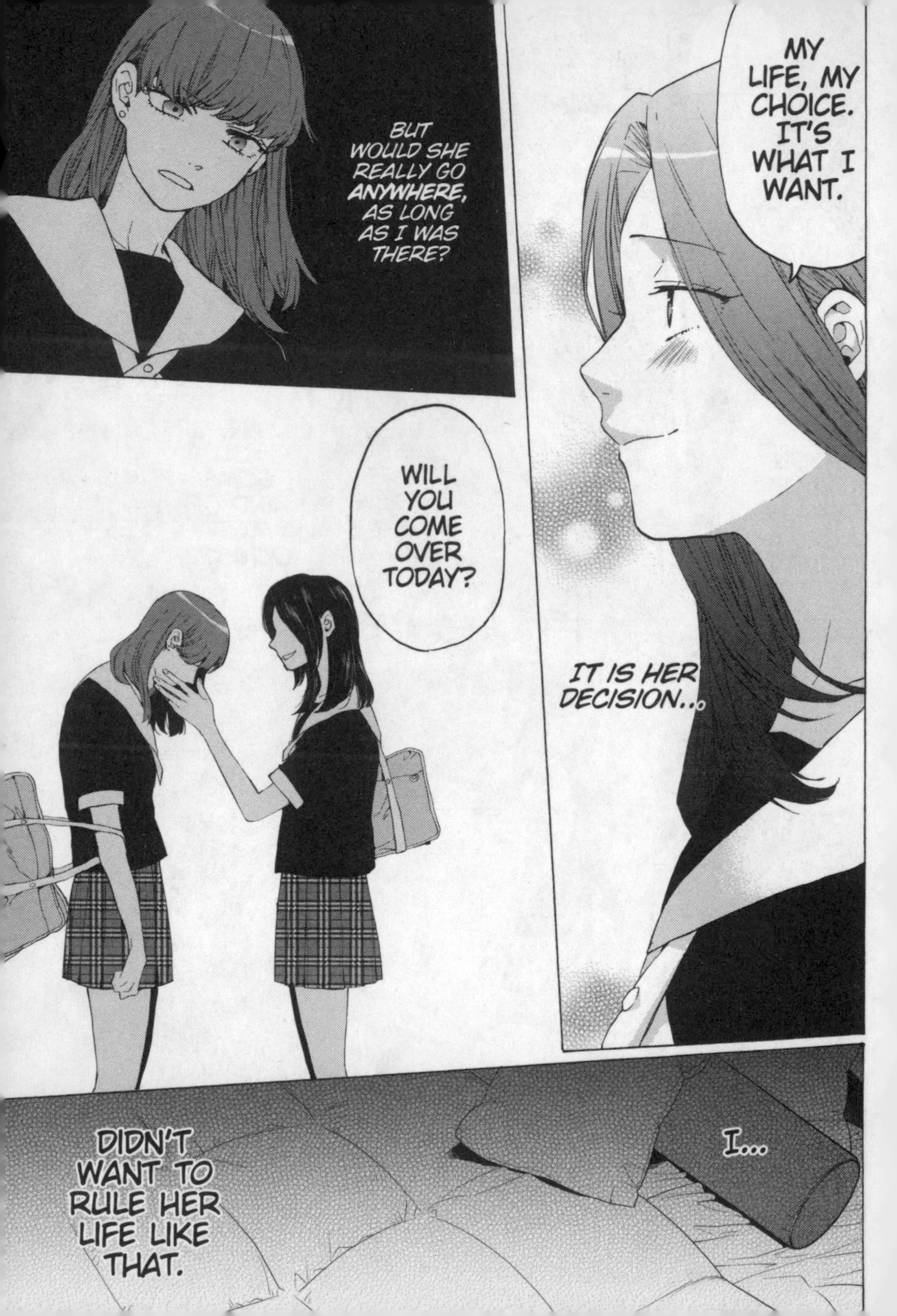
MY LIFE, MY CHOICE. IT'S WHAT I WANT.
IT IS HER DECISION...
BUT WOULD SHE REALLY GO *ANYWHERE*, AS LONG AS I WAS THERE?
WILL YOU COME OVER TODAY?
I...
DIDN'T WANT TO RULE HER LIFE LIKE THAT.

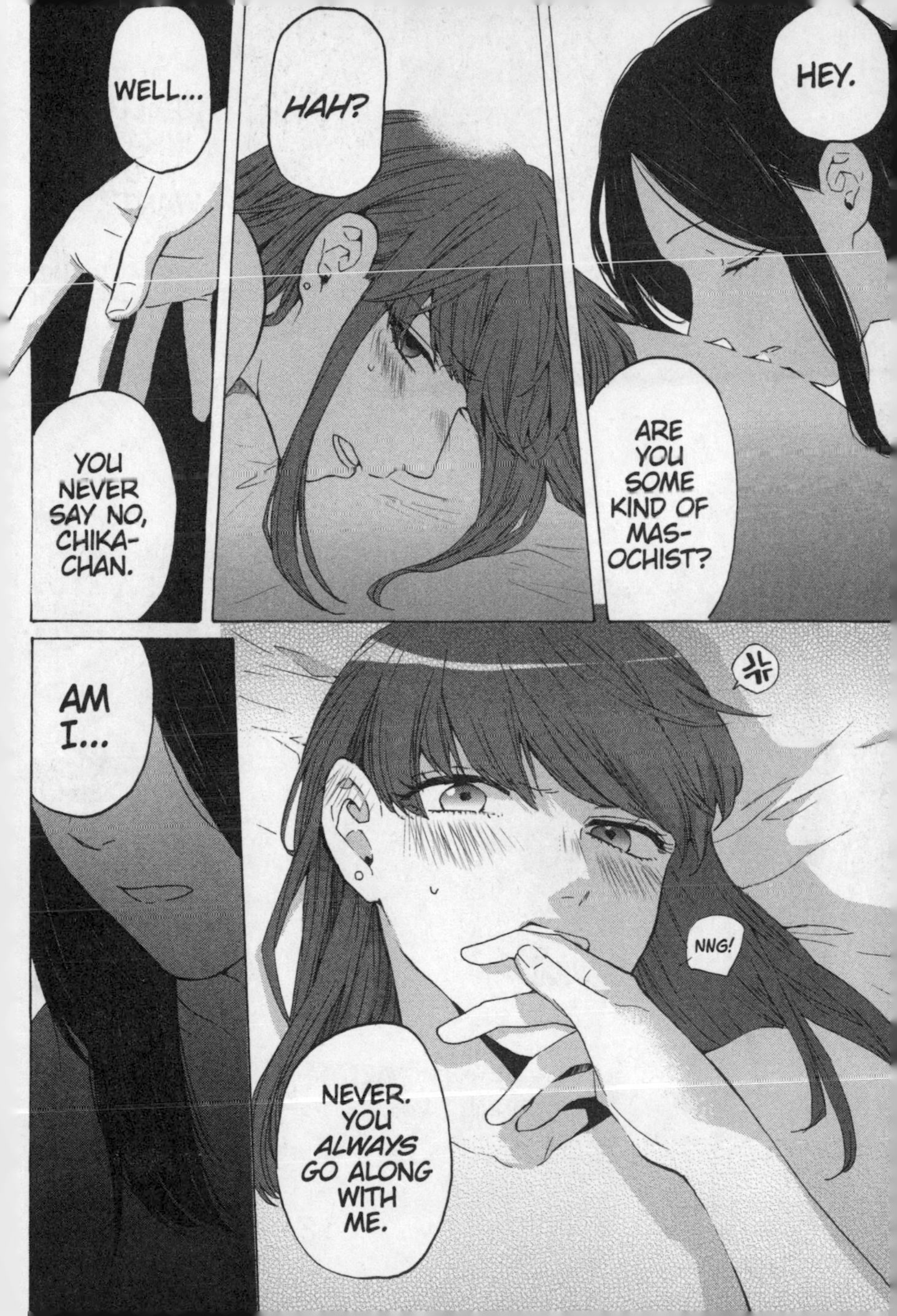
HEY.
ARE YOU SOME KIND OF MAS-OCHIST?
HAH?
WELL...
YOU NEVER SAY NO, CHIKA-CHAN.
NNG!
NEVER. YOU *ALWAYS* GO ALONG WITH ME.
AM I...

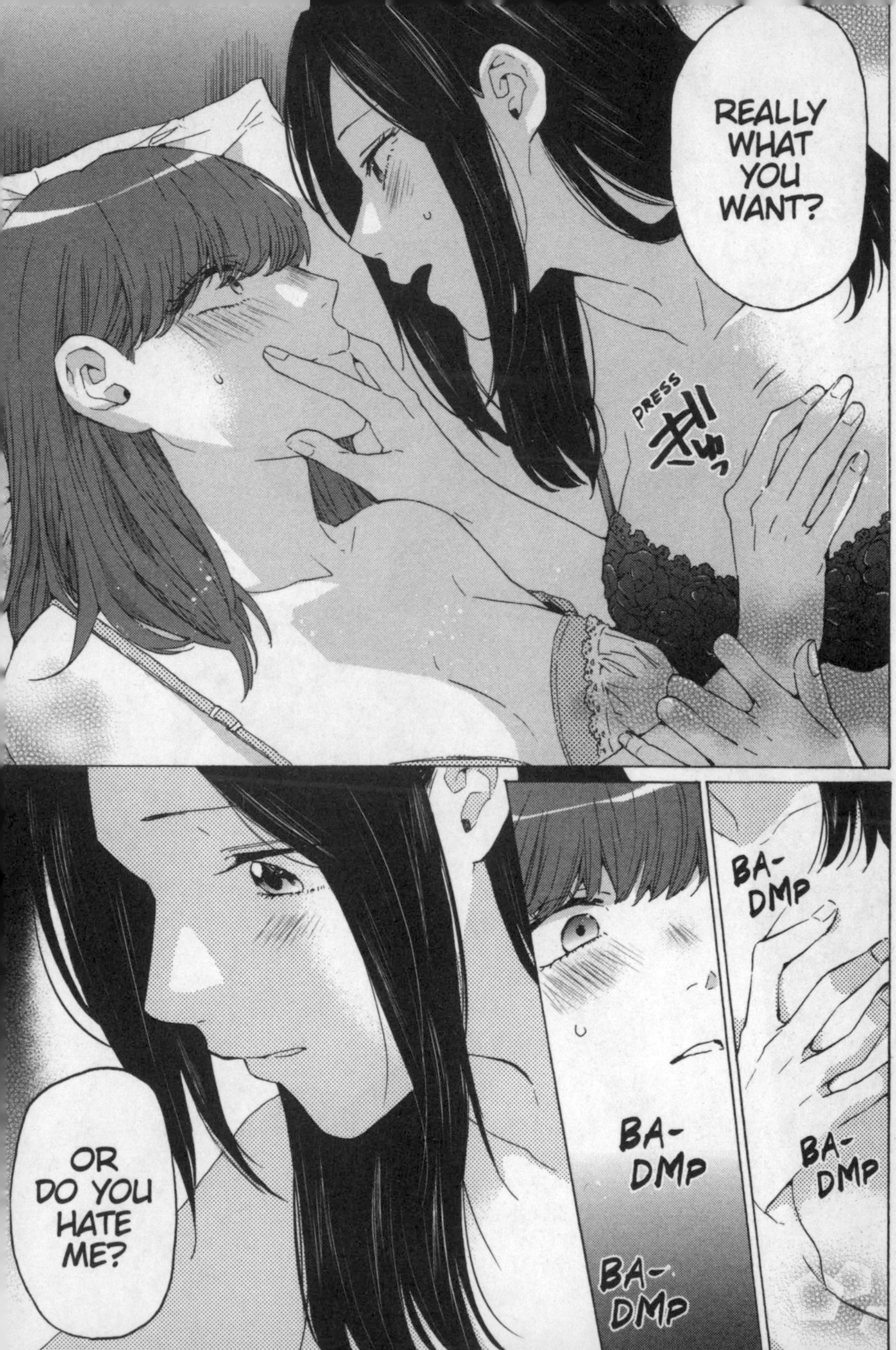
REALLY WHAT YOU WANT?
PRESS
きゅっ
BA-DMP
BA-DMP
BA-DMP
BA-DMP
OR DO YOU HATE ME?

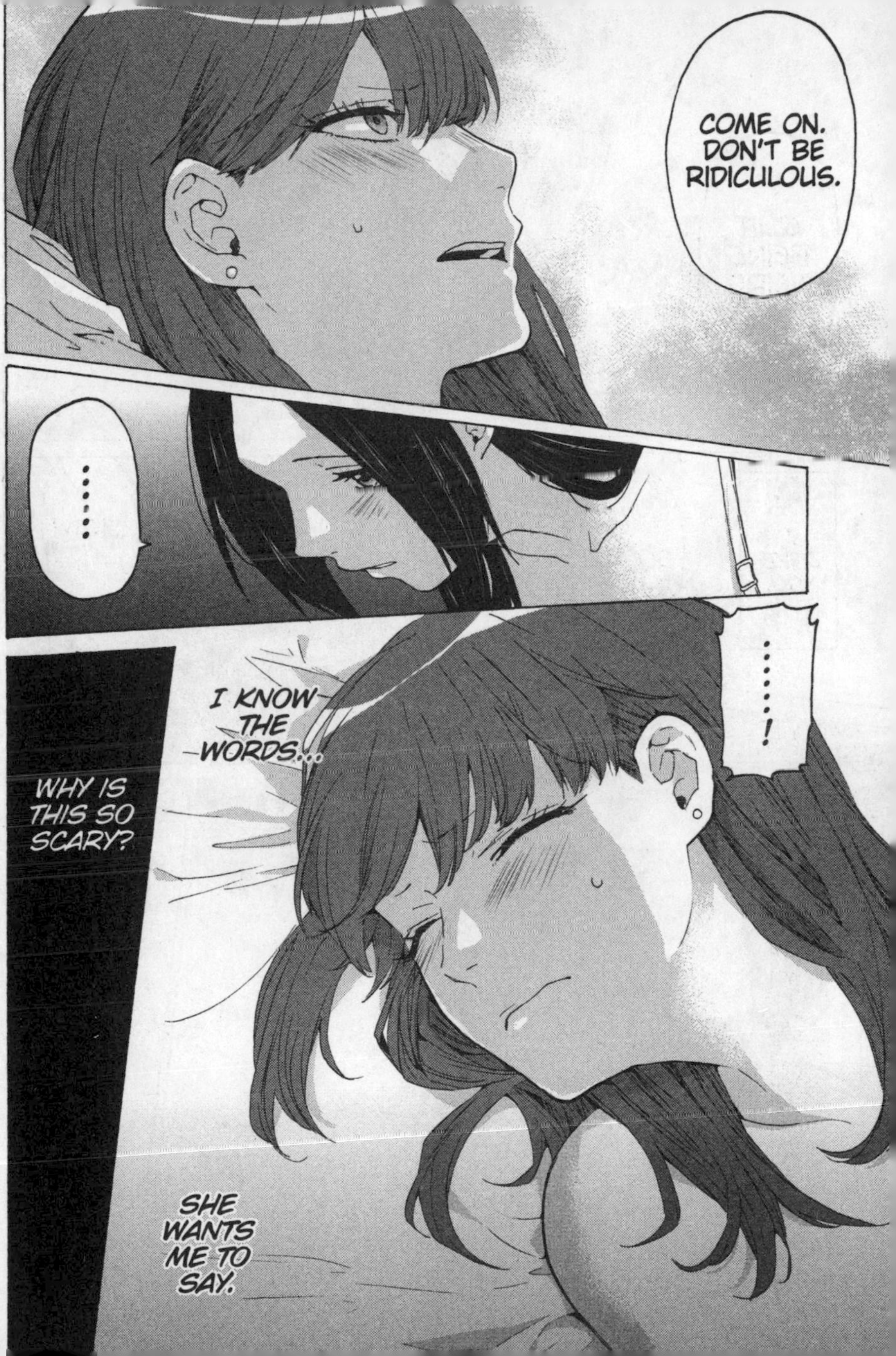
COME ON. DON'T BE RIDICULOUS.
......
......!
I KNOW THE WORDS...
WHY IS THIS SO SCARY?
SHE WANTS ME TO SAY.

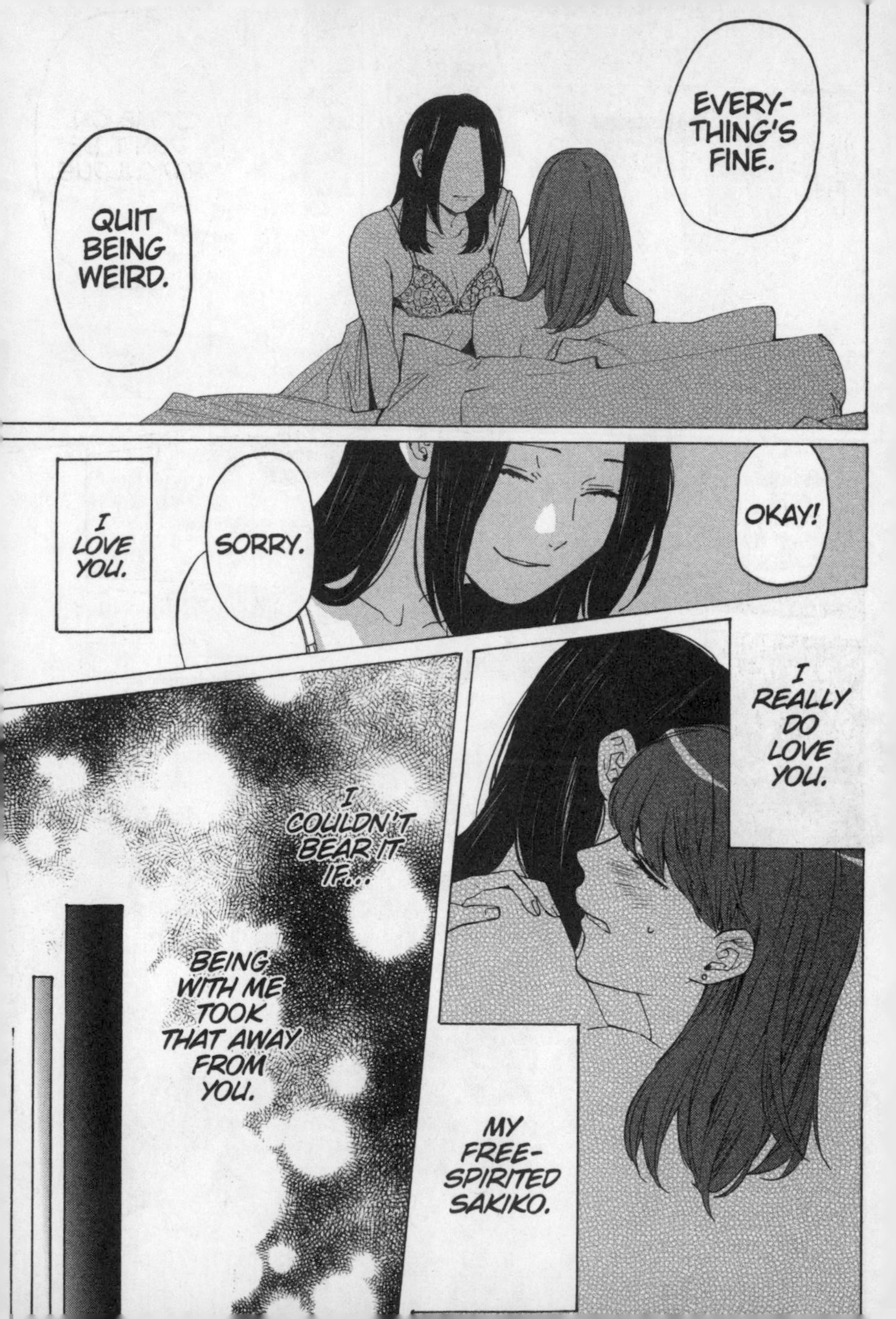
EVERY-THING'S FINE.
QUIT BEING WEIRD.
OKAY!
SORRY.
I LOVE YOU.
I REALLY DO LOVE YOU.
MY FREE-SPIRITED SAKIKO.
I COULDN'T BEAR IT IF...
BEING WITH ME TOOK THAT AWAY FROM YOU.

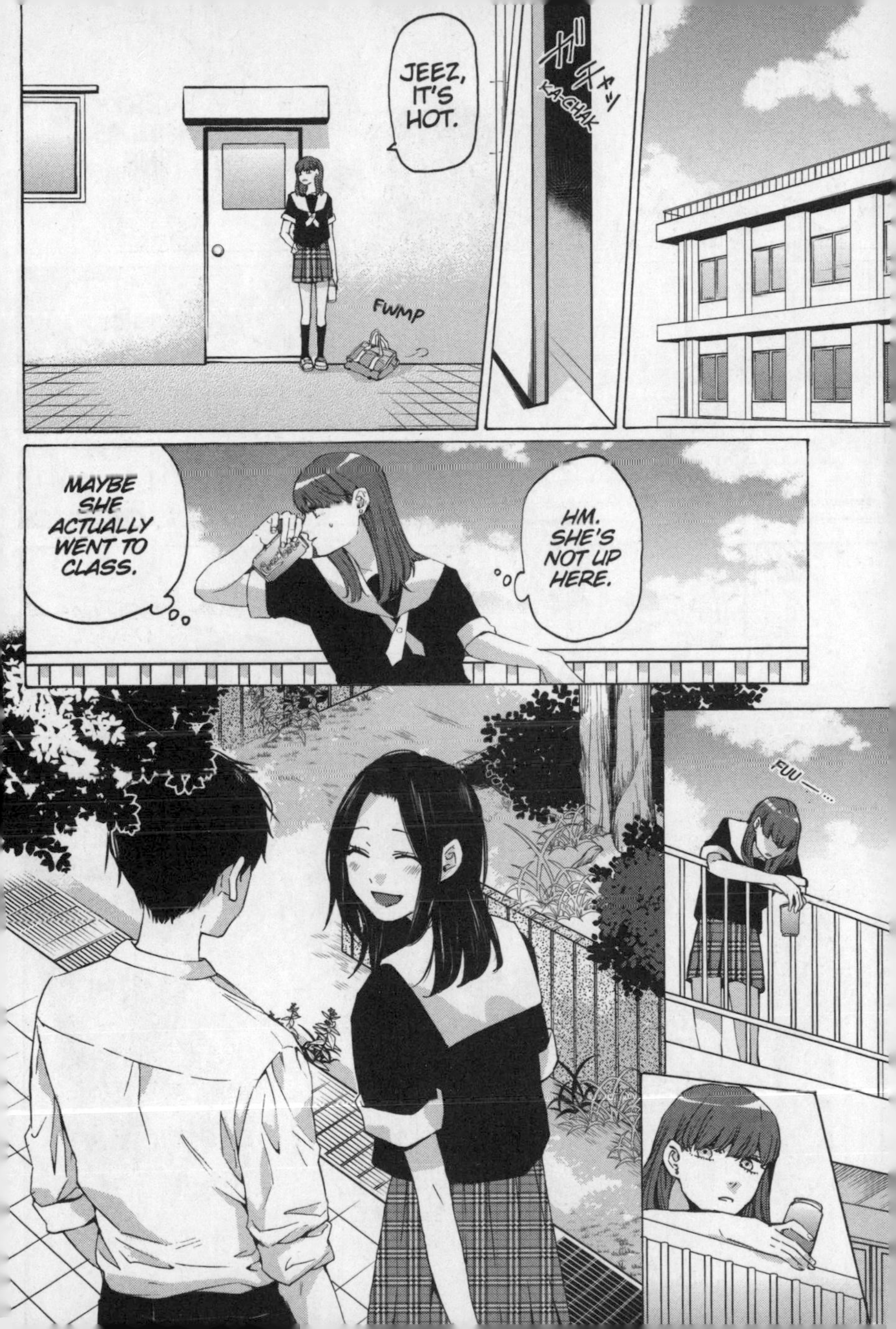
ガチャッ
KA-CHAK
JEEZ, IT'S HOT.
FWUMP
HM. SHE'S NOT UP HERE.
MAYBE SHE ACTUALLY WENT TO CLASS.
FUU—...

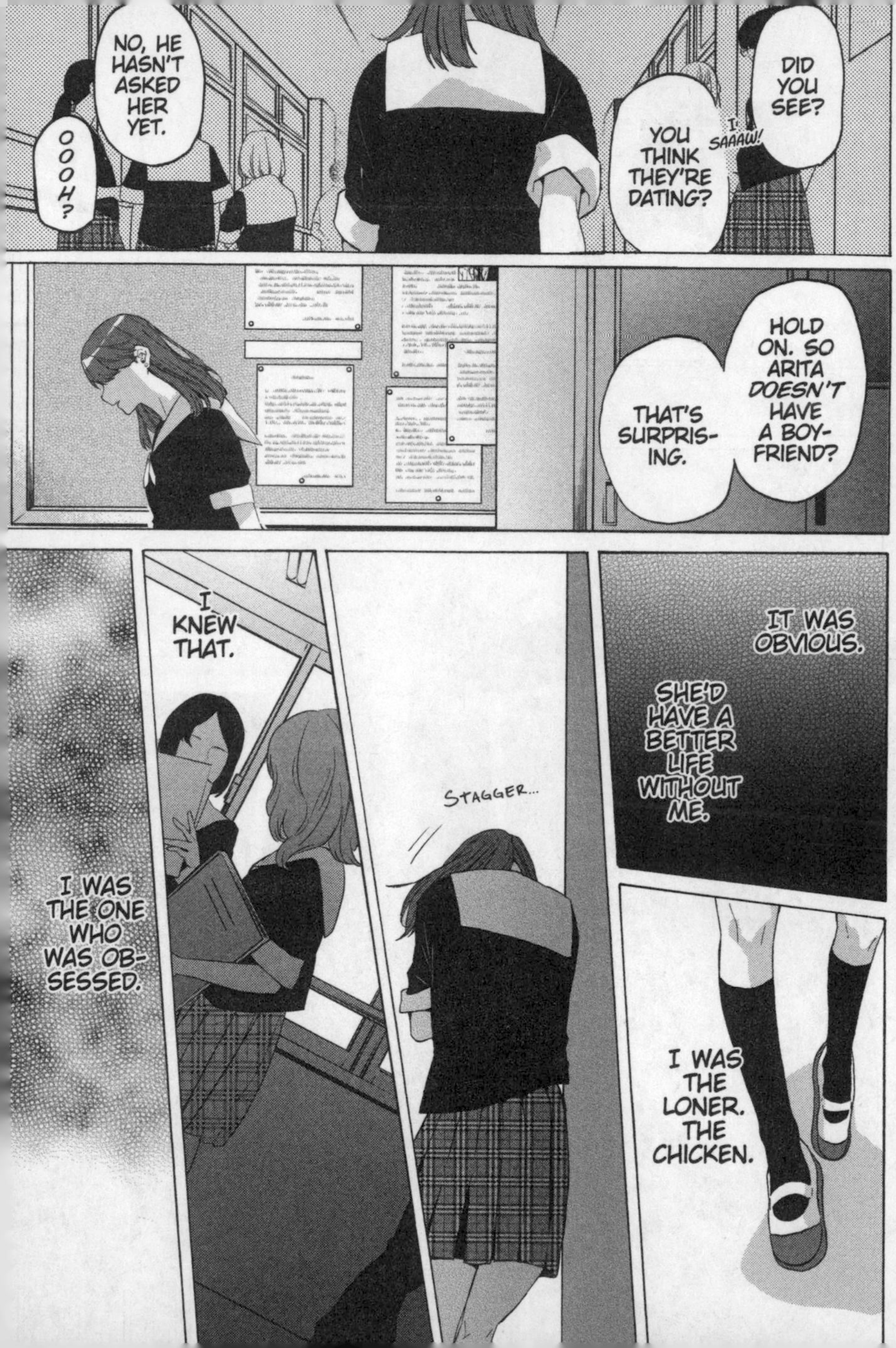
DID YOU SEE?
I SAAAW!
YOU THINK THEY'RE DATING?
NO, HE HASN'T ASKED HER YET.
OOOH?
HOLD ON. SO ARITA DOESN'T HAVE A BOY-FRIEND?
THAT'S SURPRIS-ING.
IT WAS OBVIOUS.
SHE'D HAVE A BETTER LIFE WITHOUT ME.
I WAS THE LONER. THE CHICKEN.
STAGGER...
I KNEW THAT.
I WAS THE ONE WHO WAS OB-SESSED.

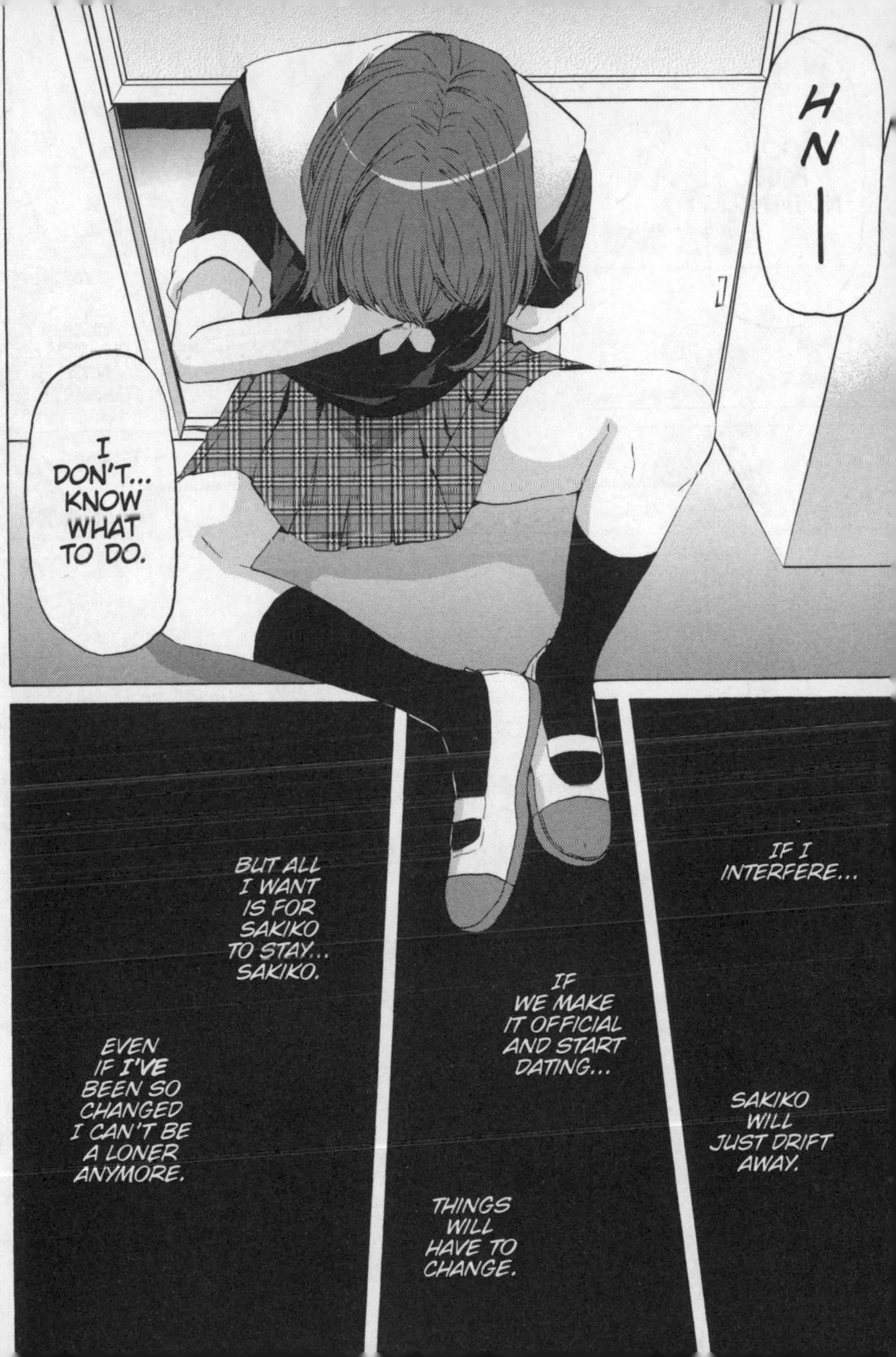

HN—
I DON'T... KNOW WHAT TO DO.
IF I INTERFERE...
SAKIKO WILL JUST DRIFT AWAY.
IF WE MAKE IT OFFICIAL AND START DATING...
THINGS WILL HAVE TO CHANGE.
BUT ALL I WANT IS FOR SAKIKO TO STAY... SAKIKO.
EVEN IF I'VE BEEN SO CHANGED I CAN'T BE A LONER ANYMORE.

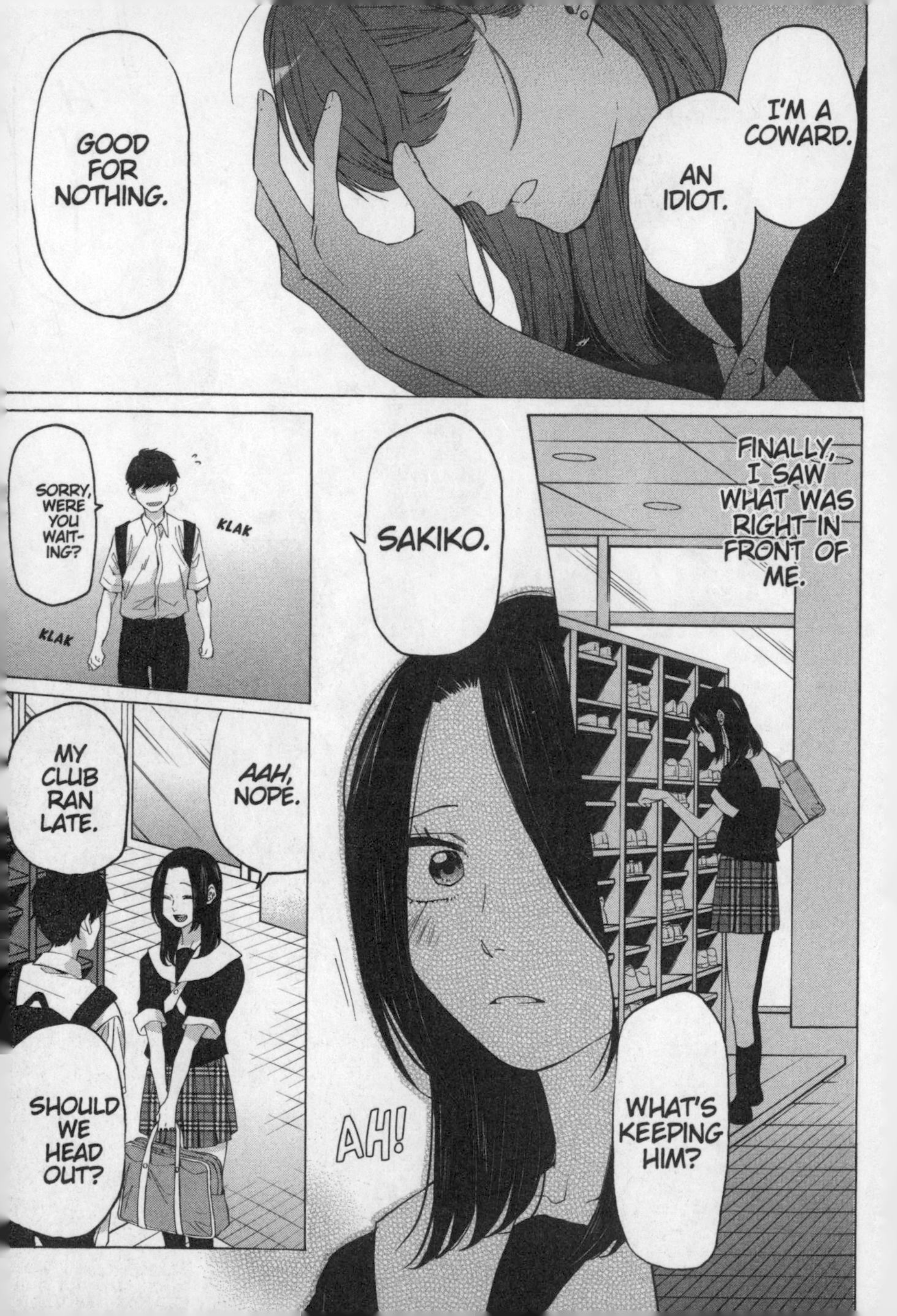
I'M A COWARD.
AN IDIOT.
GOOD FOR NOTHING.
FINALLY, I SAW WHAT WAS RIGHT IN FRONT OF ME.
SAKIKO.
WHAT'S KEEPING HIM?
AH!
SORRY, WERE YOU WAITING?
KLAK
KLAK
AAH, NOPE.
MY CLUB RAN LATE.
SHOULD WE HEAD OUT?

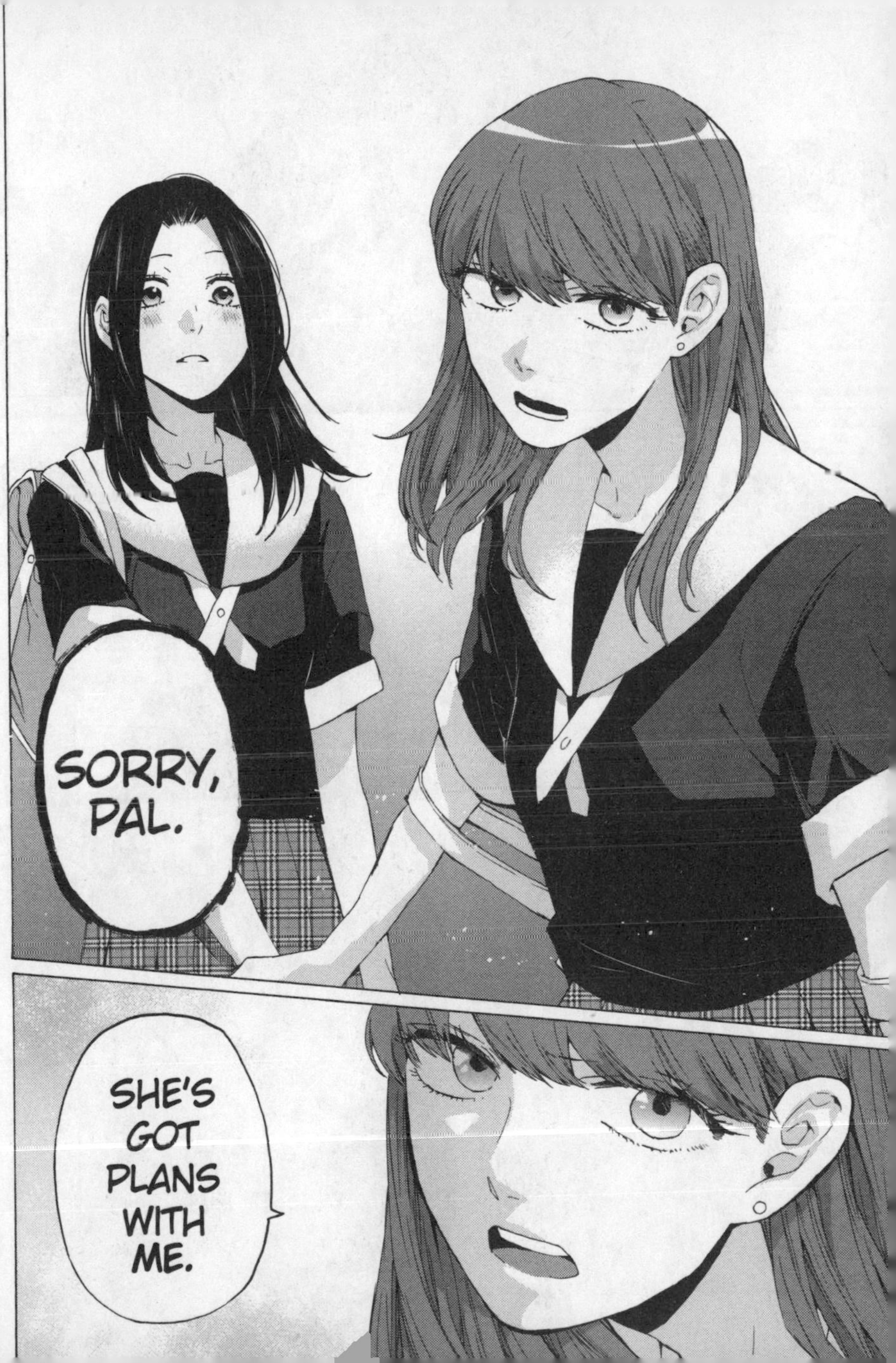
SORRY, PAL.
SHE'S GOT PLANS WITH ME.

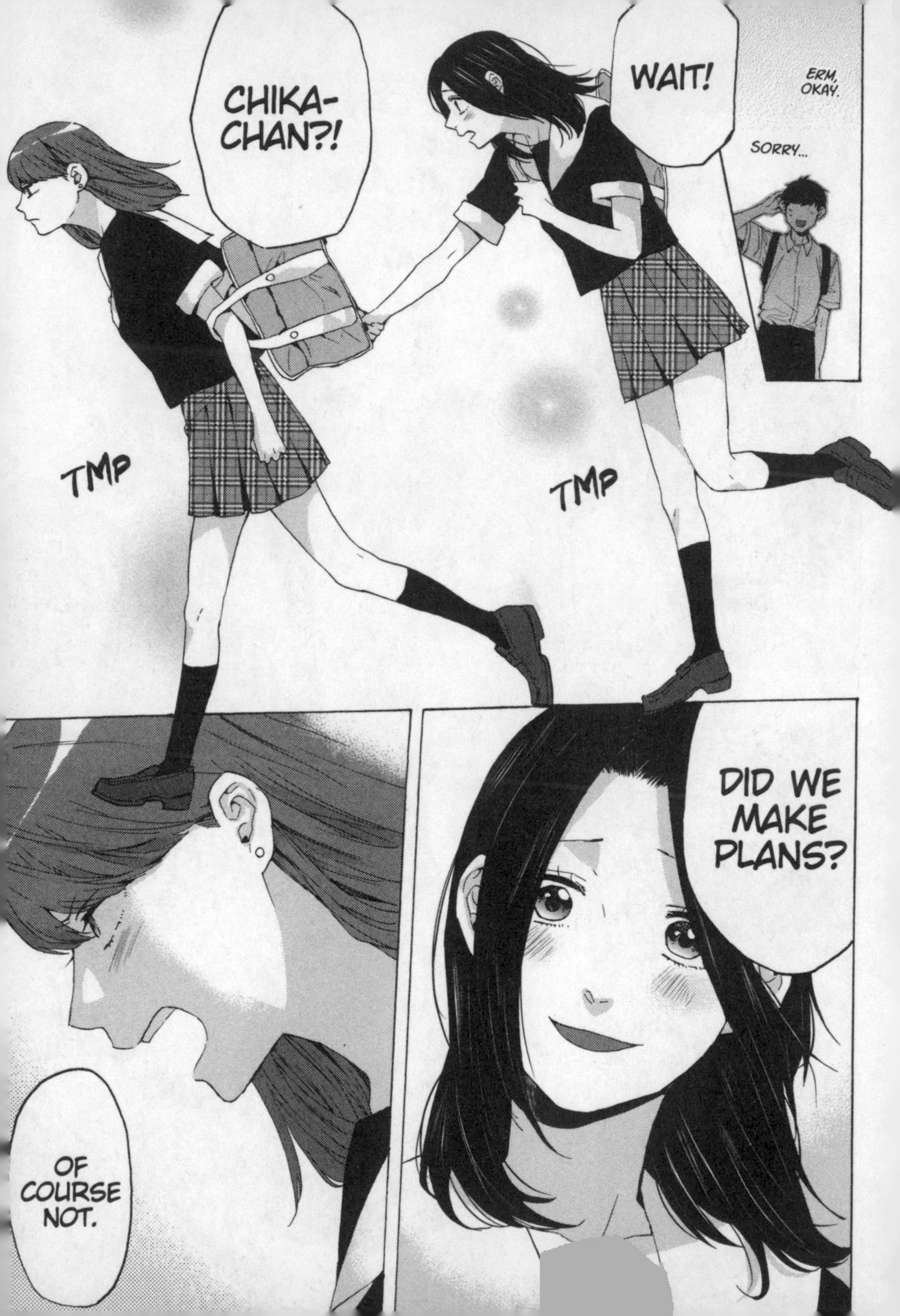
ERM, OKAY.
SORRY...
WAIT!
CHIKA-CHAN?!
TMP
TMP
DID WE MAKE PLANS?
OF COURSE NOT.

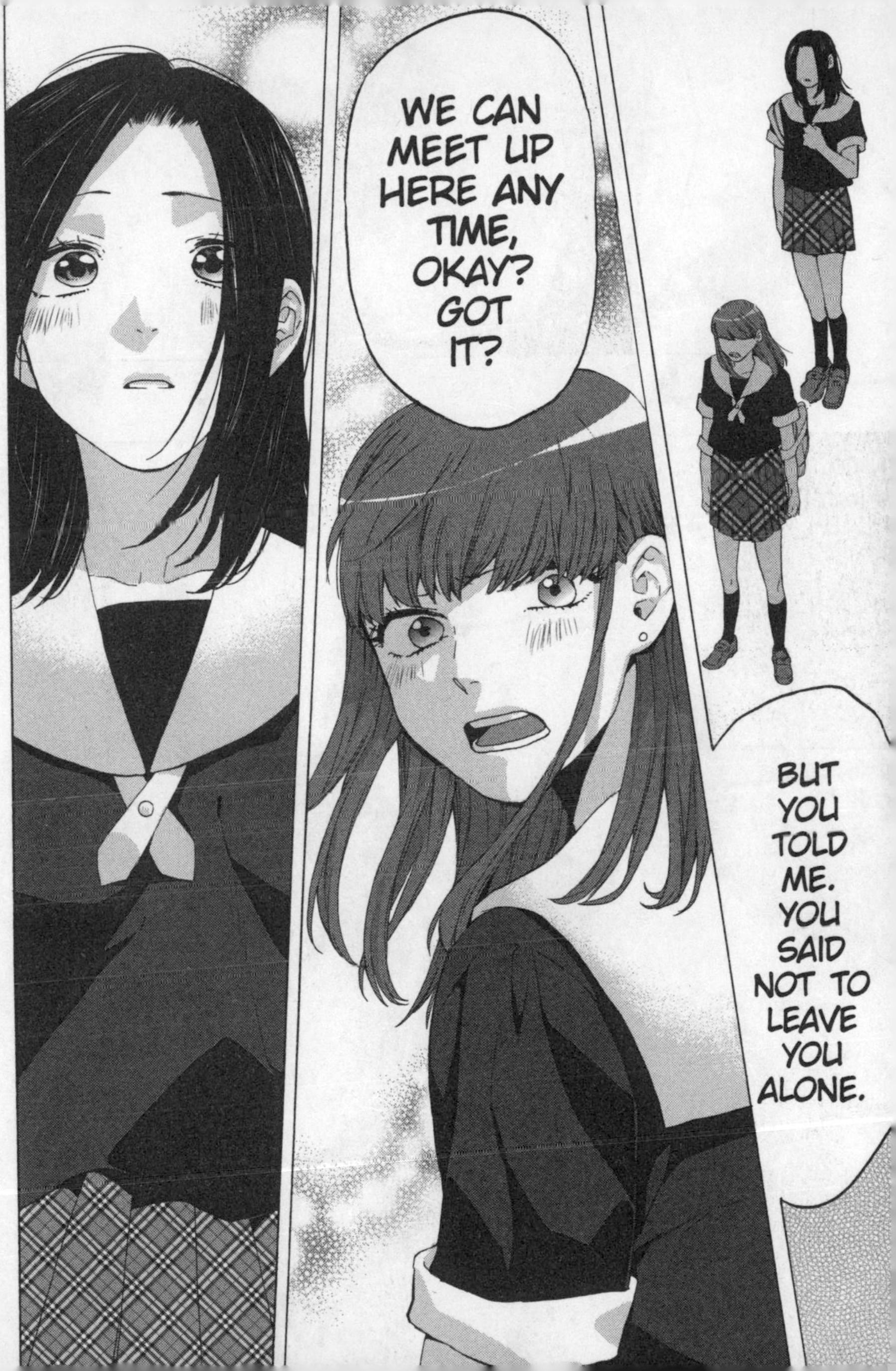
BUT YOU TOLD ME. YOU SAID NOT TO LEAVE YOU ALONE.
WE CAN MEET UP HERE ANY TIME, OKAY? GOT IT?

FWSH

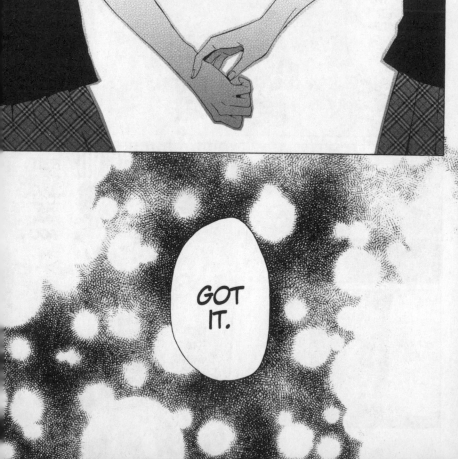

GOT IT.

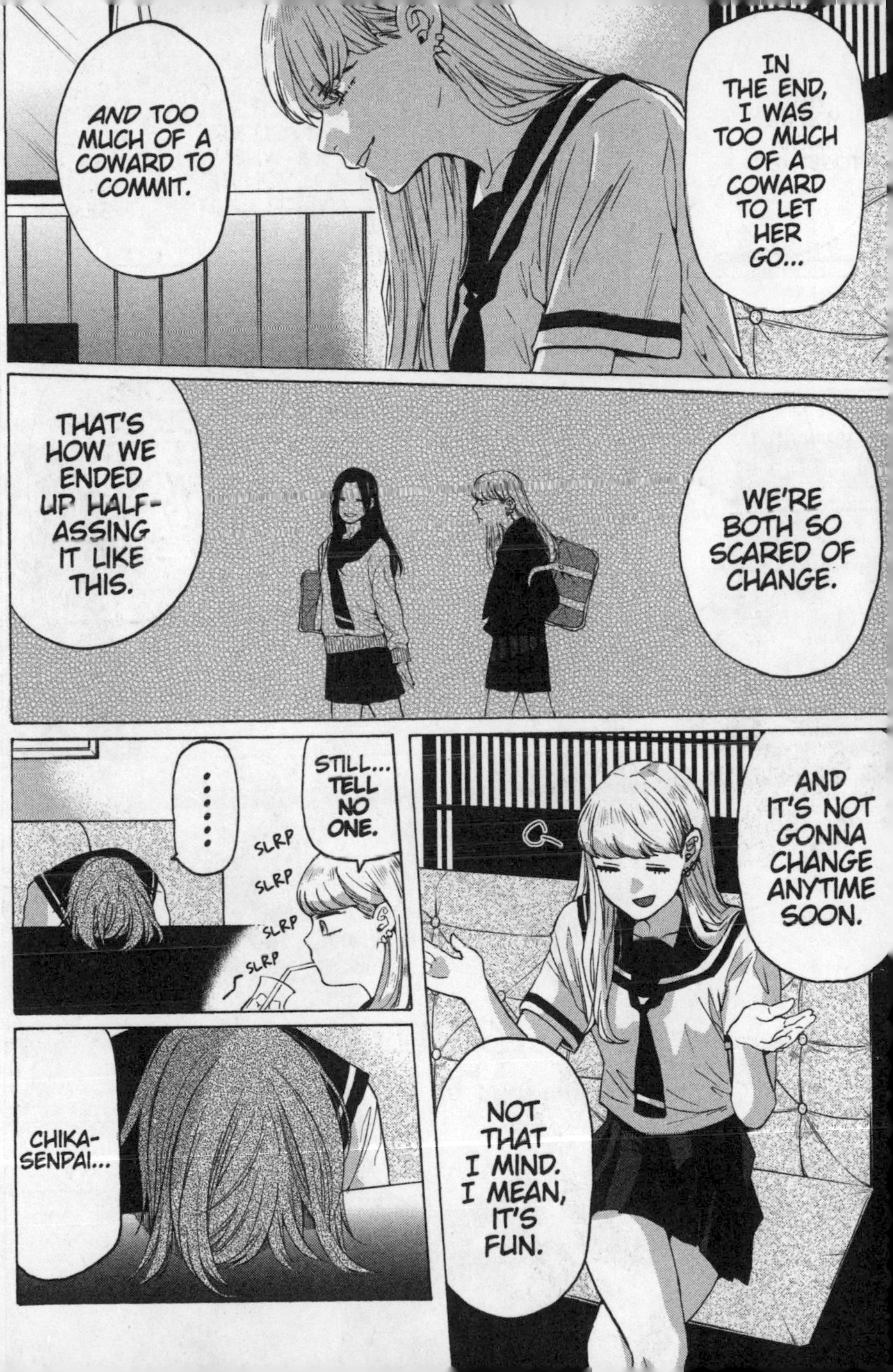
IN THE END, I WAS TOO MUCH OF A COWARD TO LET HER GO...
AND TOO MUCH OF A COWARD TO COMMIT.
WE'RE BOTH SO SCARED OF CHANGE.
THAT'S HOW WE ENDED UP HALF-ASSING IT LIKE THIS.
AND IT'S NOT GONNA CHANGE ANYTIME SOON.
NOT THAT I MIND. I MEAN, IT'S FUN.
STILL... TELL NO ONE.
SLRP
SLRP
SLRP
SLRP
......
CHIKA-SENPAI...

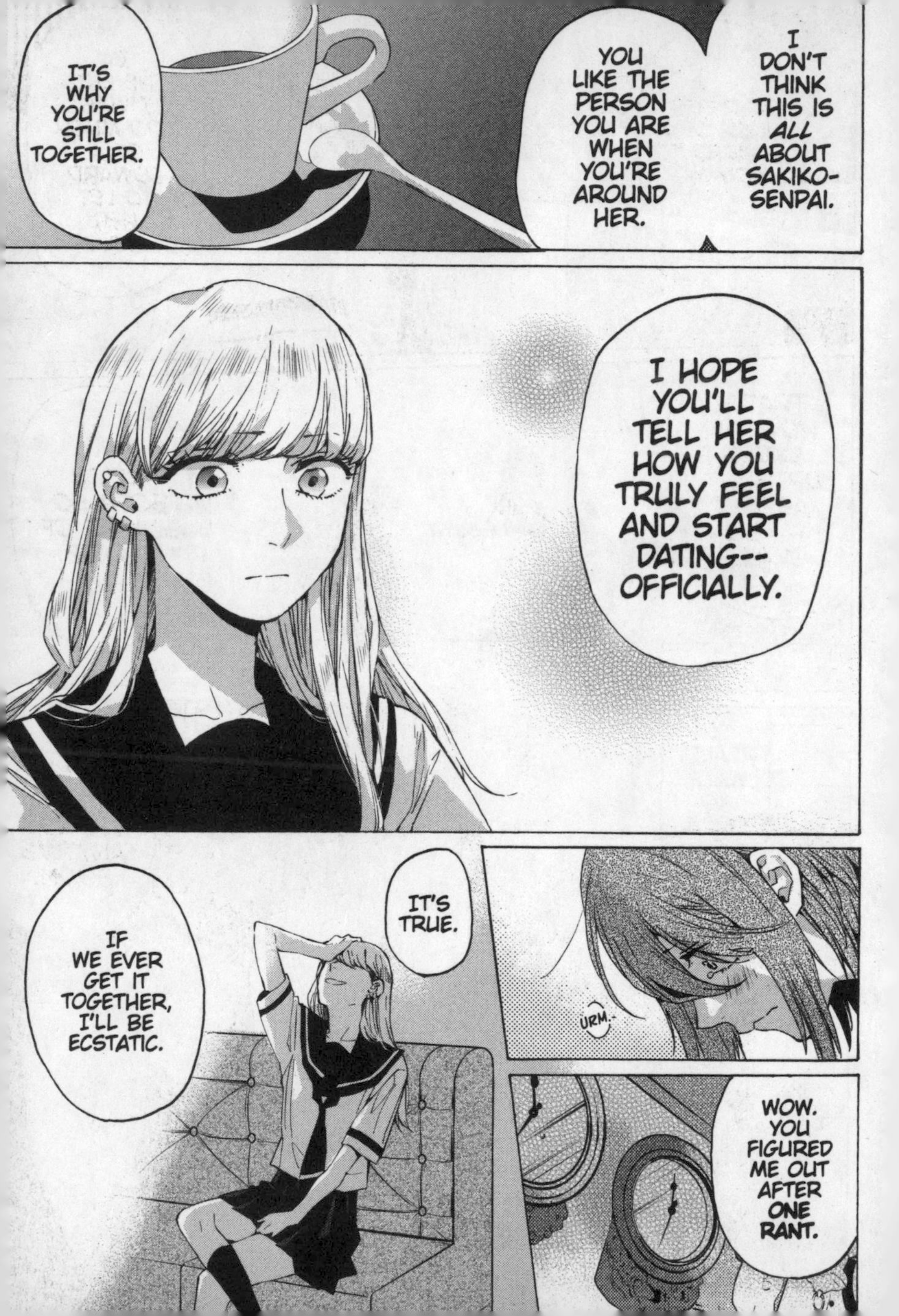
I DON'T THINK THIS IS ALL ABOUT SAKIKO-SENPAI.
YOU LIKE THE PERSON YOU ARE WHEN YOU'RE AROUND HER.
IT'S WHY YOU'RE STILL TOGETHER.
I HOPE YOU'LL TELL HER HOW YOU TRULY FEEL AND START DATING--OFFICIALLY.
URM.
WOW. YOU FIGURED ME OUT AFTER ONE RANT.
IT'S TRUE.
IF WE EVER GET IT TOGETHER, I'LL BE ECSTATIC.

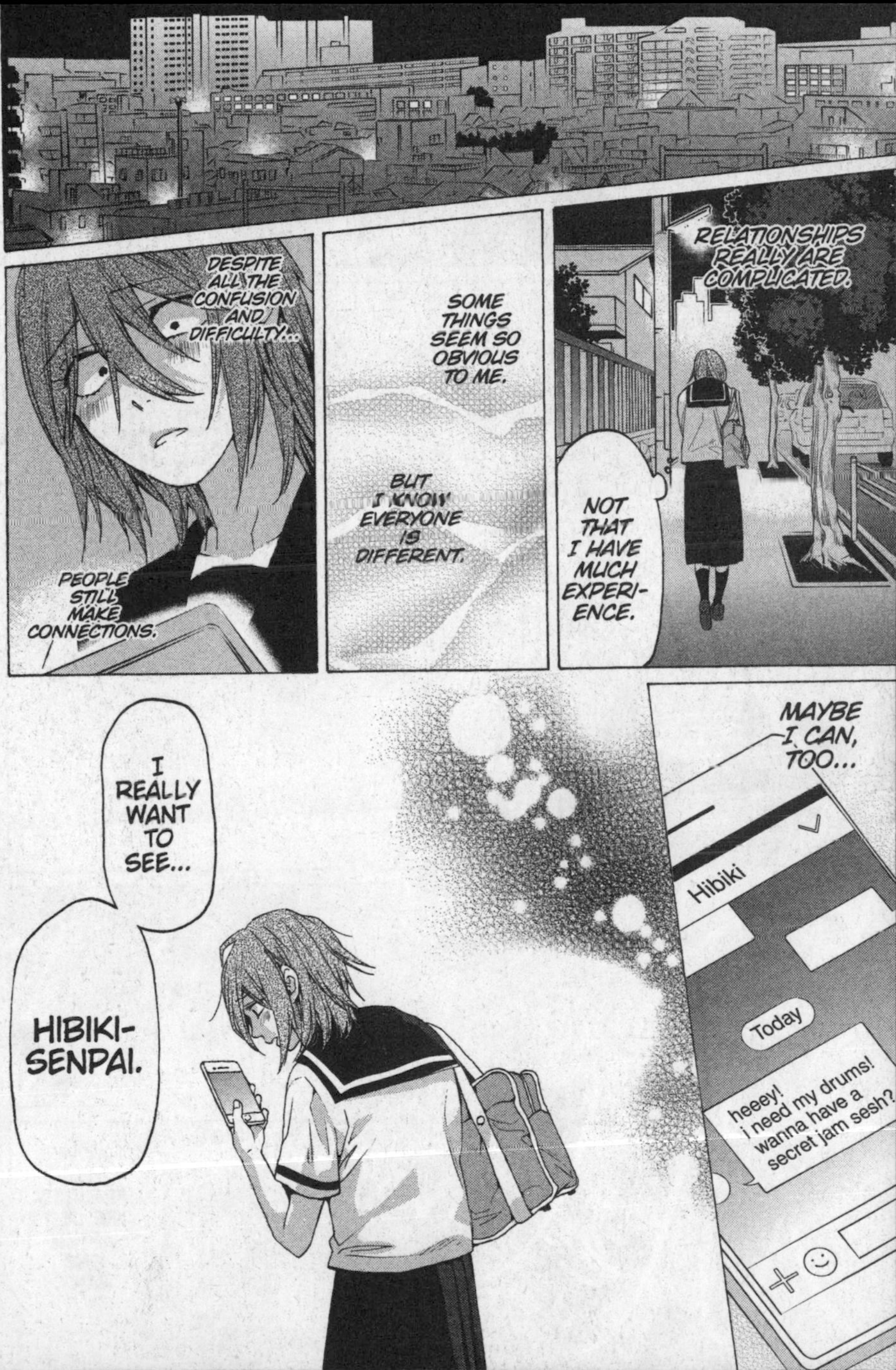
RELATIONSHIPS REALLY ARE COMPLICATED.
NOT THAT I HAVE MUCH EXPERIENCE.
SOME THINGS SEEM SO OBVIOUS TO ME.
BUT I KNOW EVERYONE IS DIFFERENT.
DESPITE ALL THE CONFUSION AND DIFFICULTY...
PEOPLE STILL MAKE CONNECTIONS.
MAYBE I CAN, TOO...
Hibiki
Today
heeey! i need my drums! wanna have a secret jam sesh?
I REALLY WANT TO SEE...
HIBIKI-SENPAI.

Hello, Melancholic!

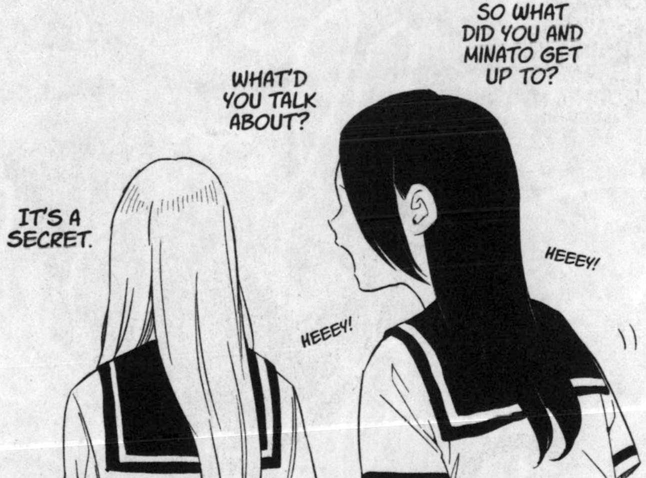
SO WHAT DID YOU AND MINATO GET UP TO?
WHAT'D YOU TALK ABOUT?
HEEEY!
IT'S A SECRET.
HEEEY!

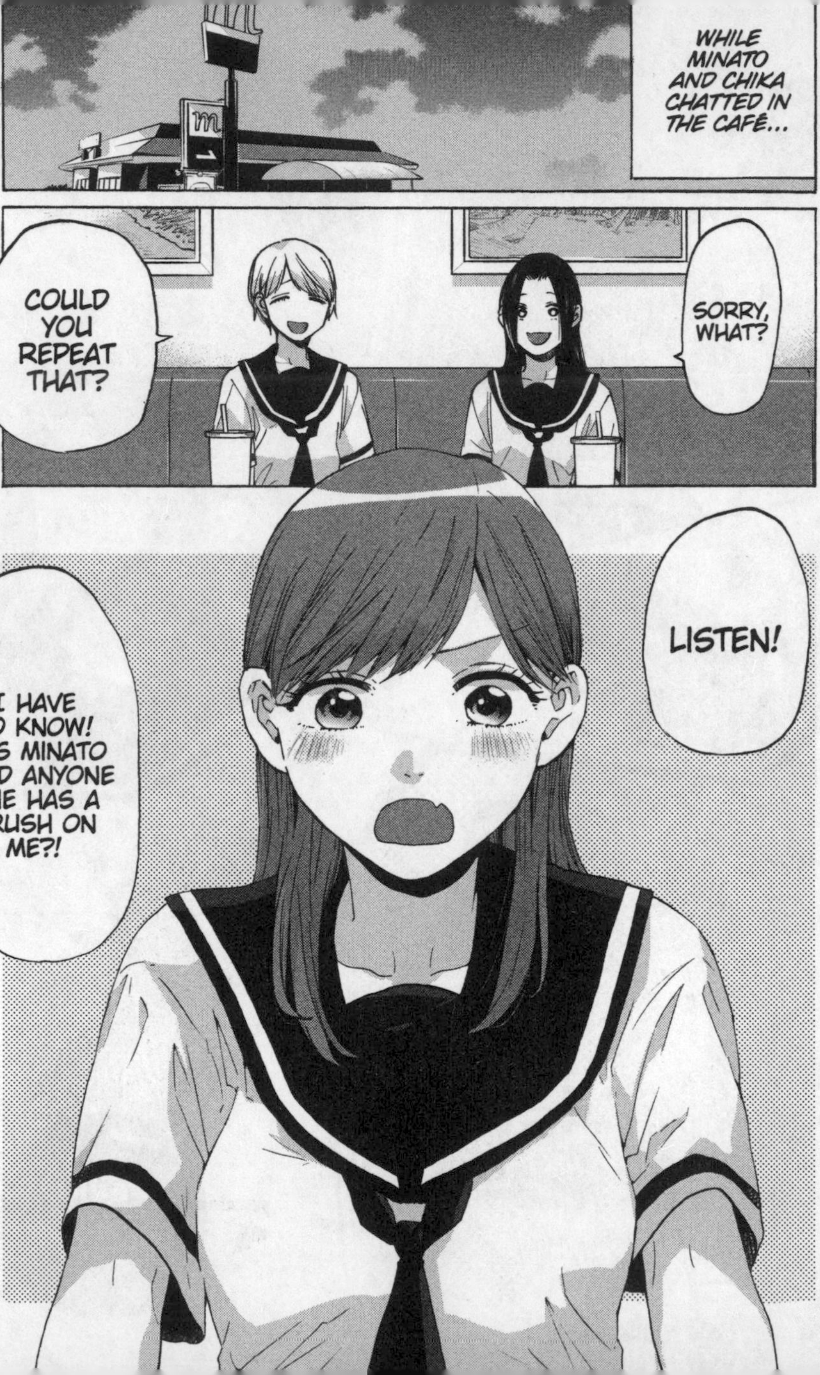
WHILE MINATO AND CHIKA CHATTED IN THE CAFÉ...
SORRY, WHAT?
COULD YOU REPEAT THAT?
LISTEN!
I HAVE TO KNOW! HAS MINATO TOLD ANYONE SHE HAS A CRUSH ON ME?!

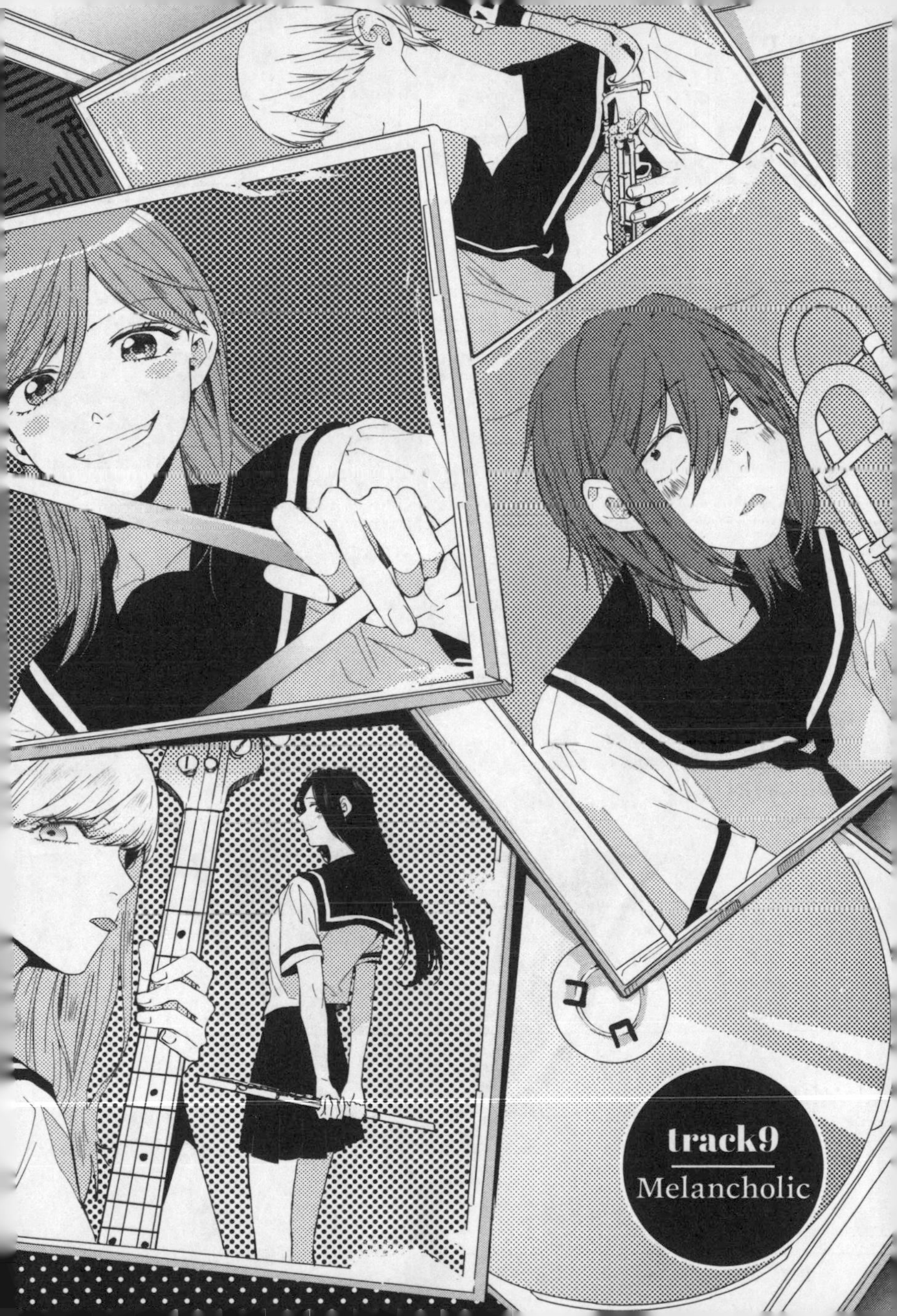
track9
Melancholic

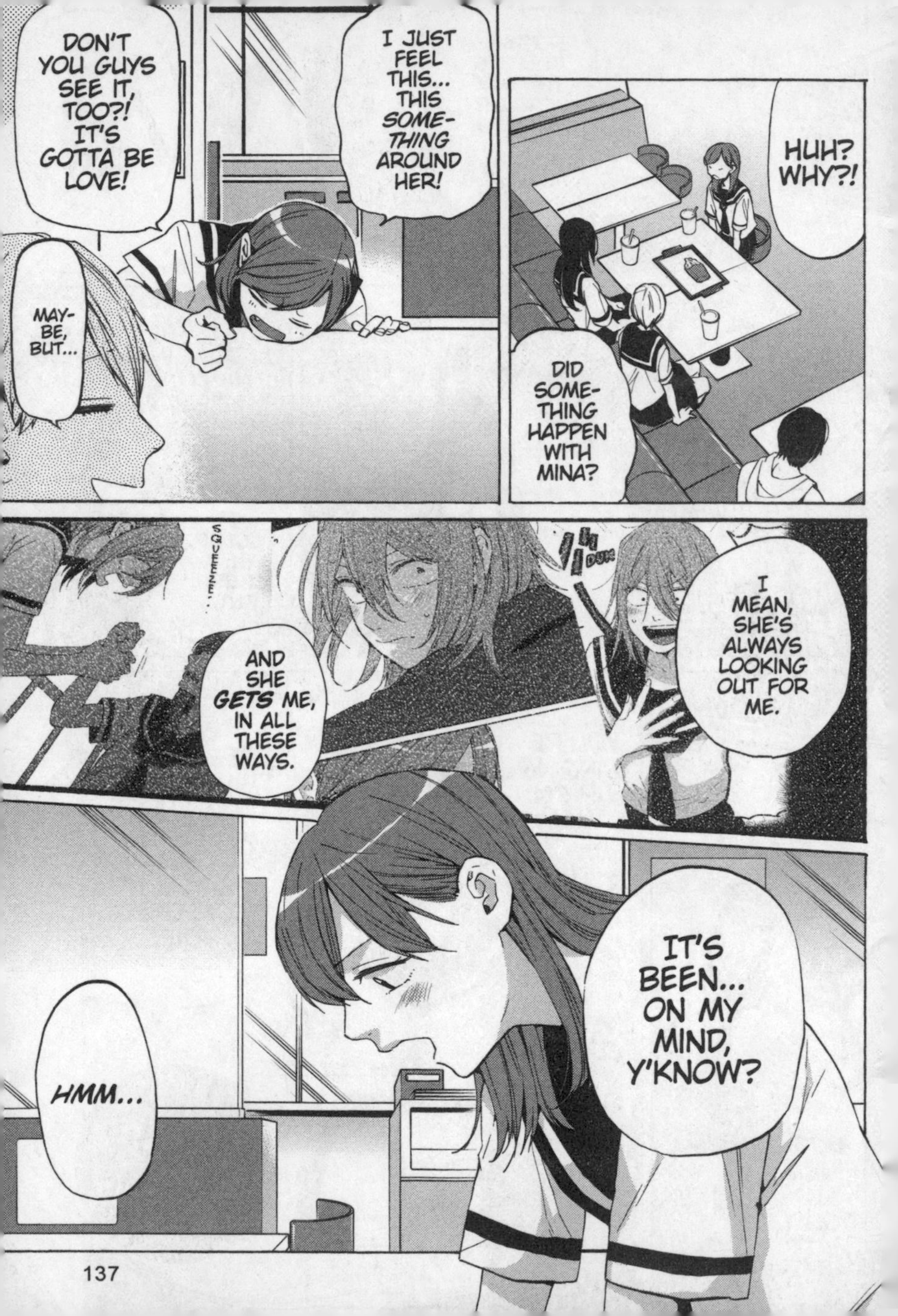
HUH? WHY?!
DID SOMETHING HAPPEN WITH MINA?
I JUST FEEL THIS... THIS *SOMETHING* AROUND HER!
DON'T YOU GUYS SEE IT, TOO?! IT'S GOTTA BE LOVE!
MAY-BE, BUT...
DUN
I MEAN, SHE'S ALWAYS LOOKING OUT FOR ME.
AND SHE **GETS** ME, IN ALL THESE WAYS.
SQUEEZE...
IT'S BEEN... ON MY MIND, Y'KNOW?
HMM...

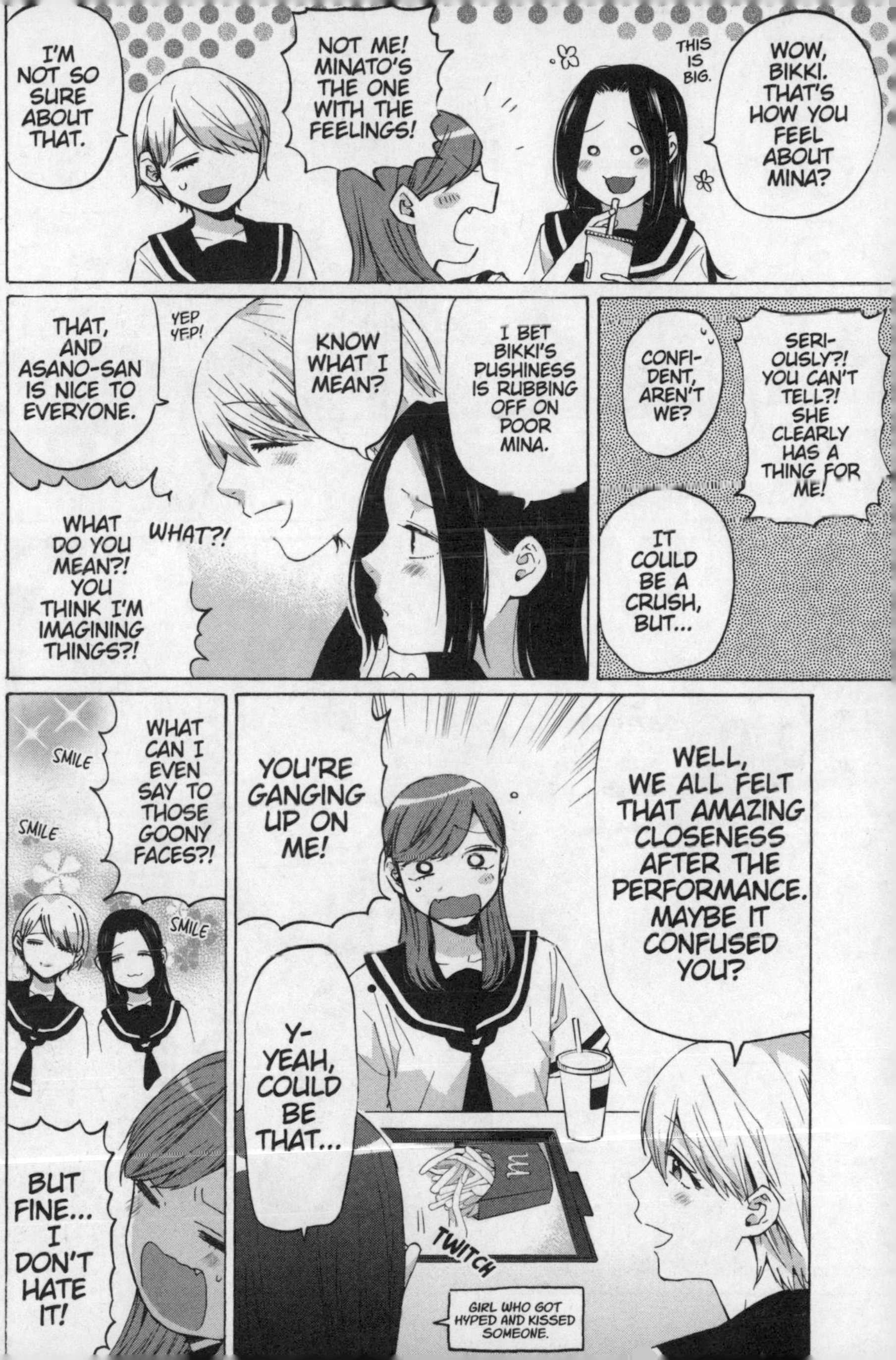
WOW, BIKKI. THAT'S HOW YOU FEEL ABOUT MINA?
THIS IS BIG.
NOT ME! MINATO'S THE ONE WITH THE FEELINGS!
I'M NOT SO SURE ABOUT THAT.
SERIOUSLY?! YOU CAN'T TELL?! SHE CLEARLY HAS A THING FOR ME!
CONFIDENT, AREN'T WE?
IT COULD BE A CRUSH, BUT...
I BET BIKKI'S PUSHINESS IS RUBBING OFF ON POOR MINA.
KNOW WHAT I MEAN?
YEP YEP!
THAT, AND ASANO-SAN IS NICE TO EVERYONE.
WHAT?!
WHAT DO YOU MEAN?! YOU THINK I'M IMAGINING THINGS?!
WELL, WE ALL FELT THAT AMAZING CLOSENESS AFTER THE PERFORMANCE. MAYBE IT CONFUSED YOU?
YOU'RE GANGING UP ON ME!
Y-YEAH, COULD BE THAT...
TWITCH
GIRL WHO GOT HYPED AND KISSED SOMEONE.
WHAT CAN I EVEN SAY TO THOSE GOONY FACES?!
SMILE
SMILE
SMILE
BUT FINE... I DON'T HATE IT!

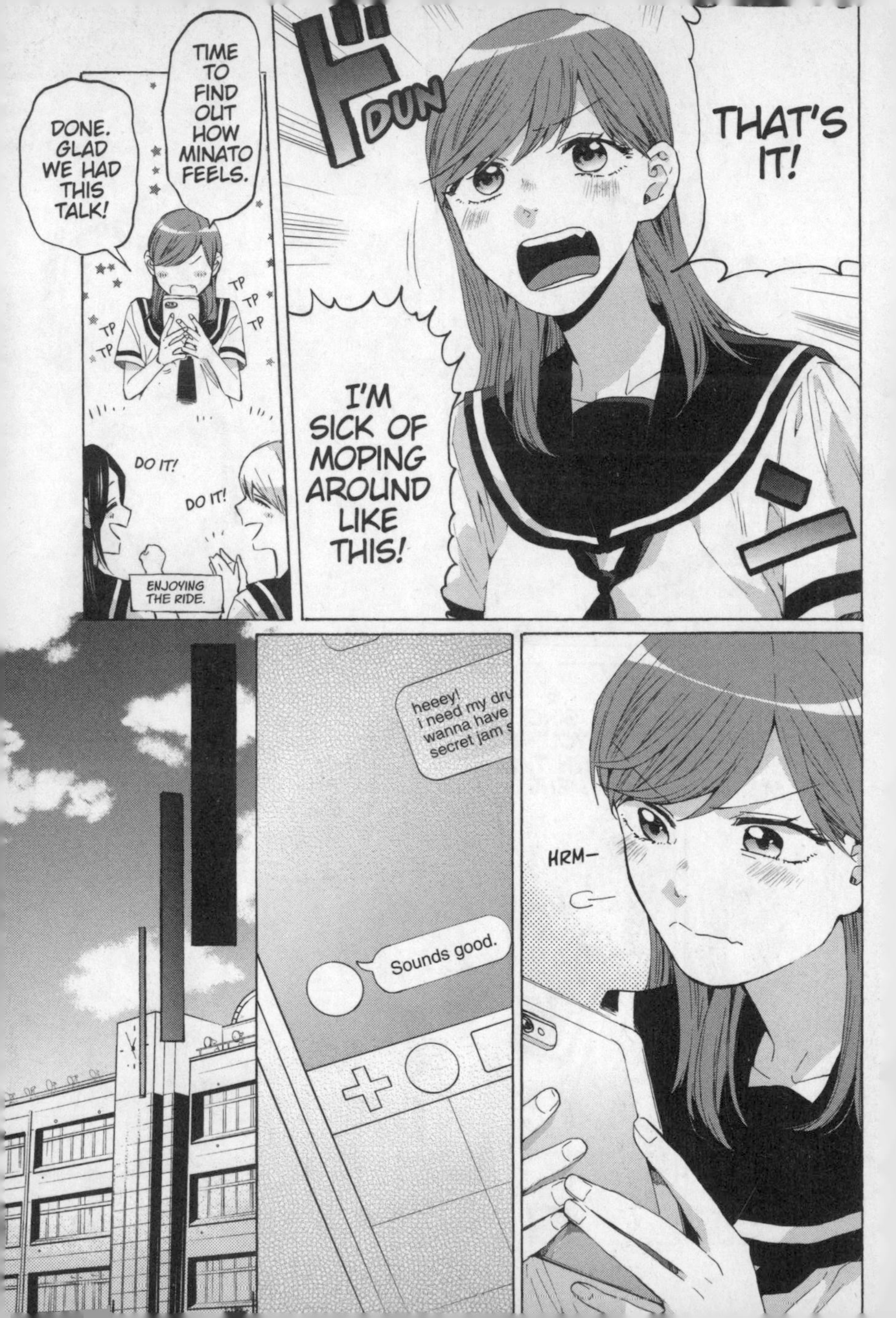
THAT'S IT!
DUN
I'M SICK OF MOPING AROUND LIKE THIS!
TIME TO FIND OUT HOW MINATO FEELS.
DONE. GLAD WE HAD THIS TALK!
TP TP TP
TP TP
DO IT!
DO IT!
ENJOYING THE RIDE.
HRM–
heeey!
i need my dru
wanna have
secret jam s
Sounds good.

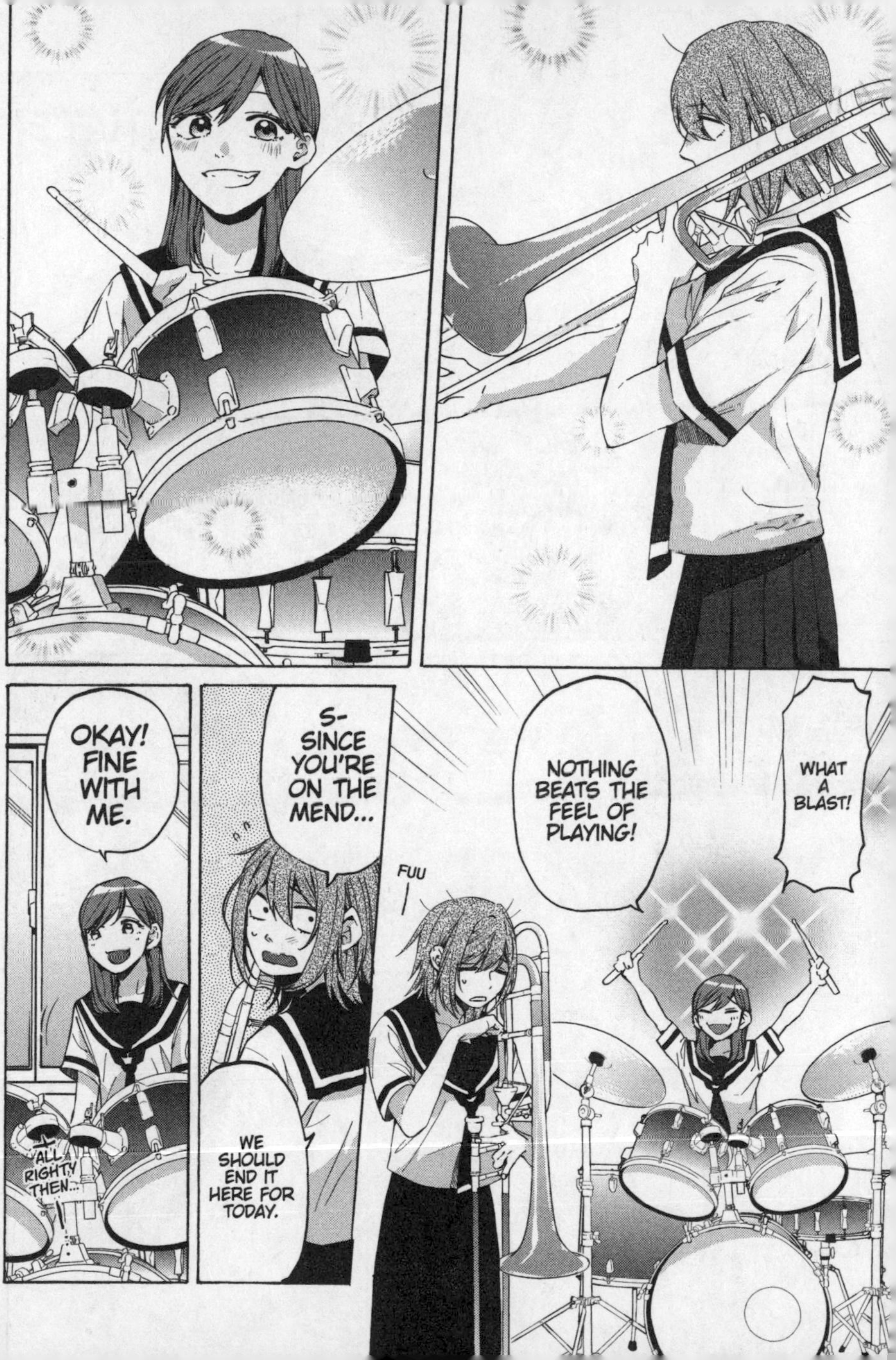
WHAT A BLAST!
NOTHING BEATS THE FEEL OF PLAYING!
FUU
S- SINCE YOU'RE ON THE MEND...
WE SHOULD END IT HERE FOR TODAY.
OKAY! FINE WITH ME.
ALL RIGHTY THEN...

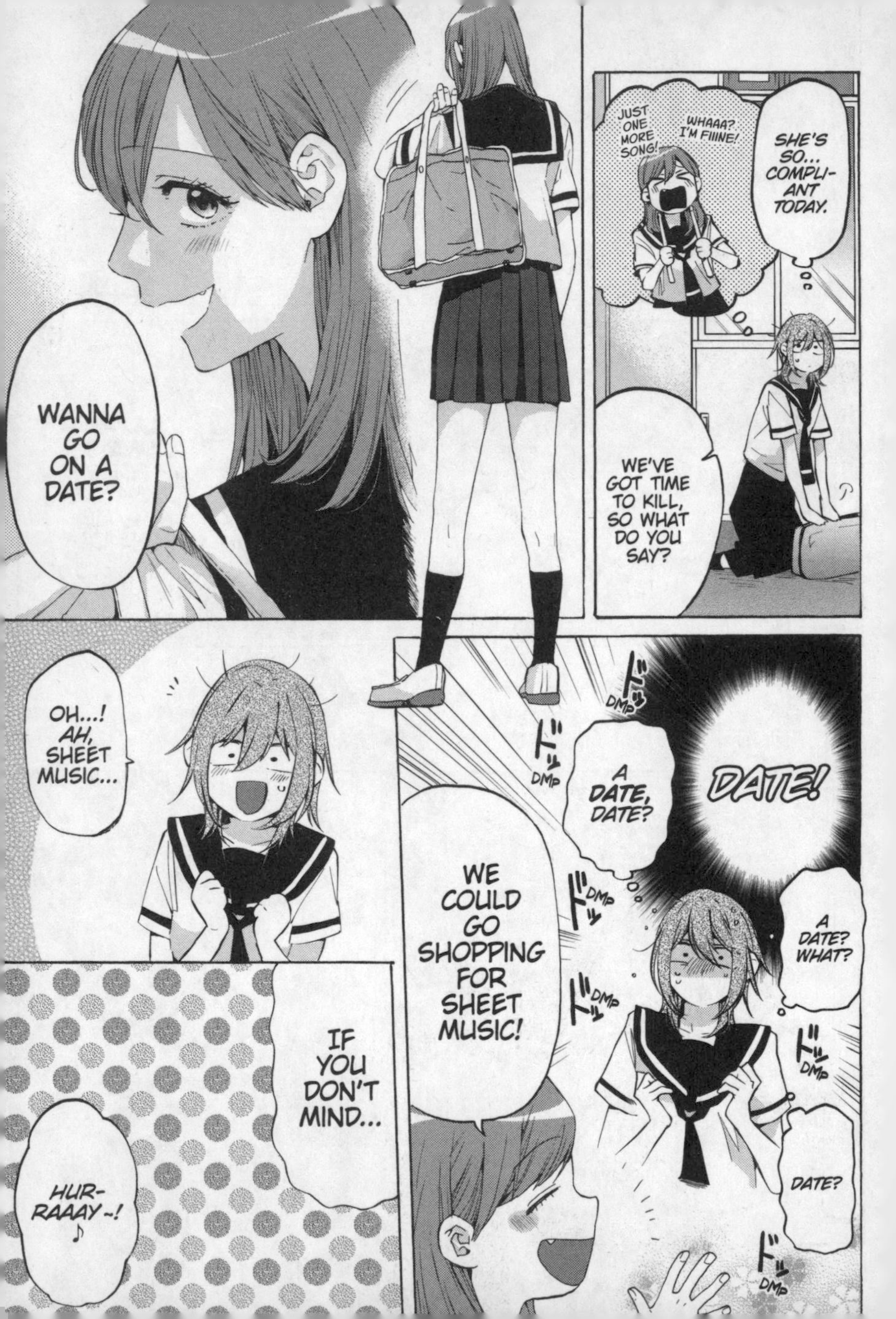
SHE'S SO... COMPLIANT TODAY.
WHAAA? I'M FIIINE!
JUST ONE MORE SONG!
WE'VE GOT TIME TO KILL, SO WHAT DO YOU SAY?
WANNA GO ON A DATE?
ドッ DMP
DATE!
ドッ DMP
A DATE, DATE?
A DATE? WHAT?
ドッ DMP
ドッ DMP
WE COULD GO SHOPPING FOR SHEET MUSIC!
ドッ DMP
DATE?
ドッ DMP
OH...! AH, SHEET MUSIC...
IF YOU DON'T MIND...
HUR-RAAAY~! ♪

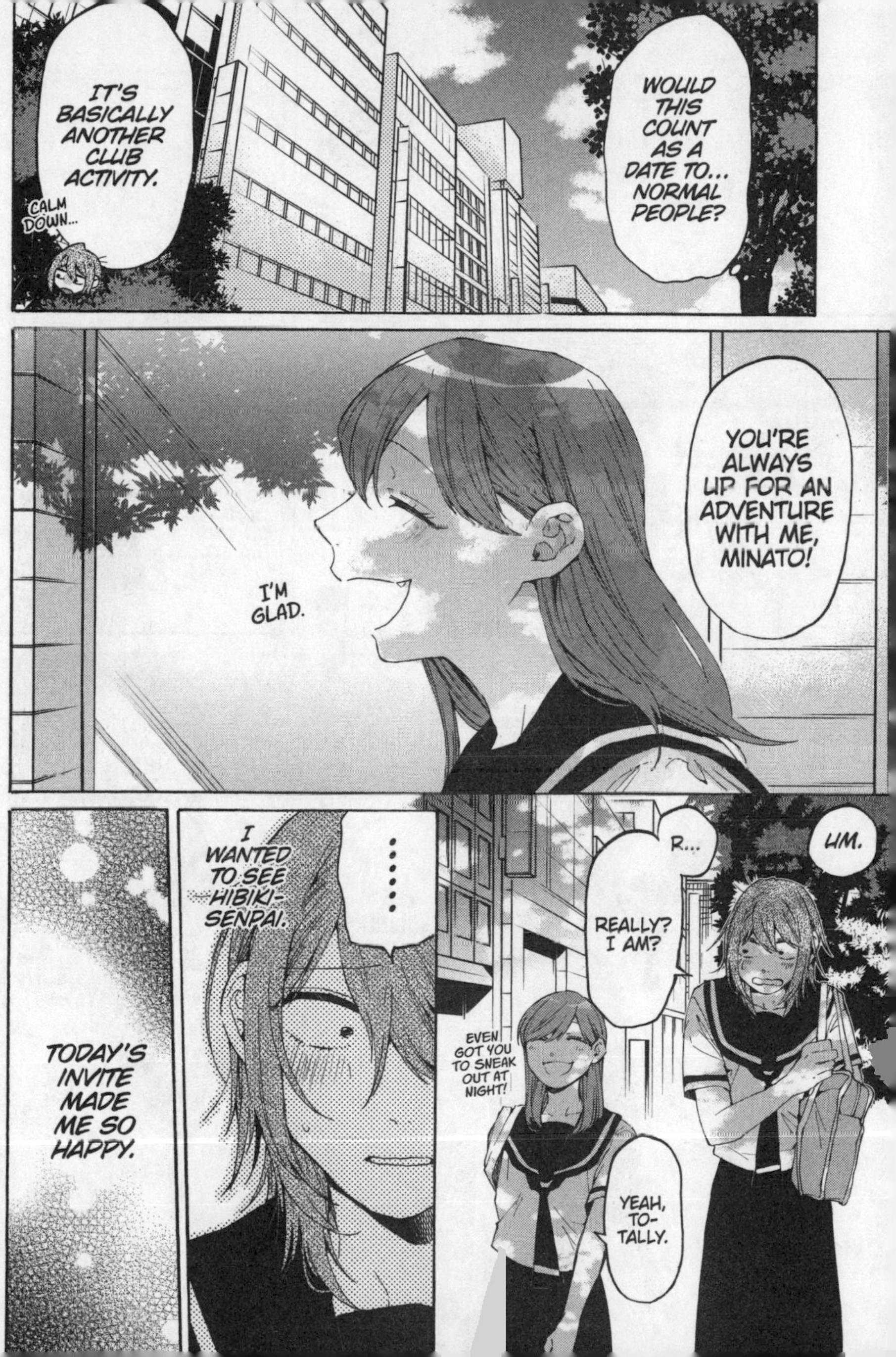
WOULD THIS COUNT AS A DATE TO... NORMAL PEOPLE?
IT'S BASICALLY ANOTHER CLUB ACTIVITY.
CALM DOWN...
YOU'RE ALWAYS UP FOR AN ADVENTURE WITH ME, MINATO!
I'M GLAD.
UM.
R...
REALLY? I AM?
EVEN GOT YOU TO SNEAK OUT AT NIGHT!
YEAH, TO-TALLY.
......
I WANTED TO SEE HIBIKI-SENPAI.
TODAY'S INVITE MADE ME SO HAPPY.

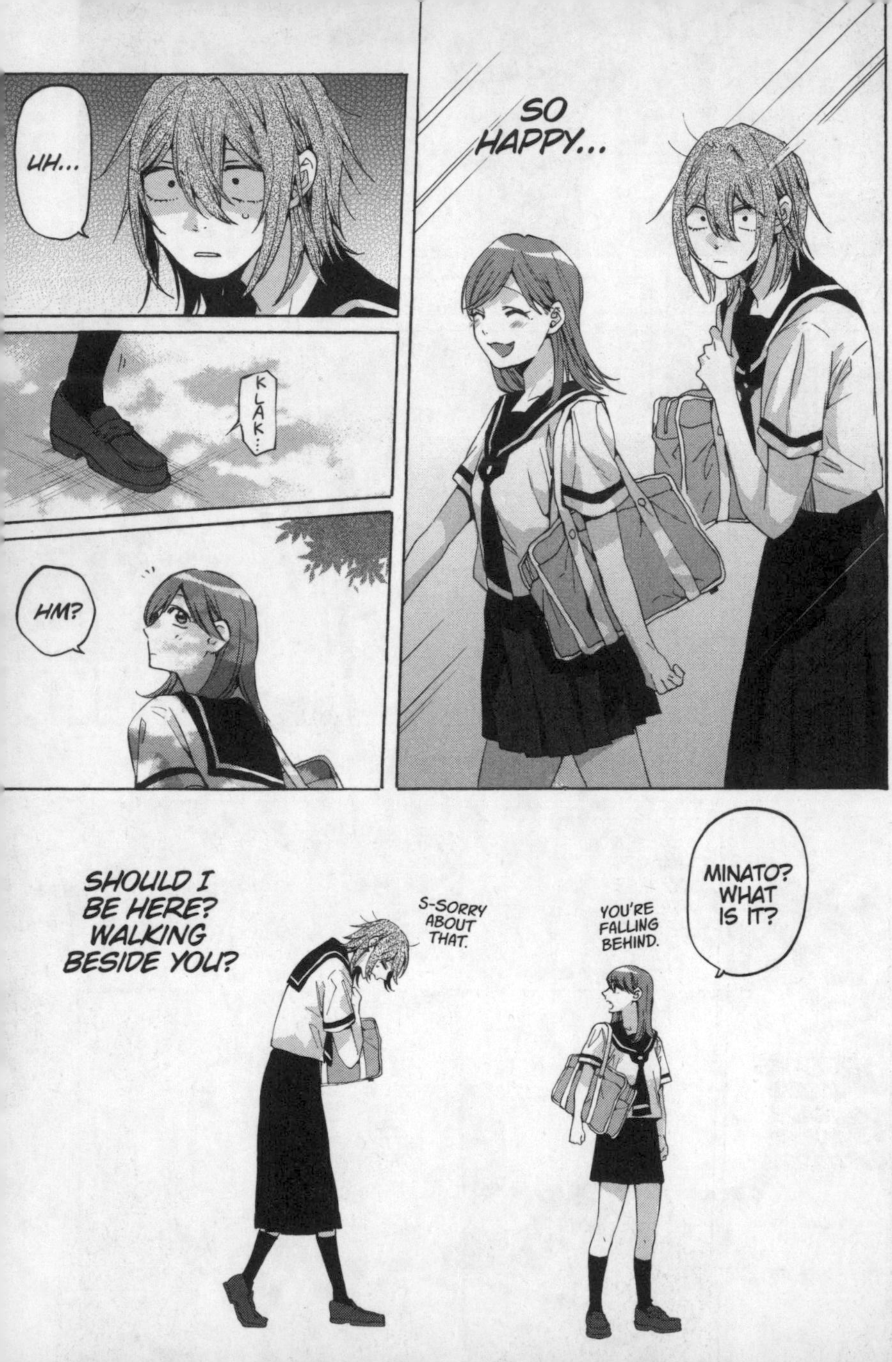
SO HAPPY...
UH...
KLAK...
HM?
MINATO? WHAT IS IT?
YOU'RE FALLING BEHIND.
S-SORRY ABOUT THAT.
SHOULD I BE HERE? WALKING BESIDE YOU?

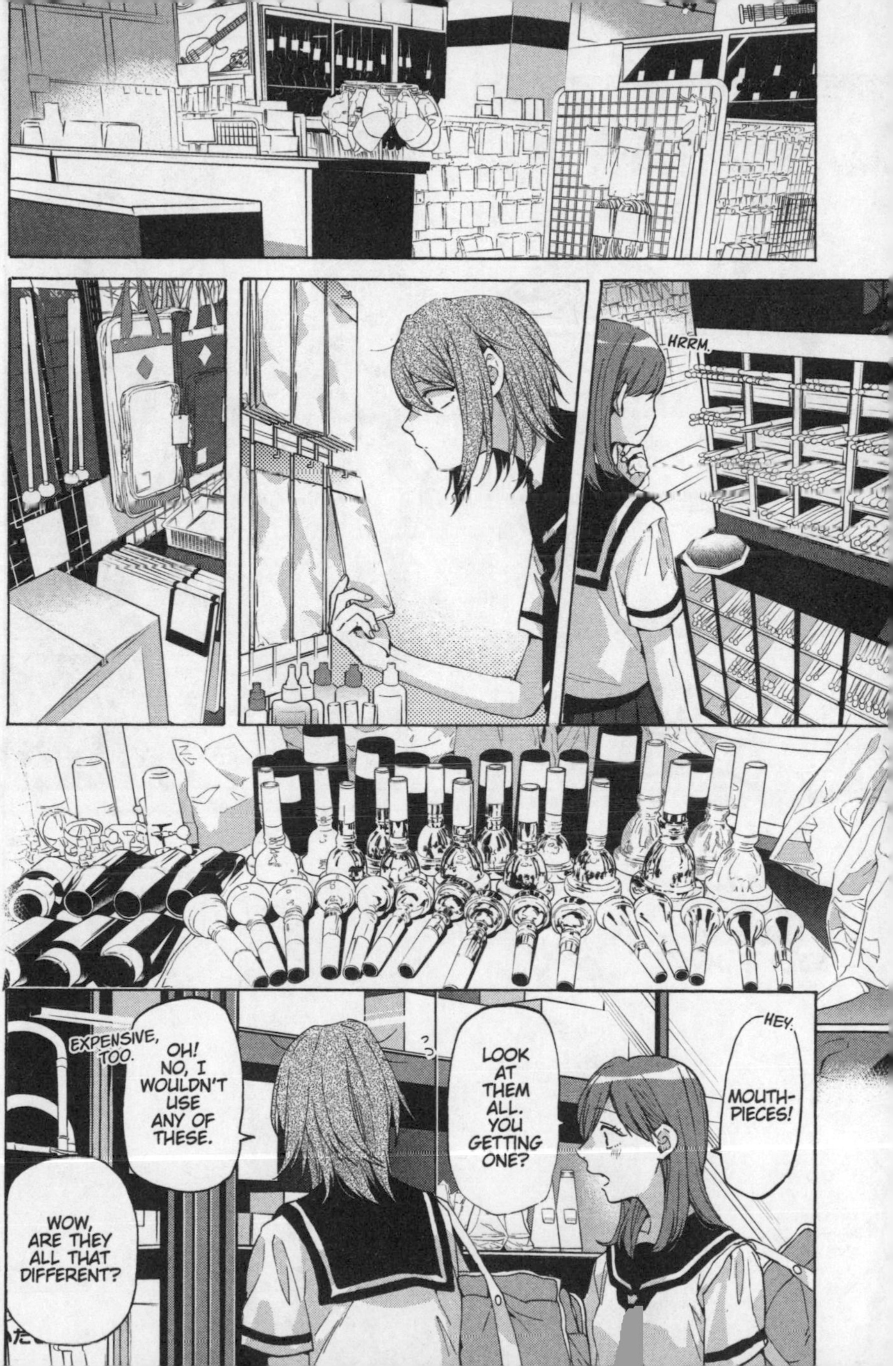
HRRM.
HEY.
MOUTH-PIECES!
LOOK AT THEM ALL. YOU GETTING ONE?
OH! NO, I WOULDN'T USE ANY OF THESE.
EXPENSIVE, TOO.
WOW, ARE THEY ALL THAT DIFFERENT?

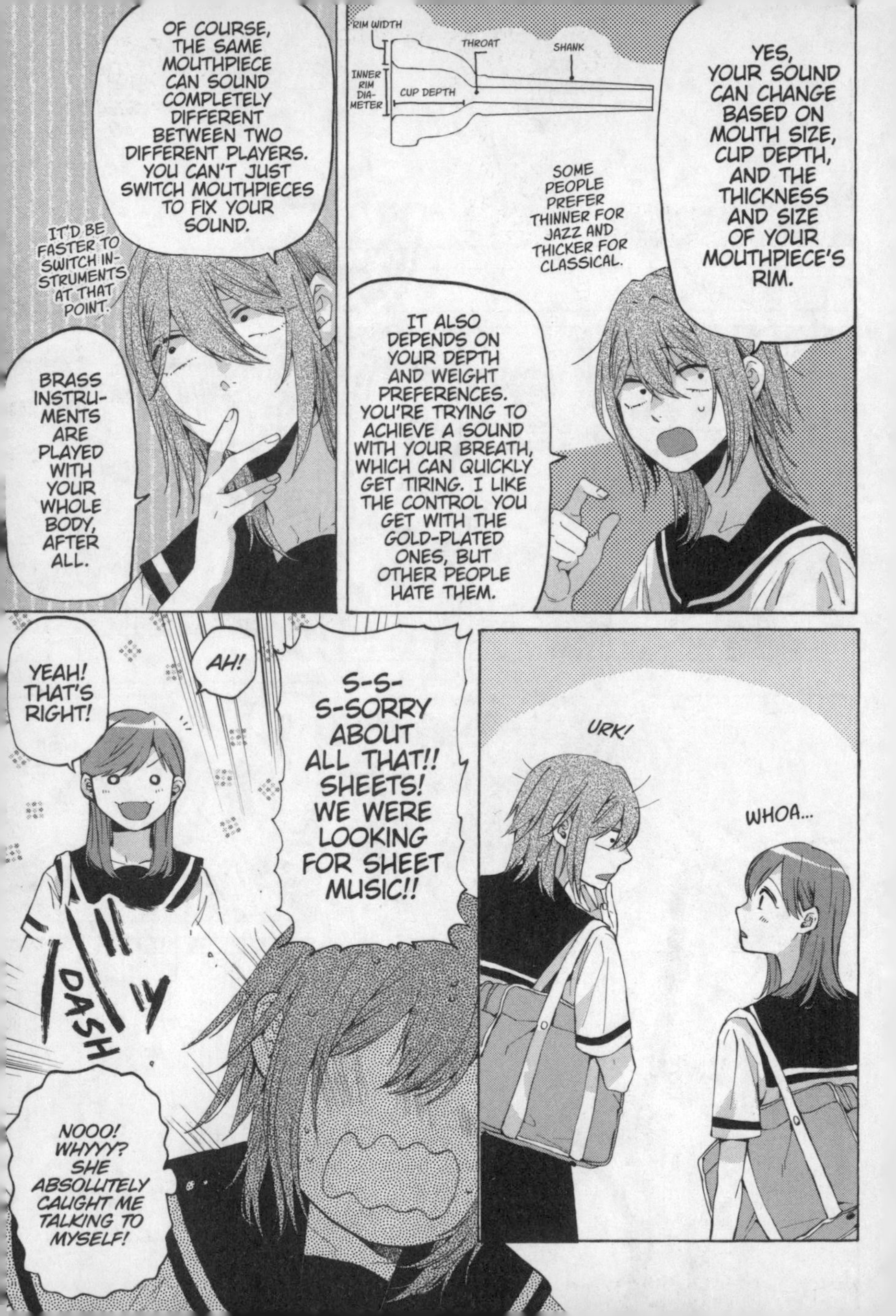
RIM WIDTH
THROAT
SHANK
INNER RIM DIA-METER
CUP DEPTH
YES, YOUR SOUND CAN CHANGE BASED ON MOUTH SIZE, CUP DEPTH, AND THE THICKNESS AND SIZE OF YOUR MOUTHPIECE'S RIM.
SOME PEOPLE PREFER THINNER FOR JAZZ AND THICKER FOR CLASSICAL.
IT ALSO DEPENDS ON YOUR DEPTH AND WEIGHT PREFERENCES. YOU'RE TRYING TO ACHIEVE A SOUND WITH YOUR BREATH, WHICH CAN QUICKLY GET TIRING. I LIKE THE CONTROL YOU GET WITH THE GOLD-PLATED ONES, BUT OTHER PEOPLE HATE THEM.
OF COURSE, THE SAME MOUTHPIECE CAN SOUND COMPLETELY DIFFERENT BETWEEN TWO DIFFERENT PLAYERS. YOU CAN'T JUST SWITCH MOUTHPIECES TO FIX YOUR SOUND.
IT'D BE FASTER TO SWITCH IN-STRUMENTS AT THAT POINT.
BRASS INSTRU-MENTS ARE PLAYED WITH YOUR WHOLE BODY, AFTER ALL.
URK!
WHOA...
AH!
S-S-S-SORRY ABOUT ALL THAT!! SHEETS! WE WERE LOOKING FOR SHEET MUSIC!!
YEAH! THAT'S RIGHT!
DASH
NOOO! WHYYY? SHE ABSOLUTELY CAUGHT ME TALKING TO MYSELF!

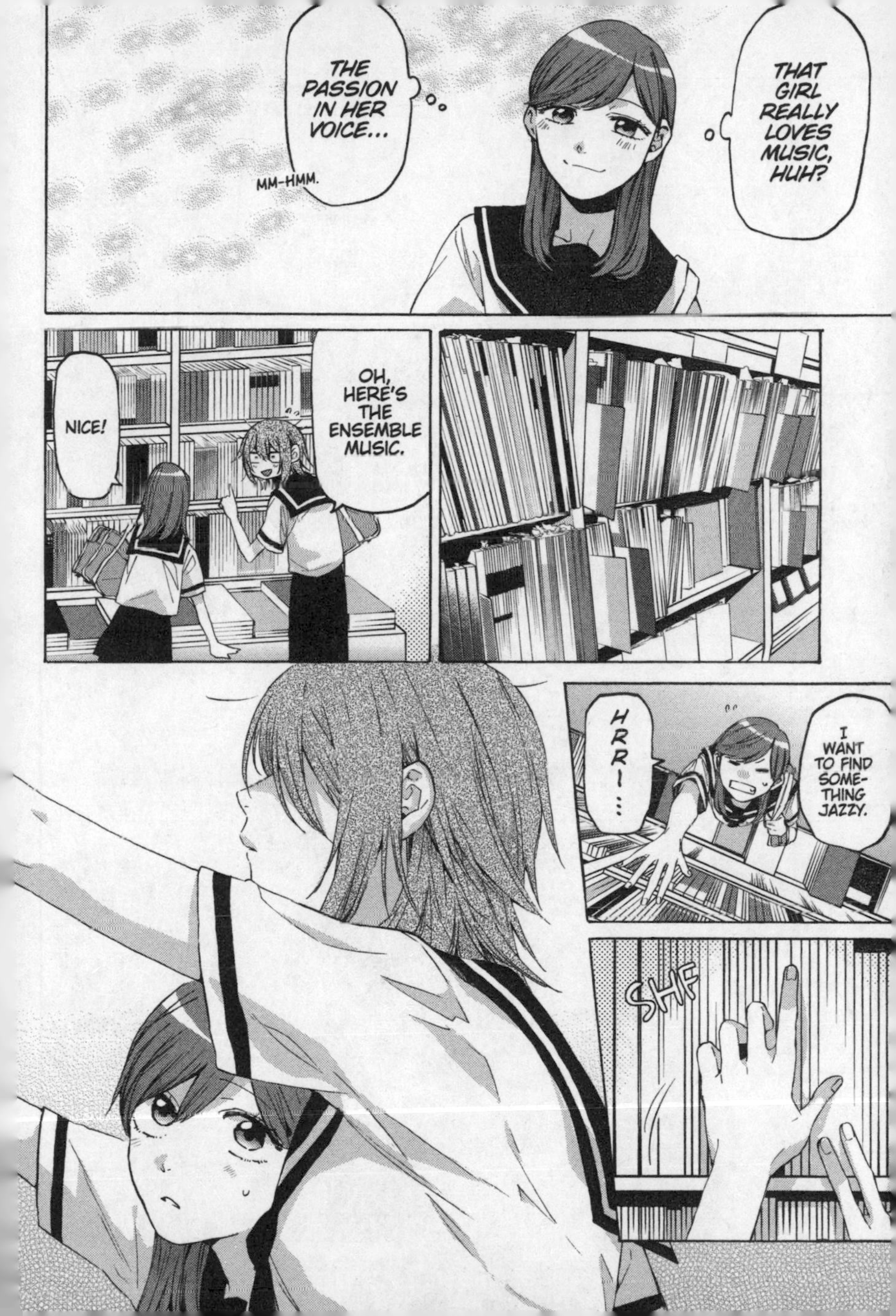
THAT GIRL REALLY LOVES MUSIC, HUH?
THE PASSION IN HER VOICE...
MM-HMM.
OH, HERE'S THE ENSEMBLE MUSIC.
NICE!
I WANT TO FIND SOMETHING JAZZY.
HRR!...
SHF

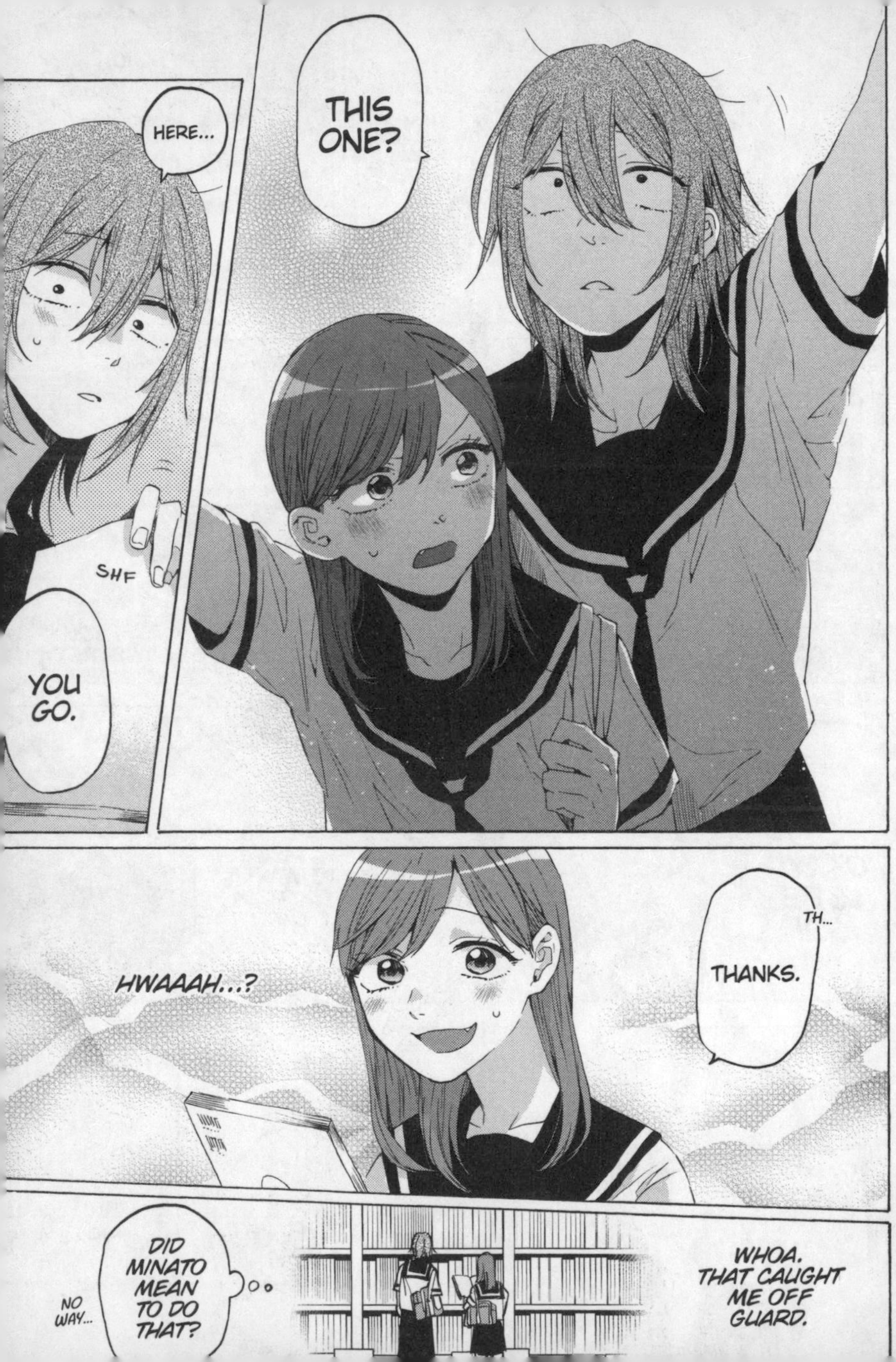
THIS ONE?
HERE...
SHF
YOU GO.
TH...
THANKS.
HWAAAH...?
WHOA. THAT CAUGHT ME OFF GUARD.
DID MINATO MEAN TO DO THAT?
NO WAY...

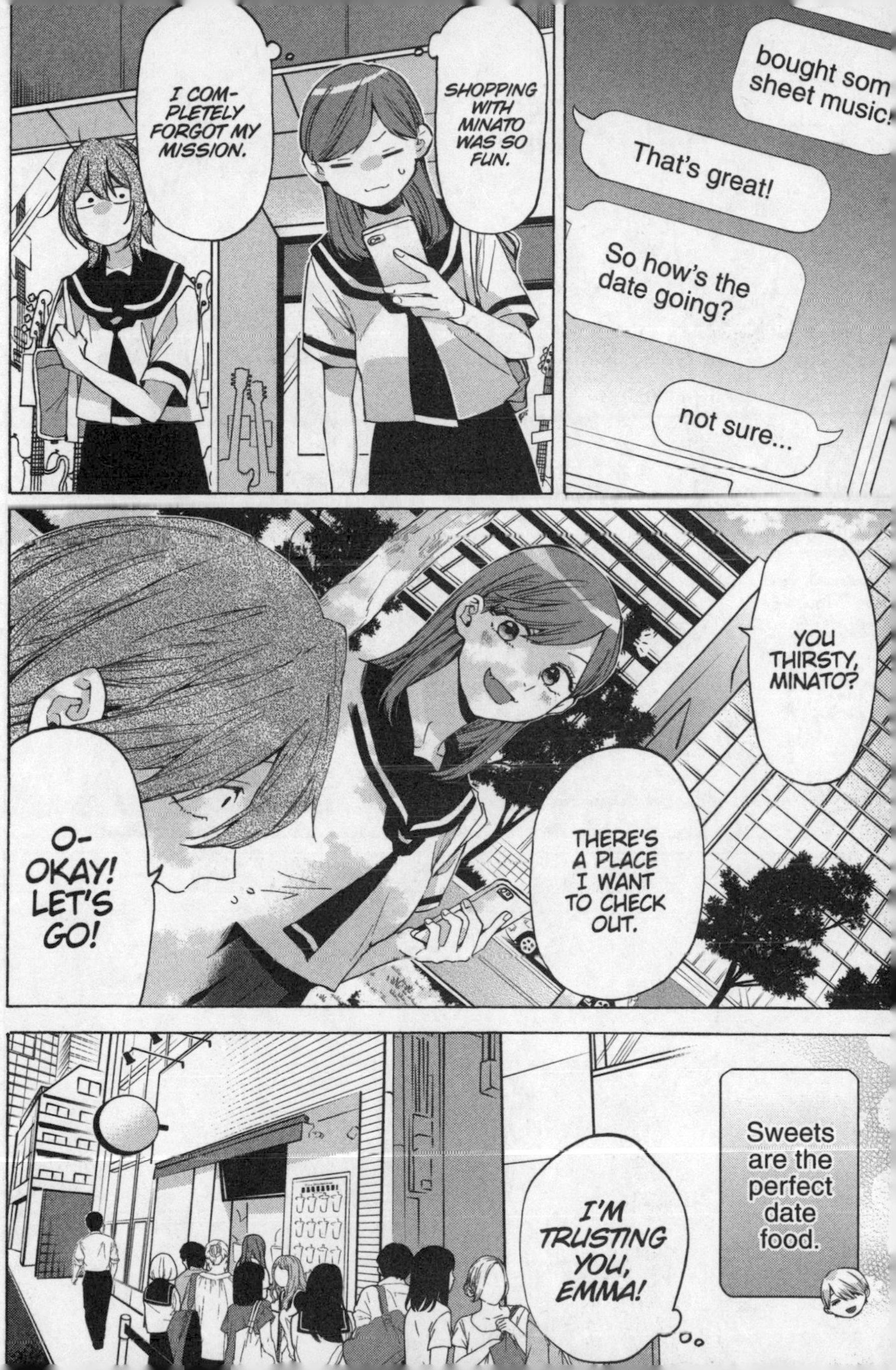
bought som sheet music!
That's great!
So how's the date going?
not sure...
SHOPPING WITH MINATO WAS SO FUN.
I COM-PLETELY FORGOT MY MISSION.
YOU THIRSTY, MINATO?
THERE'S A PLACE I WANT TO CHECK OUT.
O-OKAY! LET'S GO!
Sweets are the perfect date food.
I'M TRUSTING YOU, EMMA!

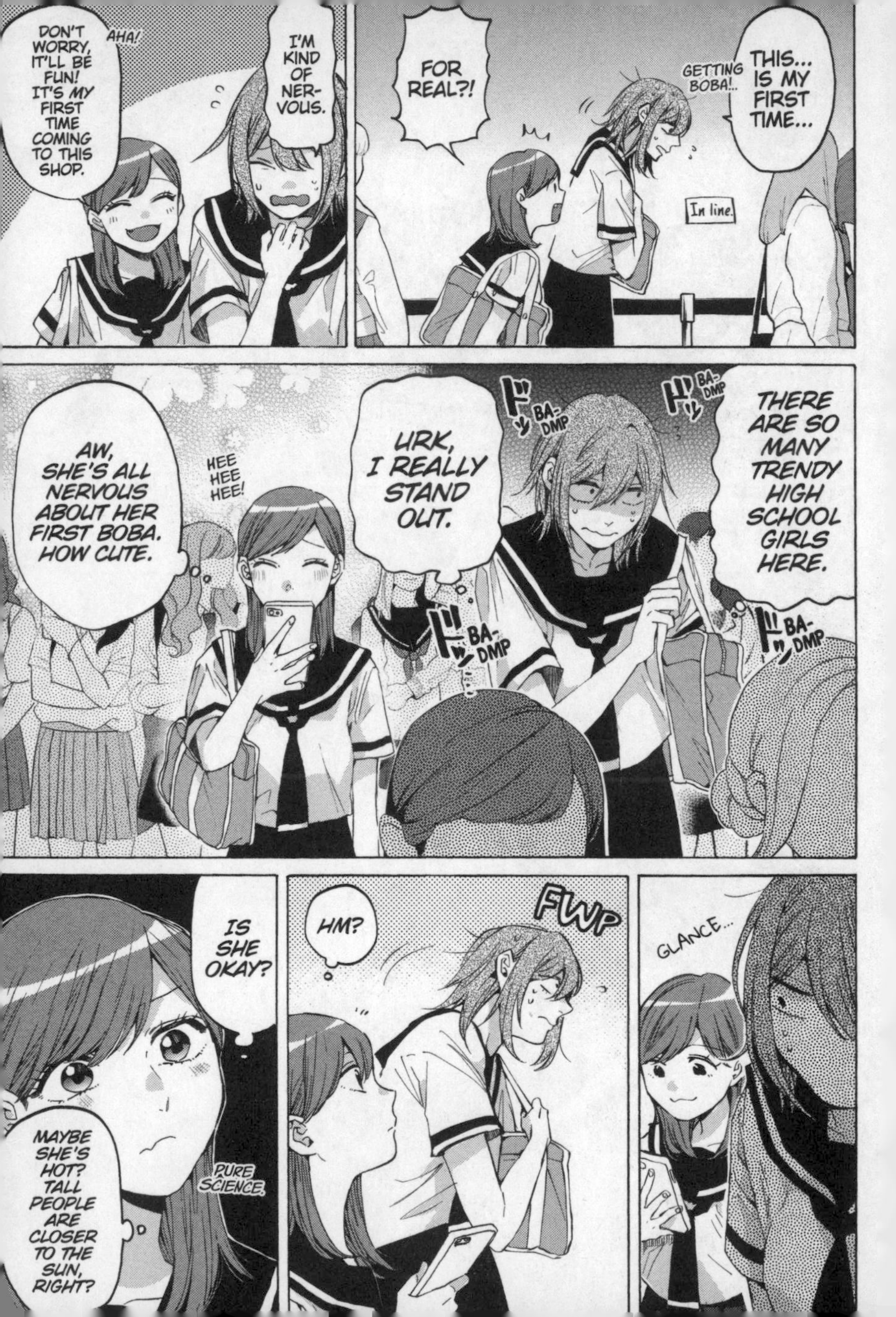
THIS... IS MY FIRST TIME...
GETTING BOBA!...
In line.
FOR REAL?!
I'M KIND OF NERVOUS.
DON'T WORRY, IT'LL BE FUN! IT'S MY FIRST TIME COMING TO THIS SHOP.
AHA!
THERE ARE SO MANY TRENDY HIGH SCHOOL GIRLS HERE.
BA-DMP
BA-DMP
BA-DMP
URK, I REALLY STAND OUT.
BA-DMP
HEE HEE HEE!
AW, SHE'S ALL NERVOUS ABOUT HER FIRST BOBA. HOW CUTE.
GLANCE...
FWP
HM?
IS SHE OKAY?
MAYBE SHE'S HOT? TALL PEOPLE ARE CLOSER TO THE SUN, RIGHT?
PURE SCIENCE.

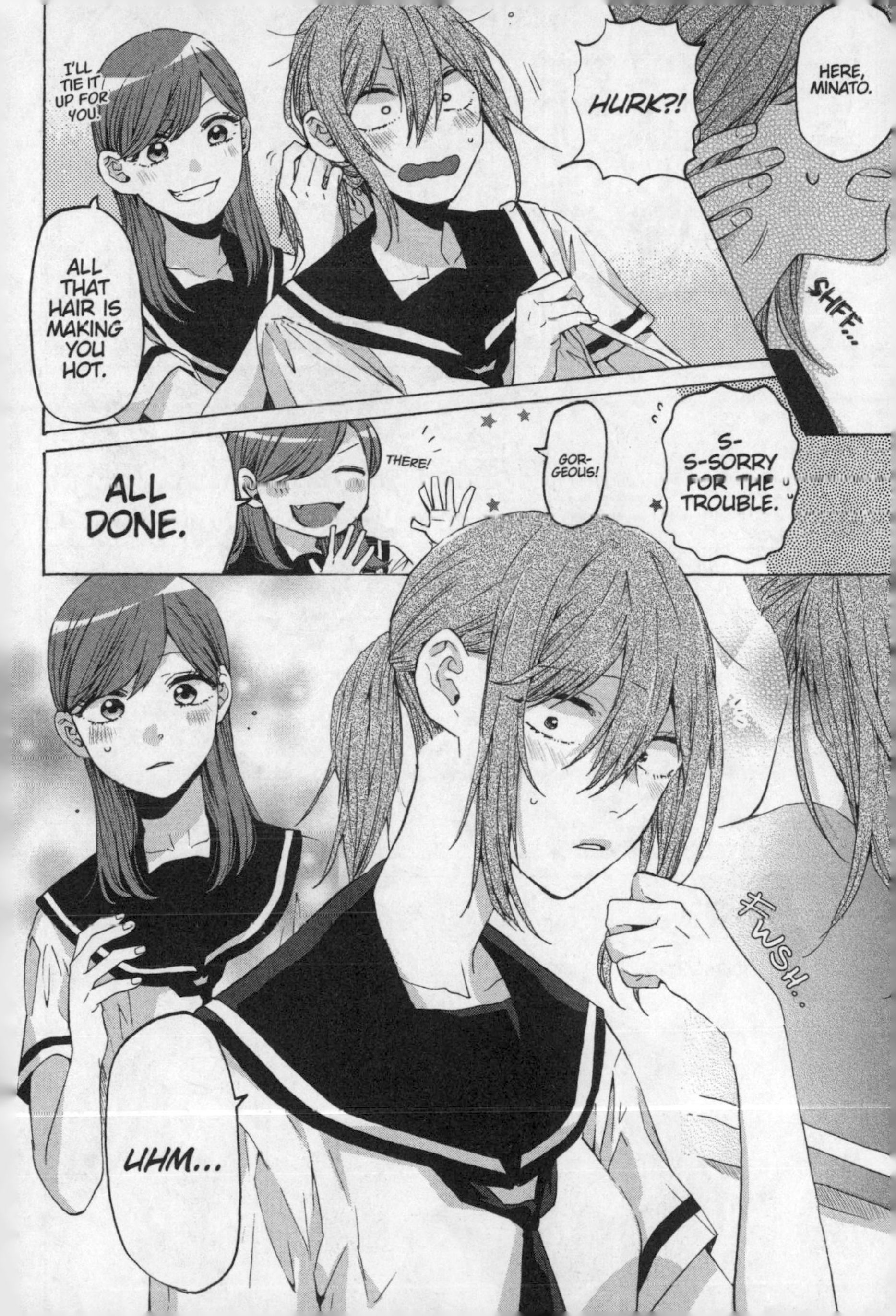
HERE, MINATO.
HURK?!
SHFF...
I'LL TIE IT UP FOR YOU.
ALL THAT HAIR IS MAKING YOU HOT.
S-S-SORRY FOR THE TROUBLE.
GOR-GEOUS!
THERE!
ALL DONE.
FWSH..
UHM...

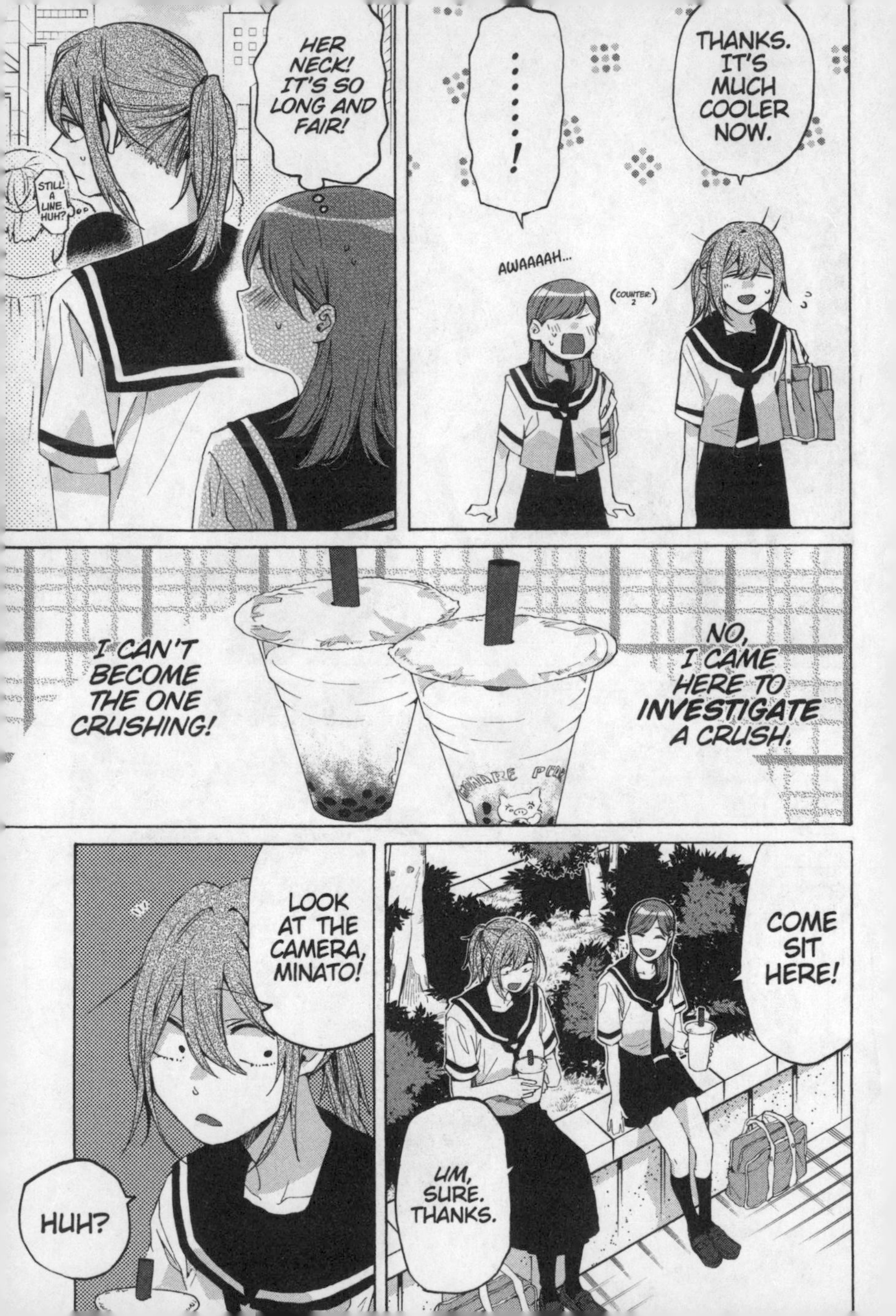
THANKS. IT'S MUCH COOLER NOW.
......!
AWAAAAH...
(COUNTER: 2)
HER NECK! IT'S SO LONG AND FAIR!
STILL A LINE, HUH?
NO, I CAME HERE TO INVESTIGATE A CRUSH.
I CAN'T BECOME THE ONE CRUSHING!
COME SIT HERE!
UM, SURE. THANKS.
LOOK AT THE CAMERA, MINATO!
HUH?

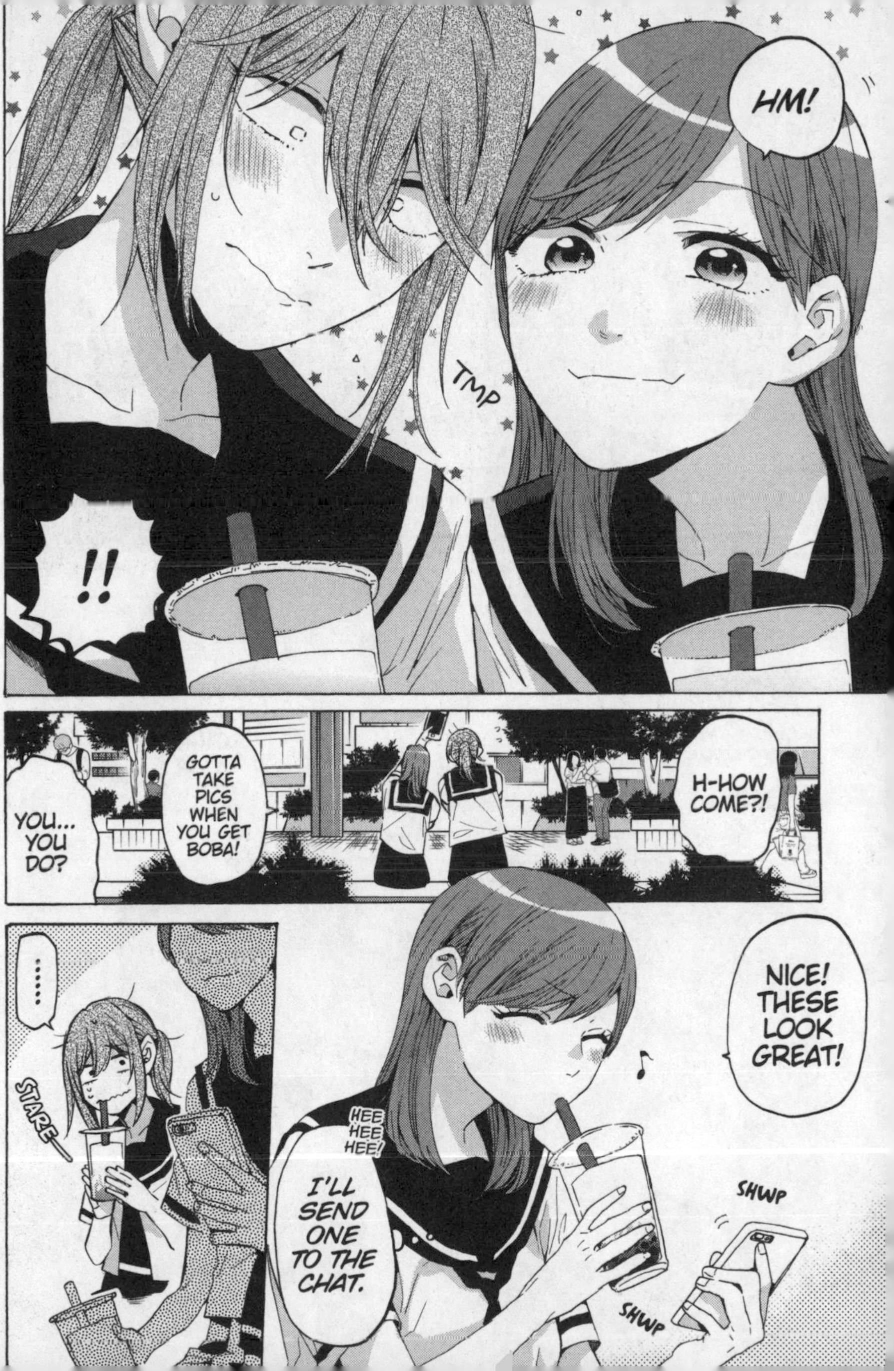
HM!
TMP
!!
H-HOW COME?!
GOTTA TAKE PICS WHEN YOU GET BOBA!
YOU... YOU DO?
NICE! THESE LOOK GREAT!
SHWP
HEE HEE HEE!
I'LL SEND ONE TO THE CHAT.
SHWP
......
STARE

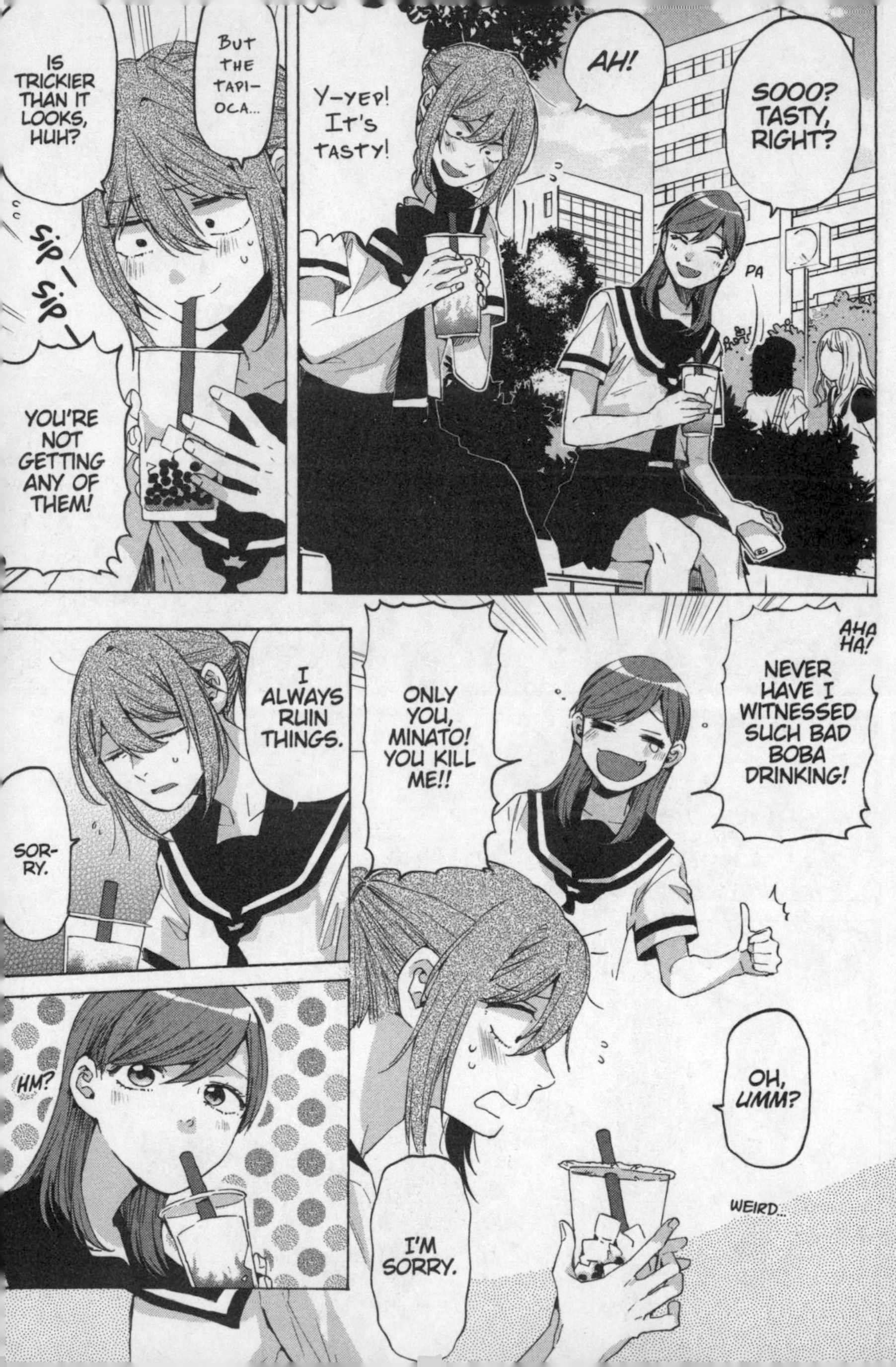
SOOO? TASTY, RIGHT?
AH!
Y-YEP! It's tasty!
PA
BUT THE TAPI-OCA...
IS TRICKIER THAN IT LOOKS, HUH?
SIP—SIP—
YOU'RE NOT GETTING ANY OF THEM!
AHAHA!
NEVER HAVE I WITNESSED SUCH BAD BOBA DRINKING!
ONLY YOU, MINATO! YOU KILL ME!!
I ALWAYS RUIN THINGS.
SOR-RY.
OH, UMM?
WEIRD...
I'M SORRY.
HM?

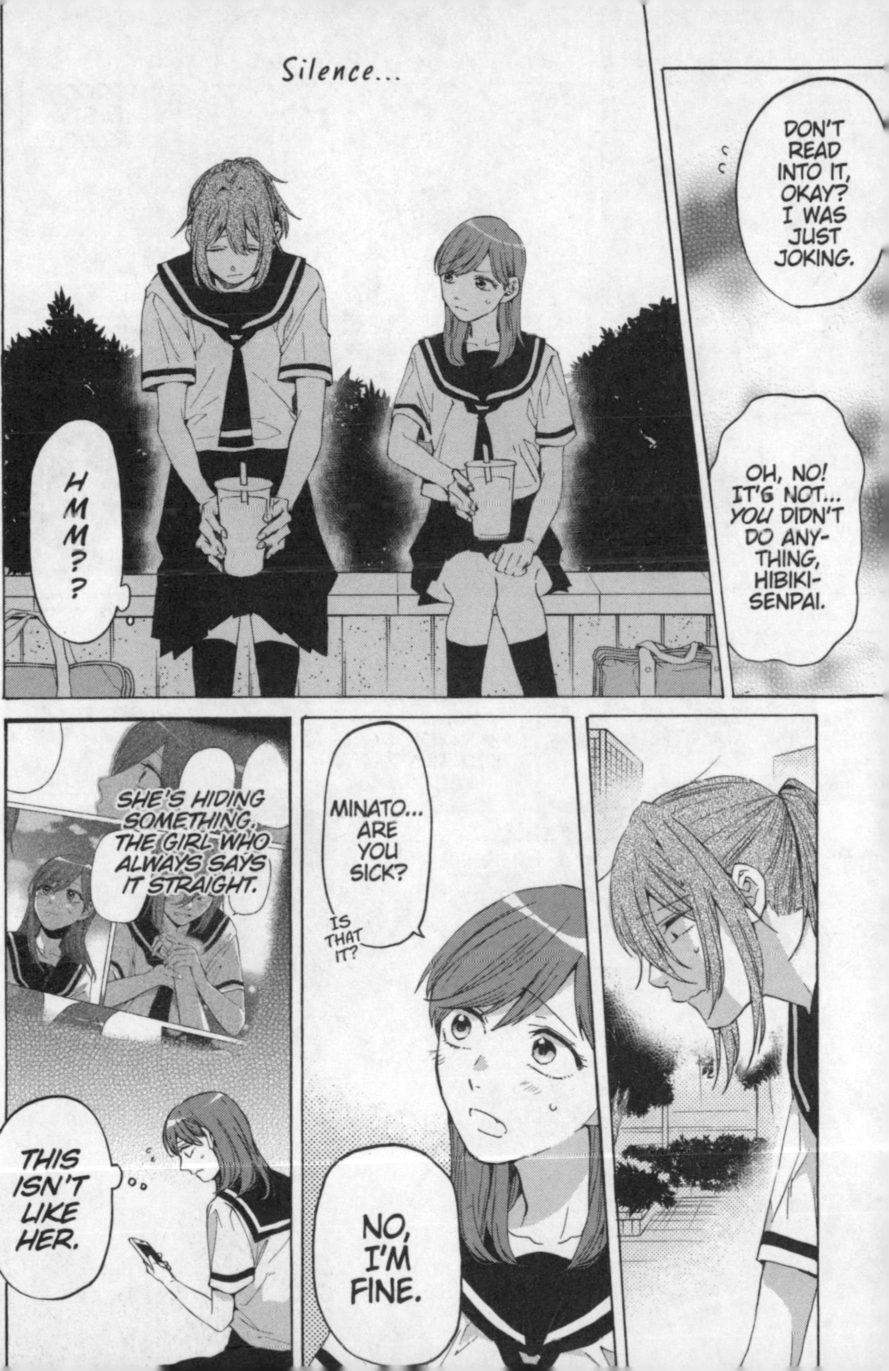
DON'T READ INTO IT, OKAY? I WAS JUST JOKING.
OH, NO! IT'S NOT... YOU DIDN'T DO ANYTHING, HIBIKI-SENPAI.
Silence...
HMM??
MINATO... ARE YOU SICK?
IS THAT IT?
NO, I'M FINE.
SHE'S HIDING SOMETHING. THE GIRL WHO ALWAYS SAYS IT STRAIGHT.
THIS ISN'T LIKE HER.

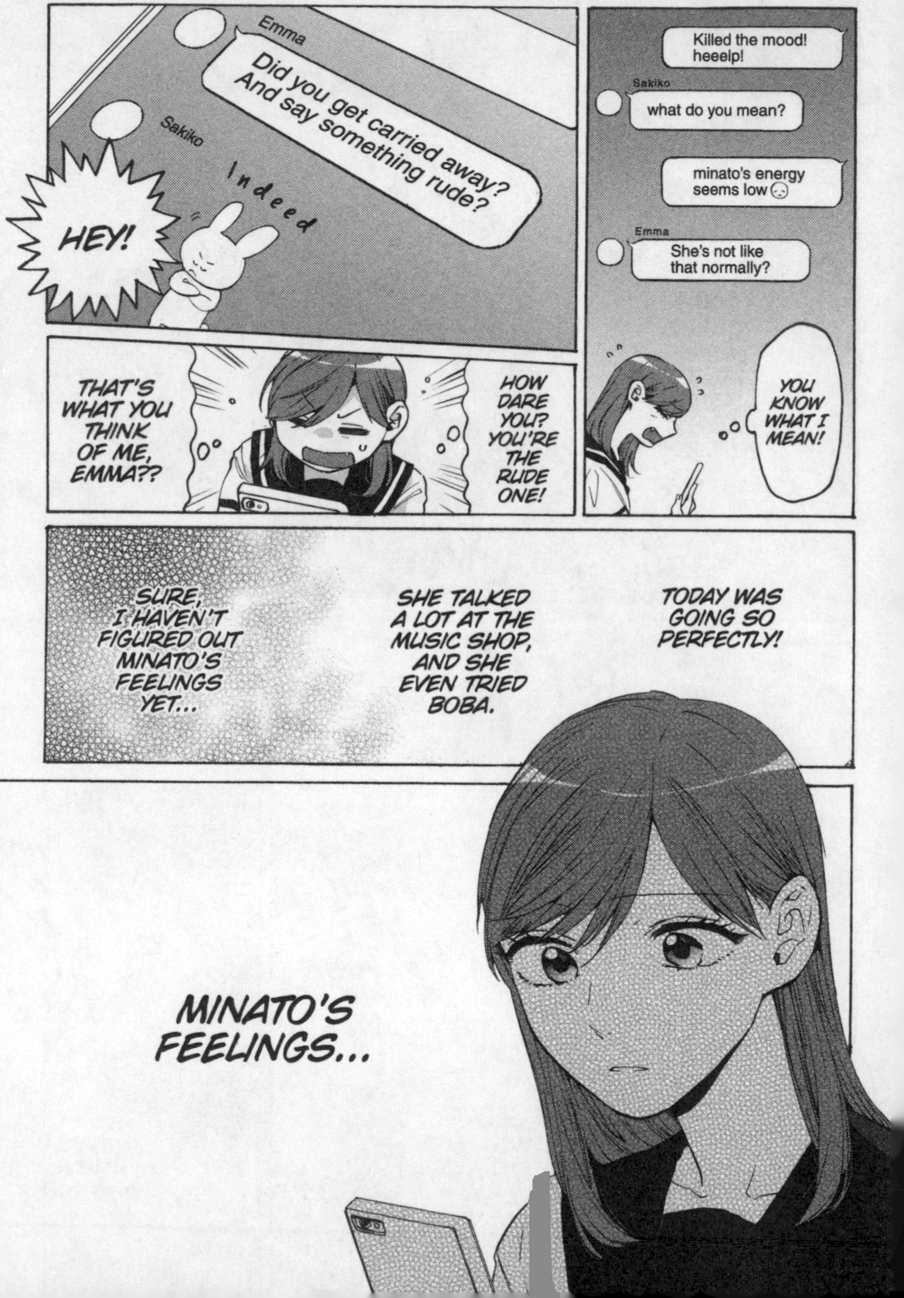
Killed the mood! heeelp!
Sakiko
what do you mean?
minato's energy seems low
Emma
She's not like that normally?
Emma
Did you get carried away? And say something rude?
Sakiko
Indeed
HEY!
YOU KNOW WHAT I MEAN!
HOW DARE YOU? YOU'RE THE RUDE ONE!
THAT'S WHAT YOU THINK OF ME, EMMA??
TODAY WAS GOING SO PERFECTLY!
SHE TALKED A LOT AT THE MUSIC SHOP, AND SHE EVEN TRIED BOBA.
SURE, I HAVEN'T FIGURED OUT MINATO'S FEELINGS YET...
MINATO'S FEELINGS...

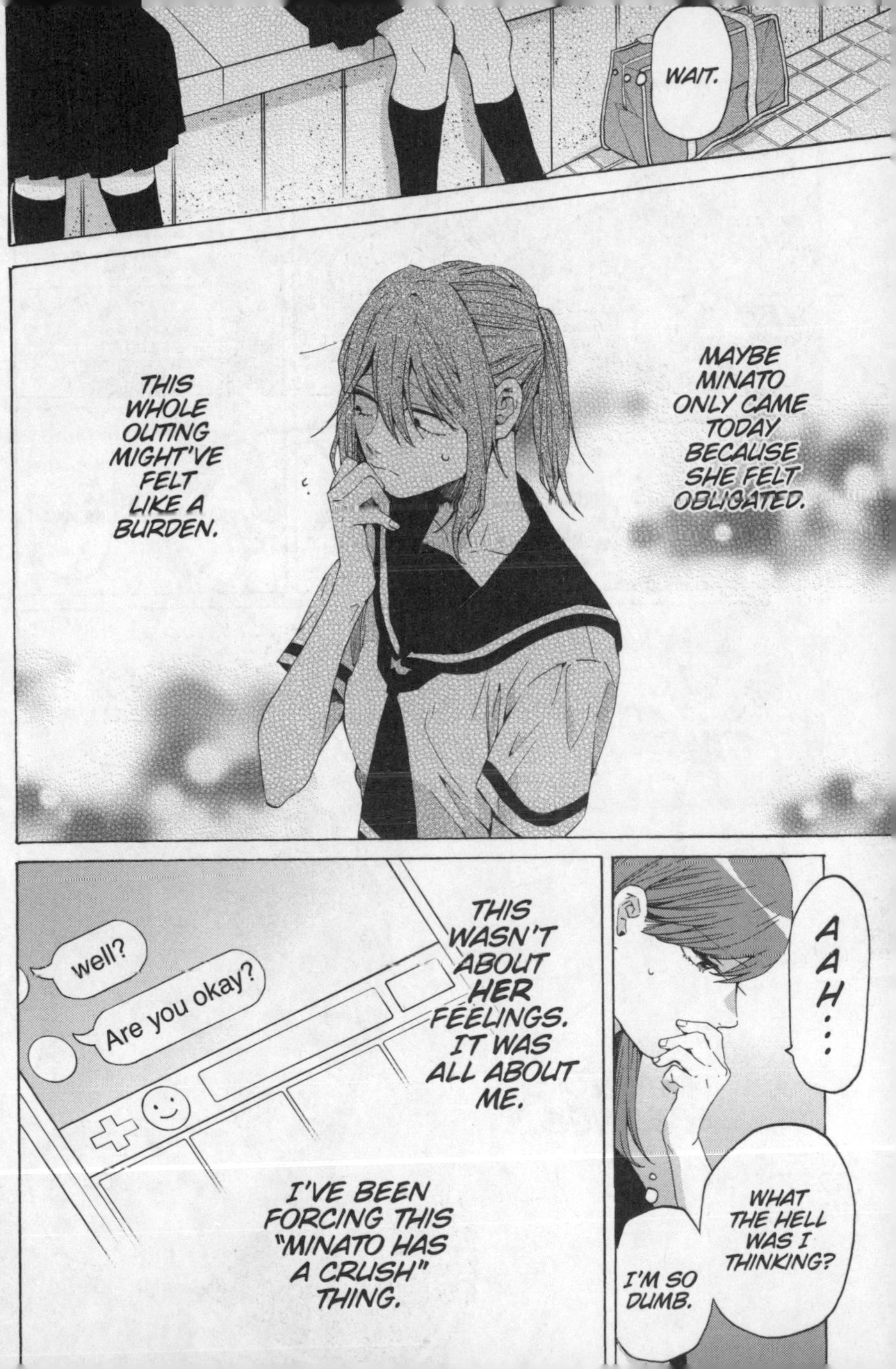
WAIT.
MAYBE MINATO ONLY CAME TODAY BECAUSE SHE FELT OBLIGATED.
THIS WHOLE OUTING MIGHT'VE FELT LIKE A BURDEN.
AAH...
WHAT THE HELL WAS I THINKING?
I'M SO DUMB.
THIS WASN'T ABOUT HER FEELINGS. IT WAS ALL ABOUT ME.
well?
Are you okay?
I'VE BEEN FORCING THIS "MINATO HAS A CRUSH" THING.

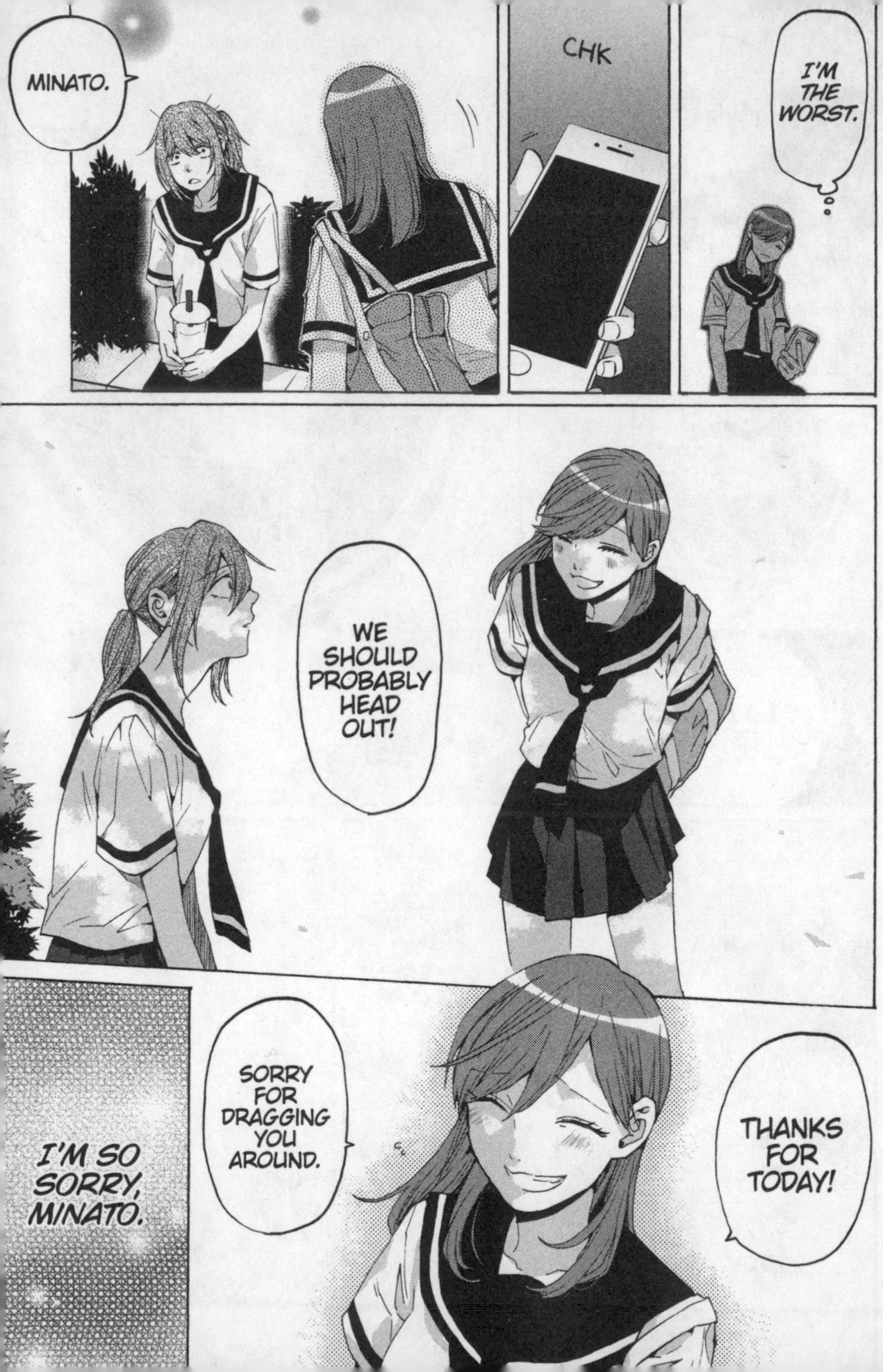
I'M THE WORST.
CHK
MINATO.
WE SHOULD PROBABLY HEAD OUT!
THANKS FOR TODAY!
SORRY FOR DRAGGING YOU AROUND.
I'M SO SORRY, MINATO.

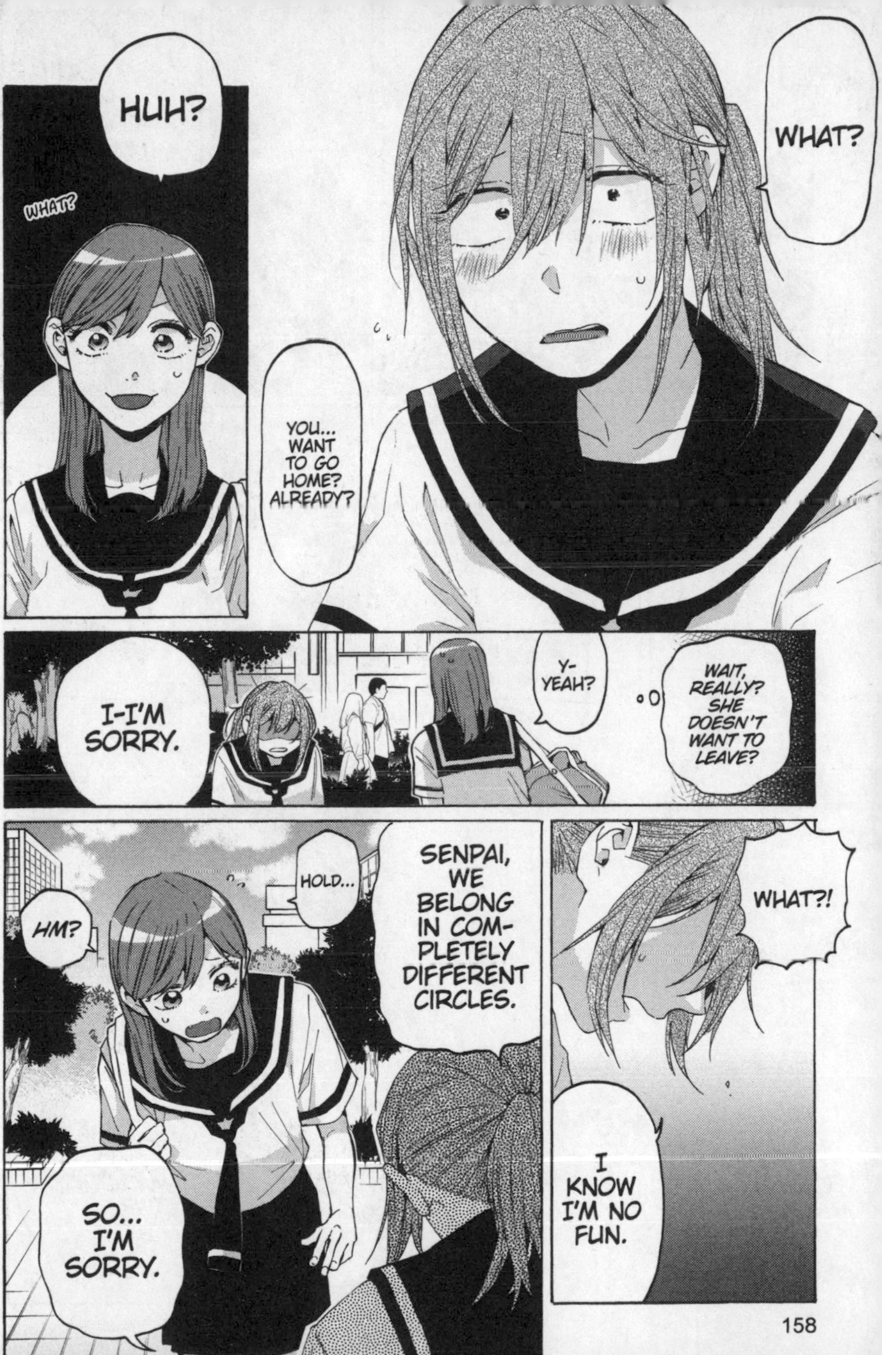
WHAT?
YOU... WANT TO GO HOME? ALREADY?
HUH?
WHAT?
WAIT, REALLY? SHE DOESN'T WANT TO LEAVE?
Y-YEAH?
I-I'M SORRY.
WHAT?!
I KNOW I'M NO FUN.
SENPAI, WE BELONG IN COM-PLETELY DIFFERENT CIRCLES.
HOLD...
HM?
SO... I'M SORRY.

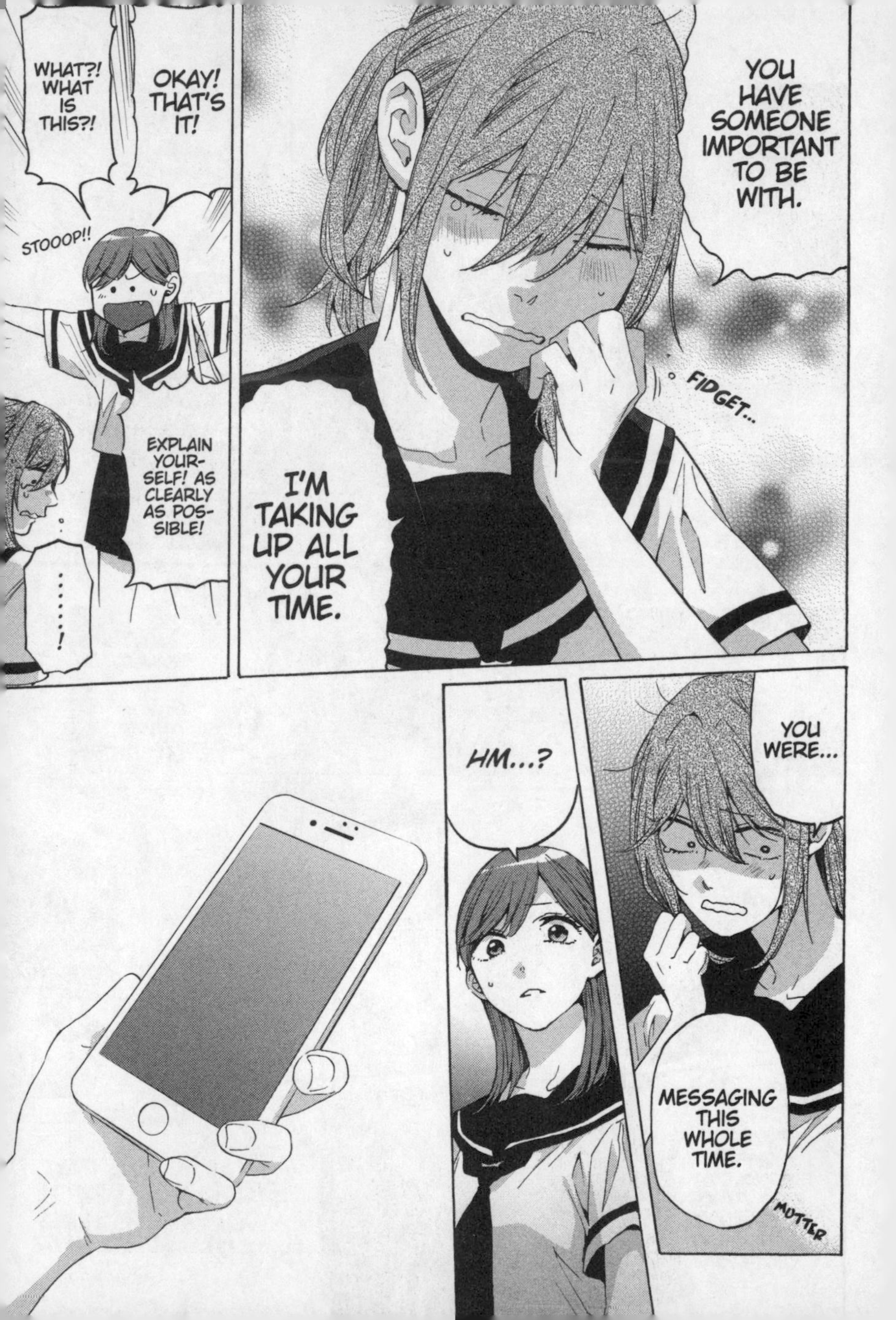
YOU HAVE SOMEONE IMPORTANT TO BE WITH.
FIDGET...
I'M TAKING UP ALL YOUR TIME.
OKAY! THAT'S IT!
WHAT?! WHAT IS THIS?!
STOOOP!!
EXPLAIN YOUR-SELF! AS CLEARLY AS POS-SIBLE!
......!
YOU WERE...
MESSAGING THIS WHOLE TIME.
MUTTER
HM...?

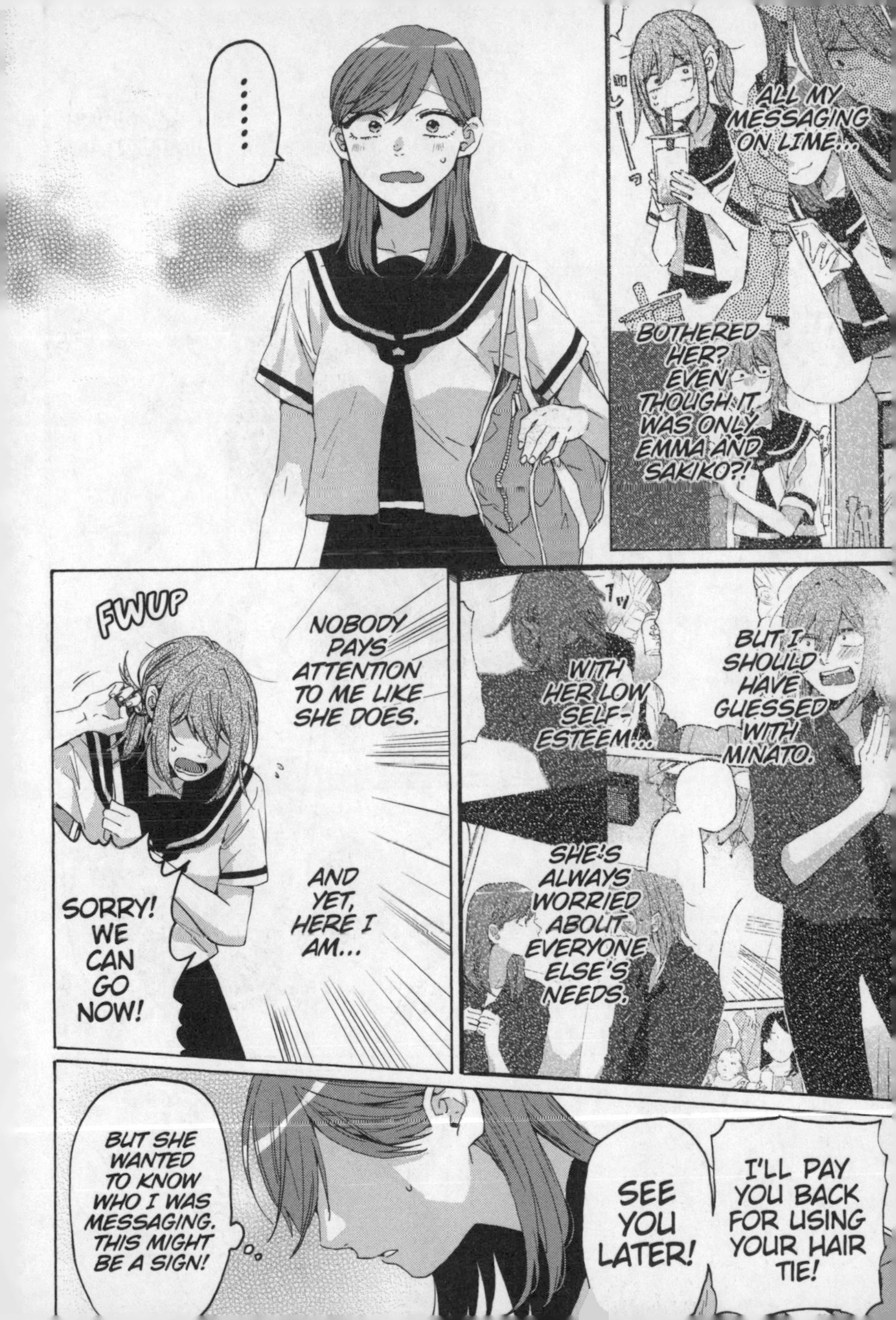
ALL MY MESSAGING ON LIME...
BOTHERED HER? EVEN THOUGH IT WAS ONLY EMMA AND SAKIKO?!
......
BUT I SHOULD HAVE GUESSED WITH MINATO.
WITH HER LOW SELF-ESTEEM...
SHE'S ALWAYS WORRIED ABOUT EVERYONE ELSE'S NEEDS.
FWUP
NOBODY PAYS ATTENTION TO ME LIKE SHE DOES.
AND YET, HERE I AM...
SORRY! WE CAN GO NOW!
I'LL PAY YOU BACK FOR USING YOUR HAIR TIE!
SEE YOU LATER!
BUT SHE WANTED TO KNOW WHO I WAS MESSAGING. THIS MIGHT BE A SIGN!

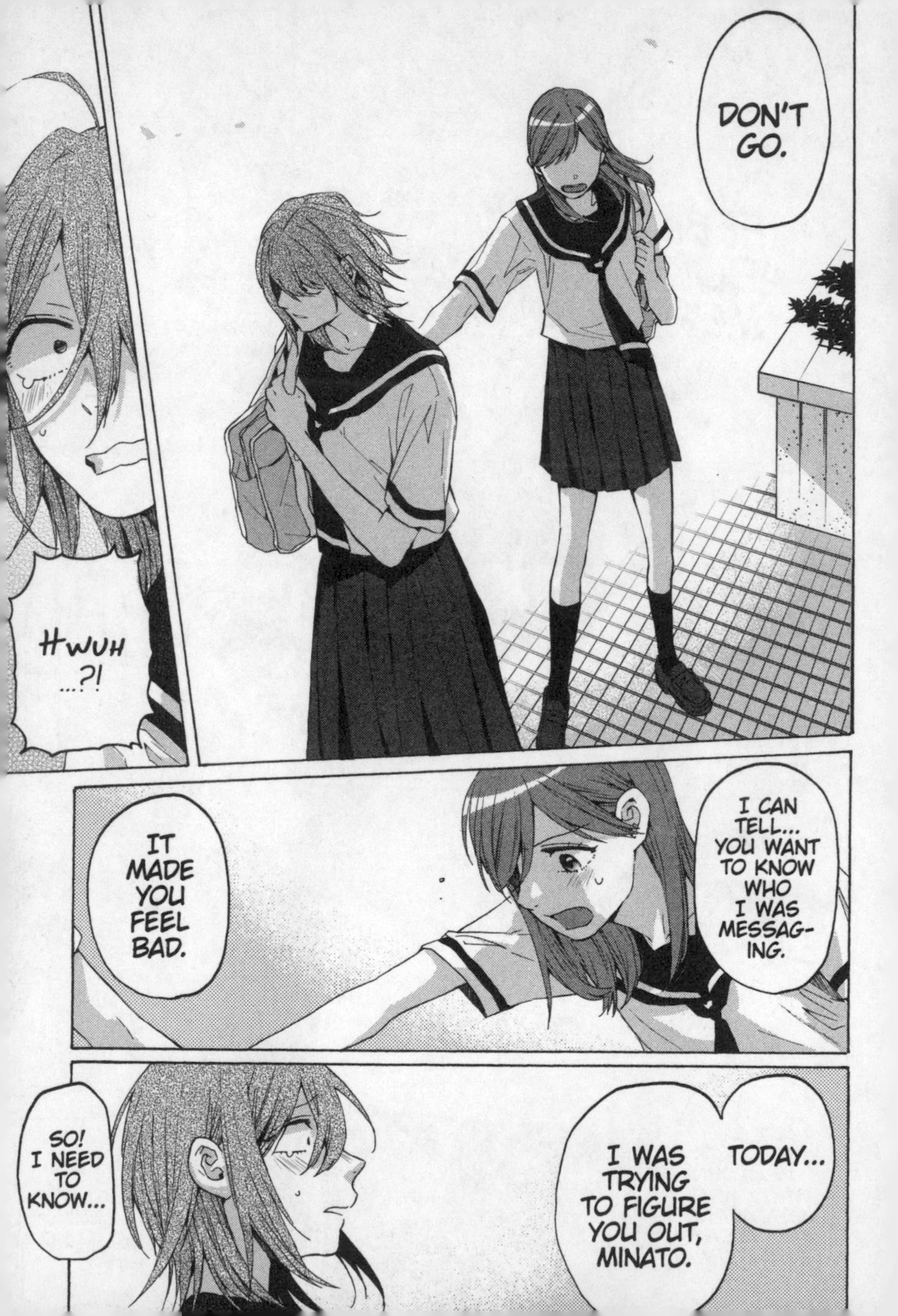
DON'T GO.
HWUH ...?!
I CAN TELL... YOU WANT TO KNOW WHO I WAS MESSAGING.
IT MADE YOU FEEL BAD.
TODAY... I WAS TRYING TO FIGURE YOU OUT, MINATO.
SO! I NEED TO KNOW...

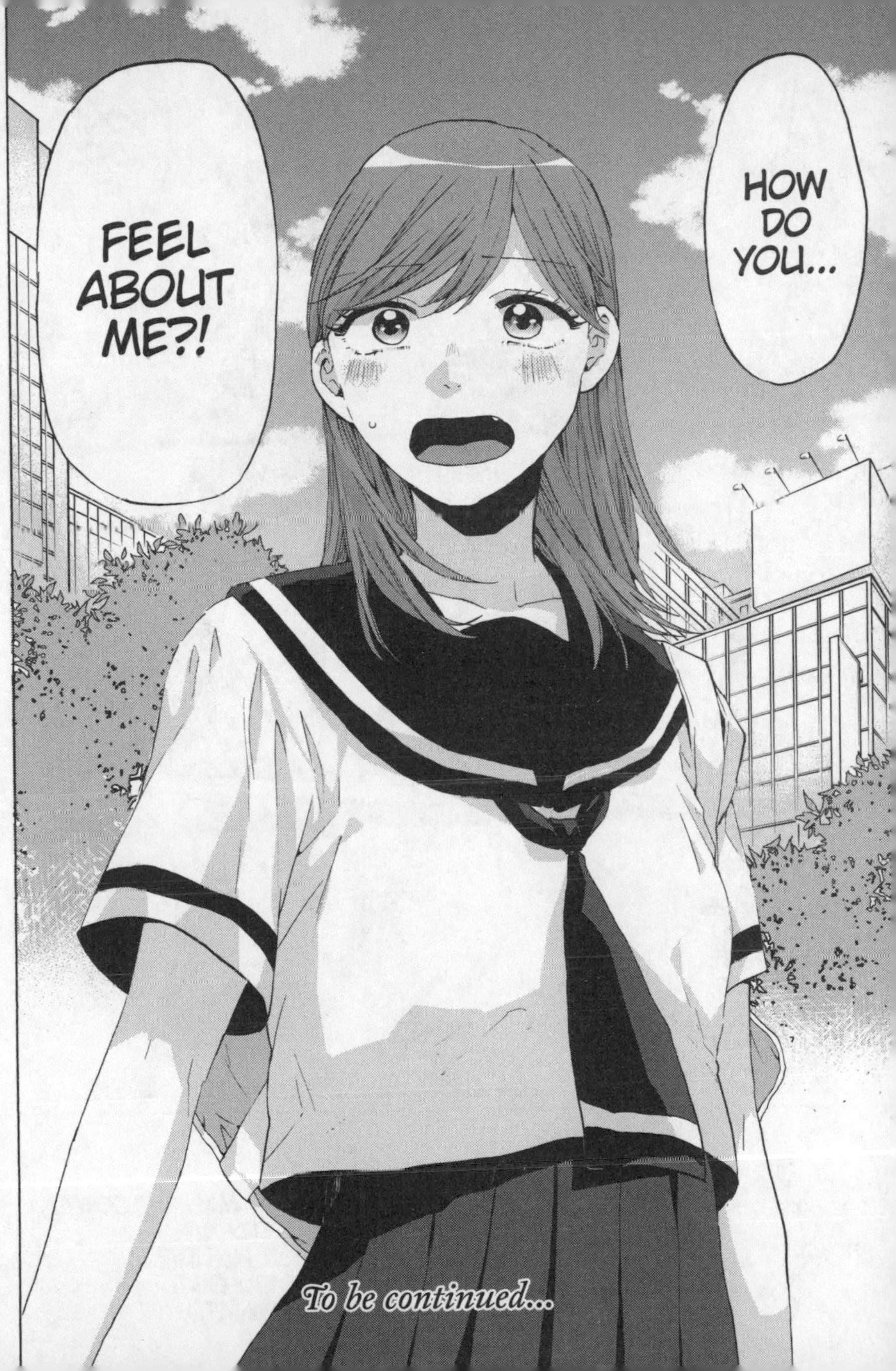
HOW DO YOU...
FEEL ABOUT ME?!
To be continued...

PONYTAIL
HIBIKI

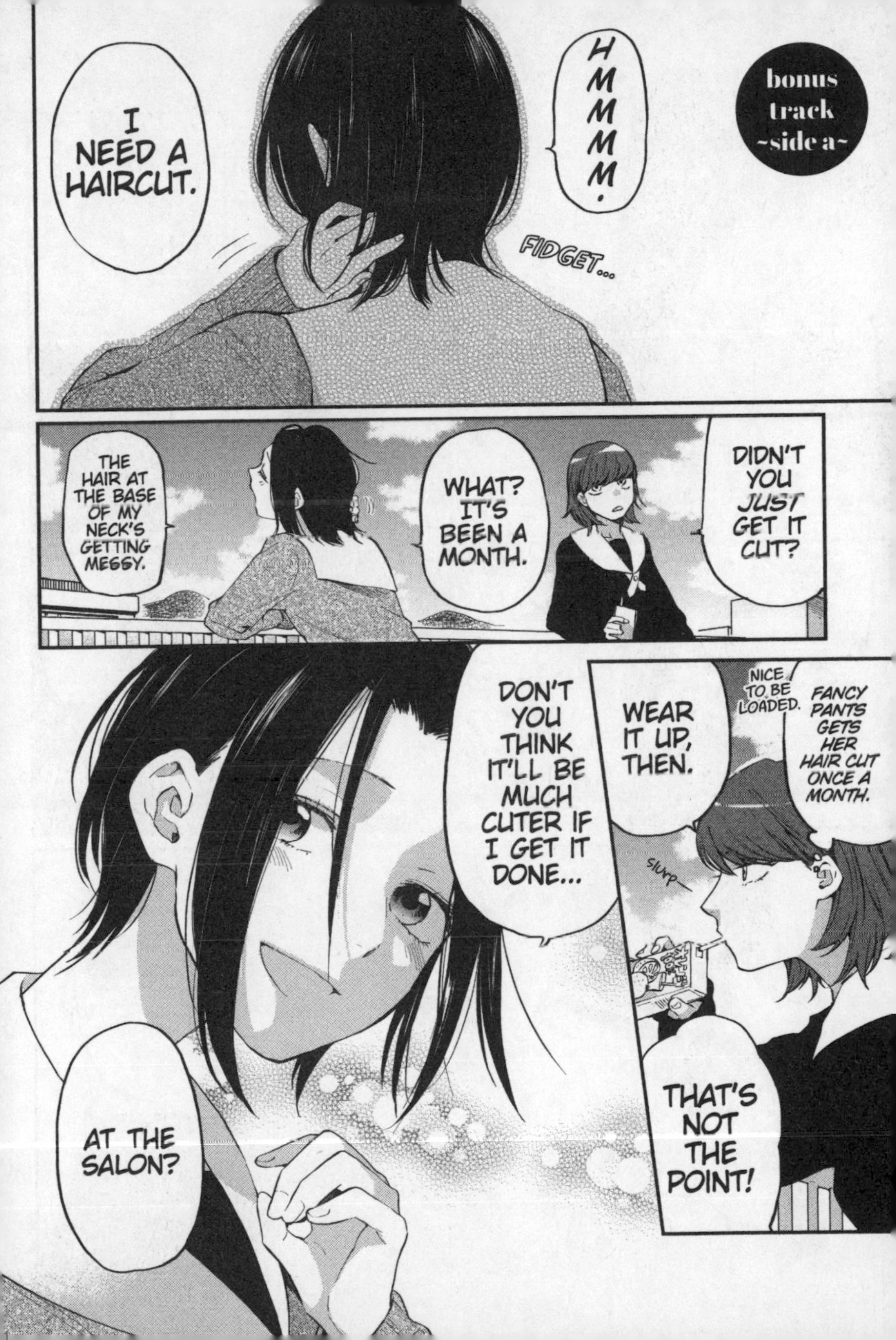
bonus track ~side a~
HMMMM.
FIDGET...
I NEED A HAIRCUT.
DIDN'T YOU JUST GET IT CUT?
WHAT? IT'S BEEN A MONTH.
THE HAIR AT THE BASE OF MY NECK'S GETTING MESSY.
FANCY PANTS GETS HER HAIR CUT ONCE A MONTH.
NICE TO BE LOADED.
WEAR IT UP, THEN.
slurp
THAT'S NOT THE POINT!
DON'T YOU THINK IT'LL BE MUCH CUTER IF I GET IT DONE...
AT THE SALON?

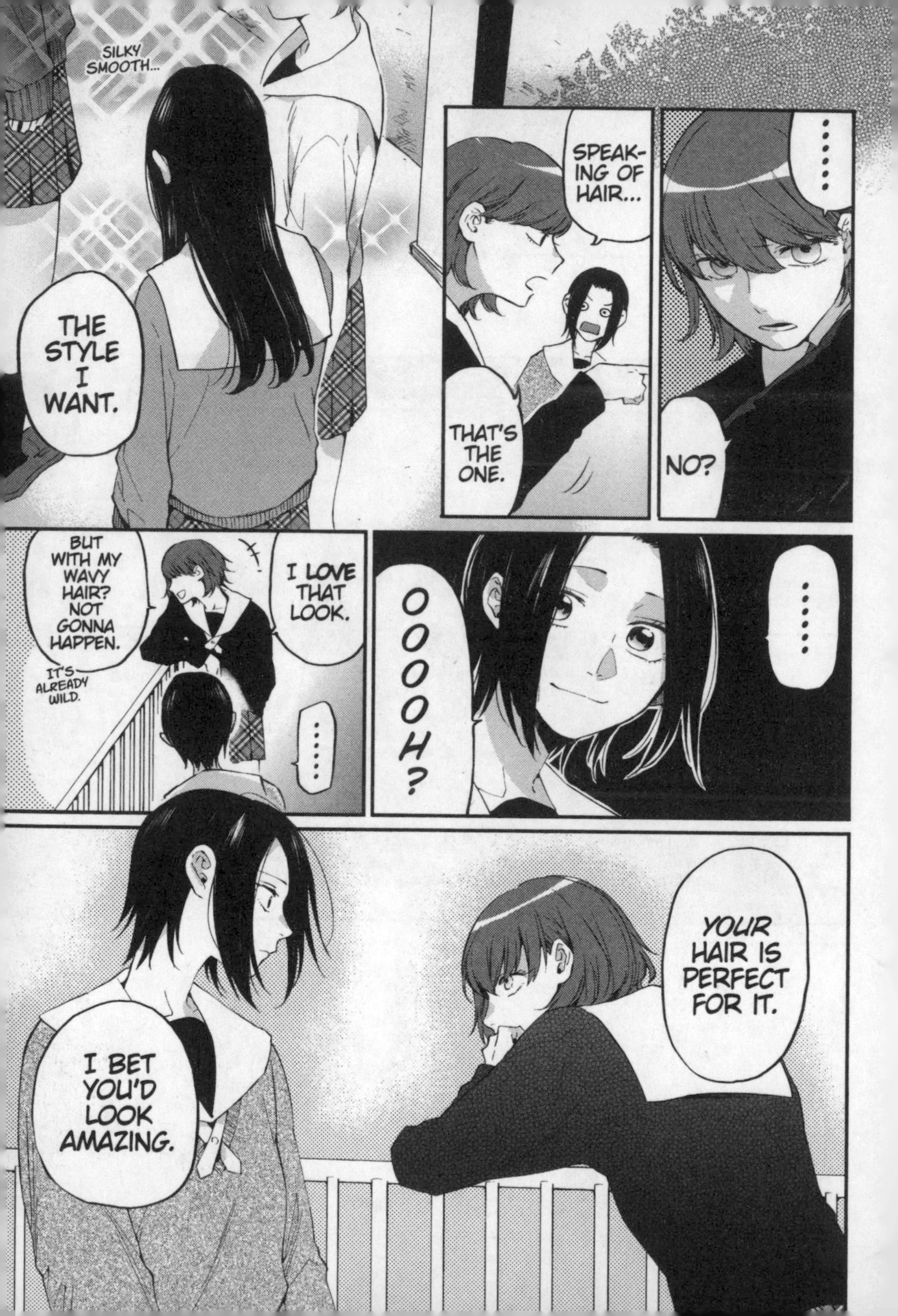
......
NO?
SPEAKING OF HAIR...
THAT'S THE ONE.
SILKY SMOOTH...
THE STYLE I WANT.
......
OOOOOH?
I LOVE THAT LOOK.
BUT WITH MY WAVY HAIR? NOT GONNA HAPPEN.
IT'S ALREADY WILD.
......
YOUR HAIR IS PERFECT FOR IT.
I BET YOU'D LOOK AMAZING.

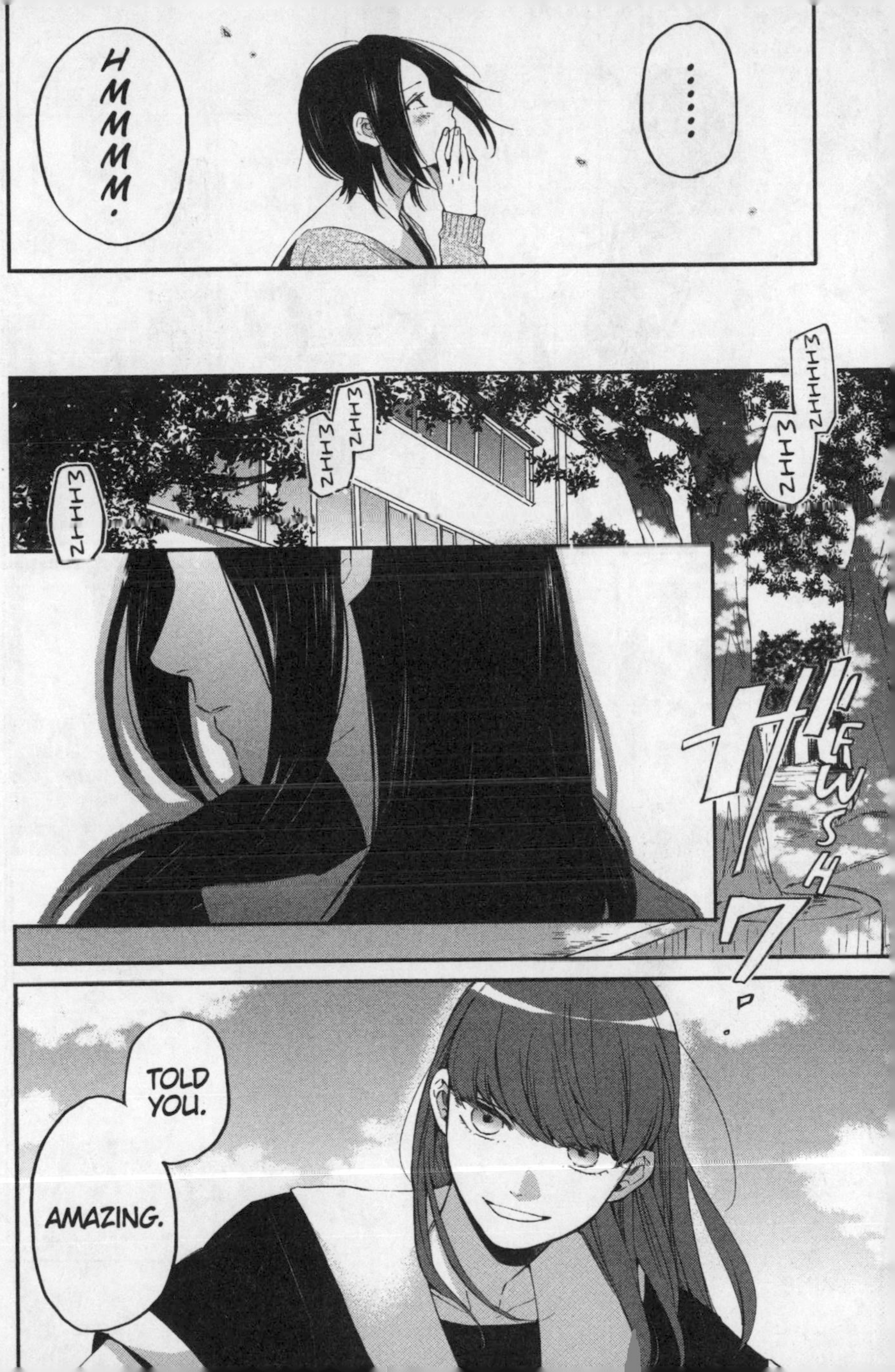
......
HMMMMM!
WHHHHZ
WHHZ
WHHZ
WHHHZ
FWSH
TOLD YOU.
AMAZING.

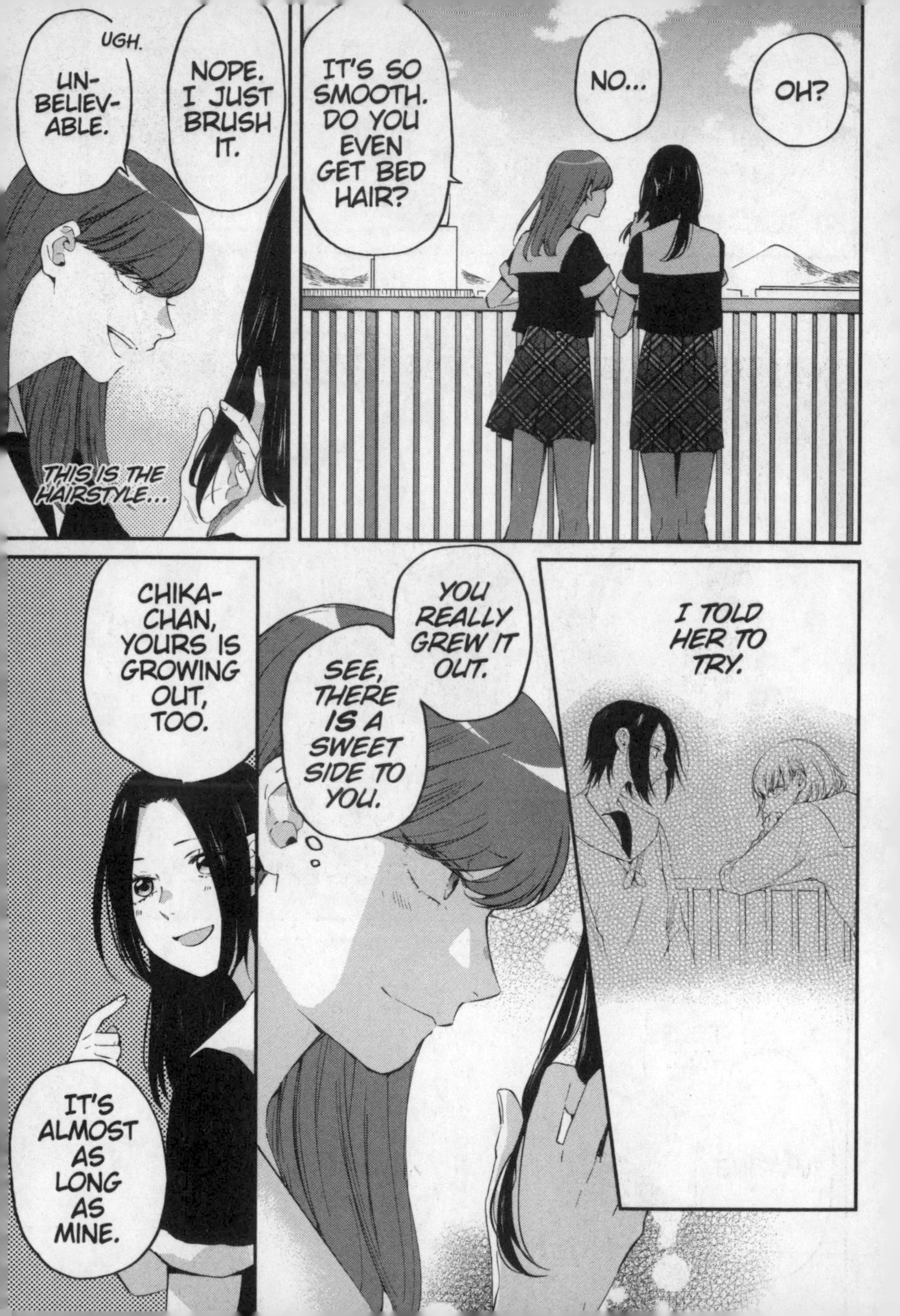
OH?
NO...
IT'S SO SMOOTH. DO YOU EVEN GET BED HAIR?
NOPE. I JUST BRUSH IT.
UGH.
UN-BELIEV-ABLE.
THIS IS THE HAIRSTYLE...
I TOLD HER TO TRY.
YOU REALLY GREW IT OUT.
SEE, THERE IS A SWEET SIDE TO YOU.
CHIKA-CHAN, YOURS IS GROWING OUT, TOO.
IT'S ALMOST AS LONG AS MINE.

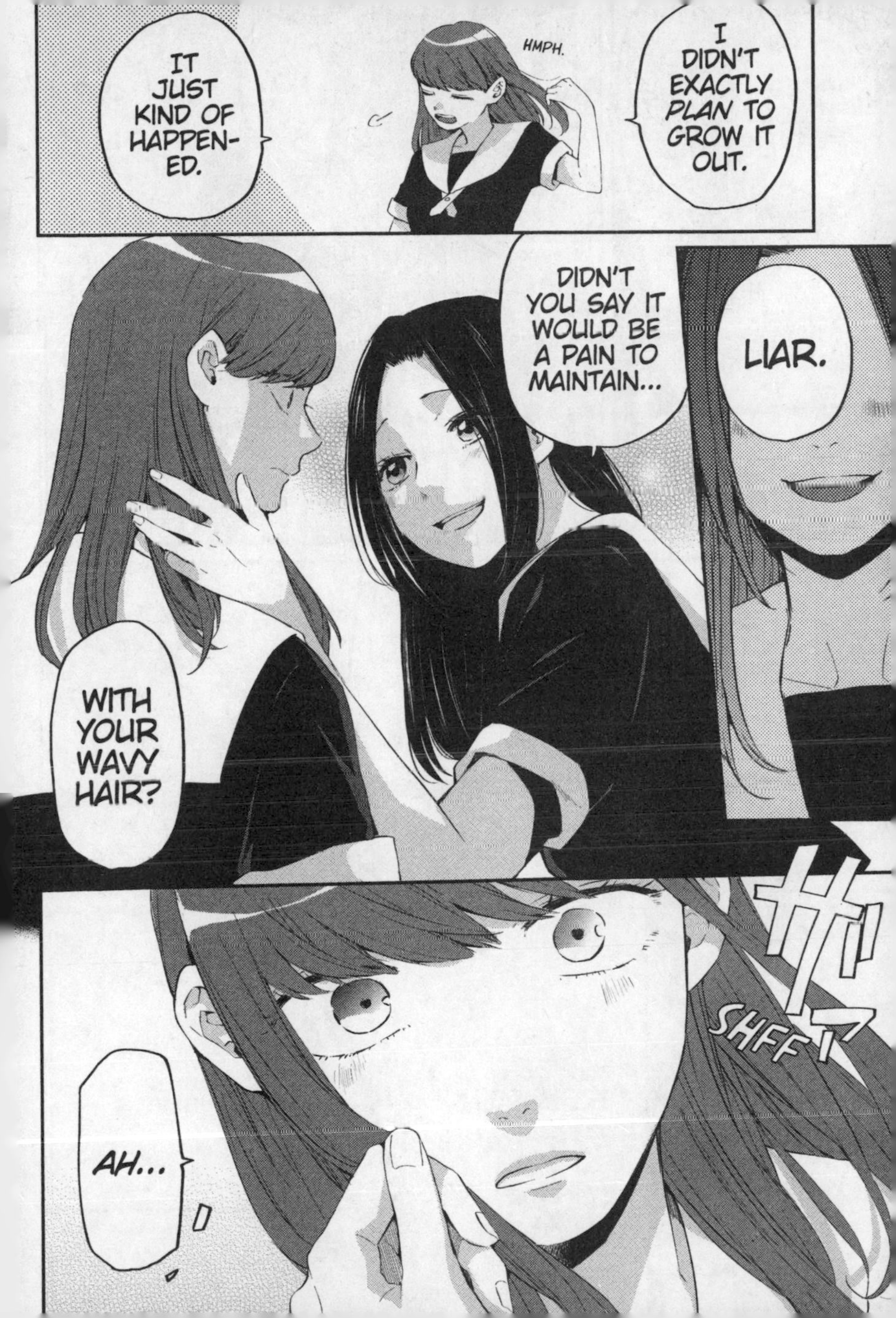
I DIDN'T EXACTLY PLAN TO GROW IT OUT.
HMPH.
IT JUST KIND OF HAPPEN-ED.
LIAR.
DIDN'T YOU SAY IT WOULD BE A PAIN TO MAINTAIN...
WITH YOUR WAVY HAIR?
SHFF
AH...

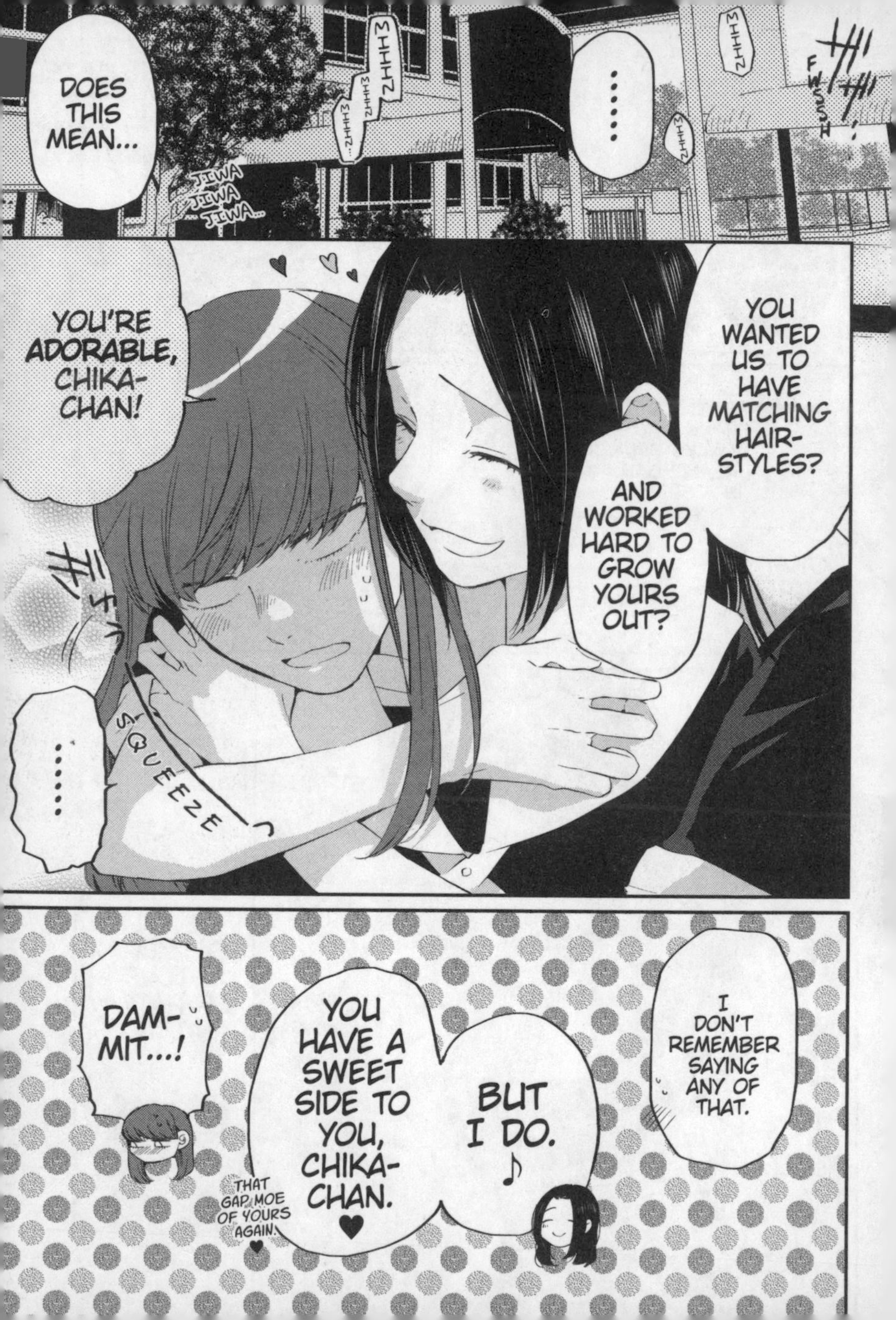
FWSH
MIHHN
......
MIHHN
MIHHN
MIHHN...
JIWA JIWA JIWA...
DOES THIS MEAN...
YOU WANTED US TO HAVE MATCHING HAIR-STYLES?
AND WORKED HARD TO GROW YOURS OUT?
YOU'RE ADORABLE, CHIKA-CHAN!
SQUEEZE
......
I DON'T REMEMBER SAYING ANY OF THAT.
BUT I DO. ♪
YOU HAVE A SWEET SIDE TO YOU, CHIKA-CHAN. ♥
THAT GAP MOE OF YOURS AGAIN. ♥
DAM-MIT....!

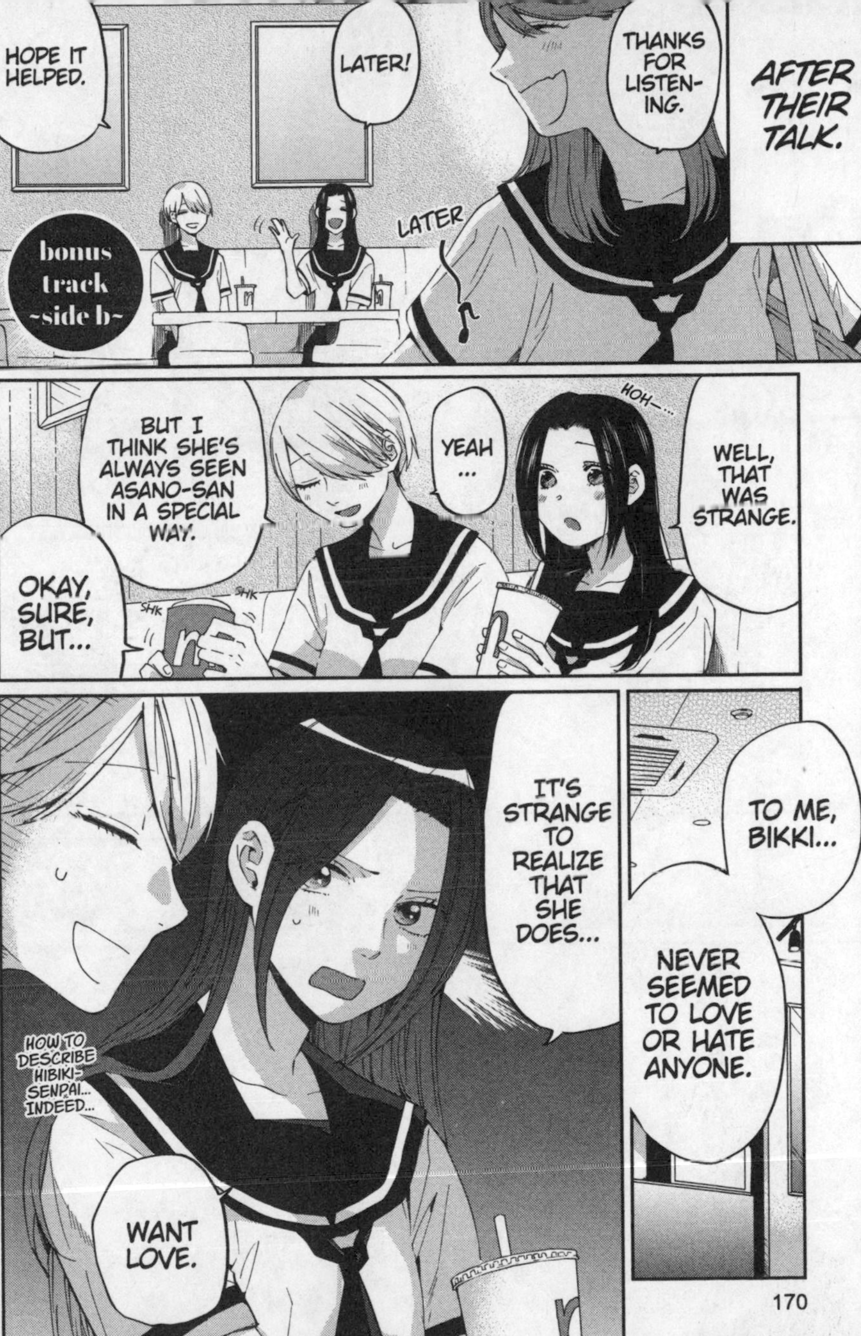
AFTER THEIR TALK.
THANKS FOR LISTEN-ING.
LATER!
HOPE IT HELPED.
LATER
bonus track ~side b~
WELL, THAT WAS STRANGE.
HOH—...
YEAH ...
BUT I THINK SHE'S ALWAYS SEEN ASANO-SAN IN A SPECIAL WAY.
OKAY, SURE, BUT...
SHK
SHK
TO ME, BIKKI...
NEVER SEEMED TO LOVE OR HATE ANYONE.
IT'S STRANGE TO REALIZE THAT SHE DOES...
WANT LOVE.
HOW TO DESCRIBE HIBIKI-SENPAI... INDEED...

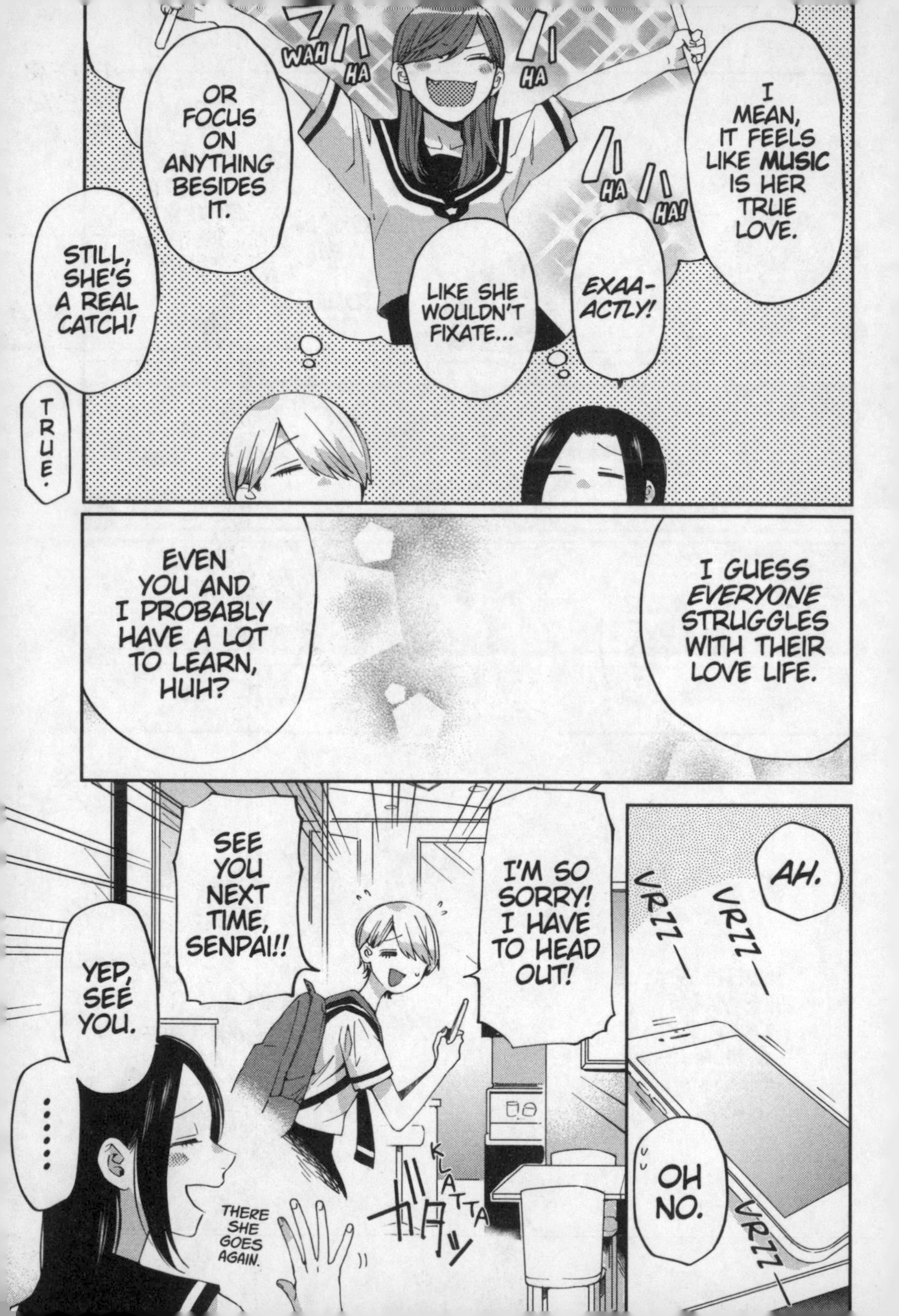
I MEAN, IT FEELS LIKE MUSIC IS HER TRUE LOVE.
WAH HA HA HA HA!
EXAA-ACTLY!
LIKE SHE WOULDN'T FIXATE...
OR FOCUS ON ANYTHING BESIDES IT.
STILL, SHE'S A REAL CATCH!
TRUE.
I GUESS EVERYONE STRUGGLES WITH THEIR LOVE LIFE.
EVEN YOU AND I PROBABLY HAVE A LOT TO LEARN, HUH?
AH.
VRZZ—
VRZZ—
OH NO.
VRZZ—
I'M SO SORRY! I HAVE TO HEAD OUT!
SEE YOU NEXT TIME, SENPAI!!
YEP, SEE YOU.
KLATTA
THERE SHE GOES AGAIN.
......

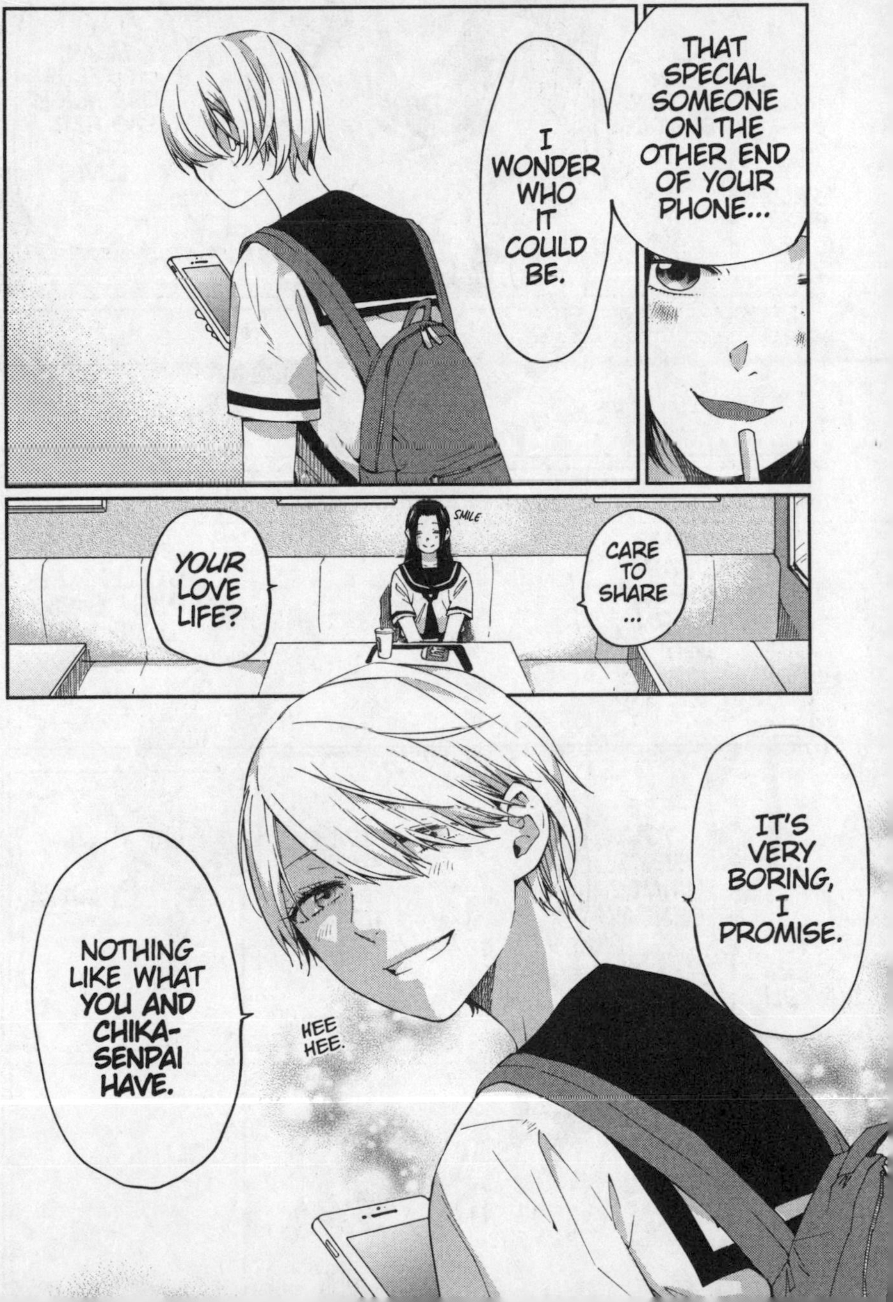
THAT SPECIAL SOMEONE ON THE OTHER END OF YOUR PHONE...
I WONDER WHO IT COULD BE.
CARE TO SHARE ...
SMILE
YOUR LOVE LIFE?
IT'S VERY BORING, I PROMISE.
HEE HEE.
NOTHING LIKE WHAT YOU AND CHIKA-SENPAI HAVE.

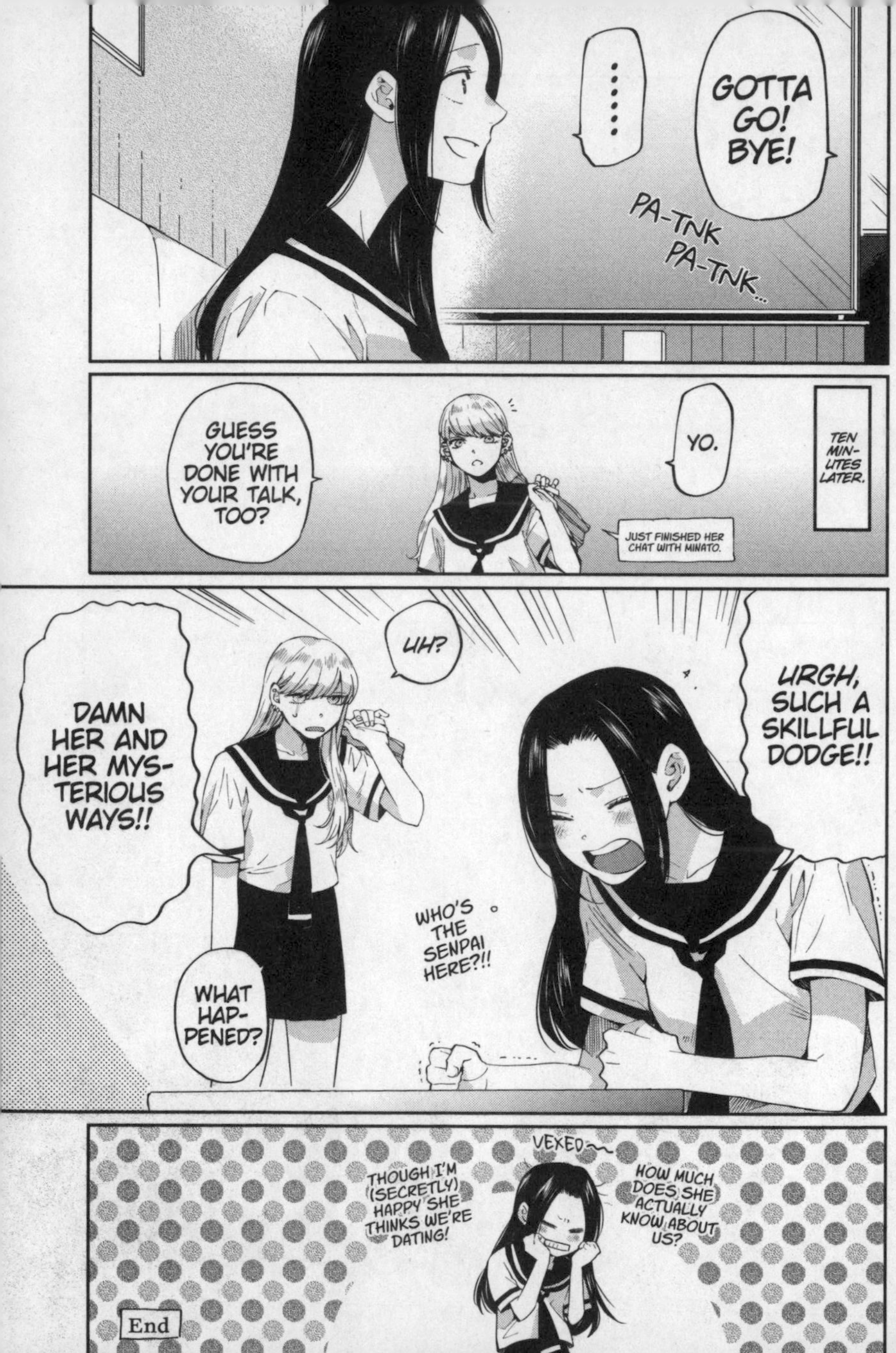
GOTTA GO! BYE!
PA-TNK PA-TNK...
......
TEN MIN-UTES LATER.
YO.
JUST FINISHED HER CHAT WITH MINATO.
GUESS YOU'RE DONE WITH YOUR TALK, TOO?
URGH, SUCH A SKILLFUL DODGE!!
UH?
DAMN HER AND HER MYS-TERIOUS WAYS!!
WHO'S THE SENPAI HERE?!!
WHAT HAP-PENED?
VEXED~
HOW MUCH DOES SHE ACTUALLY KNOW ABOUT US?
THOUGH I'M (SECRETLY) HAPPY SHE THINKS WE'RE DATING!
End

Hello, Melancholic!

Afterword

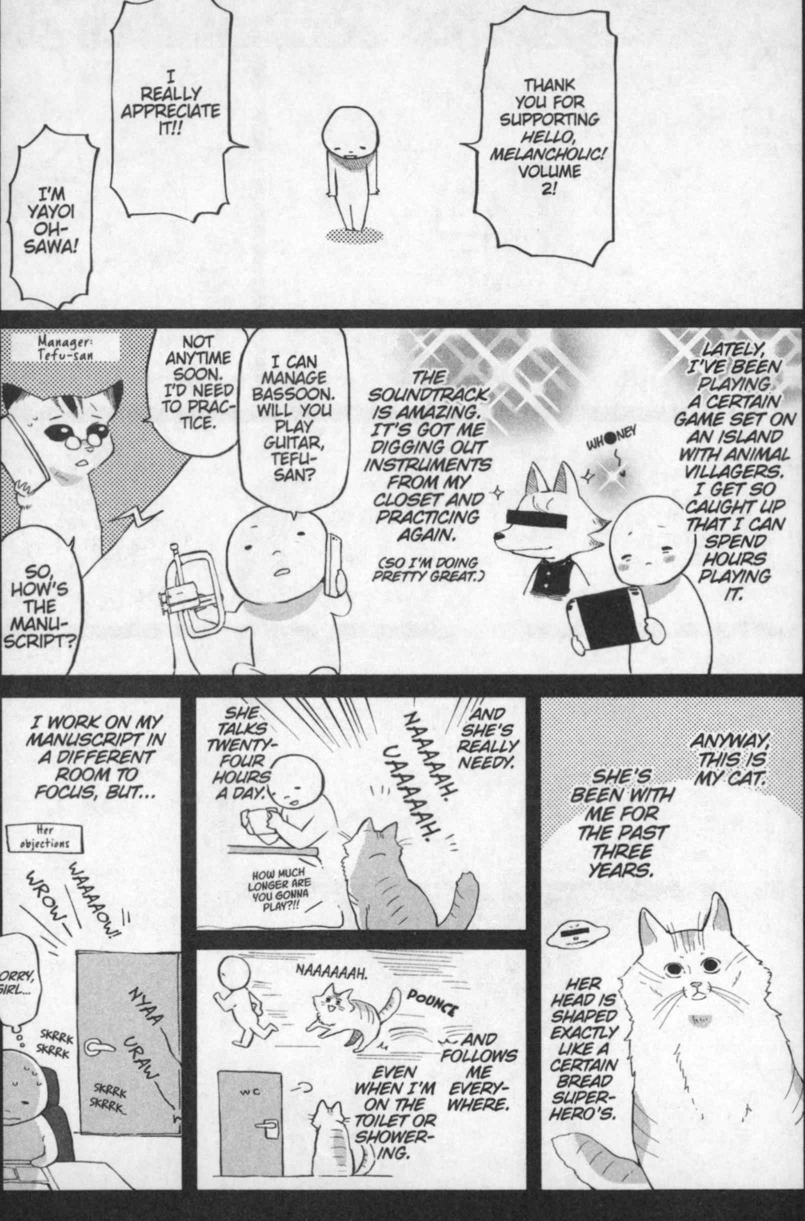
THANK YOU FOR SUPPORTING HELLO, MELANCHOLIC! VOLUME 2!
I REALLY APPRECIATE IT!!
I'M YAYOI OH-SAWA!
LATELY, I'VE BEEN PLAYING A CERTAIN GAME SET ON AN ISLAND WITH ANIMAL VILLAGERS. I GET SO CAUGHT UP THAT I CAN SPEND HOURS PLAYING IT.
WH[redacted]NEY
THE SOUNDTRACK IS AMAZING. IT'S GOT ME DIGGING OUT INSTRUMENTS FROM MY CLOSET AND PRACTICING AGAIN.
(SO I'M DOING PRETTY GREAT.)
I CAN MANAGE BASSOON. WILL YOU PLAY GUITAR, TEFU-SAN?
NOT ANYTIME SOON. I'D NEED TO PRAC-TICE.
Manager: Tefu-san
SO, HOW'S THE MANU-SCRIPT?
ANYWAY, THIS IS MY CAT.
SHE'S BEEN WITH ME FOR THE PAST THREE YEARS.
HER HEAD IS SHAPED EXACTLY LIKE A CERTAIN BREAD SUPER-HERO'S.
AND SHE'S REALLY NEEDY.
NAAAAAH. UAAAAAH.
SHE TALKS TWENTY-FOUR HOURS A DAY.
HOW MUCH LONGER ARE YOU GONNA PLAY?!!
NAAAAAAH.
POUNCE
...AND FOLLOWS ME EVERY-WHERE.
EVEN WHEN I'M ON THE TOILET OR SHOWER-ING.
WC
I WORK ON MY MANUSCRIPT IN A DIFFERENT ROOM TO FOCUS, BUT...
Her objections
WAAAAOW!
WROW
NYAA
URAW
SKRRK SKRRK
SORRY, GIRL...
SKRRK SKRRK

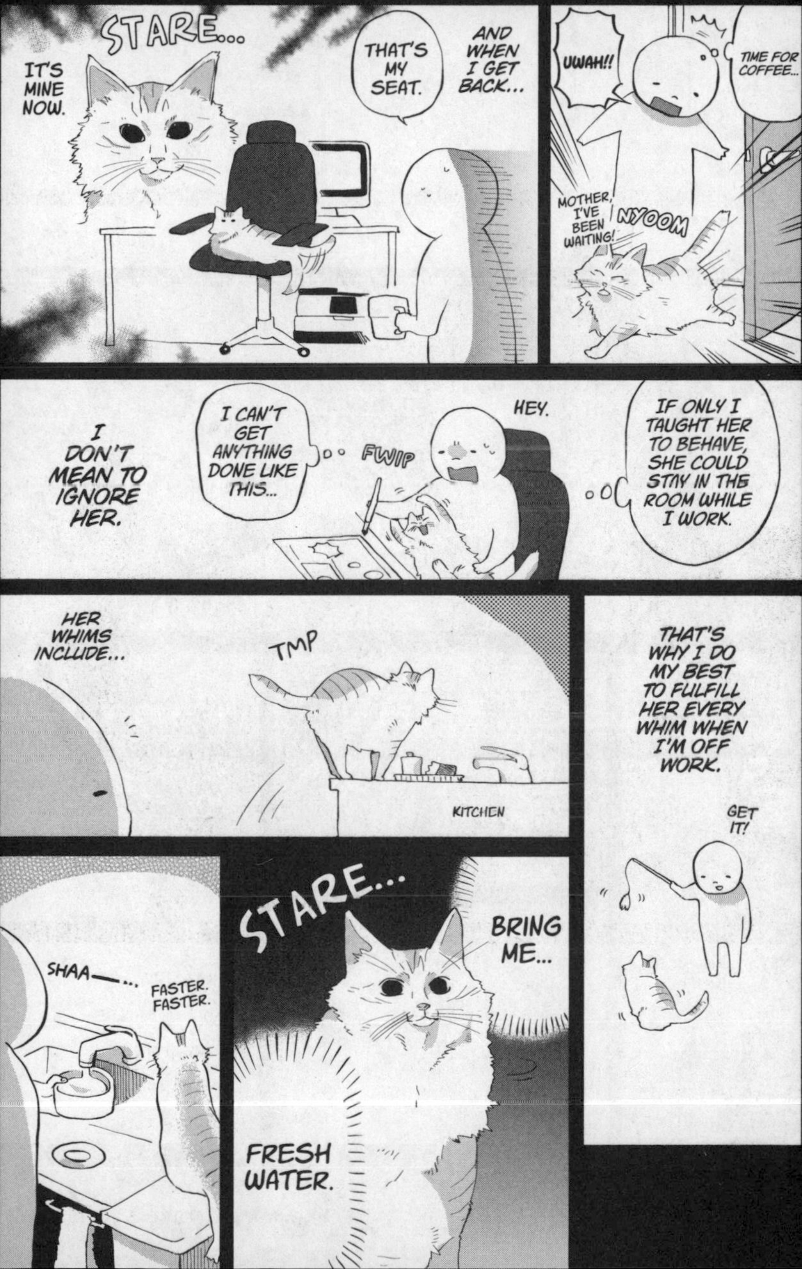
TIME FOR COFFEE...
UWAH!!
MOTHER, I'VE BEEN WAITING!
NYOOM
AND WHEN I GET BACK...
THAT'S MY SEAT.
STARE...
IT'S MINE NOW.
IF ONLY I TAUGHT HER TO BEHAVE, SHE COULD STAY IN THE ROOM WHILE I WORK.
HEY.
I CAN'T GET ANYTHING DONE LIKE THIS...
FWIP
I DON'T MEAN TO IGNORE HER.
THAT'S WHY I DO MY BEST TO FULFILL HER EVERY WHIM WHEN I'M OFF WORK.
GET IT!
TMP
KITCHEN
HER WHIMS INCLUDE...
BRING ME...
STARE...
FRESH WATER.
FASTER. FASTER.
SHAA—...

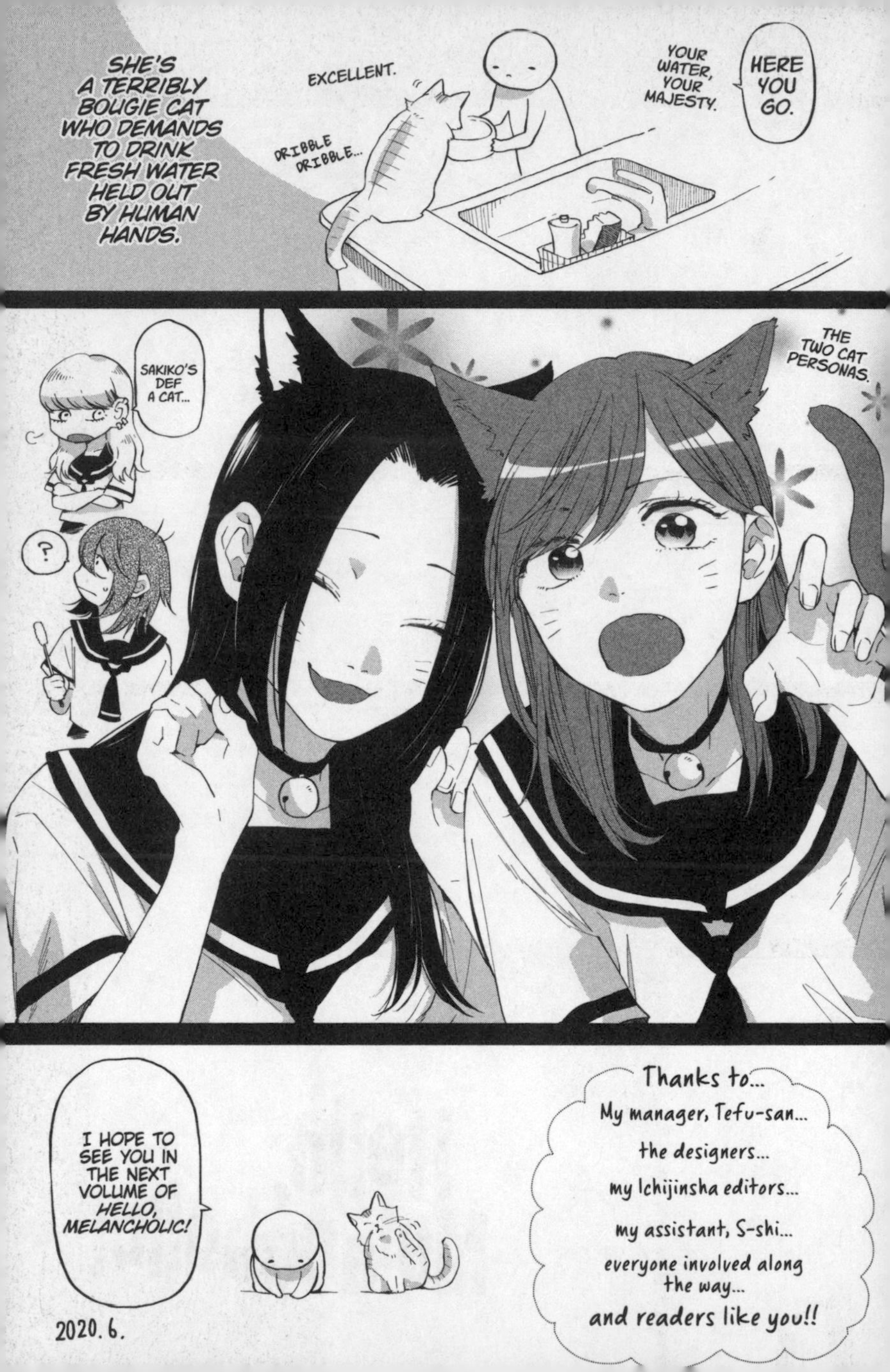
HERE YOU GO.
YOUR WATER, YOUR MAJESTY.
EXCELLENT.
DRIBBLE DRIBBLE...
SHE'S A TERRIBLY BOUGIE CAT WHO DEMANDS TO DRINK FRESH WATER HELD OUT BY HUMAN HANDS.
THE TWO CAT PERSONAS.
SAKIKO'S DEF A CAT...
?
Thanks to...
My manager, Tefu-san...
the designers...
my Ichijinsha editors...
my assistant, S-shi...
everyone involved along the way...
and readers like you!!
I HOPE TO SEE YOU IN THE NEXT VOLUME OF HELLO, MELANCHOLIC!
2020. 6.

Hello, Melancholic!

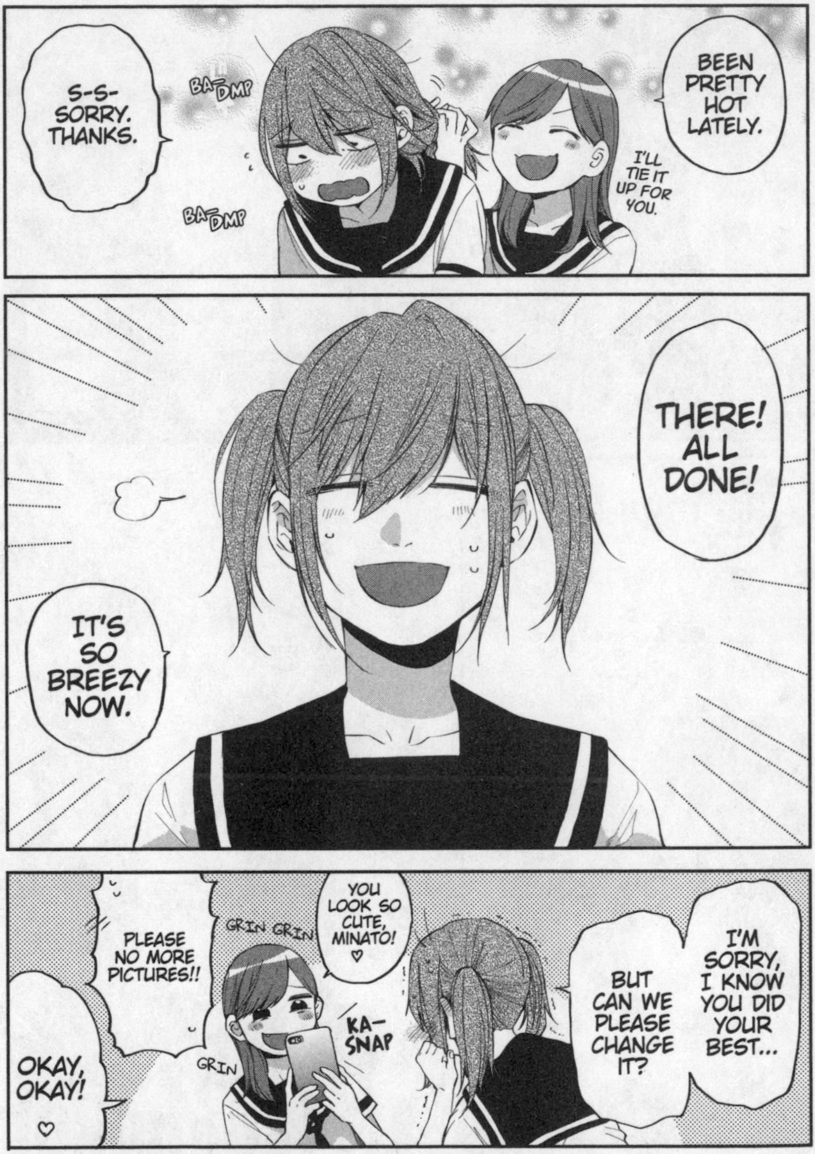
BEEN PRETTY HOT LATELY.
I'LL TIE IT UP FOR YOU.
BA-DMP
S-S-SORRY. THANKS.
BA-DMP
THERE! ALL DONE!
IT'S SO BREEZY NOW.
I'M SORRY, I KNOW YOU DID YOUR BEST...
BUT CAN WE PLEASE CHANGE IT?
YOU LOOK SO CUTE, MINATO! ♡
KA-SNAP
GRIN GRIN
GRIN
PLEASE NO MORE PICTURES!!
OKAY, OKAY! ♡

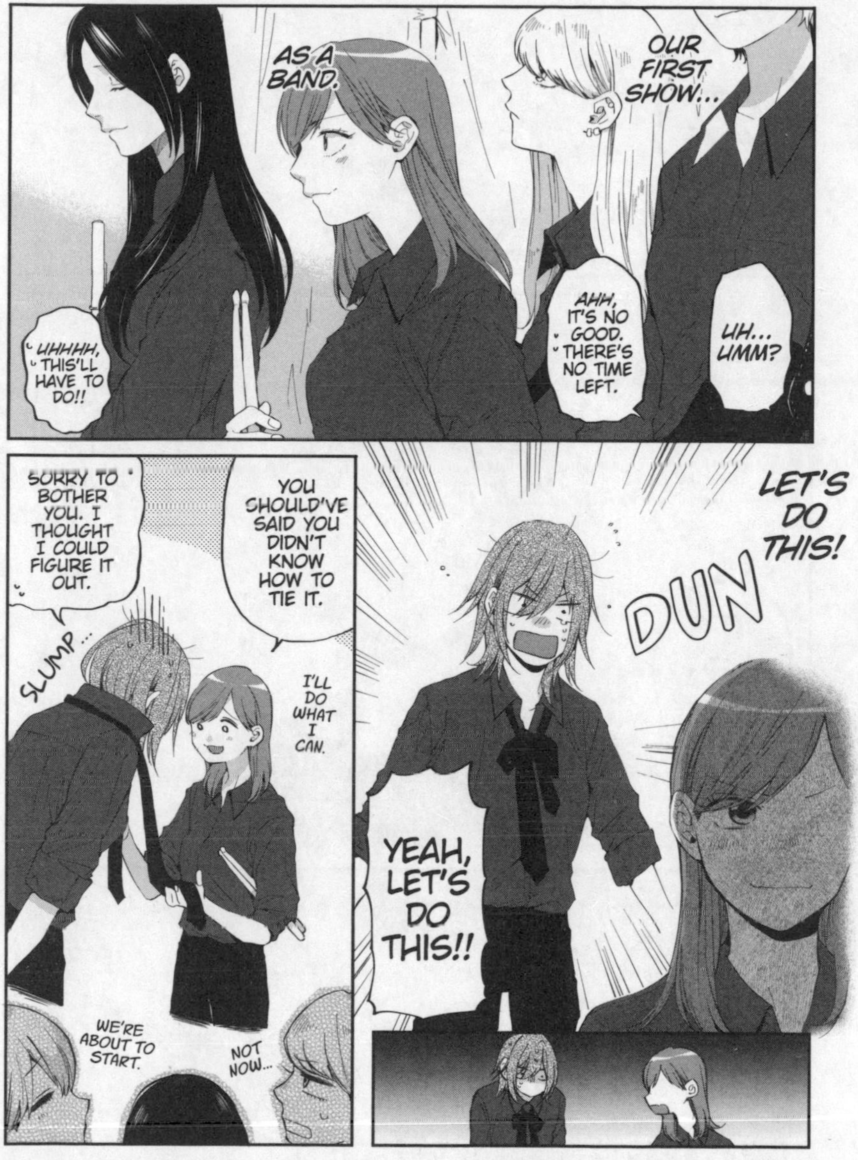
OUR FIRST SHOW...
AS A BAND.
UH... UMM?
AHH, IT'S NO GOOD. THERE'S NO TIME LEFT.
UHHHH, THIS'LL HAVE TO DO!!
LET'S DO THIS!
DUN
YEAH, LET'S DO THIS!!
YOU SHOULD'VE SAID YOU DIDN'T KNOW HOW TO TIE IT.
SORRY TO BOTHER YOU. I THOUGHT I COULD FIGURE IT OUT.
SLUMP...
I'LL DO WHAT I CAN.
NOT NOW...
WE'RE ABOUT TO START.

Hello,
Melancholic!

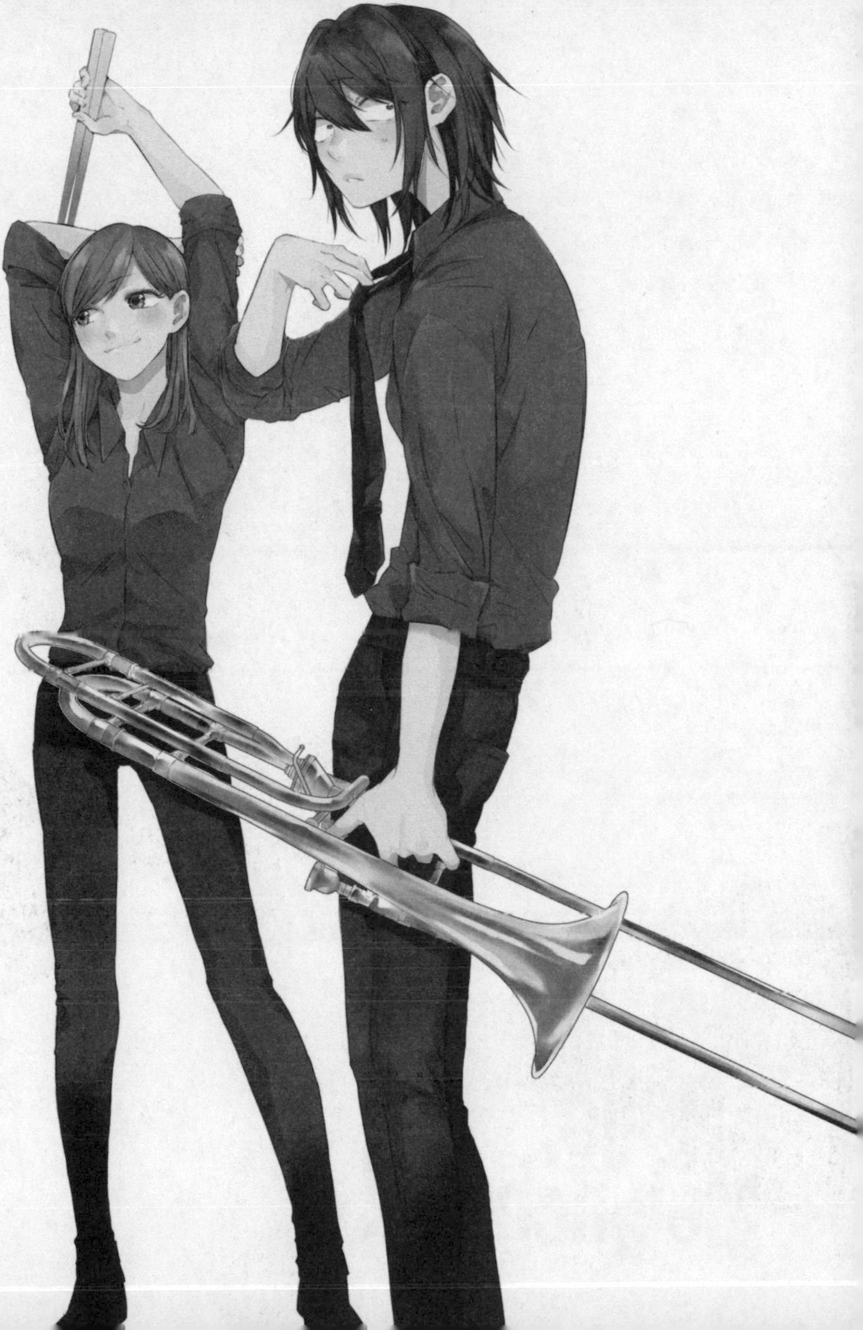

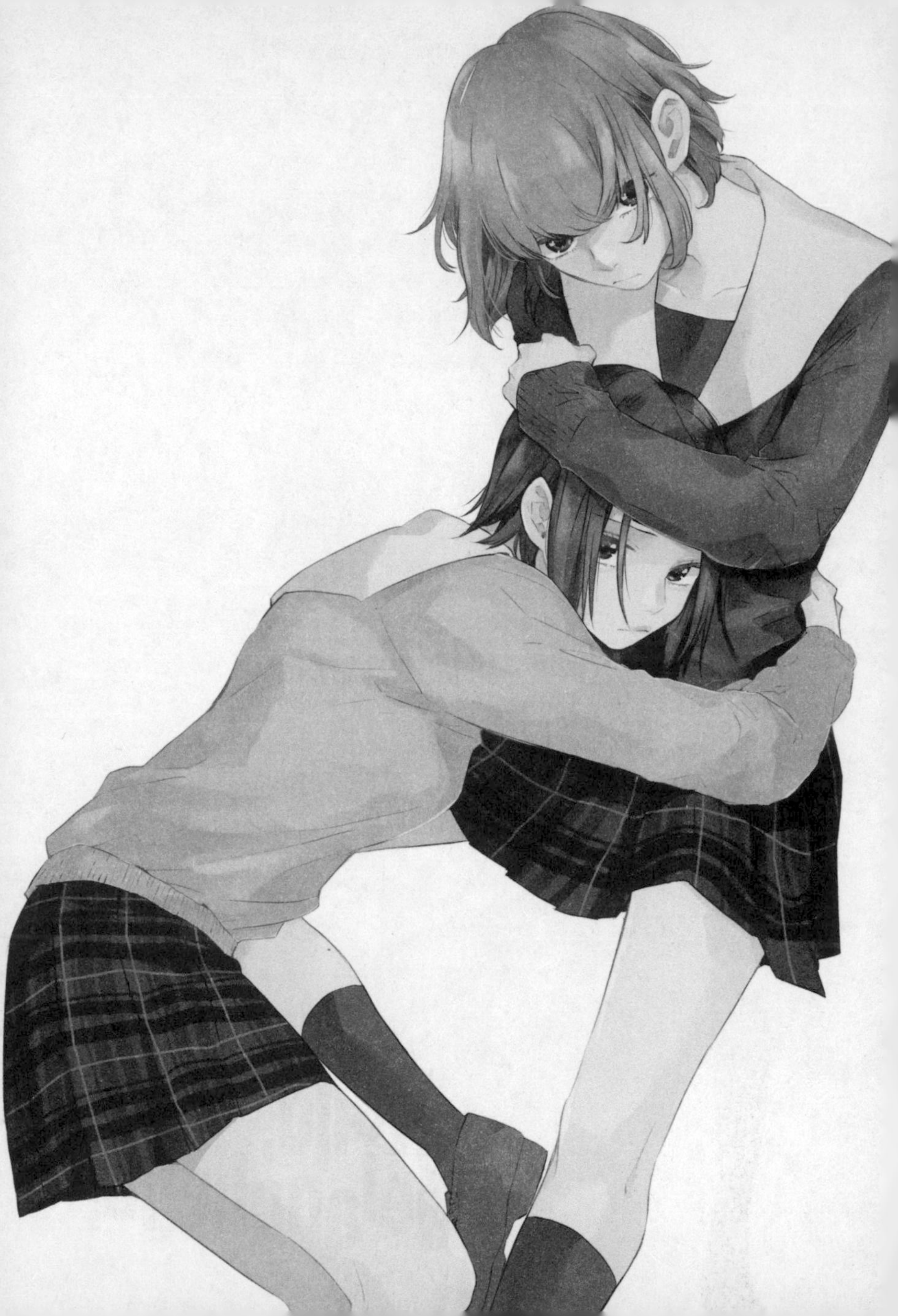

Hello,
Melancholic!